D0120135

True and Fair

TRUE AND FAIR

A History of Price Waterhouse

EDGAR JONES

HAMISH HAMILTON · LONDON

HAMISH HAMILTON LTD

Published by the Penguin Group
Penguin Books Ltd, 27 Wrights Lane, London w8 5tz, England
Penguin Books USA Inc., 375 Hudson Street, New York, New York 10014, USA
Penguin Books Australia Ltd, Ringwood, Victoria, Australia
Penguin Books Canada Ltd, 10 Alcorn Avenue, Toronto, Ontario, Canada m4v 3b2
Penguin Books (NZ) Ltd, 182–190 Wairau Road, Auckland 10, New Zealand

Penguin Books Ltd, Registered Offices: Harmondsworth, Middlesex, England

First published 1995
1 3 5 7 9 10 8 6 4 2

Copyright © Price Waterhouse, 1995

The moral right of the author has been asserted

All rights reserved.
Without limiting the rights under copyright
reserved above, no part of this publication may be
reproduced, stored in or introduced into a retrieval system,
or transmitted, in any form or by any means (electronic, mechanical,
photocopying, recording or otherwise), without the prior
written permission of both the copyright owner and
the above publisher of this book

Filmset by Datix International Limited, Bungay, Suffolk
Printed in England by Clays Ltd, St Ives plc
Set in 11/14 pt Monophoto Bembo

A CIP catalogue record for this book is available from the British Library

ISBN 0–241–00172–2

Contents

CONTENTS

vii

List of Figures

List of Tables

List of Illustrations

List of Abbreviations

BRO	Bristol Record Office
DBB	*Dictionary of Business Biography*
DNB	*Dictionary of National Biography*
ICAEW	Institute of Chartered Accountants in England and Wales
ICAI	Institute of Chartered Accountants in Ireland
LMS	London, Midland and Scottish Railway
LNER	London and North Eastern Railway
LNWR	London and North Western Railway
MCS	Management Consultancy Services
PMM	Peat Marwick McLintock
PWA	Price Waterhouse Archives
PRO	Public Record Office, Kew
RIBA	Royal Institute of British Architects Library
SEC	Securities and Exchange Comission
SER	South Eastern Railway
SSAP	Statements of Standard Accounting Practice
TFA	Trade Facilities Act Advisory Committee
WwW	*Who was Who*

Foreword

Samuel Lowell Price started in business on his own account at 5 Gresham Street in the City of London in 1849. When he and Edwin Waterhouse subsequently formed a partnership in 1865 they could not possibly have contemplated that, over a century later, there would be Price Waterhouse firms in more than 100 countries around the world employing over 50,000 people. Their working day and the clients they were serving would be unrecognisable today – everything has changed – and it has been the readiness of generations of Price Waterhouse partners and staff to recognise and adapt to change that has resulted in the Price Waterhouse of the 1990s.

It is natural to look for characteristics or qualities that have endured through the years of change. One obvious thing that has remained virtually unaltered since 1874 is the name Price Waterhouse, reflecting the fact that, unlike most of our competitors, we have grown internally without resort to major mergers. We have also inherited a clientele that includes many of the leading businesses in the country.

What else have we inherited, apart from a name and an enviable client list? I think most of our people today would say 'Pride in a firm that has a reputation for integrity, quality and service', together with a sense of responsibility to maintain and enhance that reputation for future generations.

In this book about the UK Firm Edgar Jones has performed a remarkable feat in untangling the events in the history of Price Waterhouse and placing them in their business and social context. He has made an invaluable contribution to today's generation of Price Waterhouse people in describing a firm of which we are justifiably proud.

January 1995
Ian Brindle
Senior Partner, UK Firm

Acknowledgements

This history represents the culmination of four years' work and an even longer period of gestation as Price Waterhouse prepared the ground for an in-depth study. A number of individuals within the UK Firm have supported and contributed to the project. Sir Jeffery Bowman was the senior partner who instigated the research and writing of the history; he has consistently encouraged the endeavour in a fair and open-minded manner. Ian Mills was entrusted with the chairmanship of the History Committee which guided the project in its execution and commented on various drafts of the text. His infectious enthusiasm and keen interest have both proved invaluable. The study could not have been completed without the important task of assembling and safeguarding a repository of primary sources. This task has been conscientiously performed by John Barrett, appointed as the firm's archivist in July 1983. Without his tenacity of purpose over many years, it is doubtful whether this history would ever have been commissioned. Michael Coates, Leslie Cousins and Chris Hordern were the other original members of the committee from Price Waterhouse, and were joined half-way through the project by John Barnsley, who assumed a growing executive role as other members of the committee retired from the partnership. I am indebted to all four for their commitment and assistance. In the spring of 1991 Ian Brindle succeeded Sir Jeffery Bowman as senior partner and I am thankful to him for his continued support of this project. Price Waterhouse have provided a tolerant and creative atmosphere in which to work, confident, perhaps, that their organisation deserved study and possessed sufficient integrity to benefit from critical inquiry.

To act as an external assessor and impartial source of advice, Price Waterhouse asked Professor Barry Supple, formerly of St Catharine's College, Cambridge, to serve on the History Committee, and he has proved to be an important and constructive critic. Graham Stacy was also asked to comment on key sections of the text and provided invaluable technical input. Andrew Best, literary consultant, was approached to help with the practical matters of turning a typescript into finished publication and added his editorial skills to this task. A former financial journalist and editor of *The Banker*, Colin Jones read the entire draft and made a number of helpful suggestions based upon his extensive experience.

I have received great assistance from the partners and staff of Price Waterhouse, past and present; so many that they defy listing. However, those retired members of the firm who kindly agreed to be interviewed are recorded in the 'Sources', and a particular note of thanks is due to Stanley Duncan, a former senior partner.

A debt of gratitude is owed to those individuals who have never been members of Price Waterhouse but who nevertheless offered their help and expertise. From the leading ranks of the accountancy profession, these included Lord Benson, Sir Ronald Leach and Roy Chapman. I am also grateful to Sir Jonathan Parker, who provided valuable information about his father, Sir Edmund Parker. John Garnett, formerly of the Industrial Society, and Tony Mallinson, formerly of Slaughter & May, both offered valuable insights into the firm from the perspective of an external professional. Peter Nielsen, a partner in KPMG Peat Marwick McLintock, provided access to his firm's archives, while Tim R. Newell Price made available his extensive research into the Price family. I am also grateful to Hugh B. Markus for allowing me to consult a draft of his history of the German Firm and to Peter Boys of the University of Kent for providing information on accountants in literature. Robert Furber added light to significant aspects of the Royal Mail case, and Dr John Booker granted access to the archives of Lloyds Bank. Ian Smeaton spent many hours working through the firm's financial records and I am grateful to him for producing such complete historic accounts. For her detailed reading of the text and marketing expertise, thanks are due to Valerie Moores, and to Max Grizaard, who took a number of the colour and black and white photographs, for his professional competence and care.

The entire text, in its various drafts, was typed by Glynis Haylett, and she is owed much thanks for her expertise, interest and perseverance. The author acknowledges the contribution of the publishers, and in particular of the copy-editor Bela Cunha, Keith Taylor and Andrew Franklin, who guided the book from typescript to launch.

Many have contributed to this history, but the final text is mine and I accept responsibility for any errors that remain.

London, January 1995   *Edgar Jones*

Introduction

Price Waterhouse is one of the world's largest firms of accountants. It is also one of the oldest, having been founded in December 1849 by Samuel Lowell Price, who set up on his own account at 5 Gresham Street in the City of London. In the space of a little over 140 years the practice which he established grew into an organisation of over 50,000 partners and staff, located at 450 offices in 118 countries and territories with a global fee income in 1994 of $3,975 million. This change possesses something of the drama inherent in the development of an adult from a few embryonic cells, and yet with that development, an unbroken thread of continuity has run throughout the transformation. This history seeks to explain how this evolution has occurred and to place it within the context of the accountancy profession and the financial world.

Although Price Waterhouse began in a single office in Gresham Street, it has spread territorially throughout Britain and across the globe creating a truly international organisation. In the UK the first branch office was opened at Liverpool in 1904, a second followed in Newcastle in 1912 and a third in Plymouth two years later. However, it was not until the interwar period that the firm's representation was strengthened with offices being opened in Leeds (1928), Cardiff (1932), Manchester (1932) and Birmingham (1939). Beginning in the 1960s a wave of mergers with provincial practices has led to even wider territorial coverage.

While there had been, until the 1930s, a reluctance to expand beyond London Price Waterhouse had more readily set up partnerships overseas. In a pre-airline era before the advent of efficient telecommunications, this was a virtual necessity if they wished to serve clients efficiently in foreign lands. Accordingly, during the 1890s a firm was established in the United States with offices in New York and Chicago, and other practices followed before the First World War in Egypt (1907) and Argentina (1913). Work for the British government during these hostilities led to the setting up of a Continental Firm in 1919 and this spread from France into Holland, Sweden, Germany, Switzerland and Italy before being curtailed by the rise of fascism.

The disruption caused by the global nature of the Second World War emphasised the need for an international organisation to co-ordinate the activities of the various Price Waterhouse partnerships. In March 1946 an International Firm was formally constituted. This grew in status and scale as national firms expanded and increased in number. In 1982 it was reconstituted with a more active role as the World Firm and its chairmen have commonly been the outgoing senior partners of either the UK or US practices. By 1994 there were twenty-seven member firms, including those as far afield as Korea, Malaysia, Singapore, Thailand and Venezuela.

As well as the creation of the World Firm designed to harmonise standards and procedures, in 1988 the European Combination was established as an organisational structure to co-ordinate objectives and client services both in the UK and on the Continent. Although legal and professional requirements have prevented this from being consti-tuted as a single partnership, the existing firms and companies have been treated as if they were subsidiaries within a group. At the time of its formation the Combination had 8,650 partners and staff and a total fee income of S.Fr.863 million. The expansion of the firm throughout Europe (driven in part by mergers with major national practices in France, Germany and Switzerland and the creation of a network of new offices in the former Communist states of the Eastern bloc) produced a dramatic increase in fee income which reached S.Fr.1,933 million in 1994, representing a growth rate of 124 per cent over six years. By that time the Combination had 134 offices spread throughout thirty-two countries thereby creating considerable chal-lenges in how to manage so many diverse cultures under a single organisation.

With similar territorial expansion taking place elsewhere in the globe, the worldwide representation of Price Waterhouse multiplied, and by 1994 the firm had a total of 450 offices in 118 countries and territories. Given the inherent differences in accounting regulations and company law across the globe, it set the World Firm a major task in attempting to establish minimum standards and common pro-cedures. In the nineteenth century the UK Firm declined to set up partnerships outside London because it was thought that it would dilute the internal ethic and make controls difficult to impose. The organisation of today with its twenty-seven national firms, together with the European Combination, represents a dramatically different concept.

The range of activities performed by Price Waterhouse has broadened. In the nineteenth century they had their origins in book-keeping, special investigations and a few insolvency assignments. The Companies Acts and progressive industrialisation introduced the concept of an annual audit and Price Waterhouse, together with the other leading practices in the major cities of the UK, began to consider themselves as professional consultants to business. The growing complexity of taxation and the imposition of Excess Profits Duty during the First World War brought them a new specialism as they advised companies and individuals on revenue matters.

During the interwar period some other firms engaged in systems' work, essentially cost accounting and rudimentary forms of management accounts, though this activity remained of limited scope until the rise of management consultancy in the 1960s. There are, therefore, three key areas of Price Waterhouse's practice: audit, tax and management consultancy. In 1994, when the UK Firm earned £384 million in fees, the percentage contributions of these were 38, 28 and 21 respectively. To these core activities a number of further specialisms have been added, including corporate finance and recovery (subsuming the traditional insolvency practice), which earned 13 per cent of fees in 1994, local government work, privatisation services, advice for emerging businesses and a professional recruitment function. This pattern of diversification has been replicated in all of the major Price Waterhouse firms across the world.

The broadening of the range of services offered by the major practices and their territorial expansion within countries and sometimes across national boundaries have combined to require more complex and structured management systems. In the early 1960s it was still possible for the entire UK partnership to meet around a single table on a daily basis to discuss problems. Today, when its membership exceeds 400, an executive appointed by an elected senior partner takes key management decisions, which, in turn, are monitored by a Supervisory Committee (formerly the Policy Committee). Each of the functional specialisms has its own managerial hierarchy, as do the regional offices.

Price Waterhouse has grown out of all proportion and would not be recognised by its founders. Its UK fee income in 1900, after fifty-one

3

years of practice, was a little over £43,000 and profits, including contributions from overseas, totalled £36,000. By 1945 the scale of the business had altered by a factor of ten (not accounting for inflation), fees having risen to £423,000 and profits £224,000. Nevertheless, in certain essentials (organisation, the nature of professional services), the partnership was still recognisably the same. From the 1960s the pace of change quickened. By 1965 turnover had reached £2.8 million and the number of partners and staff rose from 1,660 in 1970 to 6,580 by 1989. By 1975 fees had reached £14.2 million, £94.3 million by 1985 and exceeded £300 million in 1990.

Worldwide the statistics of growth are equally dramatic. Global fee income reached $2,881 million in 1990 and increased to $3,975 million by 1994. Following a series of mergers among the largest firms, Price Waterhouse was ranked sixth in terms of turnover in a group of six firms which by virtue of their size stand apart from the rest of the profession.

How, then, has this transformation been achieved? Price Waterhouse was fortunate in becoming a leading City practice at the time that the accountancy profession was being formally established. It was not among the oldest firms (which included Quilter, Ball & Co., W.W. Deloitte and Turquand, Youngs) but was prominent in the second generation. S.L. Price, the first senior partner, became a founder Council member of the Institute of Chartered Accountants in England and Wales, and on his death in 1887 Edwin Waterhouse was elected in his place. The earliest firms focused on what were then highly lucrative insolvency commissions and Price Waterhouse, entering the accountancy market a little later, tended to specialise in auditing. This proved fortunate as the firm built up an impressive list of clients including railway companies, banks and other financial institutions. As these grew and Price Waterhouse kept pace with their demands, so the firm's reputation was established and it attracted the attention of new enterprises seeking incorporation. By the turn of the century Price Waterhouse was unquestionably one of the country's leading accountancy practices with an outstanding audit portfolio.

The standing of the firm was raised still further during the interwar period by the meteoric rise of one of its most talented partners, Sir Gilbert Garnsey. Although he never lived to become the senior partner, Garnsey gained popular recognition for his work on government inquiries, as a company doctor and an advocate of accounting reforms. His ability to win assignments and attract new clients temporarily lifted Price Waterhouse ahead of its rivals in terms of size and public exposure. His sudden death in 1932, following not long after the Royal Mail case, which had seen one of the firm's partners in the dock at the Old Bailey charged under the 1861 Larceny Act, was a set-back to the progress of the firm. Although Price Waterhouse held its own in the thirties, the Second World War disrupted routines, drew talented staff into the forces and extended the careers of some who were due to retire. It was a complaisant and insular partnership which entered the 1950s and struggled to recapture the confidence and spirit of innovation which Garnsey had instilled.

A recovery, which had been initiated by W.E. Parker through the appointment of younger partners, was carried forward by Stanley Duncan who gave the administrative and strategic talents of Michael Coates scope to flourish. The latter, on succeeding to the senior partnership, brought these reforms to fruition and guided the firm into the modern period, while his successor, Sir Jeffery Bowman, took the UK Firm into Europe through the Combination arrangement.

What, then, are the broad themes of this history? There is an enduring Price Waterhouse ethic. Firms, like individuals, possess a sense of self – a unique character combined with continuity and a wish to preserve these features. This is particularly strong in Price Waterhouse, principally because the firm has never been subject to a merger with a partnership of equivalent size. In 1921 it turned down the chance to amalgamate with W.B. Peat & Co., in 1984 and five years later rejected unions with Deloittes and Arthur Andersen respectively. As a result the Price Waterhouse name has remained unaltered in its essentials since 1874. A powerful sense of continuity had been maintained by the traditions of training articled clerks and newly qualified accountants and appointing partners from within. Only in the last decade have professional staff been recruited from outside at senior grades, particularly into specialist departments.

Apart from generating a powerful and coherent culture, Price Waterhouse has always striven to achieve professional excellence. Edwin Waterhouse began the tradition of hiring prize-winners from the Institute examinations and setting high accounting standards. He would rather have lost a valued client than agree to sign an audit report which he considered inadequate or misleading. This probity became deeply ingrained in the partnership and even in the mediocre years of the late 1930s and 1940s the firm maintained a technical lead. Sir Thomas Robson, who in all practical purposes led the partnership during the war and was senior partner in the 1950s, had an outstanding reputation for integrity and accounting expertise.

The progressive internationalisation of the partnership is a third and important theme. Price Waterhouse was truly fortunate in having set up a US Firm which then grew rapidly. From the 1920s to the 1950s it held the largest portfolio of blue-chip audit clients in America. So long as these businesses dominated the world economy, the UK and European Firms were able to benefit from a ready supply of work from their overseas subsidiaries. The reconstruction of the practice on the Continent after the Second World War relied heavily on assignments from US parent companies. The risk of the UK and US Firms drifting apart was recognised in 1945 and an international partnership created to foster co-operation by providing a formal setting for discussion and the forging of personal relationships. So long as American and, to a lesser extent, British capital exercised a powerful influence over the international economy, Price Waterhouse had a powerful strategic position. During the 1960s, however, the rise of multinational corporations in countries other than America and the UK and the relative decline of these markets threatened the firm's fortunes.

In some respects Price Waterhouse appeared to be stronger than it really was. In the 1970s, for example, the firm had a large and very profitable practice in West Germany. Yet, over 95 per cent of its work was referred from foreign multinationals. Not only was its share of the indigenous market small but it was also poorly placed to win overseas assignments from the rising number of German multinationals. This situation pertained in many other important European and Asian countries. Price Waterhouse was compelled to take a new, active strategy abroad; this involved opening or developing offices in order to compete for a larger market share. In the past the firm had expanded only in response to the existing demands of clients. In the 1980s the requirement to invest ahead of business opportunities resulted in greater levels of expenditure and slower rewards. To spread the cost over all the Price Waterhouse partnership, the World Firm commonly shouldered the initial capital investment.

Although international development has been a key theme in the recent history of Price Waterhouse, it has not always been achieved smoothly. While the senior partners of the various national firms were enthusiastic about the role to be taken by the World Firm, in practice they were often unwilling to follow its lead. As a result progress has been uneven, and as yet it has proved difficult to replicate all the requisites of a multinational structure across a diverse range of professional partnerships.

Thus, the intention of this history is to show how Price Waterhouse grew to become an organisation of international proportions. At the turn of the nineteenth century it had a partnership of five (Waterhouse, Sneath, Fowler, Wyon and Halsey), a fee income of £43,000 and profits of £36,000. There was a single office at 3 Frederick's Place in the City of London and its overseas representation was limited to offices in New York and Chicago, together with an agency agreement concluded with Flack & Flack in Australia. Today, the UK Firm alone has a turnover of almost £400 million, twenty offices throughout the UK and a total personnel of nearly 6,200. This study seeks to chart this transformation and to explain how it could have occurred, and to elucidate the factors responsible for Price Waterhouse's continuing commercial success.

I

The Rising Profession

He that delights in his trade will delight in his books; and . . . he
that will thrive must . . . diligently keep his books, or else he will
never know whether he thrives or no.

Daniel Defoe, *The Complete English Tradesman*

'The word accountant,' wrote Beresford Worthington in 1895, 'is not
infrequently assumed by those mixed up with money lending, bogus
company promotions, book-making and other shady occupations.'[1]
Earlier in the century William Hazlitt, registrar of the court of bankruptcy and son of the essayist, had noted that 'an accountant was a
person unaccountable for his actions'.[2] These judgements stand in
dramatic contrast against contemporary assessments of their status and
probity. In 1962 Anthony Sampson identified them as 'the priesthood of
industry',[3] while Stevens in his study of America's leading accountancy
firms, the 'Big Eight', concluded that

> many of the world's best financial minds – leading accountants,
> lawyers, auditors, consultants, actuaries, and tax specialists – are on
> the staffs, serving clients, writing papers, counselling government,
> and perhaps most important, making decisions with social, political
> and economic repercussions. All of The Big Eight conduct massive
> educational programmes with a curriculum, staff and student body
> to rival that of a small college. When anyone wants to know
> anything about the world of business and finance they can turn to
> The Big Eight for the answers.[4]

So, there has been a major transformation in the way that accountants
are perceived by society and in the beliefs that they hold about
themselves.

Origins of the Profession

By way of introduction to the history of Price Waterhouse, this chapter examines the revolution which has occurred in the status attached to the accountant and the value which is placed on his expertise. Writing in 1857, H. Byerley Thomson divided the professions into two categories, the 'privileged' and the 'underprivileged'. Entry to the first was regulated by law and membership 'closed to free competition from without'. It included priests, barristers and physicians, who, he suggested, 'excel the others in numbers and wealth, receive a superior education and are generally drawn from a superior class'. The accountant belonged to the second group containing, according to Thomson, the 'painter, architect, sculptor, civil engineer, educator, parliamentary agent, actuary, average calculator etc. To these professions there is no legal restriction of entrance.'[5] The low standing of the accountant derived from his traditional role. Most were viewed as mere book-keepers, those who maintained a record of what others had made, sold or collected. Yet from the mid-nineteenth century increasing numbers were able to earn a lucrative income from insolvency assignments – winding up the growing numbers of limited liability companies that had fallen into liquidation. That they were able to profit from the misfortunes of others, however, brought further opprobrium upon their heads. Mr Justice Quain, for example, complained in 1875 that 'the whole affairs in bankruptcy had been handed over to an ignorant set of men called accountants'.[6]

Indeed, according to Worthington, writing in 1895, it was said to have been 'not an unusual phenomenon for a bankrupt who had thus gained a practical insight into business to develop into an accountant himself'.[7] Sir Robert Palmer Harding, chief official receiver and a founder of Harding, Pullein, Whinney & Gibbons (later to become Ernst & Young), was anecdotally reported as owning a hatter's shop which had run into financial difficulties. When his books were produced in court, the official observed that he had never seen better-kept records and that Harding would be more profitably employed as an accountant.

A rising tide of insolvency work and the involvement of unregulated practitioners led The Times to complain in 1868 that it has been one of the leading evils of recent times that an occupation like this, which requires the highest qualifications of commercial experience and a degree of integrity ... should have been left without a governing or ruling body to set standards.[8]

Such criticism doubtless encouraged accountants to form themselves into societies, which, in turn, sought recognition from the government. Their campaigns, mounted during the 1870s, ultimately resulted in the grant of a Royal Charter on 11 May 1880. The introduction of competitive examinations and the promulgation of a code of conduct followed, but these, in the short term, failed to lift the status of the profession to that described by Byerley Thomson as 'privileged'. Speaking during the period of his presidency of the Institute of Chartered Accountants in England and Wales (ICAEW) in 1887, Frederick Whinney conceded, 'we cannot, however, regard ourselves as on a line with the old professions'. Progressive specialisation within the economy, he believed, had 'called into existence the semi-professions, of which we form one, and that not the least distinguished'.[9]

The reluctance to accept accountants as being on a par with physicians or barristers was not simply a function of the public's perception of their work but also a reflection of the social class from which many were drawn. Young, upper-middle-class men, who had attended the old universities before embarking on a professional career, exhibited a reluctance to enter so fledgling a profession; until well into the 1950s most favoured the church, law or medicine. Such preferences were initially considered by G.O. May, later to become senior partner of Price Waterhouse in America. Having won a scholarship to Blundell's School in Devon, his ambition drew him towards winning a similar honour in mathematics at Cambridge. However, the visit of a relative, J.M. Criddle, a successful solicitor in Newcastle upon Tyne, resulted in a dramatic change of direction:

> He urged that I should give up my plans to go to Cambridge and go at once into accountancy, which he said was a rising profession ... Could I do both? To carry out my plans and then go into accountancy would have involved a delay of at least two and a half years. Had I the right to incur it with all the financial consequences it entailed?[10]

The upshot of this meeting was that May became an articled clerk in the Exeter office of Thomas Andrew, for which his father paid a premium of 100 guineas.

Speaking in 1922, Sir William Plender, then senior partner of Deloittes, observed how few chartered accountants had been to Oxford or Cambridge.[11] Rather than dwelling on this fact as a consequence of the profession's comparatively short existence, he considered it a positive asset:

> Avidity in work, the imperative need of taking pains, and keenest of perception have oft-times been neglected by the university man, whilst the student of moderate powers who has cultivated and observed these qualities passes him in the race . . . too often it is seen that the university graduate will not trouble sufficiently about the details – often mechanical, always laborious – which mark the beginnings of life in an accountant's office.[12]

The son of a grocer and draper, Plender had studied at the Royal Grammar School at Newcastle upon Tyne, and served his articles there with John G. Benson & Co. A letter of introduction from G.B. Monkhouse, a leading practitioner in the City (see p.163), had allowed him to join a more prestigious London firm, though he continued to entertain ambivalent feelings about the 'supreme advantage' of an Oxbridge education.[13]

Perhaps the greatest single advance in the standing of the profession occurred as a result of the First World War. Until then, official recognition had largely been denied to accountants; only Harding (1890) as chief official receiver, Plender (1911) for government work, Peat (1912) for public services and Harmood-Banner (1913) as Lord Mayor of Liverpool had received knighthoods. Heads of leading firms and presidents of the ICAEW, such as William Turquand, William Welch Deloitte, Edwin Waterhouse, Frederick Whinney and Ernest Cooper, went unrewarded by the state. However, the need to control and monitor the workings of an economy at war necessitated the recruitment of accountants as administrators and advisers, many being granted considerable executive authority. Consequently, a number of senior figures from the profession received honours when the hostilities ended. At Price Waterhouse for example, five of the nine wartime partners were knighted: Sir Albert Wyon, Sir Laurence Halsey, Sir Gilbert Garnsey,

Sir Arthur Lowes Dickinson and Sir Nicholas Waterhouse. Subsequently, several of the sons of the founding accountants received honours, including Sir Harry Peat (1920), Sir William McLintock (1922) and Sir Arthur Whinney (1927), while Sir William Plender received the first accountancy peerage in 1931.

During the interwar period accountants became increasingly conspicuous in the highest echelons of British society. Technical ability had drawn them into industry where they became financial controllers, while those who also demonstrated managerial acumen rose to be chief executives. Some outstanding examples included Sir Francis D'Arcy Cooper, chairman of Unilever from 1925, and J.H. Jolly, managing director of GKN from 1934. Prominent court cases, such as those involving Clarence Hatry in 1929 and the Royal Mail Steam Packet Co. in 1931, brought the profession's senior representatives further into the limelight as expert witnesses. Investigations and company reconstructions, such as those carried out by Garnsey, McLintock and Sir Mark Webster Jenkinson, also served to raise the public profile of accountants in the twenties. Senior accountants in this period became established figures and caught the public's attention to a greater extent than today.[14] These events gradually altered the general perception of their work, and in 1933 Carr-Saunders and Wilson in their survey of the professions were able to conclude that 'the part played by the accountant in the economic life of this country has become one of great importance'.[15]

Yet, in 1938, speaking at the Fifth International Accountants Congress held in Berlin, Sir Nicholas Waterhouse was forced to observe that:

> Though the work of an accountant now covers a vast field of activity and has reached a very high level of importance in this country, it is still one of the youngest of the professions.[16]

One reason why accountancy could still be described as young doubtless lay in the subject's comparative technical innocence. While science was increasingly coming to the aid of medicine, and law had exercised university minds for centuries, the study of accountancy remained, until after the Second World War, a relatively unsophisticated discipline. Although much foundation work had been laid down by writers such as Professor L.R. Dicksee, F.W. Pixley and Sir Gilbert Garnsey (and F.R.M. de Paula was to make great strides with the principles of consolidation in 1933–4), for the most part original ideas were ignored by the profession until after the passing of the 1948 Companies Act. A few, notably Sir Josiah Stamp, chairman of the London Midland & Scottish Railway, were critical of accountants during the interwar period for these very reasons. One commentator in the thirties observed:

> it is difficult to avoid the inference that the want of proper facilities (university courses etc) for theoretical training is in part responsible for the scanty interest displayed by accountants in the study of their craft.[17]

For the general practitioner, the intellectual demands of medicine and the law remained greater than those of accountancy. Hence, gifted accountants were drawn towards government committees or special investigations, rather than towards an attempt to advance the rudiments of the profession. To an extent this also reflected a general resistance on the part of clients to disclose more than they were compelled to do by *laissez-faire* company legislation. Yet, so long as the vast majority of accountants received their training *in situ* without having first graduated, and so long as accountancy remained only tenuously established as a university discipline, the ambitious and able scholar would have found either law or medicine a more exciting and challenging prospect during the interwar years.

The period from 1945 to the present may be divided into two, with a turning point around the early seventies. The first period was characterised by progressive but unspectacular change. Firms grew at a steady rather than a dramatic rate. The Partnership Act limited the size of partnerships to twenty members and although devices were employed to circumvent the restriction (the admission, for example, of London partners to regional firms), they served to inhibit planning on a truly national scale. Yet, ever-developing company and tax legislation drew accountants more deeply into business and the management of individuals' personal affairs. Nevertheless, the perception of their role and status by the public was probably not greatly different in 1970 than it had been in 1945. Symbols of reliability and probity, they were not in general viewed as dynamic or assertive interventionists, however much this image may have been at variance with the reality.

After 1970 the pace of change quickened. Encouraged by the removal of the limit on the size of partnerships effected by the 1967 Companies

Act, and in response to the concentration of industry following take-overs and nationalisation, the leading firms expanded rapidly, acquiring smaller competitors and merging with their peers. These larger organisations demanded the planned recruitment of students on an unprecedented scale and made imperative the move to modern office blocks to accommodate both expanded numbers and new technology. The scope of activity undertaken by the leading firms broadened appreciably to embrace every aspect of management consultancy, tax and general financial advice. To reflect this development, some firms, such as Price Waterhouse, no longer describe themselves as 'Chartered Accountants' in their corporate literature.

The increase in the prestige and potential rewards of the major international firms has enabled them to attract the very brightest graduates. Whereas twenty years ago the legal profession or the medical schools would have held the attention of many, today training at one of the major accountancy firms is akin to taking an MBA from a distinguished university. Once qualified, the able accountant is presented with a range of options often leading to rapid promotion and impressive rewards. The modern image of a successful accountant is a person who is assertive, committed, technically expert and ambitious. The contrast with those unqualified Victorian progenitors who congregated in City bars waiting for lucrative insolvency commissions to fall into their laps is sharp.

Public Perception

The status of the accountant as reflected in literature has also undergone considerable change over the last 150 years. Unlike the doctor or lawyer, who have featured in so many novels and stories, the accountant has made few appearances in fiction until recently. In the nineteenth and early years of the twentieth centuries his role was commonly that of a supporting character, a foil for the hero. Mycroft Holmes, for example, brother of the famous consulting detective, was described by Sir Arthur Conan Doyle in the case of *The Greek Interpreter* as having 'an extraordinary facility for figures, and [one who] audits the books in some of the government departments'.[18]

One of the earliest references in literature to a practising accountant, rather than a book-keeper or internal accountant, is to be found in *Little Dorrit* by Charles Dickens. Mr Dorrit, jailed in Marshalsea Prison for debt, was in fact the inheritor of a fortune of which he had no knowledge. The family lineage and financial circumstances of the claim were established by a Mr Rugg, who advertised himself as 'General Agent, Accountant, Debts Recovered'.[19] Practising from rooms in Pentonville, he had

> a round white visage, as if all his blushes had been drawn out of him long ago, and who had a ragged yellow head like a worn-out hearth broom . . .[20]

Rugg was depicted as a cold-hearted man of business who repeatedly observed, 'What I envy you sir, is the luxury of your own feelings. I belong to a profession in which that luxury is sometimes denied us.'[21] Rugg, whose part in the story remained a minor one, scarcely presented an impression of a distinguished practitioner with a prestigious address and clientele.

One of the fullest descriptions of an accountant's office is given by Somerset Maugham in his semi-autobiographical novel, *Of Human Bondage*. After a short period at Heidelberg University, Maugham had returned to London to seek a career. In 1892 he entered an accountancy firm in Chancery Lane, but after several months left to turn to medicine.[22] By the end of the nineteenth century a clear social distinction had emerged in City firms between the partner and clerk. In Maugham's novel, the former, called Carter, lived in Enfield, was an officer in the Hertfordshire Yeomanry and chairman of the local Conservative Association:

> He was dressed in a long frock-coat. He looked like a military man; his moustache was waxed, his grey hair was short and neat, he held himself upright.[23]

He encouraged his youthful pupil:

> He hoped that Philip [Maugham] would get on well and like the work, he mustn't miss his lectures, they were getting up the tone of the profession, they wanted gentlemen in it.[24]

The managing clerk, Mr Goodworthy, occupied a less well furnished office and was of a lower social standing:

He spoke with a patronising and at the same time timid air, as though he sought to assume an importance which he did not feel. He said he hoped Philip would like the work; there was a good deal of drudgery about it, but when you got used to it, it was interesting; and one made money, that was the chief thing, wasn't it? He laughed with an odd mixture of superiority and shyness.[25]

When choosing a profession for his novels about an upper-middle-class family, the Forsytes, Galsworthy selected a solicitor's practice. Yet Aunt Hester suggested that Nicholas Forsyte's son should become an accountant rather than serve as an officer in the Royal Navy. An admiral, she reasoned, was paid a 'pittance', while 'an accountant had many more chances, but let him be put with a good firm where there was no risk at starting'.[26] In the event he joined an insurance company.

As accountants have assumed a higher profile and as the public's estimation of their expertise has risen, so novelists have granted them greater prominence. In *Accounting for Murder* Emma Lathen (the pseudonym of Mary Jane Latsis, an economist, and Martha Henissart, a lawyer) created the character of Clarence Fortinbras, 'an authority in the field of corporate accounting' to investigate a fraud at 'National Calculating':

> Clarence Fortinbras was an accountant's accountant. When Price Waterhouse was reduced to wringing its hands in despair, Fortinbras was the man to be called in. If the problems raised by a major auto firm's going public proved very delicate, then a quiet feeler would go forth from the independent auditors – to Clarence Fortinbras.[27]

That the BBC could win the Best Single Drama award from the British Academy in March 1990 for a play entitled *The Accountant* would perhaps have been inconceivable twenty years earlier.

While lawyers, doctors and priests have been the subjects of many paintings, especially in the Victorian period, recognised British artists have failed to depict (except in formal, commissioned portraits) the accountant at work either in his office or on the premises of his client. This not only reflects the social standing and dull popular image of the accountant but is also a feature of the nature of the profession. While most individuals would have visited a solicitor or general practitioner at some stage, few attended an accountant's office.

Until 1991 the National Portrait Gallery had no picture of an individual whose egregiousness was based primarily on his career as an accountant. Only then were portraits of Sir Kenneth Cork and Lord Benson hung in the section depicting influential people of the twentieth century.

Price Waterhouse within the Profession

To what extent, then, have these changes been reflected in the literature of the accountancy profession? Given that many of the major firms can trace their foundations to the mid-Victorian period, an interest in their antecedents arose during the 1950s as centenaries approached. Cooper Brothers were among the first to commission a history, and it was recently revealed that its anonymous author was Lord Benson. Shortly afterwards Sir Russell Kettle, the senior partner, completed a study of Deloittes, and other firms encouraged partners to record past events for in-house consumption. In 1950, for example, G.E. Richards researched *History of the Firm, The First Fifty Years [of Price Waterhouse] 1850–1900*, and in the same year a similar typescript narrative was produced for Peat Marwick Mitchell but never formally released.

This pattern of internally generated studies continued throughout the 1960s and 1970s with further additions to the literature: Sir Harold Howitt's *History of the Institute of Chartered Accountants in England and Wales* and Rex Winsbury, *Thomson McLintock & Co., The First Hundred Years*. The centenary of the ICAEW encouraged Ernst & Whinney to commission the first academic history of a UK accountancy firm, and Leon Hopkins produced *The Hundredth Year*, a more general survey of the profession. *Touche Ross & Co. 1899–1981, The Origins and Growth of the United Kingdom Firm* by a retired partner, A.B. Richards, followed shortly afterwards.

In the United States other major firms have also published histories for internal circulation. The first narrative of Arthur Andersen was published in Chicago in 1963 followed by an updated edition in 1974, and Peat Marwick Mitchell launched a study of their firm in 1982 under the authorship of T.A. Wise. Other US histories had included that of *Ernst & Ernst 1903–1960* and De Mond's *Price Waterhouse & Co. in America*, which was replaced in 1993 by a newly commissioned study by D.M. Allen and K. McDermott, *Accounting for Success, a History of Price Waterhouse in America 1890–1990*. Thus, over the last thirty years the largest accountancy firms have generated a small but growing literature about themselves though their authors were drawn in the main from retired partners.

How does this history of Price Waterhouse relate to these publications and to the changes which have occurred within the profession? This study seeks to explain why particular strategies were adopted and others revised or rejected. It attempts to reveal the personalities of those who made decisions and dictated the pace of change. This history also focuses upon the organisation, structure and development of the partnership as a profession operating in a competitive marketplace, and seeks to explain how a small but respected City practice could grow to embrace 474 UK partners. In the last twenty years the firm's fee income has grown rapidly and far in excess of inflation. Fees levelled before the First World War at around £55,000, rose to between £250,000 and £380,000 per annum during the interwar period, and passed £1 million in 1958. In 1994 they were almost £400 million.

The transfer of London office, in 1975, from Frederick's Place to Southwark Towers, a purpose-built office block, symbolised the fundamental change which had occurred within Price Waterhouse. An increasingly commercial attitude was adopted to facilitate the continued expansion of the firm. New strategies of recruitment, training and career development were introduced, while a hierarchy of functional committees and procedures was introduced to manage an ever more complex organisation. It had still been possible in the 1960s for all the London partners to assemble each day at 9.00 a.m. to deal with outstanding client and administrative matters. It was, for example, a rule that all prospectuses prepared by Price Waterhouse had to be discussed at this assembly. With a firm which currently employs nearly 6,200 personnel at twenty offices in Britain, responsible for the training of over 1,000 students, it is impracticable to resort to the traditional partnership structure. A restructuring along functional lines distinguished between the main activities of audit, tax, management consultancy, and corporate finance and recovery. Reporting procedures were put in place to resolve the complexities of communicating between different elements located in a variety of places, and to emphasise the need to work within an overall strategy as well as to respond to specific problems.

The type of work that the firm is called upon to produce has also changed considerably. Clients have made new demands upon the auditor, requesting specialist advice or requiring that a network of offices be available to service growing numbers of subsidiaries both at home and overseas. The needs of the largest international clients, for example, may be seen to lie at the root of the territorial expansion of the major firms. Equally, the latter are continually alert to identify areas in the economy into which their existing expertise can be extended. A reputation for high standards, reliability and efficiency provides them with a valuable springboard to enter related fields of activity. The success of Price Waterhouse in capturing a major sector of the management consultancy market provides a graphic example of this approach.

As a generalisation, insolvency work dominated the early Victorian practices, but this declined as auditing rose to occupy a pre-eminent position, responsible for the bulk of most City practices' fee income until well after the Second World War. The need for tax advice following the introduction of death duties, surtax and increasingly high levels of income tax has proved to be a major feature of the twentieth century. More recently, management consultancy, executive recruitment, privatisation, corporate finance and assignments for local and central government have assumed a greater importance in the accountant's repertoire.

What, then, are the distinctive features of Price Waterhouse? The firm is almost unique among the major practices in retaining the same name, in essence, for over a hundred years. Having adopted the style Price, Waterhouse & Co. in 1874, the only changes have been the loss of the comma in 1940 and the abandonment of the '& Co.' in 1981. This continuity reflects a strategy of expansion through internal growth combined with the selective acquisition of smaller independent firms. Figure 1 demonstrates how few mergers have taken place in the history of Price Waterhouse. By the late 1960s the firm had, for example, opened its own offices in Birmingham, Cardiff, Edinburgh, Glasgow, Leeds, Liverpool, Manchester and Middlesbrough (Figure 2). A recent survey of the other large accountancy firms reveals that most are the product of many more amalgamations than Price Waterhouse.[28] Ernst & Whinney, for example, a predecessor firm of Ernst & Young, was the product of the union of approximately forty partnerships when formed in 1980. Deloitte, Haskins & Sells had a complex genealogical tree,[29] doubtless made more involved by their recent merger with Touche Ross[30] in America and with the firm of Coopers & Lybrand in the UK.[31]

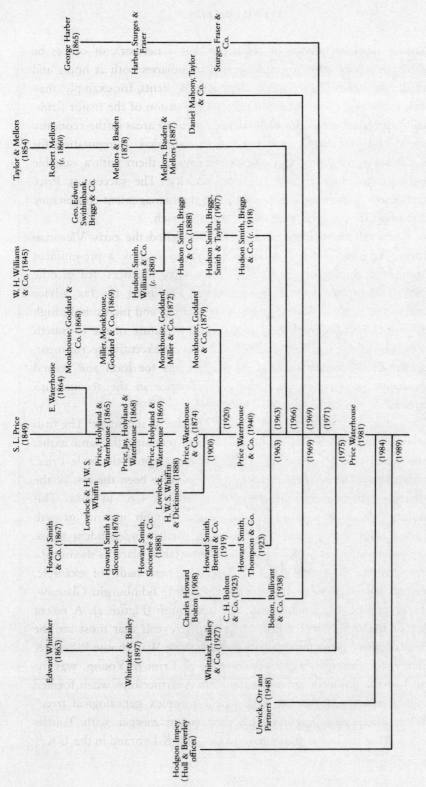

FIGURE I

A Simplified Genealogical Table of the UK Firm of Price Waterhouse

FIGURE 2

The Location and Origin of the Principal Offices of
Price Waterhouse in Britain

What are the implications of this powerful thread of continuity? It suggests that a sense of identity is particularly strong at Price Waterhouse; that there is an almost unstated feeling or appreciation of the firm's values and manner, which perhaps becomes apparent only when a novel course of action is proposed and is then abandoned because it does not accord with collective beliefs about what Price Waterhouse should be doing. This sense of identity has been strengthened by two further factors: an enduring physical location and great stability within the partnership. Between 1864 and 1975 the firm occupied only two principal offices and these were situated within several hundred yards of each other. When Price, Holyland and Waterhouse formed their partnership and it proved necessary to find larger premises to accommodate their respective businesses, rooms on several floors at 13 (now 44) Gresham Street were rented. Pressure of space forced Price Waterhouse to move in 1899 to 3 Frederick's Place where the firm expanded into adjacent offices and neighbouring buildings. It was not until 1975 that the need to integrate the firm's rapidly growing activities led to the transfer from the City to a purpose-built office block at London Bridge.

The second factor was that until recently it was virtually unknown for partners to move to other organisations and more rarely still to other firms. Admission to the partnership was regarded as being for the remainder of the individual's working life. Equally, until the 1950s seniority within the firm was based primarily on length of service which, in turn, produced few changes of leadership and a sense of continuity down the years. Edwin Waterhouse, for example, was senior partner from 1887 to 1906, some nineteen years, and his son, Sir Nicholas, held the office for fifteen years between 1945 and 1960. Sir Albert Wyon was the longest-serving senior partner, some twenty-one years, from 1916 to 1937, while Sir Laurence Halsey completed eight years in the office from 1937 to 1945. Although Sir Thomas Robson was senior partner for only six years, between 1960 and 1966, he had, in fact, performed many of the chief executive's functions as deputy to the elderly Sir Nicholas Waterhouse. Subsequent senior partners had all joined the firm either as articled clerks or newly qualified accountants and were, therefore, well versed in the traditions and values of Price Waterhouse.

In the foreword to his autobiography, *Accounting for Life*, Lord Benson observed that:

I have noticed that the basic professional principles which were laid down by the Cooper Brothers in 1854 have remained unchanged all through my lifetime, and I do not think they will alter much in the years to come. It is only the outward trappings that change.[32]

While most would agree that standards of professional conduct should have an enduring quality and that those promulgated by the Victorians largely pertain today, there is an implication that change to 'outward trappings' is of lesser consequence. It remains a moot point as to whether the transformation which has occurred in the size, structure and activities of the major accountancy firms may be, in fact, of greater significance than the continuing ethical principles which underpin them.

2

Foundations of the Partnership

If my nephew is steady, cautious, fond of a sedentary life and quiet pursuits, and at the same time proficient in arithmetic with a disposition towards the prosecution of the highest branches, he cannot follow a better line than that of an accountant. It is one in which, with attention and skill, aided by such opportunities as I may be able to procure for him, he must ultimately succeed.

Sir Walter Scott in a letter to his brother Thomas, 23 July 1820[1]

Traditionally, 24 December 1849 has been taken as the foundation of the UK Firm of Price Waterhouse,[2] for that was the date on which Samuel Lowell Price severed his links with William Edwards and set up on his own account at 5 Gresham Street. He continued to practise there for fifteen years until 1 May 1865 when he was joined in partnership by W.H. Holyland and Edwin Waterhouse. The former had worked for a warehousing business in Watling Street and latterly had been a principal clerk with Turquand, Youngs & Co., a leading City firm. Waterhouse had been articled to William Turquand but in 1864, having reached the point where he could be regarded as qualified, decided to leave in order to establish his own practice. However, scarcely a year later the advantages of joining two more experienced accountants proved compelling. The three, united in partnership, moved to larger premises at 13 (now 44) Gresham Street. Not a little mystery surrounds these early but important events. Details of the careers of Price and Holyland have not been easy to discover, while reports of their personalities and motives have proved even more elusive. Nevertheless, it has been possible to document a broad chronology of the firm's foundation.

Samuel Lowell Price

Samuel Lowell Price was born in 1821 at Bristol, the eleventh child of Charles Price.[3] The latter had served an apprenticeship with Thomas Patience, of the Patience and Gadd Pottery at 3 Counterslip, and in 1796 entered into partnership with Gadd at 124 Temple Street. The death of Gadd in 1798 left Price as the sole proprietor at about the time he had become a master potter. In 1802 he took Joseph Read into partnership and in 1803–4 Price & Read acquired James Alsop's pottery at 123 Temple Street.[4] Although trained as a potter, Read spent most of his time on accounting duties, having learned these skills as a confidential clerk in the employment of John Cave & Co., wholesale druggists and colour manufacturers of Bristol.[5] Trading alone from 1818, Charles Price brought two sons into the partnership under the style C. Price & Sons.[6] The pottery continued to be owned by the Price family until 1961 when it closed.

Little documentary evidence survives to tell of S.L. Price's early life and education. Samuel Newell Price, a nephew, stated that he had been articled to the Bristol firm of Bradley & Barnard, who described themselves as 'public accountants, auctioneers and general agents to assignees and creditors in bankruptcies'.[7] In 1842–3 S.L. Price enjoyed a salary of £120 per annum and worked in Bradley & Barnard's London office.[8]

The firm's accounts also recorded a credit of £2 for a 'cash journey' on 23 September 1842 which was presumably to refund his travel expenses from Bristol.[9] If, indeed, he had trained with this firm, it would suggest that Price had joined at some time in 1839 or slightly before as three years were generally considered an appropriate period of articles. Alternatively, it has been suggested that Price could have trained with a Samuel Delpratt Price,[10] an 'accomptant' who had been sworn in as a burgess of Bristol in September 1799.[11] The latter had a son of the same name who did not join in the family firm but became a plumber and glazier.[12] Or it has been suggested that Charles and Samuel Delpratt Senior were related and that the young Samuel Lowell entered the latter's office. It has, however, proved impossible to establish any familial link between these two Prices, and the weight of evidence suggests that Bradley & Barnard had, in fact, trained its promising clerk in Bristol before he transferred to London. Indeed, a representative from a later

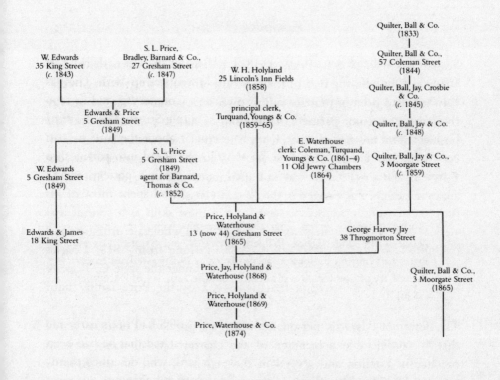

FIGURE 3

The Foundation of Price Waterhouse

generation of the family, Granville Sharp Price, son of the Rev. Dr Thomas Price, served articles with the firm in Bristol.[13]

At some date during the 1830s Bradley & Barnard opened an office in 25 St Swithin's Lane, London,[14] and it would have been to these premises that S.L. Price journeyed in 1842.[15] However, by 1844 the firm had moved to 6 Bow Church Yard and by 1847 was at 27 Gresham Street. Price was well regarded for in March 1848 he was credited with £79 14s 1d from the firm's capital account.[16] This, together with a reference to the 'Old Led[ger]' suggested that he had been admitted to the partnership at some time before 1848 and was perhaps entrusted with the running of the London office. He continued to act as the firm's agents (now called Barnard, Thomas & Co.) when in partnership with Edwards and afterwards as a sole practitioner.[17] From around 1853, Price also became an agent for another Bristol firm, Jackson, Garrard & Neale.

Edwards & Price

Sometime in 1848 S.L. Price decided to enter into partnership with William Edwards, the two of them taking offices at 5 Gresham Street.[18] Edwards had been in practice on his own since around 1843,[19] and was, therefore, the senior partner. In addition, he had in part taken over the business of his brother-in-law, Henry Threlkeld, 'accountant and auctioneer' of 2 Star Court, Bread Street.[20] Why the arrangement between Edwards and Price failed was not mentioned and only the briefest of announcements was inserted in the London Gazette:

> Notice is hereby given, that the partnership heretofore existing between the undersigned William Edwards and Samuel Lowell Price, carrying on business as accountants, at No. 5 Gresham Street in the City of London, was dissolved from the 24th day of December [1849].[21]

The nature of Edwards' personality remains a puzzle. His obituary stated that 'a considerable percentage of the chartered accountants now in practice in London and several in the provinces were at one time or other in Mr Edwards' office'.[22] It was said that W.W. Deloitte at the age of fifteen had obtained a position as assistant to a Mr Edwards who was official assignee at the Bankruptcy Court.[23] As Figure 4 reveals, Edwards participated in a number of important partnerships but rarely remained in them for long. He may have been an able but autocratic figure who could not tolerate equals but took pleasure from encouraging juniors.

The upshot of the dissolution of December 1849 was that Edwards and Price both continued to practise from 5 Gresham Street but as separate individuals.[24] Their offices were situated in a four-storey, neo-classical commercial premises on the south side of the road, slightly to the west of St Lawrence Jewry. Sadly, the building was bombed in the Second World War and subsequently demolished.[25] The nature of their business, and indeed of Price's clients for the fifteen and a half years that he practised alone, remains uncertain as no documentary evidence for either period has survived. But the proximity of their office to the bankruptcy courts, and the nature of the economy, both suggested that the bulk of their work came from insolvencies. The grant of limited liability led to a great increase in the number of joint stock companies

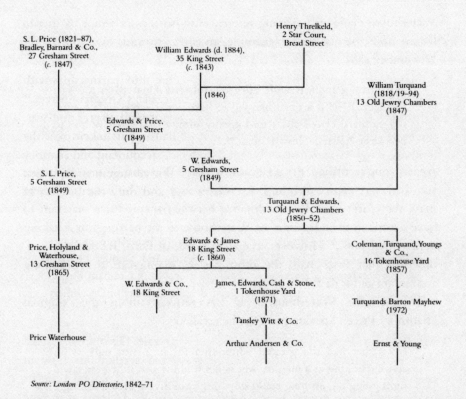

Source: London PO Directories, 1842–71

FIGURE 4

The Relationship between Price, Edwards and Turquand

but many of these ventures were speculative and had a short life. Some 25.6 per cent of all public companies set up between 1856 and 1865 ended in insolvency. The proportion of bankruptcies rose to 30.3 per cent for those founded in 1866–74 and 33.4 per cent for those established between 1875 and 1883.[26] Of the doomed companies formed between 1856 and 1865 half failed within the first six years of their existence, half of those of 1866–74 within the first five years and half of those of 1875–83 within the first four years. It was inconceivable that either Edwards or Price would not have sought a share of this potentially lucrative market.

Descriptions of Samuel Lowell Price are as vague as they are brief. A relative reported that he was a 'tall handsome man; he wore a velvet coat; in his later years he suffered from bad attacks of lumbago and would have to be helped home from the office'.[27] Sadly, Edwin

Waterhouse made only fleeting references to his former senior partner in his memoirs; he quotes, for example, an entry from his own journal for November 1865:

> My first six months with Price & Holyland expired on the 31st October. I feel it a great blessing to have come across such men as my partners. Price's character I greatly admire, and I believe him to be a large-hearted Christian man.[28]

Apart from recording Price's death in 1887, Waterhouse scarcely made any further reference to him. Price was twenty years his senior and there may, therefore, have been a distance between them. Price was said to have described the admission of Waterhouse to the partnership as taking in 'a young pup'.[29] However, the elder Ford, of Ford, Rhodes & Ford, observed that Price had 'the most perfect manner of any practising accountant of his day'.[30]

Sir Nicholas Waterhouse was less reticent about the 'original "Sammy" Price'. Speaking in 1950 he recalled:

> My father had the greatest admiration for him, not only as an accountant, but as a pugilist. My father told me that if he ever saw a fight going on, nothing could stop him from diving in and having a good time. In the days of the Fenian riots in the 80s, on several occasions . . . he turned up to the office in a very dishevelled and somewhat bloodstained condition.[31]

Waterhouse also remembered visiting the offices at 44 Gresham Street as a child:

> We stood waiting by the commissionaire's box for my father to come down. My father and Mr Price came down and I was introduced . . . There was a little whistle on the commissionaire's speaking tube – that was the horrible contraption before house telephones were invented. Mr Price removed the whistle and put the tube to his ear, and a voice belonging to someone upstairs, who thought he was addressing the commissionaire, was distinctly heard to say 'Has Old Sammy gone yet?' Mr Price replied 'I'll come up and "Sammy" you', and up the stairs he went as fast as his legs could carry him.[32]

In 1848 Price married Emma Nutter Price, eldest daughter of the Rev. Dr Thomas Price, his half-brother and secretary of the Protestant

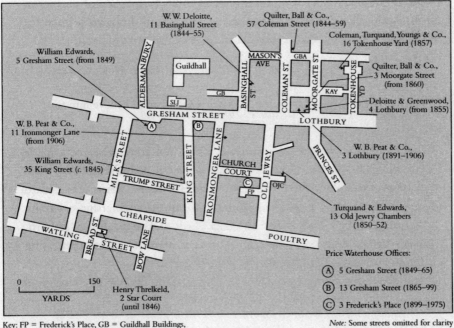

FIGURE 5

Selected Accountancy Firms in the Victorian City of London

Dissenters and General Fire and Accident Co. The wedding took place at Wansbeck in Denmark since such a union was not legal in Britain. S.L. Price lived at 94 Camden Road Villas, though when he became more affluent he moved to 37 York Terrace, Regent's Park, and on retirement also took a country house, 'The Lodge', in Farnham Royal. He died at his London home on 19 May 1887 at the age of sixty-six.

Price had been actively involved in the movement to secure official recognition for accountants. He had, for example, attended an informal meeting on 8 June 1870 at the offices of Quilter, Ball & Co. when it was decided to set up an association and had proposed William Quilter for the chairmanship. When the Institute of Accountants in London, as it was called, held its first council meeting in December, the constitution was confirmed on his proposal.[33] Throughout the decade this body, together with a number of provincial associations, campaigned for either

a Royal Charter or an Act of Parliament to secure a means of incorporation. In the event, matters were settled by the granting of a charter in
May 1880. Price became a founder member of the council and, though a
rare attender of meetings, retained his seat until his death.

William Hopkins Holyland

In his memoirs, Edwin Waterhouse recounted how frequent trips to
John Fowler's Steam Plough Works in Leeds led to several chance
meetings at the Queen's Hotel with W.H. Holyland, 'a principal clerk of
Mr Turquand's, who was engaged in winding up the Leeds Banking
Company, which had come to grief'.[34] Waterhouse had served his
articles between January 1861 and January 1864 with Coleman, Turquand, Youngs & Co. but was now in sole practice. Waterhouse wrote
that Holyland

> told me he was about to join his friend Mr S.L. Price, an accountant
> of Gresham Street, in partnership, and suggested that I should make
> a third in the arrangement. I had been doing very well for myself
> during the last few months, but the offer seemed to open out
> chances of quickly attaining a wider experience, whilst ensuring a
> more steady practice and affording me the advantages of assistance
> should I need it. After consulting my grandfather and some business
> friends, I accepted the terms offered [to] me, and we arranged to
> put up our names as a firm on 1st May 1865.[35]

How Holyland met Price is not recorded. It is conceivable that the
former was a dissenter and that an introduction had been effected
through the Society of Friends.

Little has been documented about the early career of William Hopkins
Holyland. He was born on 25 December 1807, but nothing certain is
known of his parents, education or early working life. A relative
believed that Holyland had been a partner with a Mr Prosser in a soap
manufactory which had come to grief.[36] However, no listing of such an
enterprise was recorded in London trade directories for the period.[37] In
around 1850 he joined the firm of Rogers, Lowery & Co., warehouse-
men and outfitters of 91 Watling Street and remained with them until
1856.[38] He then decided to set up an accountant's practice and in 1858

recorded his address as 25 Lincoln's Inn Fields.[39] This career change suggested that he may have been the partner responsible for the financial affairs of the warehousing business and may have been a book-keeper in his youth.

It seems that Holyland's practice did not flourish and was shortlived. He did not, for example, advertise in the *Post Office Directory* for 1859 or 1860 under the heading 'accountants', nor was he listed as renting office accommodation at 25 Lincoln's Inn Fields. Possibly he found it difficult to establish connections with clients or at the bankruptcy courts, coming from a commercial background rather than having been employed by a well-known accountancy firm. Nevertheless, his joining Coleman, Turquand, Youngs & Co., a pre-eminent City firm, to become one of their principal clerks, showed that his probity and competence were not in question.

Edwin Waterhouse

Edwin Waterhouse,[40] born on 4 June 1841 at Aigburth, Liverpool, was the seventh and youngest child of Alfred Waterhouse, a partner in the merchanting and broking business of Nicholas Waterhouse & Sons.[41] His eldest brother, Alfred, a prolific architect, was to design some of the finest public buildings of the century, including the Assize Courts (1861), Town Hall (1868–77) and Refuge Assurance (1893–1913) in Manchester, the Natural History Museum (1873–81) and University College Hospital (1897–1906), together with important commissions for the Prudential Assurance Co. (1875–9). He won the RIBA Gold Medal in 1878 and was President in 1888–91. The Waterhouse family were prominent members of the Society of Friends and as a result Edwin and an elder brother, William, were sent to University College School, a comparatively liberal institution with a reputation for scholarship, populated by the sons of middle-class dissenters.[42] Edwin proved to be an able, though not outstanding, student and in October 1857 he joined another brother, Theodore, at University College. Throughout these years of study, as Edwin himself acknowledged, Theodore served as an example to him: 'Great were the advantages to me in having one so interested in my welfare for good, as he always was ready to help and advise me.'[43] Edwin took a 'good second-class B.A. degree' having studied Greek, Latin, English and mathematics, and gained prizes in Greek and English.[44] Equally important, his undergraduate days introduced him to many members of a middle-class élite who in later life were to occupy influential posts in government, administration, commerce and the professions.

His elder brother Theodore had a natural academic talent, gaining first-class honours with prizes in moral philosophy and the history of philosophy; and in 1867 he was elected a Fellow. However, he decided to enter the law and having served articles with Clayton, Cookson & Wainwright and achieved second place in the Law Society's final examinations, he set up his own practice at 10 Lincoln's Inn Fields. His partner, William Winterbotham, later wrote of Theodore:

> He was exact and thorough in all his work, and he rarely made a mistake; never did careless work himself, and he was impatient of careless work in others. He was especially precise in all matters of account ... For some years he kept the accounts of his business himself, not only entering up the cash-book and posting the ledger, but even making a fair copy of these books in his own hand.[45]

This general description could have been applied equally well to Edwin. The fact that both Theodore, the solicitor, and Alfred, the architect, were scrupulous in keeping precise financial records, suggested that there was something in the Waterhouse family values which attracted them to regularity, order and control. Edwin, however, was the sole accountant and it may perhaps be significant that his firm was the most successful of the three.

Having sat finals at University College in 1860, Edwin Waterhouse found himself faced with the dilemma of which career to choose. There was a fortuitous element in his selection. Since Alfred was already well established as an architect and Theodore was training to be a solicitor, Edwin initially toyed with the idea of medicine, but as he felt 'no special bent that way' and 'feared a failure', he soon abandoned such a scheme.[46] 'The consideration of the subject,' he later wrote,

> gave me many painful hours, and I know was the cause of anxiety to my parents. Matters were arranged for me in a simple but unexpected way. Among our neighbours at Whiteknights [Reading] were three ladies, sisters of William Turquand, the 'accountant', to whom my parents thus became introduced. My father considered a

training in an accountant's office, giving me an insight into City
and commercial life, just what was wanted for me. I acquiesced and
it was soon arranged that after a holiday, I should go to the office of
Coleman, Turquand, Youngs & Co. of Tokenhouse Yard, E.C. and
learn something about business generally from the point of view of
the public accountant.[47]

There was a touch of irony in this decision as Edwin admitted he then
knew 'nothing of business and felt a dislike of the "city" and of the pale
and anxious faces which I saw on my infrequent visits there'.[48]

At that time Coleman, Turquand, Youngs & Co. was one of the
City's leading practices along with Quilter, Ball & Co., Harding,
Pullein, Whinney & Gibbons and W.W. Deloitte. Turquand, later to
become the first president of the ICAEW, was described by Ernest
Cooper as

> a courteous gentleman, always well dressed, an ideal professional
> man ... a bankrupt merchant in his hands call[ed] to see me and
> indignantly protesting that he had been to see Mr Turquand about
> his affairs, and all he could get was an exclamation that he might
> take his affairs to the Devil.[49]

His father having paid a premium of £210, Edwin Waterhouse began
to learn the tasks of an accountant under the overall supervision of
Mr Weise, a partner. He studied book-keeping and the various ways that
insolvent businesses could be wound up, but before long, as he recalled,

> I was given little matters of audit or investigation to carry through
> myself, and the work then soon became of interest. I remember an
> examination into the accounts of the manager of a Union Work-
> house, on which I made a long report while yet a novice at my
> work. For many weeks I was engaged in assisting a principal clerk
> in putting in order the accounts of some Army agents in Westmin-
> ster ... I was occasionally sent to the offices of the London &
> North Western Railway to assist in Mr Coleman's work as public
> accountant in the service of the auditors. Mr Coleman was connected
> also with the London, Chatham & Dover Railway, then carrying
> out its metropolitan extensions, and I gained not a little experience
> in examining into the trade claims for loss of business on change
> of premises, and in sometimes giving evidence in the court of
> arbitration.[50]

After two years, in January 1863, Edwin received his first payment, £2 6s 5d, and had the promise of a salary. In this pre-Charter period there were no qualifying examinations, and three years were considered 'long enough to educate a young man sufficiently to be in a position to take up business for himself'.[51] Accordingly, in December 1863 Edwin Waterhouse informed Turquand that he had decided to leave his employment in order to set up on his own account. They offered to keep him on so that he could extend his experience, but he adhered to the advice of his father and brother Alfred that he establish his own practice, and left Tokenhouse Yard on 7 January 1864.

On 24 February 1864, after a holiday on the Riviera and having been given £2,000 by his father, Edwin Waterhouse put up his brass plate at 11 Old Jewry Chambers in the City.[52] During the first few weeks he was largely occupied in sending out business cards and letters to friends and acquaintances, many of whom had a non-conformist connection. Among those whom he contacted were: Lewis Fry, Ransom & Sims, J.W. Richardson, Edward Ashworth, William Fowler, J.S. Fry & Sons, J.W. Pease, Crewdson & Worthington, J.B. Braithwaite, Huntley & Palmers and Henry Crosfield.[53] Because no work had materialised and he feared for the success of his practice, on Saturday 9 April, he decided to call on John Ball, of Quilter, Ball & Co., to seek his advice. This, he recorded, was possibly a mistake as Mr Ball,

> after putting some questions to me to test my abilities, which I think I was too nervous to answer properly, told me that some further practice with Coleman & Co. would be good for me. But I remembered what my brother Alfred told me of his own experience, that one little matter carried through by myself and for myself would teach me more than a month of clerkship – and I waited.[54]

Two months passed without an assignment until his brother Alfred despatched the financial records of his Manchester practice for examination and reorganisation. He balanced the accounts to 5 April 1864 and appended a 'list of a few alterations in the method of keeping accounts, which will add greatly to their efficiency and accuracy'.[55] In June, having devised a double-entry system, he prepared a profit and loss account.[56] It was subsequently reported that the managerial and financial controls maintained by Alfred Waterhouse made his the most efficient architectural practice of the day,[57] and some of the credit for these innovations must have been due to Edwin, who continued to advise him on accountancy matters.[58]

Another crucial connection was with Harmood Banner & Sons, the Liverpool accountants, to whom Edwin wrote on 2 April 1864, while anxiously searching for work:

> I need not say how happy I should be to undertake any work for such a firm as your own, and of how much greater importance to a young man like myself the obtaining of such work is than the question of a large or small amount of remuneration for it. I should of course be very unwilling ... to do business on terms which might be thought too low for a first class accountant but under the present circumstances, I beg to leave the question of terms entirely in your hands.[59]

As a result of this inquiry, Harmood W. Banner sub-contracted assignments which had been referred to him in Liverpool but required subsidiary work in London.[60] He was responsible for providing Waterhouse with his first audit, that of the Queen Insurance Co. in Leadenhall Street.[61] By July 1864 Waterhouse was able to report:

> I have completed the audit ... I have gone with great minuteness into the accounts ... I trust, however, that we may make some improvements in the method of keeping the accounts in the future ... I am anxious you should know how very glad I shall be to undertake any other work in London with which you might be willing to entrust us.[62]

However, as Table 1 (see Appendix) reveals, the bulk of the work performed by Edwin Waterhouse in his first eleven months as a sole practitioner was the preparation of accounts either for partnerships, companies or individuals. At a time when the general level of accountancy knowledge was rudimentary, practitioners had an educative role to play as the following letter to the directors of Hewett & Co. demonstrated:

> The cash vouchers agree with very few exceptions with the journal and cash book entries though there is considerable room for improvement in the method in which they are arranged ... There is considerable room for improvement to the method of opening the ledger accounts, the petty cash account, and in other details ... It is

of course highly desirable that a system of stores accounts should be in operation as early as possible: no reliable account of profit can be made without this . . .[63]

The mid-nineteenth century was a time when basic accounting knowledge and skills were still spreading throughout a rapidly expanding business community and were often entrusted to those whose primary interests lay elsewhere. Something of the wonderment at being able to record the financial consequences of commercial activities was captured by Dickens who depicted the manufacturing enterprise of Daniel Doyce & Arthur Clennam:

Arthur now showed, with pains and care, the state of their gains and losses, responsibilities and prospects. Daniel went through it all in his patient manner . . . He audited the accounts, as if they were a far more ingenious piece of mechanism than he had ever constructed, and afterwards stood looking at them . . . as if he were absorbed in the contemplation of some wonderful engine.

'It's all beautiful, Clennam, in its regularity and order. Nothing can be plainer. Nothing can be better.'[64]

Edwin Waterhouse did not secure lucrative insolvency commissions; they would have been captured by the established City firms. Neither did he perform many audits. This was partly a reflection of his youth and inexperience but also resulted from the general scarcity of audit work in the 1860s. The then well-known firm of Harding, Whinney & Gibbons, (subsequently Whinney, Smith & Whinney and latterly Ernst & Young) for example, earned only £220 (or 2.4 per cent) of its fee income in 1860 from auditing, a figure which had risen to a mere £1,506 (10.9 per cent) twenty years later.[65] Indeed, such audit work as Waterhouse secured had commonly been preceded by a request to prepare the books of account.

The tasks which Waterhouse performed for the British Ice Making Co. illustrated the pattern of mid-nineteenth century accountancy. The business had fallen into difficulties because of the exceptionally cold winter of 1863–4, 'which so completely satisfied the demand for ice that the company ceased working'.[66] He was called upon to examine the books and to prepare a balance sheet and profit and loss account in order that the viability of the enterprise could be re-assessed. Although he estimated a loss of £361 14s 5d, he concluded that the undertaking has not yet had a fair trial. It is true that hitherto, owing to the machinery having been so long idle, the expenses have amounted to something like three times the receipts; but looking at the large margin between the real cost of making ice and its present market value (even inferior ice is now selling at 30/- or 40/- per ton), there is no apparent reason why a very good dividend should not be enjoyed by the shareholders.[67]

He had earlier calculated that the plant was capable of producing twelve tons of ice a day at an average cost of less than 10 shillings a ton. *Au fond*, therefore, the business appeared to be sound but had been unfortunate in starting to trade during unusually cold weather. Waterhouse continued to negotiate with the company's directors and it seems that his report and audit presented to a general meeting[68] played a major part in the decision to recommence operations. In December 1864 he reported to his friend, Edward Burges, that 'the machinery is now at work; ice is being sold at a remunerative price'.[69]

In the event the enterprise did not prove successful. Perhaps the winter of 1864–5 had been too harsh. In April Edwin Waterhouse was again writing to the British Ice Making Co., but this time to request that they consider him as a liquidator:

> I hope that I am not offending good taste in thus formally applying for that post. The gentlemen, whom I shall in a few days join in business are of very great experience [Price and Holyland], and I feel your company would do well or at any rate die creditably in our hands.[70]

As Table 1 (see Appendix) shows, the work that Waterhouse performed for John Fowler was of great importance for his early practice, representing 36.5 per cent of chargeable hours in 1864. Fowler, a Quaker manufacturer of steam-powered agricultural machinery, was an acquaintance of his father and had approached Waterhouse with a view to 'organising and starting a system of accounts specially adapted to the business as well as taking charge of and generally superintending them for some months'.[71] In conjunction with another Quaker, Fowler had set up the Steam Plough Royalty Co. in 1859 at Leathley Road, Hunslet, Leeds, but the strain of establishing the works had caused him a nervous breakdown[72] at about the same time as he requested Edwin

Waterhouse to report upon its cost account system.[73] Sadly, Fowler contracted lockjaw (tetanus) after a riding accident and died in November 1864, a sudden end to the career of an innovative engineer and entrepreneur.

An unusual investigation was undertaken by Waterhouse on behalf of the Great Eastern Railway and West Ham Gas Co. in view of the proposed increase in their parish assessments. For the former this involved preparing 'an accurate account of the mileage of railway within the parish'[74] and provided Edwin Waterhouse with a further introduction to railway accounting, a specialism which was subsequently to bring the firm substantial fees and prestige.

Price, Holyland & Waterhouse

In March 1864, in answer to an approach from H.C. Gurney that he might consider a union, Waterhouse wrote,

> I cannot say that I have thought much about partnerships, having looked forward to making my way for the next few years if possible by myself; but I have no unalterable course before me . . .[75]

His experience as a sole practitioner proved to be shortlived. The suggestion that he join forces with Price had come from Holyland. Details of the negotiations were probably never recorded as, on 1 March 1865, Edwin Waterhouse corresponded with Holyland: 'I think I promised to write to you on the subject of our conversation on Monday but I should so much prefer a chat with you . . .'[76] An arrangement must have been concluded shortly afterwards for, on 28 March, he was in touch with Henry Plews, the landlord of his rooms at 11 Old Jewry Chambers, to inform him that 'I will let you know as early as I can how soon I shall be ready to vacate them'.[77] In the event he left the premises at the end of April.[78]

The new partnership was formally established on 1 May 1865 (Figure 6). As the most experienced accountant, rather than the eldest, Price became the senior partner. The firm was capitalised at £2,000 of which £1,000 had been contributed by Price and £500 each by Holyland and Waterhouse.[79] In addition, the latter paid £1,000 to Price and £250 to Holyland by way of premiums. Price was to take half of the profits up

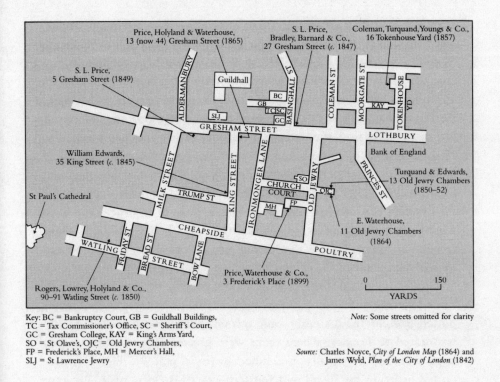

Key: BC = Bankruptcy Court, GB = Guildhall Buildings,
TC = Tax Commissioner's Office, SC = Sheriff's Court,
GC = Gresham College, KAY = King's Arms Yard,
SO = St Olave's, OJC = Old Jewry Chambers,
FP = Frederick's Place, MH = Mercer's Hall,
SLJ = St Lawrence Jewry

Note: Some streets omitted for clarity

Source: Charles Noyce, *City of London Map* (1864) and
James Wyld, *Plan of the City of London* (1842)

FIGURE 6

The Geographical Origins of Price Waterhouse in Nineteenth-century London

to £3,000, the remainder to be divided equally between Holyland and Waterhouse; those over £3,000 were to be apportioned equally between the three.[80] With a surplus of £7,440 for their first year of trading, Waterhouse would have received a gross income of £2,230. In November 1865 Waterhouse wrote in his diary:

> Financially too our partnership seems to have answered. I have this afternoon made up the profit and loss account for the six months and I find my own share will more than cover the premium [£1,250] which I paid on joining Mr Price.[81]

The accommodation at 5 Gresham Street, where Price had practised since 1848, was found to be inadequate to house the expanded partnership. Accordingly, they took rooms on the first, second and third floors in the premises of the Queens Assurance Co. A *palazzo* building of

Portland stone situated on the corner of Gresham Street (No.13 later 44) and King Street, it had been completed in 1845 by the architect Sancton Wood, at a cost of £8,000. Wood had established his reputation as a designer of stations, notably Shoreditch terminus (1849), for the Eastern Counties Railway, and subsequently completed a number of buildings for the Midland Railway on the line between Peterborough and Leicester. In an infant profession where the quality of one's premises helped to establish a sense of probity and trustworthiness, this clearly represented an important move in the history of the firm. Waterhouse observed that their image of respectability might have received an early dent but for his foresight that had 'prevented the carrying out of an order for a brass plate on our swing doors, which had the doors been ajar, would have resulted in "Price, HolyWater" being seen on one door, and "Land and House" on the other'.[82]

Thus it was that three men of comparatively diverse backgrounds came together to form a partnership. Price, the son of a non-conformist potter, had entered the embryonic accountancy profession in his youth, transferred to London where there were greater opportunities to earn large fees, and eventually established his own practice. Holyland, reported as being his friend and fourteen years his elder, may also have been a dissenter. An experienced book-keeper, he had become a partner in a City warehousing business, had briefly gone into private practice and then given this up to seek employment with the firm of Coleman, Turquand, Youngs & Co. Both men were therefore of roughly equivalent social standing, experience and age. Waterhouse, twenty years younger than Price and only twenty-four, came from a different background. His father, having retired from the family cotton-broking business in Liverpool, lived in reasonable style at Whiteknights, near Reading. He had sent Edwin to University College London, and the latter was expected to follow his elder brothers into one of the respected professions. Although brought up a Quaker, he was baptised into the Church of England in May 1864 shortly after setting up in practice. Waterhouse represented a second generation of accountants drawn from a better-educated and more socially privileged group than the founding fathers. And it was perhaps for this reason Price and Holyland were prepared to admit him to their partnership.

The foundation of Price, Holyland & Waterhouse could not have occurred at a more propitious time. In the absence of examinations and rules of conduct, entry could not have been simpler. The widespread grant of limited liability by the 1856 and 1862 Companies Acts created two sources of income for accountants: those businesses which failed generated insolvency assignments, while those which survived required advice on the keeping of financial records and production of annual accounts, and a growing number of these were appointing accountants to perform the annual audit.

As a result, the 1840s and 1850s were the decades when many of the most prestigious accountancy firms were established. Quilter Ball & Co. (now subsumed within Coopers & Lybrand), for example, began in 1844, W.W. Deloitte set up in practice in 1845, Harding & Pullein (later to become Whinney, Smith & Whinney) in 1848, Turquand & Edwards *c.*1850, and Cooper Brothers & Co. in 1854. It had been in 1849 that S.L. Price set forth on his own and practised successfully for fifteen and a half years before joining Holyland and Waterhouse. In addition, the numbers of those advertising themselves as accountants in trade directories, though not an accurate total, increased from 107 in 1840 to 205 in 1845[83] and 264 in 1850.[84] The census, too, provided an indication of the growth of the profession enumerating 4,974 accountants in 1841, 6,138 in 1851 and 6,240 in 1861.[85] Definitional changes, however, prevented these figures from being a precise population record. But in any event, the processes leading to the formation of Price, Holyland & Waterhouse in 1865 were part of a general trend, as a new profession was founded and began to root itself within the commercial fortunes of the nation.

3

The Burgeoning Practice

The auditing of the accounts of individuals, firms and public companies, also of executors and trustees and corporations, forms the foundation of the practice of professional accountants.

Francis W. Pixley, *The Profession of a Chartered Accountant*

The second half of the nineteenth century saw accountants formally recognised as a profession and a number of leading City firms establish themselves as auditors of important corporations and institutions. Until this time their principal activity had been that of liquidator.[1] However, the widespread grant of limited liability in 1856 and 1862 created a need for expert advice on the keeping of financial records by management, and, as businesses became larger and more complex, unqualified shareholder auditors increasingly sought professional assistance. In time, accountants with no personal stake in the enterprise were elected to audit the accounts and these regular, annual appointments came to form the core fee income of prestigious City firms. Price Waterhouse was one such practice. Under the leadership initially of S.L. Price and from 1887 of Edwin Waterhouse it grew steadily to become one of the largest and most respected partnerships, drawing clients from banking, insurance and the railway companies. Although not one of the oldest nor one of the first-rank practices of the 1860s, a consistent and determined commitment to auditing propelled Price Waterhouse ahead of many of its better-established rivals as it gained a sound reputation for efficiency, reliability and probity.

These business developments took place within a context of sustained and sometimes rapid economic growth. Greater numbers of enterprises were established than ever before, covering an ever wider range of activities. These companies, in turn, needed financial institutions to sell their shares, handle their assets and raise fresh capital. The rising tide of activity demanded improved transport networks, the response coming not from the state but from company promoters. Granted unparalleled opportunities to seek the protection of limited liability, management could operate within broad and sometimes indistinct boundaries. In an atmosphere of speculation and fraud, accountants found themselves attempting to establish standards of reporting and sound rules of practice. Large business enterprises concerned to present an image of probity to the public were only too ready to employ City firms. Price Waterhouse, while benefiting from the loose regulations surrounding company deal-ings, sought to impose standardised and fair principles. Thus, the last thirty years of the Victorian era represented a turning point in both the history of the accountancy profession and the fortunes of its most dynamic participants.

The Early Clients

The loss of the firm's day books has made it impossible to reconstruct the precise nature of Price, Holyland & Waterhouse's early practice. However, both the legal system and the nascent state of commercial enterprise suggested that Price in his fifteen years as a sole practitioner would have derived a substantial proportion of his fee income from insolvency work. The Bankruptcy Act of 1831 had provided for the employment of officers, designated 'official assignees' to liquidate estates on behalf of creditors. Some were accountants, while others employed practitioners to assist with the technical aspects of the work. The Companies Act of 1862 established the position of 'official liquidator' and was nicknamed by a professional, grateful for the additional opportunities that it granted, 'the accountant's friend'.[2] The Bankruptcy Act of 1861 permitted all debtors, including those who formerly would have been considered insolvent, to absolve themselves from their liabilities by becoming voluntarily bank-rupt.[3] As a result, the number of failures which were registered with the courts rose dramatically and from 1862 to 1869 never fell below 7,000 per annum.[4] Although the 1869 Bankruptcy Act tightened the requirements it also abolished the position of official assignee, so that accountants could be appointed directly as trustees to administer the debtor's estate rather than having to work through an intermediary. The 1860s and 1870s, therefore, created unprecedented scope for accountants to build insolvency practices.

Waterhouse, being a comparatively new entrant to professional practice, had not been greatly involved in bankruptcy, the bulk of his fees being earned from accounting tasks. Holyland, as a clerk of Turquand, would have gained much insolvency experience but would probably have brought few clients to the new partnership. The scale of the firm's share of the bankruptcy market may be established from the evidence presented by William Henderson to the 1867 Select Committee on the Limited Liability Acts. Himself an accountant, he produced the following statement:[5]

Liquidators in 1866	Number of companies	Total capital of liquidated companies (£)
Harding, Whinney & Gibbons[a]	61	20,259,600
Coleman, Turquand, Youngs & Co.[a]	29	18,416,000
Kemp, Cannan, Ford & Co.[b]	12	13,660,000
Price, Holyland & Waterhouse	8	5,200,000
Chatteris & Nichols[b]	5	4,915,000
Quilter, Ball & Co.[c]	5	1,100,000
Sundries consisting of 91 persons	139	28,558,600
Total	259	92,109,200

[a] – now Ernst & Young; [b] – now Touche Ross; [c] – now Coopers & Lybrand

Alas, few details have survived of the identities of these insolvent companies. It is likely that the majority of the eight companies liquidated by the firm in 1866 derived from connections established by S.L. Price. Edwin Waterhouse recalled that the Overend, Gurney failure of May 1866 did not directly affect the fortunes of Price, Holyland & Waterhouse:

> The financial crisis did not at the moment throw any heavy work upon the firm but the troubles of the Indian cotton trade which followed a month or two later led to our having to take charge of the affairs of Dadabhai Naoriji, a very interesting and virtuous Parsee merchant who failed for a large sum, of those of Jamsetzee Musserwanjee Tata, and the winding up of the Commercial Bank of India, a very heavy matter of business which occupied Holyland for some years entrusted to us by Messrs Freshfields as representing the Bank of England.[6]

Other liquidations included the Royal Copper Mines of Cobre 'an important matter put into my [Waterhouse's] hands at the instance of Mr Pasco Glyn of Lombard Street' and a Norwegian timber estate comprising 'some 1,250,000 acres of mountain, lake and forest' and the Albert Life Assurance Society 'a heavy matter of business, involving great distress among policy holders'.[7] The latter had failed spectacularly in 1869 bringing down some twenty-six other offices which it had absorbed during a period of expansion.[8] S.L. Price was appointed joint liquidator.[9]

Much of the routine accounting work that Waterhouse had under-taken in his year as a sole practitioner continued. A letter, dated November 1871, to the Hon. P.C. Glyn, illustrated the mundane but important nature of these tasks:

> I have had pleasure in examining the farm accounts of your bailiff. I have not compared the vouchers with the cash payments which I believe you did not think necessary, but have examined the costings &c. of the various books, which . . . are all correct. The statement of accounts also for the year is, with the exception of the two items . . . very nearly right.
>
> I have sent with the books a little account showing how the figures should be stated, and distinguishing between the firm's account with you – the bailiff's cash account and the firm's working account.[10]

At a time when book-keeping was a skill acquired in a rudimentary fashion without technical qualifications, major businesses often employed reputable City firms to perform basic accounting tasks. In 1873, for example, Edwin Waterhouse wrote to J.W. Richardson, the Tyneside shipbuilder, to report that 'my clerk has completed your books in the manner in which your Newcastle friends have done them before'.[11] Although it was to continue to earn fees throughout the nineteenth century (for Whinney, Smith & Whinney, a comparable City practice, income from basic accounting remained at around 10–15 per cent during this period),[12] this type of work was not responsible for the sustained expansion of the firm. Indeed, the mortality rate for registered businesses fell by half between 1883 and 1913. Of crucial importance in generating growth were the audits of major commercial enterprises.[13]

Company Legislation

The long-term prosperity of the many newly founded City accountancy practices derived from the Acts of 1856 and 1862 which created the joint stock company protected by limited liability. Without this legislation, their activities would have been largely confined to insolvency assignments and book-keeping. The evidence suggests that without these statutes the nation's economic growth might have been retarded because business organisations would have been constrained from achieving further economies of scale under existing partnership arrangements. It was the 1856 and 1862 Companies Acts, therefore, that created the commercial environment in which accountants with auditing skills could thrive.

The damaging and often fraudulent dealing which had followed wild speculation in the shares of the South Sea Co. (then managing the greater part of the national debt), had led the government to pass the Bubble Act of June 1720. Although this legislation held up the development of a capital market, it did not destroy the unincorporated company. Such organisations continued to be formed and continued to issue shares, and until the beginning of the nineteenth century few proceedings were brought against them under the Bubble Act.[14] Further, businesses of any size turned to other, sometimes complex or costly arrangements to raise capital such as an Act of Parliament or Royal Charter. The repeal of the Bubble Act in 1825 did nothing to allay fears about deception and fraud. These remained after the passing of the Chartered Companies Act of 1837, which resulted in the formation of a number of blatantly dishonest businesses, particularly in the field of assurance.[15] It was their existence which led the Board of Trade to secure the setting up of a parliamentary committee in 1841 to inquire into the conduct of joint stock companies.[16] Its report, published three years later under the chairmanship of W.E. Gladstone, concluded that corporate statute should be made more readily available but that newly created companies should be properly regulated. It suggested a register of names, including the location of offices, directors and internal rules. Further, the committee advised that public companies should present audited accounts to shareholders at the annual general meeting and that these documents should then be filed with the registrar. The Joint Stock Companies Act of 1844 gave legal effect to these recommendations and provided promoters with a straightforward means of obtaining incorporation, though it did not grant the businesses so formed the protection of limited liability.

The possibility of widening the grant of limited liability, the lever which released the brake on company promotion, was examined by a select committee in 1851 and a royal commission five years later. In 1855 legislation was passed which enabled any company registered under the 1844 Act to limit the liability of its members for its debts and obligations generally to the amount unpaid on their shares, provided that they adopt the word 'limited'.[17] In addition, the company was required to have at least twenty-five members holding £10 shares paid up to the extent of 20 per cent, and not less than three-quarters of the nominal capital was to be subscribed. The 1855 Act remained in force for only a few months. It was then repealed so that it could be incorporated in the Joint Stock Companies Act of 1856. However, virtually all the safeguards of the 1855 Act were deleted by this and the 1862 Act. It created a situation in which maximum opportunity marched with minimal control, and remained in force for almost a century until the 1948 Companies Act ended an era of *laissez-faire*.

Although the 1856 Companies Act provided a model set of articles, these remained voluntary and the compulsory accounting provisions contained within the 1844 Act were repealed.[18] The recommendation in the 1856 Act that accounts 'be kept upon the principle of double-entry, in cash book, journal and ledger'[19] was omitted from the 1862 Act perhaps because it was thought too ambitious.[20] The latter did require that a profit statement and balance sheet be presented at the annual general meeting, but while details of these were given they were not made binding. Thus were created the circumstances in which groups of individuals or existing partnerships could set themselves up as a public company in order to raise capital, protected by limited liability, and who, once in operation, would be bound by minimal rules in respect of their shareholders. Such scant procedural and accounting regulations sent investors in search of professional advice. They began to hire practising accountants to assist them in their investigations and to put pressure on directors to behave responsibly.

Set in a context of progressive industrialisation, the repercussions of this company legislation were dramatic. Within the first nine years of limited liability 4,859 companies registered, while between 1866 and 1883, 15,662 limited companies were formed.[21] Although most of these organisations were private and would not have engaged the services of a practising accountant, the result was a growing tide of audit assignments, albeit at secondhand, for the profession. The theme was set to music by W.S. Gilbert in 'When Limited Liability Was a Novelty' from *Utopia Unlimited; or, The Flowers of Progress*. The largest of these public companies –major industrial enterprises, banks, financial institutions and railways – generated important accounting issues which required the expertise of the qualified practitioner.

Auditing: Railways

In establishing Price Waterhouse as railway auditors, the appointment of Edwin Waterhouse 'in the name of the firm . . . [as] public accountant to the auditors of the London & North Western Railway in November 1866'[22] was of great significance. The incumbent J.E. Coleman, his former employer, had resigned and Waterhouse had become well known to the accounts staff of the LNWR at Euston when working there as a clerk. In these early days the auditors comprised two shareholders, elected at the annual general meeting, who were mandated to examine the accounts in order to protect the interests of their fellow investors. Yet, as railway companies became larger and their financial records became more complex, so they felt the need to consult independent advisers. Waterhouse, therefore, was not himself the auditor but was paid to assist Henry Crosfield and R.W. Hand, the elected shareholders.[23] This situation continued until May 1873, when the sudden death of Hand resulted in Waterhouse being appointed as temporary auditor. Re-elected in January 1874, he continued to serve in this capacity until his replacement by [Sir] Edward Lawrence in January 1876. Henceforth, it was Edwin Waterhouse himself who was elected as the public accountant to assist the auditors rather than the firm, an arrangement which was confirmed upon the death of Crosfield in 1882.[24] Waterhouse succeeded him as an auditor in his own right at a special meeting held on 16 February of that year, and continued to serve as such until his resignation in January 1913 (having already retired from Price Water-house in 1905) when he was followed by his son, Nicholas.[25] The board of directors recorded their appreciation of Edwin Waterhouse's sustained contribution, adding that

> not only would the proprietors [shareholders] lose the services of a guardian of their interest who has shown conspicuous ability, but the directors would miss the presence of a friend whom they held in highest esteem and with whom they had been associated for so many years.[26]

The construction of the railways required the raising of far larger sums of money from the investing public than canal building had done earlier. Initially there were few safeguards for investors, and as organisations grew in size, thus creating new opportunities for mismanagement, shareholders became increasingly concerned not only about profits but also about the maintenance of assets. Confidence was severely shaken in 1847 when Quilter, Ball & Co. produced their report on the Eastern Counties Railway. This demonstrated that the chairman, George Hudson, the so-called 'Railway King', had omitted £318,144 from the debit side of the revenue account and that £35,315 was wrongly credited.[27] The fall of the heroic Hudson was an occasion for national soul-searching concerning the nature of commercial morality, prompting Tennyson to observe in 'Maud':

> But these are days of advance, the works of men of mind,
> When who but a fool would have faith in a tradesman's ware or his word?
> When only the ledger lives, and only not all men lie;
> Peace in her vineyard – yes! – but a company forges the wine.

In response to a general atmosphere of shareholder suspicion, the LNWR took the unprecedented step in October 1848 of circulating a statement of liabilities and estimated future expenditure to shareholders. This practice was then followed by other railway companies including the Great Western. From December 1848 the LNWR issued more comprehensive accounts and this greater level of disclosure contributed to a rise in share values.

It may have been the discussion generated by the Select Committee on the Audit of Railway Accounts in 1849 which encouraged the employment of professional accountants to assist the shareholders. Quilter, as an expert witness, argued that the auditor ought 'to be an independent individual, not interested in putting a favourable appearance

upon the face of the accounts'.[28] Following the scandal at the Eastern
Counties Railway, he had been elected an auditor. It was in 1849 that J.E.
Coleman was appointed to advise the shareholder auditors at the
LNWR,[29] and that W.W. Deloitte first assisted the auditors of the Great
Western Railway in their 'laborious examination of all books, accounts
and documents of the company, having been appointed without previous
communication with any individual connected with the company'.[30]

Railway companies were among the largest organisations in Britain.
The increasing complexity of these businesses in turn demanded innovation in accounting techniques. As early as 1849 Captain Mark Huish,
general manager of the LNWR, had recommended that rolling stock
should be maintained out of revenue, while a depreciation fund should
be established to meet the cost of replacing the permanent way. Huish
argued that locomotives, carriages and wagons would be systematically
renewed by repair or replacement, while the slower deterioration of
track would bring with it a sudden cost burden.[31]

The double-account system evolved from the need to devise reporting
procedures to cope with expensive, long-lived assets. The conventional
balance sheet was divided into two accounting statements: first, the
capital account which set out the sums raised from issuing shares and
debentures and the amounts spent on the acquisition of fixed assets, and
secondly, the general balance sheet which listed the balance on the
capital account, the undistributed balance on the revenue account, and
the assets and liabilities in a state of change as a result of trading
transactions.[32] Although it had precedents in practices devised by canal
companies, the double-account system appears to have originated with
the London & Birmingham Railway.[33] However, a weakness of the
method was that during the construction period it allowed the return
paid to shareholders to be charged to the capital account. Once a line
was opened for traffic, it became increasingly difficult to make adequate
provision for investors' dividends as revenue receipts were often slow to
build up.[34] Directors were reluctant to withhold dividends as this would
make it more difficult to raise capital in the future. Some managers
overstated profits by omitting liabilities, crediting a range of capital
receipts to revenue and debiting revenue expenses to capital.[35]

Once appointed to assist the shareholder auditors, Edwin Waterhouse
upheld the open-minded accounting traditions of the LNWR. Convinced of the importance of separating capital and revenue expenditure,

he insisted that the LNWR make such a distinction,[36] and resisted any pressure to return to former practice. He introduced a similar policy to the South Eastern Railway, and in 1867 to the London, Brighton & South Coast Railway which reported that 'dividends have only been paid by a wholesale system of charging to capital not only interest on new lines but also repairs, renewals, law charges and other accruing expenses on completed lines'.[37] It has been suggested that the similarity between the form of accounts prescribed by the 1868 Railway Act and those published by the LNWR implied that Waterhouse may have been consulted by the Board of Trade when considering the form of new legislation.[38] His work for the accountancy department at Euston facilitated the compilation of operating statistics which were used, in turn, to assess performance and the allocation of resources. This served as an example of continuity with some of the earliest tasks performed by accountants for railways. For as one anonymous accountant recalled, newly established companies had retained professionals to

> gather and collate information in regard to the industries of the district through which the proposed railway would serve, and to prepare estimates of passenger and goods traffic which might be anticipated. Members of the profession who acquired a reputation for their skill in dealing with such problems were therefore prior to 1846 in constant request in Parliamentary committee rooms.[39]

Railway companies were prestigious and financially rewarding clients – truly modern elements in the Victorian economy, akin to the national airlines of today. As they grew by absorbing smaller or competing enterprises they became some of the largest business organisations in Britain. By 1873 there were 229,000 people employed by railway companies in England and Wales, a figure which had risen to 312,000 by 1884.[40]

The early audit appointment to the LNWR proved crucial for, as Waterhouse recalled, it

> led us to be chosen to assist a committee of investigation into the affairs of the London, Brighton & South Coast Railway ... The finances of the company had certainly been terribly mismanaged, dividends paid out of capital, and much money wasted, and the laxity of account keeping which was then brought to light was one of the main causes of legislation with regard to railway accounts

which followed in 1868. Our work was undertaken mainly by Mr
Holyland, for my experience in those days was but slight. Mr Price
also lent his aid but I fear that we made a bungle of our report . . .[41]

Nevertheless, the shortcomings of their investigation do not seem to
have been of devastating consequence, and in 1867 Price, Holyland &
Waterhouse were appointed auditors of the London, Brighton & South
Coast Railway.

In the same way that an auditor could grow by keeping pace with a
voracious conglomerate in the 1960s and 1970s, so Victorian accountants
benefited by being the auditors of a major railway company. Since the
British network had been laid down by hundreds of independent companies linking up with one another or at times duplicating routes, expansion
in the main could be achieved only by take-over. Originally itself the
product of a merger between the London & Birmingham, Grand
Junction and Manchester & Birmingham Railways, the LNWR proceeded to acquire smaller companies within and at the edge of
its territory, such as the Holyhead, Lancaster & Carlisle and Cambrian Railways. In this fashion additional work found its way to
Price, Holyland & Waterhouse without the auditor having to seek it
actively.

Another major railway audit fell to Edwin Waterhouse in January
1868 when George Grenfell Glyn and a partner from the bankers
Williams Deacon & Co. nominated him as debenture auditor of the
South Eastern Railway, the company which eventually dominated
Kent. As Waterhouse recalled:

> The position of the money market and wide spreading distress
> made it difficult for railways to renew their terminable debentures,
> and Sir Edward Watkin, chairman of the South Eastern, determined
> to convert the whole of that company's floating debt into debenture
> stock, the issue of which stock was to be watched by Mr Glyn and
> his colleagues, as trustees, assisted by an auditor of their own
> choosing. The conversion was satisfactorily accomplished at the
> expense of saddling the company with four per cent interest on the
> bulk of its debentures in perpetuity, but the auditorship
> continues . . .[42]

The bulk of the firm's railway work was supervised by Waterhouse, and
the audits of the LNWR, Metropolitan Railway, Shropshire Union

Railway & Canal Co. and the Isle of Wight Railway Co. were his personal appointments.[43] The fees of these clients in 1906 were £1,350, £400, £77 10s and £35 respectively. Indeed, it appears that the volume of work was such that Edwin Waterhouse declined the invitation to stand as auditor of the Midland Railway, a prestigious company. In August 1883 he replied to W.B. Paget:

> It would give me great pleasure to do so, did I not feel that just at the time of year when the work, should I be appointed, would arise, my hands are perhaps already too full to allow me to give so important a matter the personal attention it would require. As you may know I am auditor of the London & North Western Railway and each half year I find my work there increase . . .[44]

It is inconceivable today that a partner would refuse to take the audit of a major business because of pressure of work. Waterhouse proposed S.L. Price for the post but, given perhaps his lack of specialist knowledge, this proved an unacceptable suggestion. Price had been joint auditor of the Ringwood, Christchurch & Bournemouth Railway in 1859, and may also have held a similar appointment at the Bedford & Northampton Railway,[45] but both were minor enterprises and were eventually absorbed into the London & South Western and Midland Railways respectively.

In 1891–2 the largest single fee earned by Price Waterhouse was that of the LNWR (£1,199), while other substantial sums were paid by the London, Brighton & South Coast Railway (£300), Metropolitan Railway (£299) and the South Eastern Railway (£350).[46] Other audits included the Great Eastern and the Lancashire & Yorkshire Railways.

Having established a reputation as railway auditors, Price Waterhouse were called upon to perform a number of related investigations. In 1873 Edwin Waterhouse concluded 'an examination into the affairs of the Irish North Western Railway' at the request of the directors. A meeting of the London shareholders was held, he wrote,

> in order that the board might give information as to the present condition and prospects of the line. The shareholders present appeared glad to have the opportunity of learning something about their property, which though unproductive for a long time, seems likely materially to improve in value, specially in consequence of the opening of the new route to Ireland via Greenock.[47]

Broadening the Practice:
Banks and Financial Institutions

The last decade of the nineteenth century saw Price Waterhouse gain a number of important banking clients following the flotation of many smaller private ventures during the 1880s and the merger movement which ensued. In 1889, Edwin Waterhouse recalled, the firm was very busy with the audit of private banks:

> These concerns were beginning to find themselves at a disadvantage compared with the joint stock undertakings that prided themselves on the stability exhibited by their published balance sheets; and were considering the propriety of themselves circulating statements of their affairs among their customers. Several private banks, therefore, asked that balance sheets should at any rate be prepared, leaving the publication of the same to be considered afterwards.[48]

Halsey, who had just joined Price Waterhouse as an articled clerk, recollected that the prospectus work for the flotation of these private banks revealed antiquated accounting methods: 'It is a matter of some surprise to me that a large proportion of those firms had kept their books up to that time on a single entry system.'[49] In the event, the publication of these balance sheets led to a series of amalgamations among the smaller provincial companies and with the large established joint stock banks, thereby laying the foundations for a national network. Rapidly growing banks required prestigious City auditors, and Howard Lloyd, general manager of Lloyds Bank, then a Birmingham institution, asked Price Waterhouse to perform their audit.[50] Lloyd, a Quaker, was an old friend of Waterhouse, a fact which doubtless contributed to their selection ahead of the other City firms.[51]

By 1891–2 Price Waterhouse had built up an impressive list of clients in financial services. They included, with the annual fee in brackets: Atlas Assurance (£150), Bank of New Zealand (£158), Bank of Westmorland (£42), Gresham Life Assurance Society (not known), Gurneys & Co. (£210), Lloyds Bank (£350), London & Westminster Bank (£313), Lewes Bank (£200), National Provincial Bank (£210) and the County of Gloucester Bank (£174).[52] In addition, the firm was appointed auditor to the Law Debenture Corporation on its flotation in 1889, and may also have been responsible for the preparation of the prospectus. Edwin Waterhouse was listed among those who had subscribed to the 200 'Founders' shares'. Price Waterhouse had also audited the Foreign and Colonial Government Trust Co., the world's first investment trust, from its establishment in 1868.[53] The firm was fast becoming a City institution in its own right.

Special Assignments

Given the unregulated nature of business dealings and an entrepreneurial spirit, much scope existed for accountants to take on unusual assignments, and many of these were perhaps the harbingers of today's management consultancy practices. In 1870, for example, Edwin Waterhouse was employed by Fox, Head & Co., the Middlesbrough rolling mills, to institute a system of profit calculation which could then be used to allocate bonuses to the workforce in an attempt to avoid industrial disputes.[54] In the following year he was involved in an arbitration between masters and men engaged in the north-east iron industry which involved a report on the returns of some twenty-three works.[55] Following this, Messrs Richardson & Sons of Hartlepool, 'the proprietors of [iron] works amongst the largest and best organised in the district', asked Price Waterhouse 'to assist them in converting their establishment into a joint stock company'.[56]

In the summer of 1877 Edwin Waterhouse conducted an inquiry into the affairs of the Artisans, Labourers & General Dwellings Co. The business, he wrote,

> was seeking to interest the public in an extension of its operations, when its methods were severely attacked . . . During the investigation the manager and secretary, who bore the name of Mr Swindlehurst, resigned . . . In the result, it was discovered that both the chairman and the secretary had been intermediaries between the vendors of the land and the company, appropriating large sums to the company's loss.[57]

In 1894 Price Waterhouse undertook a major investigation into the financial affairs of the 8th Duke of Devonshire's estates at Eastbourne.[58]

The land had been developed for housing and the duke believed that the reserve which should have accumulated had been squandered by his agents. The report, which ran to thirty-five pages of foolscap, drew attention to the idiosyncratic accounting methods and a failure to produce either

> a balance sheet, or ... an account showing the expenditure under
> any capital heading ... In our opinion the most careful separation
> of purely revenue expenditure from outlay in improvements and in
> developments is necessary in such a case.[59]

Price Waterhouse drew up an income and expenditure account which summarised the financial position of the estate for a period of fifty years and served as a guide to its future management. The duke was sufficiently impressed with their work to employ them again in 1901 to investigate the management of his Sussex estate. Price Waterhouse discovered that the agents and their chief cashier had indeed been fraudulent.[60]

The detection of fraud was an important part of the Victorian accountant's tasks – perhaps to a greater extent than today. During a period when uniformity in account keeping was regarded at best as undesirable, the opportunities for embezzlement were plentiful. In 1880, having been appointed auditor of the Metropolitan Railway, Waterhouse recorded that a clerk had

> manipulated the depositors' passbooks in every conceivable way,
> duplicating some, and stitching duplicate leaves into others with
> singular cleverness. There was great difficulty in ascertaining the full
> amount of his frauds.[61]

Fortunes of the Firm

Within two years of the foundation of Price, Holyland & Waterhouse, the fees earned by the partnership rose to around £15,000 per annum, and remained at about that level until 1889 (Table 2, see Appendix). Indexing this income to even out the effects of price movements does not greatly alter the picture. This pattern of turnover stood in contrast to that of some of the older City firms. Far greater fluctuations in fees, for example, are observable from the accounts of Turquand, Youngs & Co. and Whinney, Smith & Whinney.[62] Being older practices, they had a greater involvement in insolvency work which could produce enormous fees of a short-term nature, while accounting and auditing generated smaller but regular sums. By the end of the century, however, bankruptcy assignments contributed less to the fees of these older firms so that fluctuations in their annual income evened out.

The profit figures for Price, Holyland & Waterhouse (Table 3, see Appendix) reflect the peaks and troughs observed for the firm's fees. At a time when office expenses were comparatively low, when staff overheads were limited and articled clerks had to pay a substantial premium, it was not surprising that a close relationship existed between fee income and profits. In 1866, for example, profits were 80 per cent of fees; in 1870, 1875, 1880 and 1885 the percentages were 81, 64, 70 and 69 respectively.

As Edwin Waterhouse explained in a letter to R.L. Pratt of Darlington, there was no fixed rate for an accountant's fees. 'Some,' he observed,

> charge £3 3s a day for a principal's time and £1 11s 6d or £1 1s for clerks. Others £2 2s a day 'all round'. The custom in this office is usually to name a lump sum, having regard to the amount of principals' and clerks' time, sometimes mentioning the amount of each – and having regard also specially to the nature of the work and the value of the work done. £3 3s is of course much less than I estimate my own time as worth and get for it.[63]

No details of how much partners charged for their time have survived. If the £14,677 profit for 1870 were to be divided according to the partnership deed of January 1869, then Price would have earned £7,788 (26/49ths), Holyland £4,193 (14/49ths) and Waterhouse £2,696 (9/49ths). Judged by other middle-class incomes of the period, these were considerable.

In terms of turnover, Price Waterhouse grew at a more rapid rate after 1889, its fees rising from £21,560 in that year to £47,821 in 1901 (Table 2, see Appendix). Price Waterhouse moved ahead of several of its older City rivals – overtaking both Turquand, Youngs & Co. and Whinney, Smith & Whinney by 1901. It was probably an expanding audit practice which was responsible for this change in the league tables. Price Waterhouse had assembled an impressive list of railway companies as clients, and from the 1890s attracted a number of banks and financial

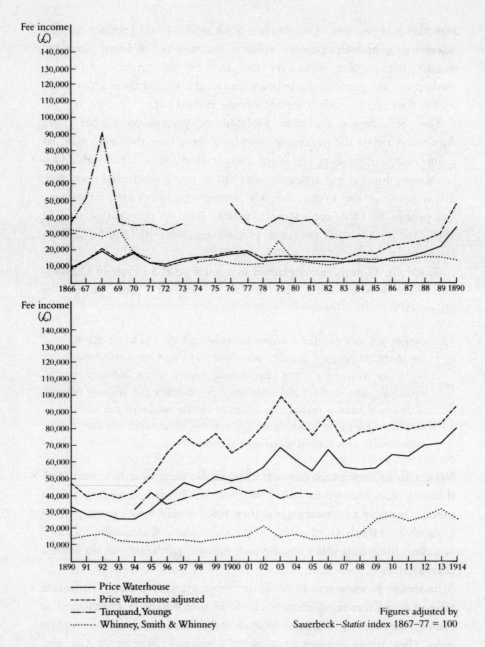

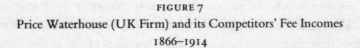

Price Waterhouse
Price Waterhouse adjusted
Turquand, Youngs
Whinney, Smith & Whinney

Figures adjusted by
Sauerbeck–*Statist* index 1867–77 = 100

FIGURE 7

Price Waterhouse (UK Firm) and its Competitors' Fee Incomes
1866–1914

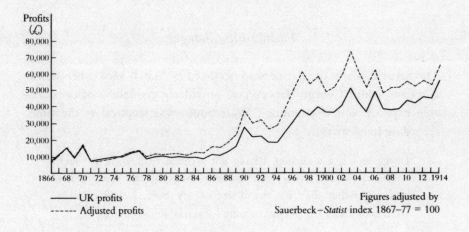

FIGURE 8
Price Waterhouse (UK Firm) Profits 1866–1914

institutions. By comparison Whinney, Smith & Whinney still earned 60 per cent of its fees in 1885 from insolvency work. Although this percentage fell to 15 in 1895, it had risen to 20 per cent by 1900 and to 53 per cent in 1910, remaining over 30 per cent until the early 1920s.[64] The fee income of Turquand, Youngs may have divided in similar proportions. Although such statistics cannot be calculated for Price Waterhouse, it may be conjectured that they did not need to restructure their business during the 1890s, but were able to develop their audit practice, already a core activity.

As in the middle years of the century, profits marched broadly in step with turnover, both rising dramatically after 1889 (Table 3, see Appendix). However, overheads also increased marginally, reducing the ratio of profits to fees from 78 per cent in 1890 to 72 per cent in 1895, and to 68 per cent in 1901. Although the United States Firm (established at New York in 1890) began to make a contribution to UK profits from 1891, these sums remained comparatively small until the Edwardian period.

Partnership Changes

The first change in the partnership occurred in March 1868 when it was agreed to admit George Harvey Jay, 'an elderly gentleman of considerable experience in accounting'. Waterhouse was sceptical at the time, recording in his diary:

> I hope this is a wise step. I have not acceded to it without much consideration for it has been brought about by the wish of my partners, rather than by any desire of my own. I shall have to sacrifice some of my present income for uncertain advantages . . .[65]

The style of the firm became Price, Jay, Holyland & Waterhouse.

Jay had originally worked as a clerk in the office of Quilter, Ball & Co. and had been admitted to the partnership in around 1846. He appears to have retired from that firm around 1864, though he was listed in the *Post Office Directory* for 1852 as manager to the Monarch Fire & Life Assurance Co. at 4 Adelaide Place.[66] The partnership deed of July 1868, which recorded Jay as being an accountant of 38 Throgmorton Street, granted him a 15/64ths share, ahead of Holyland (14/64) and Waterhouse (9/64).[67] For what reason Jay left the partnership on 31 December in the same year is not recorded, though Waterhouse recollected that he had not proved sufficiently useful to justify his share of the profits. He was, however, 'the first to acknowledge the position, asking to retire after the experience of a few months'.[68] Jay was subsequently listed as a 'stockjobber' at 17 Old Broad Street.[69]

In 1871, aged sixty-four, Holyland asked to retire after some six years of partnership.[70] William Edwards served as arbitrator in setting the terms of Holyland's withdrawal, and he departed on 18 March.[71] Nevertheless, he retained a room at 13 Gresham Street in order to undertake a few private assignments, such as the liquidation of the Commercial Bank of India. On 31 October 1874 S.L. Price wrote to Holyland to inform him that it had been decided to change the name of the firm to Price, Waterhouse & Co. (as from 2 November) in order to avoid any possible confusion over the membership of the partnership.[72] Henceforth, Holyland practised in his own name until his death on 20 January 1882.

In order to cope with the growing volume of work, two additional partners were admitted on 1 July 1875 – James Alexander Mann and

George Sneath. Little is recorded of Mann, except that he decided to retire from the firm in June 1880 in order to emigrate to Halifax, Nova Scotia, where he set up in practice. The local *Morning Herald* for October carried his advertisement and an edition in January 1881 announced that he had been appointed agent to Sharp Stewart & Co., locomotive builders at the Atlas Works in Manchester, to Ransome & Napier and to the Machen Tin Works.[73] There was subsequently a suggestion that Mann was attempting to poach Price Waterhouse clients, since the firm wrote to him:

> We take this opportunity to express our regret that you should have sent circulars to many of our business friends, whose acquaintance you can have made only through your connection with us, asking that accountant's business should be entrusted to you. This appears to us an endeavour to intercept business that might externally flow to this office, and much at variance with the spirit with which we entered our late partnership.[74]

Mann appears to have departed Halifax by August 1881, leaving no further trace of his whereabouts or subsequent career.

George Sneath, the son of a yeoman farmer, was born at Baston, Lincolnshire, on 6 April 1842.[75] Moving to Leicester, he was employed by a firm of solicitors, spending much of his time on the preparation of estate accounts. In 1865 Sneath came to London to work as a clerk to Price. He was admitted to membership of the ICAEW without having to pass an examination, on the basis of his experience. His son, Rupert Sneath, told the story that when Price died leaving just two partners in the firm, Waterhouse offered to change the style to Waterhouse, Sneath & Co.[76] Sneath, to his credit, thought the change injudicious given the reputation attached to the established name.

Described by Halsey, later a senior partner, as 'a rapid worker with an amazing facility for marshalling and analysing figures', he had 'a different intellectual background to that possessed by his senior partner. He was well liked by the staff but not held in awe by them.'[77] A less flattering judgement was passed by Tull, a clerk later to become a partner, who was perhaps embittered by a duodenal ulcer which had forced his retirement. He suggested that Sneath 'although clever was illiterate' and was 'very often drunk in the office and had no manners'.[78] Undoubtedly, Sneath did not possess the formal, academic training of

Waterhouse. He was perhaps a bright, self-educated clerk whose ability alone secured his advancement. He probably held the senior partnership beyond his best years (p. 86). Sneath specialised in the audit of banks and played an important part in their merger movement of the 1890s.[79] He served on the council of the ICAEW from 1896 to 1914.[80] [Sir] Nicholas Waterhouse, himself later to be senior partner, described George Sneath as a 'philanthropist and a great character, beloved to all'.[81] He had indeed been a benefactor of Hendon Cottage Hospital, living as he did nearby at Gloucester Lodge.

Sneath was a prominent freemason, having been initiated to the Royal Athelston Lodge, London, in December 1878. He was probably the first mason at Price Waterhouse (neither Price, Holyland or Waterhouse had joined), and may have been responsible for establishing a tradition of freemasonry in the firm. He was a founder member of the Chartered Accountants Lodge, set up in 1906, and served as its senior warden in 1908.[82] Although never a large lodge (numbers rose to forty-six within ten years), it attracted several leading figures within the profession, including Sir William Plender, F.W. Pixley and Sir Arthur Whinney.[83] Among its masters were W.C. Sneath (1922–3) and Sir Gilbert Garnsey (1928–9), who had been initiated to the Constitutional Lodge in 1911. Other masons within Price Waterhouse included Sir Laurence Halsey, who joined Bayard Lodge in 1906 and the Chartered Accountants Lodge in the following year.

Sneath married a Miss Young and had nine children. Of these Harry George Sneath served his articles with Price Waterhouse and was asked in about 1889, to travel to America to undertake a brewery investigation.[84] Although the task was expected to take only two months, he remained there for almost a year. Another son, William Cecil, was seconded to the Chicago office in 1897, and ten years later was admitted to the UK partnership. A third son, Rupert, after qualifying with Price Waterhouse, transferred to the South American Firm where he subsequently became senior partner.

When S.L. Price died in office on 19 May 1887, he was succeeded as senior partner by Edwin Waterhouse. In his later years Price, who suffered from lumbago, had handed over a greater share of the management and direction of the firm to his nominated successor. During the following eighteen years Waterhouse set standards of behaviour and inculcated the morality of the Christian gentleman within the firm. He also insisted on high quality of work and personal integrity – a wise policy, given that accountancy was not yet regarded as a first-rank profession. G.O. May recalled how he had worked on an audit of a large company for which Waterhouse was responsible:

> The methods of accounting employed by the company made it difficult to prepare accounts in standard form, and in doing so I had to cut one or two corners. When I laid these before Mr Waterhouse, he said with acid politeness, 'Is this a form of account, Mr May, that commends itself to your judgement?' When I replied 'Not altogether, sir', he continued, 'Then do you think it is altogether courteous to me to submit to me accounts that do not even commend themselves to your own judgement?'[85]

[Sir] Nicholas Waterhouse, son of the founder, observed that his father found it 'very difficult indeed to suffer fools gladly', but 'had a wonderful insight into character, and those who really knew him held him in the highest respect and affection'.[86] H.J. Morland and G.F. Garnsey, two promising qualified clerks, later to become partners, would squint through the crack in Waterhouse's door to discover his mood before presenting him with a contentious issue. A red face would deter their entry.[87] An inability to tolerate any behaviour which might pass as slackness, and his ingrained Quaker mores, led to a prohibition of smoking. If Waterhouse 'found a pipe or pouch lying around in the office or in the audit room of a client, he thought nothing of throwing them on the fire but, then relenting, would compensate the offender with the price of a new outfit'.[88]

According to G.O. May, he

> liked to bring into the office men who had taken good positions in the examinations and then place heavy responsibilities on them to see how they stood up under pressure.[89]

May himself was one such recruit who was entrusted with a series of investigations to test his abilities and stamina.

Summarising the achievements of Waterhouse as senior partner, Halsey remarked:

> the character and ability of Edwin Waterhouse stood out far above the others as he did in the profession generally; it was without any doubt the standards of thoroughness and integrity set by him which

the firm has always striven to uphold that made the name of the firm in those days.[90]

Waterhouse was one of the outstanding leaders of the partnership and was not surpassed in his contribution by any but Garnsey until after the Second World War.

Despite his success in steering Price Waterhouse to the front rank of accountancy firms, it would be wrong to view Edwin Waterhouse as one of the original thinkers of the profession. He was not a Dicksee, Fells, de Paula, Garnsey or May. His abilities lay not so much in the introduction of radical ideas as in the practical organisation and running of a major City partnership; he had the contacts and personality to acquire new clients and maintain established connections, combined with the toughness and attention to detail to ensure that assignments were performed fairly and efficiently. The capacity for sheer hard work and application which Waterhouse exhibited should not be forgotten in an assessment of his commercial success. On occasion, as his mother recorded, his exertions affected his health. In April 1879 she wrote:

> Dear Edwin returned from the north [Middlesbrough] about four o'clock yesterday morning, very weary with his night's journey and exceedingly busy after he came home. I fear my precious sons are often too busy for their *bodies'* good.[91]

There were three further admissions to the partnership in the nineteenth century: J. Gurney Fowler in 1887, A.W. Wyon in 1893 and L.E. Halsey in 1900. Fowler was the son of Henry Fowler and had been introduced to the firm by way of his father's younger brother John, owner of the Leeds Steam Plough Manufactory, for whom Edwin Waterhouse had performed cost accounting work when a sole practitioner. J.G. Fowler and his two brothers all served their articles with Price Waterhouse. Having recently passed his final examinations he was admitted to the partnership to fill the vacancy created by the death of Price. Halsey recalled that Fowler

> came from Quaker stock and he was a massive figure physically. I think he had been a footballer in his youth and he developed into a formidable golfer . . . Later in life he became an enthusiastic orchid breeder. He was seldom seen without some rare orchid in his

buttonhole. The growers used to bring priceless plants for his inspection to the offices and we juniors were called in to admire. He became the Treasurer of the Royal Horticultural Society and was always inaccessible at the time of their great shows ... he was possessed of considerable professional knowledge as well as business acumen and a great fund of common sense.[92]

[Sir] Nicholas Waterhouse said of him that a 'somewhat forbidding exterior and a rather gruff voice' concealed the 'kindest of hearts'.[93]

Albert William Wyon, destined to serve as senior partner for twenty-one years, had originally been articled to Price in 1885. He was a gifted accountant and won first prize in the 1890 final examination. His grandfather, William Wyon R.A., was England's chief medal-die engraver, having become the senior engraver at the Royal Mint on the premature death of his cousin, Thomas, aged twenty-five.[94] William Wyon was subsequently succeeded in this post by his son, Leonard Charles, father of Albert Wyon. In 1851 L.C. Wyon became chief engraver at the Royal Mint and was responsible for the design of English and foreign coins, and a number of campaign medals, including that to mark the Indian Mutiny. Albert Wyon, educated at Clewer House School, Windsor, did not, however, follow in the family tradition of engraving at the Royal Mint. He appears to have devoted the greater part of his life to Price Waterhouse, though his single-minded commitment also reflected a rather limited vision. Sir Nicholas Waterhouse described him as a 'wonderful clear thinker', with 'few, if any, hobbies outside the office'.[95]

One member of staff recalled that Wyon regularly came to the office on Saturday mornings and remained beyond the official closing time of 1 p.m. to finish his work before Monday.[96] Despite his intelligence and application, Wyon did not mature into a dynamic and imaginative senior partner, and his conservative approach retarded the firm's development in the late thirties (p. 126).

Admitted to the partnership in July 1900, Laurence Edward Halsey had also served his articles with Price Waterhouse. Educated at Haileybury and entering the firm in 1890,[97] he was described by Richards, a junior colleague, as being of 'a modest and retiring nature but all who knew him were impressed by his charm, his sincerity and his outstanding ability'.[98]

Thus, Sneath, Fowler, Wyon and Halsey had all been trained within the firm and none had attended university. Advancement in most cases had been relatively rapid: Fowler became a partner shortly after qualifying, Wyon in two years and Halsey in five years. Given that there was a total staff of around fifty (in 1898 Edwin Waterhouse invited forty-eight of the more senior members of staff to a garden party and dinner at 'Feldemore'), it would seem that there was a policy of selection on merit rather than seniority. Edwin Waterhouse was keen to recruit able qualifiers from the provinces and seems to have selected bright men for partnership responsibilities at an early age.

Staff and Office Routines

In the nineteenth century the progressive march of industrialisation offered offices little scope for mechanisation or the introduction of labour-saving devices. Letters were written by hand and copied in primitive presses using damp sheets of thin paper; calculations were by mental arithmetic or made on paper by the less proficient. It was said, for example, that Gilbert Garnsey could glance down a column of figures and cast them with comparative ease. Copying and calculating machines are, by and large, features of the post-1918 world. As a result, when professional firms expanded they had to take on larger numbers of clerks. In the absence of systematic records, it has been difficult to estimate the number of staff employed by Price Waterhouse in the Victorian period. When Price, Holyland and Waterhouse moved to their new premises at 44 Gresham Street in 1865 they probably had a total of around a dozen employees. A salary list drawn up in December 1894 detailed fifty-two names (including articled clerks),[99] another for December 1896 showed forty-seven receiving wages and a further nine articled clerks. Most of these had joined after 1890, only eleven having had more than six years' service, while eleven had less than two years with the firm.[100] A list for 1900 recorded a total of fifty-seven employees.[101]

The position of clerk embraced a wide spectrum of tasks, financial rewards and status. To work for a prestigious City firm of accountants such as Price Waterhouse was to be at the upper end of the scale, akin to a position in insurance and some branches of the Civil Service. An article in *The Accountant* for February 1892 observed that 'the great thing about being a clerk is the powerful respectability of the calling'.[102] The pace of work was not rapid and there was often a relaxed atmosphere. Sir Nicholas Waterhouse recalled:

> the work was not so exacting and grim in those days and generally speaking a good time was had by all especially if they were among the happy band that conducted the audit of the Gordon Hotels in London and occasionally at Monte Carlo ... It is strange that in those days when office hours were longer and no one, except occasionally a partner, left work till 2 o'clock on Saturdays every-thing seemed much more leisurely.[103]

In the slack season, around the month of August, avoided by companies as a time for the end of their financial year, Waterhouse recalled it was so quiet that staff on holiday were sometimes told to stay away 'for another week or even two'.[104]

In the Victorian era there was no formal structure of promotion and work organisation. The various grades of manager had not yet been created. Clerks earned salary increments and greater responsibility through length of service and ability. As a clerk became more experienced he tended to be given the same clients each year and, as Sir Nicholas Waterhouse added, 'it was a very rare thing for any senior clerk to be engaged on more than one job at a time'.[105] The absence of managers and the fact that in the early days some audit appointments were personal to individuals resulted in partners having a greater supervisory role than in the interwar period. With the founding of the ICAEW in 1880 and the imposition of professional examinations, a division emerged between those who were qualified and those who owed their jobs to practical experience. The latter were described in the early 1920s as lacking

> self confidence and tended to talk quietly to one another in corners. They could be very knowledgeable about their particular work (which usually required a great deal of detailed checking and vouching) and, given adequate guidance, could be very useful on an investigation or a liquidation.[106]

The social background and educational achievements of clerks at Price Waterhouse in the period to 1900 was, therefore, varied. Increasingly they were drawn from middle-class families and a growing proportion had qualified through the ICAEW. They were expected to be responsible, hard-working when occasion demanded, provident and self-reliant. Yet they were not expected to face the world alone. The firm adopted a paternalistic attitude, helping staff in times of trouble and illness, though clerks could not be certain of the size or even the possibility of a pension. Nevertheless, the firm took pride in not making staff redundant and should a clerk wish to retire he was guaranteed – in Trollope's phrase – 'a respectable maintenance for life'.[107]

Dress was formal in the late nineteenth century. Staff engaged on audits or other visits to clients were expected to wear a top hat and tail coat (the more conservative wearing a frock coat), while clerks who worked at Gresham Street wore bowler hats, short coats, and had paper shields to protect stiffly starched shirt cuffs.[108] The pin-striped suit, adopted by some City professionals during the interwar period, was said to have derived its inspiration from the lines drawn vertically in books of account.[109]

3 Frederick's Place

By the turn of the century the rented office accommodation at 44 Gresham Street had become too cramped for the growing firm and it was decided to move to larger premises. A description of these offices by Halsey, who entered the firm in 1890, has survived:

> The gods lived on the first floor, Edwin Waterhouse in a room looking out over Gresham Street and George Sneath one overlooking King Street, with two or three general office rooms in the intervening angle. Gurney Fowler's room looked out at the back towards Ironmonger Lane. There was a room for liquidations staff next to George Sneath's room but so far as I remember no one else had any allotted rooms, except Mathison (an old soldier), the cashier, who lived in a glass cage by the entrance and saw everybody who went in and out. He was aided by a commissionaire, Smythe, who had ridden with [Sir Frederick] Roberts to Kandahar . . . The third floor was seldom visited by any member of the firm and was used in times of pressure by temporary staff and in times of less pressure as the place of recreation for the pupils and articled clerks when they were disengaged, as occasionally happened.[110]

Standards of furnishing followed the status of the office's occupant.

Partners had solid mahogany desks and chairs, Turkish carpets and an ornate fireplace, while the clerks had less imposing rooms. Somerset Maugham, who had briefly entered a City practice, recalled his own experience of a general office:

> It was dark and very dingy. It was lit by a sky-light. There were three rows of desks in it and against them high stools. Over the chimney-piece was a dirty engraving of a prize fight.[111]

In March 1899 Price Waterhouse transferred to 3 Frederick's Place, part of a terrace of four-storey houses built by the Adam brothers in 1776, situated in a quiet cul-de-sac off Old Jewry.[112] It had originally been a residential street, but, by degrees, had been converted for commercial use. Although the house was 'old fashioned and rather ramshackle' it represented, according to Halsey,

> an immense improvement on the cramped quarters at Gresham Street but within a few years it was too small and we decided to rebuild. Alan Vigers, the brother of Leslie Vigers, a very well-known surveyor, and our next door neighbour, was our architect. He was a great craftsman and produced an admirably planned and built house for us.[113]

In 1915–16, while this reconstruction was in hand, Price Waterhouse moved to the two upper floors of Gresham College, situated at the junction of Basinghall and Gresham Streets. The work was completed in the autumn of 1916, and when Edwin Waterhouse paid a visit to the modernised premises he was presented with 'a painting of the old offices before they were pulled down'.[114] He hung the picture in the library of his country home, 'Feldemore'.

Overseas: New York and Chicago

Since the establishment of the colonies the British had always maintained important trade links with America. However, the ending of the Civil War in 1865, combined with sustained economic growth in the UK, generated both market opportunities and capital surpluses for investment. By 1869, for example, the input of foreign funds to the United States had reached $1.5 billion.[115] A key figure in the administration of UK investments was Henry Osborne O'Hagan, an independent company promoter, who had developed specialisms in tramways and in English and American breweries. In 1882 O'Hagan founded the City of London Contract Corporation as the vehicle for his enterprises.[116] His first American flotation, completed in 1889, involved the amalgamation of three breweries based in Rochester and New York into the Bartholomay Brewing Co.[117] In preparation for the union, O'Hagan asked Price Waterhouse to investigate the breweries' current financial position and historical earnings, determine floating assets and payments due to vendors, and to open books for the merged organisation. George Sneath and Joseph Gurney Fowler, together with some junior staff, crossed the Atlantic to undertake the work.[118] This proved to be the beginning of a profitable association as O'Hagan became involved with meat-packing companies, industrial concerns and stockyard operations.

However, the visits by Sneath and Fowler in 1889 were not the first they had made to America. These had begun in 1873 and increased in regularity. Despite a disinclination to open branch offices, Edwin Waterhouse acknowledged in 1887 that 'the business was growing and an American connection was springing up which made it necessary for us to send Mr Sneath, or a principal clerk, frequently across the Atlantic'.[119]

Price Waterhouse was not alone among UK accountancy firms in seeking assignments in the United States. In 1883 Thomas Wade, Guthrie & Co., the Manchester firm, set up a New York office to undertake investigations and audits. With the volume of work from O'Hagan increasing and the delay entailed in crossing the Atlantic, Waterhouse decided that it was necessary to open an office in New York.

In August 1890 a 'Heads of Agreement' was drawn up between Lewis D. Jones and Price Waterhouse, followed by a formal agreement signed on 11 September.[120] Jones was to give his 'whole time and energy' to the business of the new 'agency' of Price Waterhouse to be established in New York. The firm was to provide him with staff and working capital but he undertook to seek authorisation before signing its name to any accounts. An office was opened at 45 Broadway and the profits of the business were to be divided between Price Waterhouse (80 per cent) and Jones (20 per cent). Jones, a Welshman, had joined the London firm in February 1877, and though he did not formally serve articles, passed

his final examination in second place in March 1887.[121] Described by
W.C. Sneath as a 'very kindly man',[122] it was reported that his 'genial
nature and ready wit won him many friends and contacts for the
firm'.[123]

During its first year of business, the New York office took part in
two capitalisations, one of $25 million for O'Hagan's Chicago Junction
Railways & Union Stockyards Co. and the other for the New York
Belting and Packing Co. However, brewery clients (notably the United
States Breweries, Chicago Brewing & Malt Co., P. Schoenhofer Brewing
Co., Pittsburgh Breweries and Buckeye Brewery) provided the bulk of
their fee income.[124] In the following year, 1891, their client list expanded
and included: Detroit Dry Docks ($800), G.H. Hammond & Co.
($1,800), J.I. Case Threshing Machine Co. ($1,100), International
Okonite Co. ($500), International Grain Elevating Co. ($1,300) and the
Union Ferry Co. ($1,300).[125]

As the volume of business rose so in the spring of 1891 Jones wrote to
London for more assistance. Because much of the work originated from
Britain as a result of investments, the firm was careful about whom they
employed: 'so long as our staff in America are Englishmen, we do not
think our clients will be likely to have the objection ... namely the
examination of accounts by Americans. At the same time you must be
especially careful in engaging men who have been for any length of time
in America.'[126] Accordingly, when Jones asked for another senior
accountant Price Waterhouse sent W.J. Caesar, a member of the Society
of Accountants in Edinburgh, who had recently joined the staff of their
London office. Caesar had served his apprenticeship from 1876 to 1881
with A. & J. Robertson of 33 Charlotte Square,[127] and subsequently set
up in Edinburgh on his own account.[128] He then established commercial
links with America, becoming secretary of the Florida Mortgage and
Investment Co., and in 1888 came to London to launch, in his own
words,

> a large American and Colonial company with a capital of two
> millions sterling, which I proposed to raise here and invest at a
> profit in Chicago and other large cities ... Unfortunately the whole
> matter fell through.[129]

The job had necessitated two visits to Florida by Caesar to assist
with the reorganisation of the local management and this, he believed,

provided him with practical experience of American methods. After this venture he was 'induced to go to Paris and join a stockjobber there, with a view to becoming a partner'. This never materialised and having lost money he was forced to seek work in London. In retrospect, Caesar was not perhaps such a wise selection. His experience of American business undoubtedly recommended him to Price Waterhouse, but his inconsistent career record and what was to prove a difficult personality might have discouraged his appointment.

In 1891 Caesar joined Jones in New York and was soon sent to open an office in Chicago. Price Waterhouse had important brewery clients there and were also auditors of G.H. Hammond & Co. and the Union Stockyard and Transit Co., so that the staff soon referred to themselves as the 'beer and beef boys'.[130] Marr, the first partner to have been engaged in the US, recalled that the Chicago office had initially been 'located in the Adams Express or the American Express building'.[131] In May 1892 it moved to the eighth storey of the Monadnock Building, a distinguished structure designed by Burnham and Root. Fee income for the year ending June 1893 totalled $24,375 and profits were calculated to be $10,431.[132]

However, the abrasive personality exhibited by Caesar began to alienate clients. In December 1893 Winston & Meagher, the Chicago lawyers, complained to J.G. Fowler who was on a visit to the US:

> We have tried for a long time to get on with Mr Caesar but his manner and methods are not satisfactory ... it is only just that we should have someone here on your behalf, like Mr Jones, with whom we could take up matters without friction.[133]

In order to restore amicable relations Jones transferred to Chicago and sent Caesar to New York to take his place there.[134] The general level of business activity in America fell throughout 1893, and Caesar took a pessimistic view of the future. He even applied to become manager of the US branch of the London Guarantee & Accident Co. but was turned down, on the grounds that he was not an American citizen.[135]

Further difficulties arose in 1894. In the depressed economic climate, holding companies based in London had problems paying a dividend to US shareholders on their brewery investments. They proposed to reduce charges for depreciation as a way of creating a profit so as to allow such payments. Fowler resisted this action. The Chicago newspapers took the shareholders' side and blamed the 'tiresome English accountants'.[136] Price Waterhouse held firm and though the breweries remained unprofitable they did not fall into bankruptcy.[137]

When the partners of Price Waterhouse reviewed the performance of their American enterprise in the summer of 1894, they were appalled to discover that its debts were on a rising trend.[138] Seeking to be 'free from risk of loss attending establishments of our own at New York and Chicago',[139] they agreed that Jones and Caesar would establish their own independent practice and that this, in turn, would serve as agents to the UK Firm. Price Waterhouse agreed to guarantee the new partnership a minimum income for three years.[140]

Thus on 1 January 1895 Jones, Caesar & Co. came into being. It was not that Jones and Caesar broke away from a reluctant Price Waterhouse; rather that the latter, concerned by the failure to generate adequate profits, had sought to distance themselves from this embryonic venture. This event proved to be of considerable significance for the future as it granted Jones and Caesar full autonomy over their affairs just at the time when the economy revived and when American businesses were alerted to the importance of having a reputable auditor. Now there could be no doubt that Jones, Caesar & Co. was an American firm, rather than the offshoot of a UK partnership. Even when the partnership returned to the Price Waterhouse fold in 1899, it rejoined not as an agency under the absolute control of London but as an autonomous organisation which had generated a client list of its own making.

The reconstituted firm of Jones, Caesar & Co. comprised three partners (the third being S.B. Foster, who resigned in 1897 to join the Bartholomay Brewing Co. of Rochester), thirteen clerks and five office men and stenographers, divided between New York and Chicago. Although Price Waterhouse continued to refer work to Jones, Caesar & Co., the firm had now developed a momentum of its own. In 1895, for example, it acquired the audit of an important client, the Norfolk & Western Railroad, and this, in turn, led to audits or special examinations for almost a dozen lines in the next five years. As the economy revived, the practice attracted an increasing number of special investigations, including that into the Baltimore & Ohio Railroad to determine how the proceeds of certain bond issues had been spent. In September 1896 Caesar wrote to Fowler in London that

> J.P. Morgan . . . have asked us to examine the receivership account of the Northern Pacific R.R. Co. This will be a very good connection indeed and I understand that we (i.e. your firm) shall almost certainly get the annual audit. You ask as to our staff. It *now* consists of six permanent and five temporary assistants, the latter being good men to whom we pay $15 day and expenses.[141]

In 1897 Jones, Caesar & Co. began to audit the companies which subsequently merged to form the American Steel & Wire Co. Instructions for the work also came from J.P. Morgan, the bankers, and the annual fee Jones, Caesar & Co. earned from this client exceeded their total turnover in each of the six years that they had been in practice.[142] By December 1897 the number of employees had risen to twenty, of whom nine were in New York and eleven in Chicago.

In the financial year 1897–8 Jones, Caesar & Co. earned respectable profits, and Price Waterhouse began to doubt the wisdom of the new agency arrangement. The proportion of indigenous work, as distinct from that referred from Britain, had risen appreciably. In April 1896 the state of New York had passed legislation providing for the title of 'certified public accountant' (CPA). The qualification could be awarded only to US citizens or those who intended to become citizens. Caesar, who was based in New York, became a CPA shortly afterwards. In June 1897 he wrote to Price Waterhouse in London and reported:

> So far as the profession of accounting is concerned, considerable changes have taken place since you established an agency here. Properly constituted societies under state and federal control are being established very much on the lines of the English Societies. (Mr Jones is president of the Illinois Society and Mr Caesar has been asked to act as one of the trustees of the New York Society).[143]

There was a danger that should Jones, Caesar & Co. become a CPA firm, they would gradually slip away from the influence of their progenitor. So, in the spring of 1898 the two partnerships entered into a short-term agreement, pending a more comprehensive association.

However, as negotiations were drawing to a conclusion, Jones suddenly died aged forty, apparently of diabetic complications. He had just returned from a visit to the UK in November 1898 to discuss the pooling of work and profits. Having agreed in June 1899 that the style of the firm would revert to Price, Waterhouse & Co., the London partners were, nevertheless, reluctant to conclude the negotiations with Caesar alone and requested the introduction of a further partner. After the death of Jones, Caesar reorganised the firm. He placed Charles J. Marr in charge of the Chicago office and G.O. May in charge of New York.[144] Nevertheless, the London partners remained insistent that another partner be introduced. Abruptly, Caesar nominated Henry W. Wilmot, an accountant on the staff in London since December 1894, whom he had met when the latter had been assigned to the United States on Wire Company audits.[145]

Then, in 1900, aged only forty-one, the impetuous Caesar announced his resignation. According to Berger, a partner, he possessed 'a real affection for his co-founder ... and the latter's death doubtless heightened his desire to retire at an early date and return to Paris'.[146] Caesar had been an 'exacting leader', observed Berger, who had

> established some rather rigid office and staff rules which were more productive of discontent than of esprit de corps. His salary policy was hardly in keeping with the growing importance of the profession, with the firm's prosperity, or the policy of other accounting organisations ... These developments created a feeling of uncertainty on the part of certain members of the organisation which was not relieved by the introduction of Wilmot ... During 1900 the firm lost four of the top Chicago men to other accounting organisations ... as well as a number of others at both offices of lesser standing in the organisation.[147]

A serious crisis of executive authority had arisen. It was ironic that at its most profitable period to date (a surplus of over $100,000 was recorded for 1899),[148] the American partnership found itself without a partner of recognised authority and experience. However, the name of Price Waterhouse had been established and had an unrivalled prestige in the United States. The firm had an impressive list of clients drawn from the railroads, breweries, steel makers and insurance companies. It had forged valuable contacts with prominent banking firms such as J.P. Morgan & Co. and Speyer & Co., and with New York lawyers. The organisation comprised around thirty members of staff by 1901 while somewhat deficient at the senior and semi-senior grades.[149] There had been a rapid turnover of staff, probably the result of poor pay and prospects: of eighteen accountants employed in December 1897 only seven remained when Caesar departed in June 1901.[150] Thus, it was important that a devolved managerial framework be introduced, together with one or two partner promotions, in order to create a period of stability.

4

Consolidation and Succession

The character of the City of London and the firms that work within it have altered dramatically since the end of the nineteenth century. In his 'Observations on Half a Century of Business Life', Lord Plender alluded to this transformation:

> When I first entered the City of London some fifty years ago [c.1883] to take up my duties in a chartered accountant's office [Deloitte & Co.], life was quieter; the place less lively; clerks dressed more soberly in morning coat and silk hat; the scale of pay was appreciably lower and the office hours were elastic with a tendency to longer rather than shorter working day ... Female clerks were not employed and it was a rare occasion to see ladies in the city streets.[1]

Given the size of Price Waterhouse in 1900, organisational routines were basic. The partners met every morning for about half an hour to deal with the post, allocate new work and record the receipt of fees, while all staff had to report every morning on work in progress. Later, as audits became larger and the firm increased in size employees were required to present themselves only on Mondays and Fridays.

At Frederick's Place, each partner had his own office, panelled in mahogany. The porters fuelled the open coal fires and served afternoon tea of either thinly sliced bread or arrowroot biscuits. Every morning the commissionaires sharpened pencils, changed nibs in pens, and filled pots of paper clips and pins. The entrance hall was finished in oak with a solid counter for the reception.[2] A partners' board indicated whether they were 'in' or 'out' – subsequently a less grand version was installed for managers. Sir Albert Wyon, when senior partner, insisted that the dark green railings outside Frederick's Place were polished regularly. With its understated hierarchy based on occupation and class, the offices of Price Waterhouse have been likened to an extended family. Indeed, personal introductions were customarily needed to obtain a position, and a respectful, gentlemanly atmosphere pervaded the building.

For Price Waterhouse the Edwardian years were not characterised by dramatic or radical developments – rather, the changes which happened were more of a portent for the future. Edwin Waterhouse had reached an age where retirement beckoned and he was replaced by an able but less talented leader, George Sneath, whose senior partnership saw no strategic reorientation. Although no startling growth in fee income occurred, the introduction of supertax and estate duties began what was to develop into a major area of consultancy work in the interwar period, though for the time their contribution to turnover remained minimal. The opening of regional branch offices in Liverpool and Newcastle, not momentous events in themselves, did, nevertheless, establish the principle of national representation for the UK Firm. Similarly the setting up of partnerships in Egypt and South America reflected thinking on a wider territorial basis. The rapid expansion of the US Firm and its decision to recruit indigenously trained staff created tension in the relationship with its UK progenitor, and practical steps were taken to strengthen formal links. For Price Waterhouse the Edwardian era was one characterised by consolidation and continuity in which the elements of change were primed rather than activated.

The Retirement of Edwin Waterhouse

During 1904 a discussion paper was circulated among the partners, and possibly kept from the eyes of Edwin Waterhouse himself, as to whether he should 'retire at once from this firm'.[3] Given that he was sixty-four, there would inevitably be, it was argued, 'an increasingly half-hearted service from the one who draws, quite properly, more in profit to his services *in management* than the other partners, should he continue in office'.[4] His immediate departure would have the advantage of allowing arrangements to be made for the future, while Waterhouse would still be available to offer advice and oversee the smooth transfer of his personal audits (London & Westminster Bank, National Provincial Bank, LNWR and so forth) to the partnership. Yet a precipitate retirement would have raised doubts over the style of the firm, since the partnership agreement of October 1895 provided that the name 'Price, Waterhouse & Co.' belonged exclusively to Edwin Waterhouse.[5] The 1904 deed, which presumably followed this discussion document, granted the partners the opportunity, when acquiring their share of the goodwill to purchase the name of the firm as well.[6]

Throughout 1905 Edwin Waterhouse pondered his future. As senior partner, he was the undisputed head of the firm. Sneath, Fowler and Wyon, his fellow partners, did not possess the authority to prevent him from continuing in office should he have chosen to do so. Waterhouse was well rewarded for his responsibilities retaining almost half of the partnership's profits. Why then did he decide to retire? The death of Alfred, his elder brother, in August 1905, left him as the last survivor of seven children and served perhaps as a poignant reminder of his own mortality. 'A symptom or feeling of a little over fatigue', wrote Edwin, led him to consult his physician, Napper, and

> at his recommendation I made up my mind to withdraw from the firm at the year's end, thus reducing my responsibilities. This had to a certain extent been made easy when our articles of partnership were last revised [1904] by arranging the terms on which anyone of us . . . might retire.[7]

In a sense Price Waterhouse was Edwin Waterhouse's creation. Many of the leading clients, and particularly the railway companies and financial institutions, had been won by him, the work falling to his supervision. Indeed, many audit appointments were personal to Edwin rather than the firm – including the National Provincial Bank, London & Westminster Bank, Law Fire Insurance Society, Bank of New Zealand, Equity & Law Life Assurance Co., Wilts & Dorset Banking Co., Metropolitan Railway, Oxford University and, of course, the largest client of all, the London & North Western Railway.[8] Edwin Waterhouse dominated the partnership in virtually every respect. He alone of the partners had received a university education, and as a member of an upper-middle-class professional élite possessed a range of social contacts not available to other members of his firm. As Halsey, then a clerk but later to be senior partner, observed, he exercised a powerful and dominating authority over the practice.

The heavy responsibility which Waterhouse carried, combined with a thirst for work, had exhausted him. Photographs taken around 1907 reveal a man aged beyond his years. He had been reluctant, or perhaps unable, to delegate or to devolve authority. The answer was to retire completely from the running of the firm. Such, however, was his degree of involvement that it proved impossible to divorce himself from its activities so abruptly. Indeed, his fellow partners initially sought to dissuade him from retirement as they believed that such an action might lead to the loss of those audits held in his name.[9] Accordingly, the new partnership deed of 1906 agreed that he should retain a number of his personal appointments, but that the fees would be divided between him and the firm, and Waterhouse promised to exercise his influence to encourage their transfer to Price Waterhouse. A reason for admitting his son, Nicholas, to the partnership in 1906 was that he might be able, as Edwin himself recorded, to supplant 'his father in the affections of my business friends'.[10]

In 1913, for example, when Edwin Waterhouse decided to give up the audits of the National Provincial Bank, Wilts & Dorset Bank and the LNWR, he was succeeded in each case by Nicholas; in October 1913 the latter also replaced him as auditor of the Danish Gas Co. and in the following year at the North London Railway. It was not until 1915 that Edwin resigned from the Council of the ICAEW and in January 1916 as auditor to the Dean and Chapter of Westminster Abbey; in both offices he was followed by Nicholas.[11]

How can the career of Edwin Waterhouse be summarised? He, more than any other figure, was responsible for creating the firm of Price Waterhouse. He succeeded in gathering together perhaps the most impressive list of audit clients held by any City partnership in the Victorian era. Waterhouse achieved this through undoubted expertise, which included a specialist knowledge in the fields of railways and banking, and by establishing a reputation for reliability and probity. As a supervisor of clerks, he insisted on the highest standards of work and was recognised as possessing an unimpeachable integrity. His liberal and broadly based education at University College School and University College London had provided him with the academic skills to solve accounting problems, though he never developed into an innovative or radical thinker. His Quaker upbringing generated a sense of justice and the need to set an example to others, though occasionally his strictures fell over the edge into prudery or silliness. Through his family and early friendships, Waterhouse had a valuable introduction to the City, the professions and government institutions, which subsequently served to establish his firm within a powerful socio-economic matrix.

Edwin Waterhouse had perhaps one major failing. His reluctance to delegate or to prepare the ground for a successor resulted in his being followed by senior partners of lesser ability. Neither Sneath, Fowler nor Wyon possessed his talent or advantages, nor during his period of office had they been granted responsibilities beyond that of partner which might, in turn, have allowed them to develop a broader vision. Not until after the First World War, when Sir Gilbert Garnsey came to the fore, did a figure of comparable stature occupy a position of authority within the firm. Waterhouse had hoped that his sons would prosper within the firm, and in 1897 a clause had been inserted in the partnership deed which granted him the 'liberty at any time during the partnership to introduce either of his sons, William Waterhouse and Nicholas Edwin Waterhouse, into the partnership business' so long as they qualified as chartered accountants. Although the latter did eventually become senior partner in 1945, neither was technically distinguished nor initially, at least, particularly enthused by the profession.

Although he surrendered executive authority in January 1906 to George Sneath, Waterhouse continued to visit Frederick's Place on a regular basis to supervise his audits and conduct Institute matters. His son, Nicholas, observed that he 'became much mellowed after he retired'.[12] He gave up his London home, 33 Sussex Gardens, in February 1907 and lived exclusively at 'Feldemore', a house which had been commissioned from the architect George T. Redmayne and first occupied in November 1880. It was situated between Dorking and Guildford in the parish of Holmbury St Mary, a district much desired by monied Victorians. His neighbours included G.E. Street, the architect who designed the local church of St Mary's, Sir William Bowman, an oculist, Sir Frederick Mirrielees, MP, head of the merchant bank Currie & Co., and the Hon. Frederick Leveson Gower, a relative of the Duke of Sutherland.[13] The village, disguised under the name 'Summer Street', featured in *A Room with a View* by E.M. Forster, who observed how its rural charm had attracted 'great mansions'.[14] It was at 'Feldemore' that Edwin died on 17 September 1917, to be buried in the nearby churchyard of St Mary's.

William Waterhouse, the eldest, had been educated at New College, Oxford, and having passed his finals without honours in 1897 concurred with Edwin's long-standing wish that he join Price Waterhouse as an articled clerk. William was given a seat in Edwin's office, doubtless so that he could be groomed for a partnership. Sadly, in May 1900, before he had been able to take his final examination to become a chartered accountant, William succumbed to a particularly virulent form of pneumonia and died.[15] Edwin Waterhouse subsequently described his son as having been

> always good and patient and unselfish but taking perhaps a too questioning view of things to allow his surroundings to give him the pleasure they might give; and in an almost too earnest desire to do the wisest thing falling with a certain amount of indecision . . . I looked forward to his developing, in time, a strong personality, full of goodness and truth . . .[16]

It was highly likely, given the tradition of dynastic succession, that had he lived William Waterhouse would have eventually held the post of senior partner. As it was, his younger brother, Nicholas, took his place as the nominated family member in the firm.

Born three years after William, Nicholas Waterhouse was educated at Winchester College, but recalled that he had not been a happy student there, on one occasion writing home to his mother using his own blood for ink to express his misery:

> Owing to having outgrown my strength – I was over 6ft tall at the age of 14 – and also to a groggy knee, I was not allowed to play football and other games for the first two years and this disability, combined with timidity and a horrible inferiority complex brought me into great disfavour with several elder boys . . .[17]

In 1896 Nicholas followed his brother to New College, Oxford, where he read jurisprudence. This choice may, in part, have been determined by his father as being the discipline closest to accountancy which then (as today) was not taught at that university. He would have preferred 'a career in medicine, spending much time in the dissecting rooms up the Banbury Road'.[18] Perhaps it was at college that Nicholas found his self-confidence. He won a Blue for cross-country running, and spent most of his time socialising. In the event he obtained a third, and on coming down in 1899 entered Price Waterhouse as an articled clerk attached to A.W. Wyon. Nicholas qualified in 1903, having passed, he later discovered, by the barest of margins. This enabled Edwin Waterhouse to insist that his son be elected to the partnership when he retired. Accordingly, *The Times* for 2 January 1906 carried the notice:

> Messrs Price, Waterhouse & Co. announce that Mr Edwin Water-house, being desirous of partially withdrawing from the active business practice which has occupied him for more than 40 years, has retired from his position as a member of their firm. He will continue, however, to conduct those matters of business in which he holds a personal appointment, and will remain available for the purpose of consultation. The firm will be continued under the same name of the remaining partners with the addition of Mr Nicholas E. Waterhouse A.C.A. the son of the senior now retiring.[19]

Today it would be unthinkable that a senior partner could insist that his son, who had been qualified for only two years, should be so promoted. As Nicholas himself observed, it was a 'blatant example of nepotism', and some of the senior clerks, men more able than himself, 'Frank Price, Willy Sneath and Harold Morland felt "pretty sore" but their turns came soon afterwards'.[20]

Why, then, would such an elevation prove acceptable to the other partners? In the nineteenth century, it was common for fathers to introduce close relatives to partnerships (as evidenced by Cooper Brothers, Whinney, Smith & Whinney and W.B. Peat). The Victorians placed great emphasis on heredity. Edwin Waterhouse himself had attached

> considerable importance to what he considered to be 'good family' and [observed Nicholas] I think he was rather pleased when a cousin worked out a family tree claiming to trace his descent ... to that fine old Welshman, Caractacus, who was taken prisoner by the Romans in A.D.51.[21]

In other words, if a client saw the Waterhouse name in the list of partners, it suggested the continuity of those characteristics which had helped to establish the firm's reputation. At a time when accounting standards were rudimentary despite qualifying examinations, and uniformity in the presentation of financial records was considered an impossibility, an outward and tangible sign of respectability was of great importance. An established family name seemed a sure guarantee of probity and reliability.

Having no natural aptitude for accountancy, Nicholas Waterhouse did not exhibit enthusiasm for the mundane or routine aspects of auditing. His father chided him for his attitude: '"My dear boy, though you are pretty hopeless in your work, for goodness sake be one of the first in the queue every morning so at least my partners will think you are trying." '[22] The duties of a partner probably matched Nicholas' character far better than those of an audit clerk. He developed considerable charm and manifested many of the qualities of the English gentleman. Nicholas Waterhouse was, therefore, ideally suited to liaising with clients, overseeing those engaged in the detailed work of auditing and maintaining an equable atmosphere between all. As his father recorded, the additional pressure brought to bear in the First World War by government appointments resulted in his being 'very busy',[23] and perhaps provoked some belated diligence in him.

Partnership Changes

As the longest-serving member of the partnership, George Sneath succeeded Edwin Waterhouse and was to hold the post of senior partner for eight years, retiring in June 1913. He was not an innovator and no radically new strategies were developed. Although a competent practitioner, Sneath was not an original thinker in the mould of May (p. 95) or Garnsey (p.122). The fact that the firm's fee income grew gradually in real terms during his period of office suggested that few, if any, major clients were gained but equally that none were lost. His was, therefore, a caretaker administration which gave the firm time to adjust to the withdrawal of the dominant and driving force of Edwin Waterhouse.

A number of Sneath's relatives joined Price Waterhouse. His eldest son, William Cecil, became a partner in 1907. Like Edwin Waterhouse he had been educated at University College School, but had then been articled to Price Waterhouse in 1891. In tune with the firm's policy of sending promising clerks to America to gain experience, W.C. Sneath was employed in the Chicago office during 1896. Sneath, having been at school in Germany for a year and acquired a working knowledge of the language, travelled regularly to the Continent on investigations and audits. These included Hotchkiss & Co., Kodak and the Gresham Life Assurance Co. (all in Paris in connection with the UK audit), the S.G. Pauli Brewery in Bremen, Dortmund Breweries Co., Danish Gas Co. at Copenhagen and John Fowler & Co. in Magdeburg.[24] The obituary of W.C. Sneath in *The Accountant* described him as 'a kindly, unassuming man . . . [who] won the affection of his associates and employees and played a devoted part in public and charitable work'.[25] Nicholas Waterhouse recalled him as being

> a most conscientious and hard worker who took on most of the jobs previously supervised by his father [notably the audits of Lloyds Bank and the L.B. & S.C.R.] . . . He often seemed rather snowed under with work and I sometimes thought this was due to other partners . . . shifting their less interesting jobs on to him. He was so very obliging.[26]

Southall, a qualified clerk at Price Waterhouse in the twenties, observed of Sneath: 'He lacked the thrust of his father and was the least forceful of the partners.'[27]

Other admissions to the partnership in the Edwardian period included Harold John Morland in 1907, and [Sir] Arthur Lowes Dickinson, Frank Steane Price and [Sir] Gilbert Garnsey in 1913. Morland came from an old Quaker family and had been educated at Whitgift and Bootham Schools, subsequently attending University College London and King's College, Cambridge, where he obtained a first in the mathematics tripos. On graduating he worked initially as a schoolmaster and gave this up to pursue a career in accountancy, passing his finals with Sellars, Dicksee & Co. in 1900.[28] Having a naturally academic mind, he came first in his year and then joined Price Waterhouse.

Sir Nicholas Waterhouse recalled that one of Morland's earliest tasks was the first audit of Harland & Wolff following its public flotation. His high intelligence enabled him to achieve without great effort and Morland developed an off-hand manner. When Edwin Waterhouse inquired about an unusual credit to the profit and loss account, Morland replied, 'Oh, I thought that would make you scratch your head a bit, but it is really quite simple.'[29] A devout Quaker prominent in the Society of Friends, he served as a 'model' to Nicholas Waterhouse, who observed of him: 'in spite of his wonderful brain and high principles, I always thought that at heart he was bone lazy and I respected him for it'.[30] Southall, who knew him well, concluded that he had not the 'extraordinary psychic gifts of Sir Gilbert Garnsey or perhaps the unflagging persistence of Sir Albert Wyon, but in sheer width and power of mind was first among the partners'.[31] During 1931 he was, however, to be subjected to public gaze when as auditor of the Royal Mail Steam Packet Co. he was called to defend his actions at the Old Bailey (p.151).

Frank Steane Price was a great nephew of S.L. Price and the fourth son of Charles Price who founded the London firm of Price, Forbes & Co., insurance brokers. Born in Hampstead and educated at University College School, he worked in his father's business for about eighteen months before joining Price Waterhouse as a pupil of J. Gurney Fowler. Qualifying in 1898, he then travelled extensively on the Continent and to South America and South Africa. Frank's son described him as 'a quiet, serious and reticent man. Tall and alarmingly thin, he had a poor physique and a weak heart'.[32]

Nevertheless, the real coup for the firm was the recruitment in 1905 of Gilbert Garnsey, then a newly qualified accountant.[33] Destined to be one of the outstanding accountants of his generation, he rose from comparatively humble beginnings and gained admission to the partnership by sheer ability and determination. His father, William Samuel Garnsey, was a butcher in Wellington, Somerset. Gilbert was his fifth son and was educated locally at Wellington School, where he played centre-forward for the first eleven.[34] His natural scholastic and sporting abilities brought him to the attention of the Rev. E.C. Harries, the second master, who, in turn, introduced him to the Walsall firm of chartered accountants, Muras, Harries & Higginson. Garnsey played soccer for Aston Villa's second eleven as an amateur between 1902 and 1904,[35] though Sir Nicholas Waterhouse believed he had been financially rewarded by the club, using the money to pay for his articles.[36] He achieved the rare double of coming first in both the intermediate and final examinations of the ICAEW in 1903 and 1905. Aged twenty-two and of an ambitious disposition, he wrote to three of the leading firms in London for a position.[37] Following their policy of recruiting prize winners, Price Waterhouse offered him an interview. He was engaged at £2 per week and initially worked almost entirely for Nicholas Waterhouse since none of the other partners had noticed his talent. When Nicholas took the youthful Garnsey to 'Feldemore' to meet his father, retired from the partnership, the latter proved to be more perspicacious and commented ambiguously, 'you be very careful of that young man'.[38] Impressed by his intellect, Nicholas Waterhouse recollected his 'masterly' investigation of Cornells, a Smithfield business seeking public flotation. Although only twenty-four, Garnsey detected irregularities which resulted in prolonged but successful litigation. Spencer, later to become a partner, recalled that shortly after joining Price Waterhouse, Garnsey had been sent to Paris to assist him in an investigation of the New York Life Insurance Co. 'I quickly found,' he wrote, 'that he was worth most of the other assistants put together and he greatly assisted me in the completion of the work which had to be done under high pressure.'[39]

A seemingly inexhaustible capacity for hard work combined with high intelligence and a natural aptitude for accountancy resulted in Garnsey being made a partner in 1913, aged thirty, a remarkable achievement in an era when experience and family connections tended to be highly valued. He developed an uncanny skill with numbers and once observed:

> To me figures have always possessed individuality. I can remember
> a figure connected with an individual long after I may have
> forgotten his features and his form.[40]

In the years before the First World War, Garnsey travelled extensively on the Continent on audits and investigations for Price Waterhouse. It was said that he overcame difficulties of language by use of phrasebooks and would acquire a passing knowledge in a few days.[41]

Branch Offices: Liverpool and Newcastle

By 1904 the volume of work for shipping lines had risen to such proportions that it was decided to transfer these audits from Frederick's Place to a new branch office in Liverpool.[42] Its principal clients included the White Star, Dominion and Leyland companies. The office was originally supervised by a Mr Murray, but he was succeeded in 1908 by A.T. Serle, a manager, who had been employed by Lovelock, H.W.S. Whiffin & Dickinson; the latter remained in Liverpool until his retirement in 1933.

When work in the north-east of England required detailed on-site examination, it was entrusted to a Mr Williams who lived in Darlington. When he left Price Waterhouse to become chief accountant to the

North Eastern Railway, his post was taken by W.G. Brocklehurst, then senior clerk in charge of liquidations at Frederick's Place, who also took up residence in Darlington.[43] In 1912, however, Percy Parmeter, a former articled clerk of the London office and a nephew of Laurence Halsey, gave notice that he wished to leave Price Waterhouse and to set up in practice on his own account in Newcastle where he had some business connections. As he was considered an able accountant and the firm's clientele in the north-east was growing, it was decided to open a branch office in the city with Parmeter as a resident local partner, and Brocklehurst as his first assistant. Thus, in 1912 the first Price Waterhouse partnership was established in the UK outside London, and although further branches were opened during the interwar period under the supervision of managers, the principle was not extended.

The American Firm

Speaking in Sheffield in 1910 Sir William Plender referred to the 'great growth of our profession in the United States of America':

> In my occasional visits to that continent I see year by year a constant increase in the number of practising accountants, and a widening demand for their services with banking and commercial firms and companies.[44]

Although the US partnership of Price Waterhouse was flourishing commercially, it struck a managerial crisis following Caesar's decision in June 1900 to retire. As May noted, this created

> a considerable organisational problem. The professional demands of the London firm were such that they could not afford to send one of the London partners to take charge of the American practice, and they did not feel that there was anyone in the American organisation with sufficient experience and maturity to be safely entrusted with this responsibility. They found a solution, however, which was ideal ... Mr Waterhouse, through an interest in an extensive orange grove development [the Riverside Trust Co.], had come to know Arthur Lowes Dickinson, who was also a member of the board of directors of this Californian company.[45]

It was arranged that Dickinson, then senior partner in the small City firm of Lovelock, H.W.S. Whiffin & Dickinson, should sail for America in April 1901 to take charge of the US partnership from 1 July. His London practice was absorbed within Price Waterhouse.

A.L. Dickinson was the eldest son of Lowes (Cato) Dickinson of Hanwell. His father won some distinction as a portrait painter and exhibited regularly at the Royal Academy. E.M. Forster, a close friend of his younger brother, described Lowes Dickinson as a man of 'courtesy and intelligence' who would return from his London studio to 'read Scott, Shakespeare or Coleridge aloud' to his children.[46] He was a leading Christian Socialist, helping to found the Working Men's College, together with Charles Kingsley and Tom Hughes. His son, A.L. Dickinson, was educated at Charterhouse and King's College, Cambridge, where in 1882 he obtained a first in mathematics. His younger brother, Goldsworthy Lowes Dickinson, followed him to King's and, after a brief flirtation with medicine, was elected to a fellowship in modern history. He achieved fame as a lecturer, writer and advocate of pacifism during the First World War. A.L. Dickinson served his articles with Edwards, Jackson & Browning, being awarded first place in the intermediate examination of 1883 and joint first place in the final of 1886.[47] Two years later he joined Lovelock, H.W.S. Whiffin & Dickinson as a junior partner.[48] Sir Nicholas Waterhouse described him as 'a man of terrific and unbounded energy' and as having 'the kindest and most sympathetic disposition'. He 'would go out of his way to any extent to help anyone who was in difficulty'.[49] Taking 'a broad intellectual and professional interest in accountancy beyond the practical work of the firm', he was, as May recalled, 'an inspiring person to work for and with';[50] Dickinson possessed a 'transparent honesty' which

> enabled him to be fearlessly outspoken in discussions with clients. In dealing with professional matters he obtained his information on engagements first-hand, going directly to the assistant who did the work in the field. Young assistants sometimes felt his manner to be gruff but they admired and respected him.[51]

On arriving in America, Dickinson immediately took steps to strengthen the firm by appointing qualified men from England and Scotland to fill the gaps created by the resignations which had occurred under the mercurial Caesar. Charles James Marr and George Oliver May were both admitted to the partnership in January 1902, the former in Chicago and the latter in New York.[52] Dickinson soon grasped the realities of American business life, and the paramount importance of being able to tender competitively. To do this it was essential to build up a network of branch offices. By keeping a manager and small staff at the branches, Dickinson argued that the firm 'should be able to carry out local work without any travelling or hotel expenses'.[53] His first step towards geographical expansion was to open the St Louis office in November 1901, established under the familiar style of Jones, Caesar & Co. Situated in the fourth-largest US city, it prospered and soon attracted favourable comment in the local press.

However, Dickinson also learned about the uncertainties of the American business environment. As he explained to the London partners, work in America was 'more speculative' than he had realised:

> By this I mean that annual audits which in England are always the backbone of the business are comparatively few in number and the largest of them being dependent on the caprice of a few individuals cannot be considered as certain in their recurrence as they are with you.[54]

Having just lost the audits of the American Steel & Wire Co., Dickinson suggested that 'the prospects of our getting any annual auditing work from the US Steel Company are for similar reasons somewhat remote'.[55] It was essential, Dickinson believed, to raise the public profile of the partnership. For, as he wrote to London in November 1901,

> Jones, Caesar & Co. is certainly a whole lot better known than Price, Waterhouse & Co., the latter name being only employed in the case of railway companies and of breweries and insurance companies whose head offices are in England. The latter is also looked upon as being an English firm, whereas Jones, Caesar & Co. is regarded as the name of the firm in America.[56]

To correct this public impression Dickinson dispatched 36,000 announcements of his joining the US Firm to leading bankers, lawyers and merchants, and to the financial press. The London partnership were disturbed by this strategy which conflicted with their professional rules. In response Dickinson quoted a letter he had received from Wilmot, a colleague:

We are all agreed that regular and systematic advertising is deroga-
tory to the dignity of the firm, but the point is whether on
important occasions such as opening new branches, it is not unfair
to handicap ourselves by preventing a little judicious advertising. It
is not too much to say that [Edward] Stanley [the manager at St
Louis] would not have done so well except for his little burst of
advertising. Everyone in St Louis knows us and everyone can be
made to know us in Pittsburgh in the same way. America is not
England ... We just have to think about ourselves the same as
every other accountant.[57]

To the surprise of Dickinson the stockholders of US Steel chose Price
Waterhouse rather than Jones, Caesar & Co. as their auditors in February
1902, and this immediately raised the question of opening an office in
Pittsburgh.[58] This assignment proved to be of great worth to the firm.
The US Steel Corporation controlled three-quarters of the steel business
in America, and represented a major technical challenge for the accountants. Dickinson believed that stockholders could only be informed
adequately of its true financial state by a consolidation, and the published
statements for 1902 were regarded as a landmark in accounting
history.[59]

The rapid growth in the size of the New York office (from fifteen
employees in 1901 to seventy-three by 1903)[60] required that Dickinson
seek new premises. They were unable to find suitable offices in Wall
Street and decided to rent a portion of the eleventh floor of a new
building erected by the Caledonian Insurance Co. at 50 Pine Street from
May 1902.[61] However, these offices rapidly proved to be too small and
in October they were again seeking larger premises[62] – which were
found at 54 William Street.

The firm prospered, earning profits of $184,500 in 1903, a threefold
increase over the previous year.[63] However, the collapse of the corporate
merger movement and the downturn in the economy brought several
years of 'much hard work, continuous strain and poor results
financially'.[64] Profits (Table 4, see Appendix) fell accordingly, and it
was not until 1907 that Price Waterhouse entered a further period of
sustained growth in America.

In February 1906 Dickinson raised the issue of the partnership arrangements with London. 'Every additional $5,000 of profits which come to
Wilmot and myself jointly,' he complained,

means a very large amount of extra hard work and strain but it also means a clear addition to yourselves of $2,500 without raising a finger.[65]

In order to spread the burden of executive authority, he proposed admitting George R. Webster and W.E. Seatree to the partnership and requested that the London Firm surrender a portion of their shareholding. Initially the latter refused.[66] This drew from Dickinson a powerful protest. He demonstrated that London had drawn substantial profits (29 per cent of total US earnings in 1902–3, and 21 per cent in 1904–5), and concluded:

> We here feel that you [London] take little or no interest in the American business and, in fact, hardly care to understand it. We are doing a very large business under great difficulties and have pulled through ... but this has been done at an enormous cost, both physical and mental upon partners and managers ... which has simply converted life into slavery.[67]

Dickinson, who had collapsed from 'overwork', had been told by his physician to take a complete rest and doubted 'whether I can go on much longer'.[68] Wilmot, too, wrote observing 'the American business is no mere child dependent on London. It has a personality of its own.'[69] Edwin Waterhouse had just retired as senior partner, so that it fell to George Sneath to accede to the American demands and in June 1906 sufficient shares were relinquished to permit the admission of Webster and Seatree.[70]

The UK Firm had failed to appreciate just how large its American counterpart had become and the extent to which it had developed into an autonomous being. It was no longer appropriate or proper to regard this as a subsidiary partnership. Henceforth it was an equal, with characteristics of its own making.

The US Firm had grown rapidly since 1901, from twenty-four professional staff to 145 by 1911, while the number of offices had increased from two to eleven.[71] Seven new offices were opened in the period of Dickinson's senior partnership: at San Francisco (1904), Mexico City (1906), Seattle (1907), Montreal (1907), Boston (1909) and Toronto (1910) and, by taking over the practice of J.E. Sterrett, at Philadelphia (1907).

In 1909, having reached the age of fifty and wishing to return to Britain, Dickinson declared his intention to retire from the US practice in two years' time. His successor, G.O. May, was appointed by the London Firm in December 1910 and took up his duties in the new year.[72] Dickinson remained as a partner in the UK practice and was given responsibility for any matter that might arise in London concerning America. As well as overseeing the expansion in the US Firm, Dickinson had played an important part in establishing the accountancy profession in America. Through his appointment as president of the Federation of Societies of Public Accountants in 1904 and as secretary of the American Association of Public Accountants in 1905, he helped to bring about the merger of the two bodies. He had also been a leading organiser of the 1904 International Congress on Accounting, addressing it with a paper entitled 'Profits of a Corporation'. At the time of Dickinson's retirement in 1911 the US Firm comprised eleven offices in America, Canada and Mexico, and employed a total of 200 staff; it had, therefore, outgrown its UK progenitor.[73] His departure also signalled the abandonment of the Jones, Caesar style.

The appointment of May as senior partner represented a turning point in the relationship between the UK and American partnerships of Price Waterhouse. In essence, Dickinson was a British accountant who had transferred to the United States to perform a specific managerial role. He felt no special loyalty to America and his attitudes and mores would have been English. May, by comparison, had emigrated at the age of twenty-three, made his permanent home in New York, become a part-time lecturer at the Harvard Graduate School of Business Administration and was, in his thinking and allegiance, an American citizen. When May succeeded to the leadership of the firm in July 1911 two junior partners, R.O. Berger and A.B. Brodie, were admitted, which resulted in three of the then seven partners having gained their accountancy experience wholly in the United States.[74] In 1914 John Hall Bowman, who had joined the American staff in July 1897,[75] was one of seven new admissions to the partnership. Thus, the authority of the UK Firm found itself on the wane and was set to decline further.

Under May the number of offices doubled. Such territorial expansion may have reduced the rate at which profits grew. For the three years ending 30 June 1911, 1912 and 1913 profits were respectively $250,000, $276,000 and $288,000,[76] which did not represent a dramatic increase. As the US Firm grew in size and autonomy, so new partnership arrangements progressively reduced the share held by the UK partners. In June 1901, for example, A.L. Dickinson, and H.W. Wilmot each held a 30 per cent share in the firm, while London had the greatest holding, 40 per cent.[77] By 1905 when May and Marr had been admitted, London's share had fallen to 27 per cent,[78] and by 1907, after the admission of Seatree and Webster, it was 12.5 per cent. It remained at this level until the July 1919 partnership agreement when it reduced still further to 7.5 per cent.[79] When, in 1914, the US partnership doubled in size with the admission of seven new members,[80] four of these had qualified in the UK and three in America, bringing the totals respectively to eight and six.

In January 1914 May wrote to his former superior, Dickinson, in London to suggest that an exchange scheme be incorporated:

> I have given considerable thought to the question whether we could not make some arrangement by which a few of the more promising Americans on our staff could get the benefit of some English experience . . . The great defect of American business men generally was their provincial character – that they had no adequate knowledge of business methods outside their own country . . .[81]

His motive, May explained, was to attract 'the best men' by making 'them feel that the best positions are open to them'. The firm's policy had been to reduce 'the importation of men as much as possible'[82] and to recruit from the local population, and the offer of an exchange to London would act as a powerful incentive. Agreement was soon reached in principle and Dickinson replied in February:

> As a corollary to your suggestion it has occurred to us that it might be made reciprocal, that is . . . we might send out some picked men from this office . . . to learn American methods.[83]

Concerned, perhaps, that the UK and American partnerships might be drifting apart, Dickinson saw the scheme as a means of reinforcing the relationship. He wrote to May a week later to report that

> some of us have been considering the desirability of keeping the ranks of the men belonging to the Institute of Chartered Account-' ants in England in your office filled up with men likely to turn out well in order that there may be a continuous succession in the future

of such chartered men available for admission as partners and to keep up the London connection with the American firm ... There is a young man here who is just out of articles who might be a very good man for you to have on the American staff with a view to his staying permanently ... He is spoken well of by everybody as the sort of man with whom, in the ordinary course, we should not want to part. There is a feeling, however, that to preserve the continuity suggests some sacrifice of this sort might well be made.[84]

Egypt, South America and Australia

Price Waterhouse did not confine their overseas ambitions to America. In 1907 it was decided to set up an Egyptian partnership and F.G. Bonham Carter opened an office in Cairo. He had been articled to Edwin Waterhouse, had qualified in 1903, left the firm in the following year to take up a government appointment in South Africa, returning four years later. By the terms of the deed, Bonham Carter was to receive a salary of £800 per annum. The first £200 of any net profits were to be paid to him and the remainder divided in the proportion 80 per cent to the UK Firm and 20 per cent to Bonham Carter.[85] However, the arrangement proved shortlived. In January 1911, in order to spread costs and widen the opportunities open to what were comparatively small businesses, W.B. Peat and Price Waterhouse announced that their respective Egyptian practices would merge under the style Messrs Peat, Waterhouse & Co.[86] with offices at Savoy Chambers, Kasr-el-Nil, Cairo, and 15 Boulevard de Ramleh, Alexandria (originally opened by Peats in 1908).[87]

A further overseas development was initiated in October 1912 when Halsey, accompanied by F.S. Tull, a qualified member of the London staff, sailed for Buenos Aires on the SS *Asturias*. They had planned to form an association with the local firm of Leng Roberts & Co., who had diversified beyond accountancy and also served as agents in Argentina for the City merchant bankers, Baring Bros & Co. The accountancy side of the business was supervised by Albert Faller, who had worked for Price Waterhouse in London. The possible conflict of interest which this development of the practice had occasioned prevented any arrangement being concluded between the two firms. Halsey recommended that Price Waterhouse set up on its own and in April 1913 a room was taken in Leng Roberts' building at 376 Bartolome Milne; Tull remained as resident partner.[88] The office initially had very little work but the practice developed steadily through instructions received from local organisations and referrals from the UK and US Firms. Early clients included Morris, Little & Co. of Doncaster, manufacturers of sheep dips, C.H. Walker & Co., contractors engaged in extending the Buenos Aires port and docks, while local audits were performed for the Australian Mercantile Land & Finance Co. and the Chilean Transandine Railway.[89] Towards the end of 1914 a second South American office was established in Valparaiso, Chile. Profits for the first fifteen months totalled £1,500.

Early in 1896 Price Waterhouse entered into an agency agreement with Davey Flack & Co. of Melbourne. Joseph Henry Flack had originally joined the staff of the London office in 1870 and remained there until September 1874 when he emigrated to Australia to set up in practice.[90] His sons, E.H. and H.R. Flack, were sent to London to train with Price Waterhouse, and the former while working in Gresham Street accumulated sufficient leave to enable him to compete in the 1896 Olympic Games held in Athens. He later wrote:

> My main concern was lest Mr Edwin Waterhouse . . . might hear of what I was doing and probably disapprove of a member of staff of Price, Waterhouse & Co. careering across Europe to take part in athletics contests. My fears, however, were quite unfounded as when I returned to London after having the good luck to win the 800 metres and 1,500 metres, Mr Waterhouse sent for me . . . He congratulated me and followed it with an invitation to spend the following weekend at his country home.[91]

E.H. Flack was, in fact, the first Australian to win an Olympic athletic event. The firm of Flack & Flack, as it became in 1904, expanded across the sub-continent, opening offices in Perth (1904), Sydney (1908) and Brisbane (1911).[92]

Fees, Profits and Staff Numbers

As Table 2 (see Appendix) reveals, in cash terms the fee income of Price Waterhouse grew by 61 per cent between 1900 (£43,365) and 1914 (£69,927). In real terms the expansion was less dramatic due to inflationary pressures in the economy – a rise of 42 per cent. The graph (Fig.7) shows that the dramatic acceleration in income from 1894 to 1903 was not sustained, and something of a plateau formed in the decade before the First World War. In real terms fees were slightly higher in 1903 than in 1914. These trends were mirrored by profits (Table 3, see Appendix) which also peaked in real terms in 1903, though showing a 1914 maximum in cash terms.

The American Firm made an important contribution to UK profits, averaging around 15 per cent annually from 1900 to 1914, though its proportion was noticeably higher in 1903 (when it accounted for £11,244 or 22.2 per cent) and 1906 (£14,151 or 29.3 per cent). In 1914 both partnerships in South America and Egypt also generated profits, though the amounts transferred to the UK Firm remained comparatively small.

Why, then, was the rapid growth in fee income, evident from 1894 to 1903 and in profits from 1894 to 1901, not sustained in the Edwardian period? It is impossible to say whether this was a reflection of the comparatively sluggish performance of the British economy or of the transfer of authority from an ageing Edwin Waterhouse to the less dynamic figure of George Sneath. In reality both factors probably contributed to a period of relative quiescence.

A salary list drawn up in 1900 contained fifty-seven names.[93] On the retirement of George Sneath in June 1913 the total workforce of Price Waterhouse in London was 107, including eleven partners.[94] It has not proved possible to provide a comprehensive breakdown by occupation of these staff numbers, though the majority appear to have been audit clerks, a total of thirty-nine having been identified, together with a further four who were engaged on railway audits.

Taxation and Death Duties

The Edwardian era witnessed the beginnings of an important new area of work for accountants – taxation. Although a system of income tax had been devised by Pitt the Younger in 1799 as a temporary expedient to fund the French Revolutionary Wars, it was not until the 1840s that it became a regular source of peacetime revenue. In his 1842 and 1845 budgets, Sir Robert Peel switched from customs and excise duties to income tax as the principal means of collecting the state's funding. Yet the standard rate remained low, varying between 2d (0.8p) to 1s (5p) in the pound between 1843 and 1900 with a mean of 5–7d (2.1p–2.9p), while collection and assessment procedures were so straightforward that accountants in general did not become involved in revenue matters.

In a period of increasingly interventionist state policies (including the introduction of such benefits as old age pensions and unemployment insurance), Asquith's Liberal government acted not simply to raise money for public expenditure but with the deliberate intention of redistributing wealth. The administration's second budget, introduced by Lloyd George in 1909, accepted the principle of graduation in the form of a supertax fixed at 6d (2.5p) in the pound on all incomes over £5,000, and levied after the first £3,000. In addition, a distinction was made between earned income (not exceeding £2,000) which was to be charged at 9d (3.75p) in the pound, as against the 1s (5p) charged on unearned income.

The cost of the Boer War had resulted in income tax being raised beyond 1s (5p) and the 1901 budget was the first which estimated a larger revenue from direct, as against indirect, taxation. With the exception of 1904 when it was 11d (4.6p), the standard rate never fell back below 1s (5p).

The question of estate duty had originally been raised by Harcourt's budget of 1894. It had been introduced with the intention of reforming death duties (which were then divided into five classes: probate, account, estate, legacy and succession, and a graduated income tax) but in the event after a hard fought parliamentary battle the Chancellor had to settle for an amalgamation of the five under the generic title of estate duty, and the imposition of a graduated rate from 1 per cent up to £5,000 to 8 per cent on sums over £1 million.[95] These charges were increased in severity following Lloyd George's 1909 budget. Hence, the question of personal taxation for the rich and for major companies became both financially pressing and increasingly complex. The advice of an accountant could make a significant difference to a client's liability through a carefully considered strategy to minimise payments.

Involvement with the Institute

Formed by Royal Charter in 1880, the Institute of Chartered Accountants in England and Wales became one of the chief regulating bodies for the profession. Price had been an original council member, remaining as such until his death. Edwin Waterhouse became a founder member, granted admission on the strength of his experience. Three years later, in November 1883, he stood for election to the council. Ten candidates were proposed for the three vacancies. Waterhouse, however, came bottom of the first ballot with nine votes and was eliminated.[96] Price rarely attended council meetings in the mid-1880s[97] and on his death in May 1887, Waterhouse was unanimously elected in his place.[98] He took an active interest in Institute affairs, serving on the building committee which supervised the design and construction of their new offices in Moorgate Place.[99] In 1892, on the retirement of T.A. Welton, as Waterhouse recorded,

> my fellows on the council did me the honour of electing me, without any previous training as vice-president for the post [of president]. The appointment was likely to throw more than usual responsibility on its holder, as, during the year of office our new building would have to be inaugurated, and it was naturally the desire of the Institute that the occasion should be made use of to bring our profession a little before the public.[100]

Edwin Waterhouse served as president for the customary two years, retiring from office in 1894. He remained an active council member until July 1915, and also held the presidency of the Chartered Accountants' Benevolent Association from 1898 to 1915.[101] Nicholas Waterhouse, his son, succeeded him in the council and, like his father, in due course became president.

George Sneath was also elected to the council, and served upon it from 1896 to 1914, increasing the representation of Price Waterhouse to two. His place was taken by A.L. Dickinson who retired in 1928.[102]

At a time when accountants saw themselves as an emerging profession, rather than as business consultants, the ICAEW had an important part to play. It was responsible for setting qualifying examinations, establishing and enforcing standards of practice, and representing the membership with regard to legislation. As a result, the leading City firms all considered it important to have representation on its council, and to have a partner as president was a particular mark of distinction. When firms remained comparatively small in terms of their number of staff, it was vital that they have recourse to a larger institution to defend their actions and promote their principles. The ICAEW was a unifying force, a formal body in which the leaders of the profession met, exchanged views, formed friendships and made representations to governments.

Companies Acts

A principal area of concern for the ICAEW was the minimal state of company regulation. In essence, the law had remained unaltered since 1862 and there was growing concern that statutory safeguards should be introduced to protect the public from unscrupulous directors or lax auditors. The Davey Committee, set up in 1894 to investigate the question, included Edwin Waterhouse, then president of the ICAEW, among its members. He recorded in his memoirs:

> there had been so many scandals in connection with public compan-
> ies, showing fraud in their inception and formation, and dereliction
> of duty on the part of promotors and directors, that in November
> the Board of Trade, under the presidency of Mr James Bryce,
> desired to consider the possibility of amending the Joint Stock
> Companies Acts . . . The committee had a heavy work before them,
> and we met for sometimes thrice a week at 4 o'clock or so, at the
> Board of Trade offices.[103]

Their report, completed in June 1895, did not directly result in legislation. It was not until a House of Lords Select Committee, reporting over three years between 1896 and 1898, had presented its findings to Parliament that a new Bill was framed. The 1900 Companies Act required that the auditors declare whether the balance sheet laid before the annual general meeting showed 'a true and correct view of the state of the company's affairs'. It recognised, therefore, that the auditor's principal responsibility was to the shareholders rather than to the directors, though the Act fell short of defining any qualifications for the individual entrusted with the audit or specifying the contents of the balance sheet. *The Economic Journal* remarked with some accuracy, 'considering the time spent upon it, it is a pity that the Act achieves so little'.[104]

The Loreburn Committee, under the chairmanship of Sir Robert Reid, was appointed in 1905 to make further improvements to the company statutes and reported in the following year. Edwin Waterhouse was again appointed to represent English chartered accountants and found that their 'deliberations were lengthy'.[105] The main recommendation, codified in the 1907 Act, was that public companies file with the registrar

> an audited statement, in the form of a balance sheet, containing a summary of its capital, its liabilities and its assets, giving such particulars as may generally disclose the nature of such liabilities and assets, and how the values at which the fixed assets stand are arrived at.[106]

Omission of any reference to the profit and loss account in this context was to provide directors with the option of withholding a submission if they felt it was detrimental to the company's interest.[107] This Act, widely flouted in spirit, remained in force until 1928, when public pressure compelled the government to introduce tighter regulations. Even so, these revisions, too, were considered inadequate by many commentators.

Thus the 1900 and 1907 Companies Acts, both the product of much discussion, did not materially affect reporting procedures and the general disclosure of information, apart from re-establishing the registrar of companies together with the legal requirement to submit a balance sheet once a year. Many, for example, sent in the same document as before, as there was no stipulation that it had to be current. Similarly, profit figures were exempted from disclosure, as were private companies. Some groups would transfer important operations to private subsidiaries in order to avoid public scrutiny.[108] Why, then, were Waterhouse and his colleagues so reluctant to impose regulations upon companies and their auditors? This was still an age of *laissez-faire* when state intervention was kept to a minimum and the role of the individual was felt to be paramount. It was believed to be more important that directors and accountants be given maximum scope for action (the former to create profits and the latter to exercise proper professional responsibility) than that the few unscrupulous businessmen be inhibited by legislation from practising fraud or deception. The result of this statutory weakness was to place great emphasis on the goodwill and honesty of boards and sometimes to put considerable pressure on auditors required to enforce the spirit rather than the letter of the law. Suffice it to say that these Companies Acts did not generate additional work for accountants and the drive for higher standards of financial reporting came from imaginative and determined members of the profession working with enlightened businessmen and not from the legislature or their advisers.

5

The First World War

In general, a knowledge of accounts is not considered any part of the necessary education of a business officer, who accordingly is often quite ignorant of the uses that accounts have for him ... What is really required, in my opinion, to improve this ... is that the 'Accounts Department' should occupy a position in relation to the business as a whole, similar to that which the Royal Engineers, or the Army Service Corps, occupy in the Army.

Lawrence R. Dicksee, *Business Methods and the War*

The First World War brought to Price Waterhouse the first major discontinuity in its history. Until 1914 the partnership had been able to grow without interruption. The scale of the fighting, and the high mortality rates which resulted, demanded for the first time a nationwide system of conscription. In total over half the firm's employees were recruited into the forces where many were killed or disabled. Established client procedures were disrupted either by government controls or by shortages of labour occasioned by the demand for munitions and the other matériel of war. Taxation rose to unprecedented levels and new duties were imposed to keep pace with escalating expenditure. For the first time the industrial and commercial demands of modern warfare involved the entire nation in the conflict. To record and monitor all the transactions that the war effort involved, and as a safeguard against profiteering, accountants became the state's book-keepers and auditors. Great temporary offices were constructed in London's parks to accommodate them and their clerks. The First World War offered perhaps the most public and tangible demonstration of the accountant's skills and though the tide of state intervention ebbed after the armistice, the high-water mark of their involvement remained as evidence of their professional usefulness.

Partnership Changes

The principal change to the partnership during the war years was that J. Gurney Fowler died, aged sixty, in April 1916, after almost three years in office as senior partner.[1] Little is known of Fowler apart from his professional commitments. He appears to have been an able but by no means charismatic leader. An obituary in the *Staff War Bulletin* described him as having 'a reserved manner and occasionally gruff address'.[2] Like so many early City accountants, he was a non-conformist,[3] and not a graduate;[4] he had spent his entire working life with Price Waterhouse.[5] Described as having 'excellent business abilities',[6] Fowler was perhaps in the mould of Sneath and Wyon: cautious, conservative and correct. Certainly he lacked the flair and innovative spirit of Garnsey. At the time of his death he was acting for the government to determine the amount of compensation due to those railway companies under state control, and was a member of the Board of Referees appointed in connection with the assessment of Excess Profits Duty. His main outside interest was the cultivation of orchids and he won the Royal Horticultural Society's Lawrence Medal in 1915 for their culture.[7] Nicholas Waterhouse recalled that in 1910 he had purchased a Rolls-Royce from Fowler for £750. Although it had travelled only 40,000 miles, Fowler had become dissatisfied with the bodywork and was impatient for something newer.[8]

Length of service determined that Wyon, aged forty-seven and admitted to the partnership in 1895, should become the new senior partner. He, too, was fully engaged in work for the nation. Given Price Waterhouse's expertise in railway auditing, it was natural that members of the firm should be appointed to oversee their financial operations now that the railways had been placed under government control. Wyon was one of the two railway auditors selected by the state in 1916.[9] The pervasive and persistent demands of war prevented Wyon from impressing his personality on the firm until the 1920s. The partners were so hard pressed with duties for the government and in attempting to hold together their peacetime practice that there was little opportunity for strategic policy change.

The only other changes to the UK partnership of Price Waterhouse during the war years were the admission of G.O. May in 1914 and of

M.C. Spencer in July 1918. The former was, of course, senior partner of the US Firm and his election was designed to maintain a formal relationship between the two partnerships rather than influence daily management in Britain. At the end of the war, therefore, the firm consisted of Wyon at its head and nine other partners: Halsey, N.E. Waterhouse, W.C. Sneath, Morland, Dickinson, F.S. Price, Garnsey, May and Spencer.

M.C. Spencer had been educated at Bath College, and moved to London in 1893 to join the accounts department of the Buenos Aires & Pacific Railway. Perceiving that his career could advance further if he qualified as a chartered accountant, Spencer served articles with Miall, Wilkins, Randall & Co. in the City. Having been placed first in the intermediate and final examinations of the ICAEW, he entered Price Waterhouse in October 1903.[10] Spencer spent much of his early years with the firm abroad on investigations which, in 1905, included six months in Singapore on a dock arbitration between the local government and the merchant owners. In 1909–10 he travelled to South America to examine the accounts of the Arquco Railway, Chilean Transandine Railway, Lima Electric Tramways and a number of rubber companies in La Paz, Bolivia. At other times Spencer was engaged on audits or investigations throughout the Continent, including the Galician oilfields.

Government Assignments

Initially, it was thought by generals and politicians alike that the war would be brought to a decisive conclusion by Christmas 1914. Accordingly, there seemed little need for the state to intervene in the running of the economy and indeed in practical terms its machinery remained rudimentary. A degree of public control was established over the railways, shipping and other vital areas of industry under the Defence of the Realm Act (DORA) but in general life continued much as before. Robert Graves, on leave from the front, observed in 1915 that

> London seemed unreally itself. Despite the number of uniforms in the streets, the general indifference to, and ignorance about, the war surprised me. Enlistment remained voluntary. The universal catchword was 'Business as Usual'.[11]

Soon, however, the war ground to a stalemate, a battle of attrition fought from trenches dug in opposing lines from the Channel to the Alps. By the spring of 1915 it had become apparent that the army's voracious demand for the matériel of war required planning on a national level. In an attempt to ensure the efficient manufacture of munitions in the vast quantities required and to guard against profiteering by those so fortunately placed, the government took an increasingly interventionist role, and accountancy techniques became major instruments of assessment and control.

The most pressing problem swiftly became the inadequate provision of pensions and allowances allocated to the dependants of men in the forces. So great had been the public outcry that voluntary societies felt compelled to investigate. Reluctantly the government assumed responsibility for the payment of war pensions to those injured or dependants of those killed in the conflict, with Sir William Plender of Deloittes serving on the Civil Liabilities Commission. Nevertheless, in the absence of a comprehensive state service, charities continued to perform much valuable work. Halsey, for example, was honorary accountant to the Prince of Wales' National Relief Fund,[12] established in 1914 to distribute funds to service families. He was assisted in this by Nicholas Waterhouse who himself worked for Princess Mary's Fund.[13]

Such charitable work, though notable, did not represent the accountants' principal contribution to the war effort; that flowed from their recruitment into the civil service and particularly into the Ministry of Munitions, set up to expedite the manufacture of the matériel of war. This new ministry, established in 1915 at the behest of Lloyd George, became the instrument for direct government intervention. Gilbert Garnsey, thirty-two years of age when war broke out, volunteered for military service but was rejected on health grounds. In 1916 he joined the finance department of the ministry in an honorary capacity and in the following year was appointed Director of Internal Audits and Controller of Munitions Accounts.[14] He eventually served as chairman of the Finance Committee and Finance Member of the Munitions Council. Aware of the terrible sacrifices and hardships at the front, Garnsey worked a punishing seven-day week, starting at Frederick's Place at eight in the morning, crossing London to work in Whitehall and then returning to his office, remaining there often until midnight.

Other leading accountants recruited by the Ministry of Munitions included A.L. Dickinson of Price Waterhouse, who served as financial

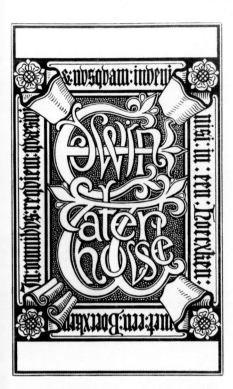

1. (*Left*) The bookplate of Edwin Waterhouse, used in the library at 'Feldemore', his country home in the village of Holmbury St Mary, Surrey.

2. (*Below*) A pen and watercolour sketch entitled 'A Merchant's Office' (1789) by Thomas Rowlandson. It depicts some of the account books required for double-entry book-keeping and shows the conditions under which clerks worked for much of the century. (*Yale Center for British Art*)

3. Samuel Lowell Price, who set up in practice on his own in December 1849, having dissolved his partnership with William Edwards.

4. The junction of Basinghall and Gresham Streets, photographed in 1914. Bradley, Barnard & Co. moved their London office to this corner building in 1847 when it was under the supervision of S.L. Price. Opposite, out of picture, were the Bankruptcy Courts, an important source of work for the pioneer accountants. (*Guildhall Library*)

5. A rare photograph showing No. 5 Gresham Street (*on the left*) beyond the church of St Lawrence Jewry. It was in these offices that both Price and Edwards practised in 1849. (*Guildhall Library*)

6. William Hopkins Holyland had a brief period in practice on his own account before seeking salaried employment with Coleman, Turquand, Youngs & Co.

7. A view looking westwards along Watling Street, showing No. 91 where W.H. Holyland worked for the outfitters Rogers, Lowery & Co. (*RCHME Crown Copyright*)

8. William Turquand, one of the first generation of accountants in practice. This is the only known photograph of the first President of the Institute of Chartered Accountants in England and Wales. It was in his firm that Edwin Waterhouse received his training.

9. Edwin Waterhouse photographed *c.* 1864, the year that he set up his own accountancy practice at No. 11 Old Jewry in the City of London.

10. The business diary and letter book of Edwin Waterhouse with his photograph.

11. The partnership deed of 1 May 1865 with the signatures of Price, Holyland and Waterhouse.

12. The Queens Assurance building on the corner of Gresham and King Streets, designed by Sancton Wood and completed in 1845. Price, Holyland & Waterhouse took rooms on the first, second and third floors in 1865 and remained there until 1899. (*British Architectural Library, RIBA*)

13. The shareholders' meeting room at Euston Station. It was here that Edwin Waterhouse would have presented the annual accounts of the London & North Western Railway.
(*National Railway Museum*)

14. (*Top left*) A letter signed by Edwin Waterhouse addressed to Mr L.V.J. Randolph, Treasurer of the Illinois Central Rail Road Co., dated 10 November 1875. It shows the firm's new style, 'Price, Waterhouse & Co.', introduced in the previous year.

15. (*Top right*) George Sneath, admitted to the partnership in 1875 and senior partner from 1 January 1906.

16. (*Left*) Edwin Waterhouse photographed in middle age, possibly in 1887 when, at the age of forty-six, he succeeded to the senior partnership.

17. John Gurney Fowler (*far left*) and his three brothers, Alfred, John Wilfred and Robert Henry (*left to right*), pose for the photographer at a shooting party in Norfolk. (*Institute of Agricultural History, University of Reading*)

18. A group assembled in the grounds of 'Feldemore' in 1898. Standing (*left to right*) are William Waterhouse, Theresa Waterhouse with 'Rob', Valentine Waterhouse with 'Laddie' and J.G. Fowler. Seated (*left to right*) are Helen Waterhouse (Edwin's second wife), Edwin Waterhouse, May Weber and Albert Wyon.

19. (*Left*) No. 3 Frederick's Place before the rebuilding in 1915–16, situated in a quiet cul-de-sac off Old Jewry. The four-storey, eighteenth-century houses had been converted into offices and were occupied by professional practices.

20. (*Below*) An interior of the New Oxford Street offices of Pears soap. The photograph, taken in 1888, revealed the ordered formality of the Victorian office, with its high desks and rigid dress code. Price Waterhouse were for many years the joint auditors of Lever Brothers, the manufacturers of Pears soap. (*RCHME Crown Copyright*)

21. (*Above*) Lewis Davies Jones, who in 1890 travelled to New York to set up an agency for Price Waterhouse.

22. (*Right*) Aldrich Court, 45 Broadway, New York, where L.D. Jones rented his first offices.

23. (*Above*) William J. Caesar, an Edinburgh chartered accountant, whom Price Waterhouse engaged in 1891 to assist Jones in America.

24. (*Left*) The Monadnock Building in Chicago, designed by Burnham and Root, in which W.J. Caesar took rooms in 1892.
(*Chicago Historical Society*)

25. (*Left*) Edwin Waterhouse in 1906, aged sixty-five, at about the time of his retirement from the partnership.

26. (*Below*) The west elevation of 'Feldemore' (*c.* 1890) where Edwin Waterhouse lived from 1880. The house was designed by George Redmayne, though the veranda and projecting dormer windows were conceived by Edwin Waterhouse in an early sketch which Redmayne adapted.

27. William Cecil Sneath, eldest son of George Sneath, who became a partner in 1907, having worked in Chicago and on the Continent.

28. Sir Arthur Lowes Dickinson, recruited by Price Waterhouse in 1901 to take charge of the US partnership.

29. A group of Price Waterhouse staff from the San Francisco office at a brewery client, *c.* 1908.

30. The partners and managers of Price Waterhouse in Dickinson's New York office, photographed in October 1910. From left to right (*front row*) G.R. Webster, H. Wilmot, A.L. Dickinson, G.O. May, C.S. Marr, W.E. Seatree, J.E. Sterrett; (*second row*) D. McClelland, J.H. Bowman, J.E. Masters, J.C. Scobie, J.R. Lynn, D.L. Grey, J. Medlock; (*third row*) C.A. Moore, Stagg, R.O. Berger, W.E. Lovejoy, A.B. Brodie.

31. The offices of the Prudential Assurance Co. at Holborn, designed by Alfred Waterhouse, elder brother of Edwin, and seen here in 1905 showing the conditions under which many clerks worked. Price Waterhouse were appointed auditors to the Prudential in 1991. (*RCHME Crown Copyright*)

32. (*Top*) An office interior, photographed in 1919, from the Pearl Assurance Co.'s building. The furniture and fixtures were typical of those which adorned the Frederick's Place office. (*RCHME Crown Copyright*)

33. (*Middle*) Another office from the Pearl Assurance building. In terms of the quality of the furniture it could have been a partner's room. Note the early telephones on the desk. (*RCHME Crown Copyright*)

34. (*Right*) A pencil sketch of Frederick's Place drawn by A. Friedenson in 1914 just before Price Waterhouse commissioned the reconstruction of their offices.

35. (*Left*) John Gurney Fowler, admitted to the partnership in 1900 and the fourth senior partner.

36. (*Below*) The temporary offices erected in the gardens beside the Victoria Embankment to house the Ministry of Munitions. (*Imperial War Museum*)

37. (*Above*) Office workers enlist in the Royal Fusiliers (City of London Regiment) during the early stages of the war. (*Imperial War Museum*)

38. (*Right*) Volunteers march behind a band along Villiers Street beside Charing Cross Station on their way to enlist in the forces. (*Imperial War Museum*)

adviser to the controlled establishment division,[15] and the sole practitioner, Mark Webster Jenkinson, later to achieve fame as a company
doctor, who became Controller of the Department of Factory Audit and
Costs. Webster Jenkinson later boasted that he had cut by £1 million
the cost of one of the first contracts submitted to him. He and his
colleagues uncovered appallingly lax accounting systems in government
and state munitions works: the audit of the Woolwich Arsenal, for
example, did not include a systematic investigation of the cash balance
which fluctuated in total from £70,000 to £250,000.[16]

While Garnsey rose to be one of the senior executives in the Ministry
of Munitions, other accountants were recruited to work as managers,
commercial superintendents, cost accountants and stores accountants.
The audit section employed qualified men who had been invalided out
of the army. Many of them thus gained experience of costing systems
and industrial management which had been denied them in their civilian
practices.[17]

As Nicholas Waterhouse observed, no fewer than five of Price Waterhouse's partners were, for part of the war at least, engaged on full-time
work for government departments.[18] He too had been rejected for
military service, and so was anxious to contribute to the war effort in
some capacity. He joined the War Office to help the Director of Army
Contracts administer contracts with textile manufacturers.[19] 'At one
time,' Waterhouse recollected, 'when the Army clothing department
were doubtful whether supplies of raw wool would be adequate, he
[Andrew Weir, later Lord Inverforth, his superior as Surveyor General
of Supply] purchased the whole of the Australian wool clip for the next
two or three years.[20] Waterhouse eventually became Director of Costings
at the War Office. He wrote in a letter to his father that

> the individual partners in W. Peat & Co. and P.W. & Co. are to
> undertake to attend at the War Office to advise as to the prices to
> be paid to contractors for goods to be purchased on the basis of
> their costs. We should have power to make, or instruct local
> accountants to make, investigations where it seemed to us necessary.
> The advisory work would of course be honorary.[21]

Waterhouse also sat on the War Office committee set up to provide for
prisoners of war held in enemy territory,[22] and after the armistice, but
before returning full-time to Frederick's Place, served as a member of

the Disposals Commission. Composed of Lord Inverforth, as Minister of Munitions, Sir Howard Frank and Waterhouse, it met on a single occasion to create the Disposals Board which, in turn, had the task of selling the vast quantities of materials acquired for the army, now no longer needed. It also established the Liquidation Committee, of which Waterhouse was appointed chairman, to wind up the hundreds of contracts still effective after the ceasefire.[23]

Although the commercial practice of Price Waterhouse undoubtedly suffered because its partners were seconded to government departments, two indirect gains resulted. First, as Waterhouse recalled, government work introduced the firm to many leading civil servants, industrialists and politicians and demonstrated to them the value of the accountant's skills. Waterhouse believed that these contacts generated new assignments in the 1920s.[24]

Secondly, on the cessation of hostilities, a large number of accountants received honours which raised the public profile not only of the profession but also of specific firms such as Price Waterhouse. Garnsey, for example, was awarded a KBE in June 1918 for his work as Controller of Munitions Accounts,[25] and at the same time Mark Webster Jenkinson received a CBE.[26] Eventually five Price Waterhouse partners were knighted (Garnsey, Halsey, Dickinson, Wyon and Waterhouse) for government work. This led to a number of jokes – that No.3 Frederick's Place should be called 'the house of the dreadful knights', or that the firm should adopt the style 'Knights and Chartered Accountants'[27] – but it undoubtedly focused the attention of the City and industry upon the partnership.

Staff in the Forces

The outbreak of hostilities in August 1914 was greeted by many with enthusiasm; the coming battle was viewed as a glorious, patriotic adventure. In the space of a little under six months nearly two million men had volunteered for active service and it was all that the army could do to house, equip and train them. Appeals were made to workplace or regional loyalties to encourage recruitment and bind units together when in the field. 'Pals' battalions were formed so that office and factory workers, farm labourers, and friends could fight alongside one another.[28]

Throughout 1914 and 1915 *The Accountant* encouraged its readership to volunteer. One editorial remarked:

> In our last week's issue we reproduced a letter from a correspondent who asked the very pertinent question whether a duly qualified professional accountant could serve his country better in the present crisis than by enlisting. So far as we are aware the answer to this question is 'No'.[29]

In October 1915, following urgent appeals from the War Office, *The Accountant* urged all firms to release men aged between nineteen and forty into the forces, suggesting that an offer of reinstatement after the hostilities might serve as a strong inducement. It added, 'undoubtedly a much larger number of accountants' clerks could be released from their present duties if . . . practitioners and their clients were to overcome a not altogether unnatural prejudice against the employment of women'.[30]

Around 50 per cent of Price Waterhouse (forty-nine members of staff) had enlisted in the forces by 1915, and some of those who had joined territorial units or obtained Officer Training Course certificates soon became casualties.[31] Lt C.D. Sneath, for example, son of the deceased senior partner, was killed early in 1915 while serving with the Middlesex Regiment. The effectiveness of the appeal to arms was recognised by Siegfried Sassoon who wrote of a visit to the 2nd Battalion of Royal Welch Fusiliers:

> At headquarters I found the Adjutant alone, worried and pre-occupied with clerical work. He had worked in an office, at accountancy, I believe, before the war; and now most of his fighting was done in writing, though he had served an apprenticeship as a brave and indefatigable platoon commander.[32]

Because so many had volunteered in such a short space of time and because the regular troops were already committed in France, considerable problems arose in training and leading the new Kitchener battalions. Initially many selected their own NCOs and few were allotted more than three officers, most of whom were unfit for active service. Since convention dictated that officers had to be gentlemen, it fell to the public schools and universities to provide platoon and company commanders.[33] Accordingly a high proportion of Price Waterhouse staff who volunteered found themselves either as lieutenants or NCOs helping to lead the chaotic New Armies. Of the fifty-three listed as serving in the forces from Price Waterhouse offices by February 1915, twenty held commissions and ten were NCOs,[34] while of the 101 current members of staff listed in December 1916, sixty-six were officers and eleven NCOs.[35] The nation was unprepared for the scale of the conflict and many units arrived in France without sufficient training, some having received their proper complement of weapons shortly before they crossed the Channel.[36]

The Accountant observed that by March 1917 voluntary recruitment and conscription had starved many London offices of

> 70 to 90 per cent of men in their employ between 18 and 41 years
> of age, and it has been impossible to replace them with either men
> or women having like experience and capacity.[37]

The December 1916 edition of the *Staff War Bulletin* recorded that 110 current employees (including twenty-two from overseas offices) of Price Waterhouse were in the forces, together with thirty former members.[38] Given that the total London office staff had numbered only 107 in June 1913,[39] this suggests that a high proportion of those under forty-one had joined up. Casualties were high. The UK Firm's war memorial recorded that fifteen had been killed during the conflict, which represented 17 per cent of those serving in 1916.

Three *Bulletins* were published and distributed among staff at home and away on military service. Extracts from letters written by those at the front were included. These accounts brought home some of the horrors of war. G.S. Craggs, from Price Waterhouse's Winnipeg office, serving as adjutant to the 10th Battalion of the 2nd Canadian Infantry Brigade suggested,

> if you want to know what it is like, move your office every five
> days. Put in one spell in a hole dug in the ground ... another in a
> loose box lately vacated by its tenant, a third in a cellar full of
> debris, a fourth in a bell tent, a fifth in the corner of a kitchen,
> and so forth. Then you will know what sort of a time I have. Its
> very largely routine office work but carried on under these
> conditions.[40]

The international nature of some accountancy work led to bizarre coincidences. The *Bulletin* reported:

Private G. O'Connor (late of San Francisco office) enlisted in Australia and has been twice wounded. After coming out of hospital recently he saw Mr Dickinson and related to him how one day when in the trenches he saw a German lying in a shell hole and whilst he was watching him, hesitating to shoot at a man in cold blood, the man turned round and surrendered and he instantly recognised him as a man he had known quite well who was at the Pabst Brewery at Milwaukee.[41]

The third *Staff War Bulletin*, at Christmas 1916, came after a delay of eighteen months which was attributed chiefly to 'pressure of other work'[42] occasioned by shortages of labour. Any further editions, however, may have been discouraged by a critical letter in *The Accountant* for February 1917, which suggested that in reporting men's units, locations and experiences it might have contravened a War Office restriction and inadvertently assisted the enemy in reconstructing the 'order of battle; that is the distribution of his troops between the various fronts . . .'[43] Although this was a far-fetched claim, no fourth issue appeared.

The career of A.E. Jones, later to become a partner of Price Waterhouse, illustrated the impact which war could have on an individual. Having served his articles with the firm and qualified in 1909, he enlisted in 1914, gaining a commission in the 5th Battalion, Royal Welch Fusiliers.[44] Decorated for his part in the battle of Romani, in which the British won command of the Sinai Desert, he decided in 1916 to transfer to the Royal Flying Corps, but in the following year was invalided out. For the remainder of the hostilities Jones exercised his accountancy skills working for Nicholas Waterhouse in the costings department of the War Office.

The acute demand for troops to replace those disabled or killed resulted in the introduction of conscription in May 1916. In order that vital war work would not be impeded, a system of 'certified occupations' was devised. As *The Accountant* recorded in that month,

> skilled technical labour has been recognised as of more value to the state employed on technical work than when used in the firing line, and we are pleased to note from recent indications that the professional knowledge and training of qualified accountants is, to some extent, beginning to receive similar recognition.[45]

Because accountants were now employed in large numbers on

government-related duties accountancy was included among the 'certified occupations' whose members were excused from military service, though only from the age of thirty-one, if married, and forty-one, if single. In addition, exemptions were granted only if a tribunal could be satisfied that their professional work was in the national interest. Chartered and Incorporated Accountants, an editorial in the professional press observed, should not 'ipso facto assume that they are absolved from military service'.[46] Indeed, public criticism of their inclusion within the certified category led to their omission from a second list. It was not until 1917, when shortages of staff had reduced practices to near chaos, that *The Accountant* changed its opinion and argued, 'the time has now been reached when it is to the interest of the nation that it should be recognised by Tribunals that accountants are performing work of national importance'.[47] They advocated that they be returned to the list of certified occupations 'without any qualifications'.[48] When the new list was issued in July 1917 qualified accountants and their clerks were included

> provided they were 35 years of age on 4 April 1916; or, if married, 31 years of age on that date. But as regards clerks, a man will not be entitled to be treated as in a certified occupation under this reservation unless he has been engaged in the same occupation for at least 10 years.[49]

A major social consequence of the First World War was the admission of women into employment on a wide scale. With qualified staff, clerks, messengers and porters away at the front, Price Waterhouse, like other City firms, became desperately short of manpower. Pride was swallowed, and women were offered jobs as telephonists, typists, clerks and even as auditors. Women were employed at Price Waterhouse as secretaries and for clerical duties within Frederick's Place, though it does not appear that they were sent to the premises of clients on professional work.[50] As secretaries to partners, some could exercise considerable influence. Miss Wolseley, a relative of the Victorian Field Marshal who worked for Garnsey, was described as a 'queenly woman', who had been to a finishing school in Lausanne and with whom it 'was well to be on good terms'.[51]

In the past the ICAEW had steadfastly refused to countenance the idea that women might qualify as chartered accountants. In 1894, for example, the Society for Promoting the Employment of Women had approached its council to explore possibilities for admitting females. The Society was strongly discouraged and *The Accountant* added its own absurd conclusion that 'there are few occupations more unsuitable to women'.[52] In 1910 the London Association of Accountants agreed to grant membership to females and *The Accountant* was prepared to consider training them provided that they had first obtained the degree of Bachelor of Commerce.[53] However, the ICAEW remained resolutely opposed to their admission and in 1912 declared:

> We have no desire to say anything that might tend to encourage women to embark upon accountancy, for although many women might make excellent bookkeepers, there is much in accountancy proper that is, we think, altogether unsuitable for them.[54]

The Institute declined to specify its reasons, and its argument appeared empty given that there were, for example, 477 female doctors in 1911.[55]

It was curious that women should have been so vigorously excluded from genteel clerical and professional employment when in the nineteenth century they had often been employed in manufacturing and in occupations involving heavy physical labour. Their recruitment into clerical and commercial posts was most dramatic in 1915 when labour shortages became acute. They were not, however, granted equal pay.

The return of the troops in 1919 resulted in about two-thirds of those women who had found work during the war being made redundant.[56] Yet, a number of accountancy firms, glad of their secretarial competence, retained their services. Price Waterhouse employed a number of women during the twenties, stipulating that they must be single. Some who married concealed this fact from their employer (by removing their wedding rings in the office) in order to retain their posts. Nevertheless, the ICAEW did not admit its first woman member, Miss E. Watts, until 1924,[57] having been preceded by the Irish Institute in May 1919,[58] and the Society of Incorporated Accountants in 1920.[59]

Fortunes of the Firm

Judged by purely commercial considerations, the war years were not beneficial to Price Waterhouse. Although fee income rose in monetary terms from £69,927 in 1914 to £102,398 in 1918, the effect of inflation undermined any gains and it fell in real terms by about 35 per cent. A similar pattern presented itself for the firm's total profits. In monetary terms these rose from £55,619 in 1914 to £72,638 in 1918, but after adjusting for the effects of inflation there was a fall of some 42 per cent. This reduction would have been greater had it not been for a significant increase in the contribution from overseas, in particular from America (see Table 6 in Appendix).

It was not difficult to discover an explanation for this downturn in the fortunes of Price Waterhouse. With so many members of staff absent in the forces it was impossible to maintain peacetime levels of working, with the result that audit fees would have been reduced or, rather, not increased in line with inflation. Because of labour shortages the nature of an audit changed. Nicholas Waterhouse recalled that before the war

> tests of certain details were the exception rather than the rule except in the larger undertakings. I can well remember spending days vouching and initialling every single dividend warrant (and even interest coupons on bonds) in order to verify the small liability on the balance sheet for dividends and interest outstanding. From 1914 onwards audit work became less and less detailed partly no doubt owing to shortage of staff and also . . . to the rush of government and other work.[60]

Many assignments undertaken for the state were voluntary, particularly those concerned with forces charities, while others were perhaps not as well remunerated as comparable tasks for a company or private clients.

While the audit practice of Price Waterhouse undoubtedly suffered, there were two areas where gains were made: taxation and cost accounting. Because the scale and duration of the conflict was underestimated by the planners, initially there was no attempt to place taxation on a war footing. With expenditure having risen to £4.5 million a day, the budget of September 1915, introduced by Reginald McKenna, a former banker, raised income tax to an unprecedented 3s 6d (17.5p) and surtax to 6s 10d (34.2p). Eventually the former rose to 5 shillings (25p) in the pound by 1917 and six shillings (30p) in 1919, having been 1s 2d (5.8p) in 1914. Supertax rates were also raised. These increments drew a greater number of personal clients to accountants for professional advice. By 1918 income tax had changed out of all recognition. No longer the simple Victorian mechanism with a uniform rate in the pound, it was becoming a complex apparatus, comprising both differentiation (in the form of an earned income relief) and graduation (the introduction of supertax). Further, a limited range of personal reliefs had also been introduced, and for industry an embryonic system of capital allowances.[61]

The imposition of an Excess Profits Duty on businesses in 1915 also had major implications for accountants. Companies with contracts to supply the government were required to demonstrate a standard level of peacetime profit, and all gains in excess of that figure were to be taxed at 50 per cent, a figure which in 1917 was raised to 80 per cent.[62] The rules were complex: businesses could select any three-year period from their previous decade of trading as the basis for this benchmark. Auditors were commissioned to discover the most favourable period. The steel and engineering group, Guest, Keen & Nettlefolds, for instance, consulted Wyon in 1917 for an expert opinion on the operation of excess profits duty, despite the fact that Price Waterhouse were not their auditors.[63] As a result of his advice, they were permitted to value stocks with no allowance for inflation and saved themselves several thousand pounds in duty. At the time of his death in 1916, J.G. Fowler had been serving as a member of the Board of Referees set up to assess claims for Excess Profits Duty.

The other area into which accountants were increasingly drawn was costing. Industry had to be regulated in order to obtain maximum output at fair prices – prices that would offer a reasonable rate of return, while not exploiting the prevailing circumstances of imperative demand and shortages of supply to produce extortionate profits. To determine the median of reasonable charges, independent checks on costs were undertaken by accountants seconded from private practice. Cost accountants had been employed in industry much more widely in America than in Britain. So, in 1915, when the Ministry of Munitions were looking for an administrator to ensure that costing techniques and controls were being effectively applied, they appointed Samuel Hardman Lever as Assistant Financial Secretary.[64] Shortly after qualifying as a chartered accountant, Lever had moved to New York to work for Barrow, Wade, Guthrie & Co. where he became an expert in cost accounting. He remained with the Ministry of Munitions until 1917 when he was appointed Financial Secretary to the Treasury. Many accountants who had been drawn into costing exercises during the war remained in government posts or factories afterwards and were to found, in 1919, the Institute of Cost and Works Accountants.

Although Price Waterhouse recognised the new commercial opportunities provided by cost accounting, they were slow to exploit them until after 1945. Nevertheless, in 1919 they recruited Albert Cathles, an Edinburgh accountant, who had been employed by the Ministry of Munitions as Deputy Controller of Factory Audit Costs.[65] He undertook a variety of business investigations specialising in works and cost accounting. However, this branch of accountancy remained a minor one throughout the interwar period partly because industry continued to undervalue the merit of these inquiries and partly because Price Waterhouse primarily considered themselves to be auditors, regarding other functions as subsidiary.

For the greater part of the war Price Waterhouse had the benefit of modernised and expanded office premises. In 1913 pressure on space had forced the partners first to consider a complete reconstruction of No. 3 Frederick's Place and then to seek alternative accommodation. In December of that year the firm moved to Gresham College, at the corner of Gresham and Basinghall Streets.[66] The work was completed by September 1915[67] and as the *Staff War Bulletin* observed,

> the old building has been entirely pulled down, and the upper floors of No. 2 . . . have been incorporated into it. The new building is planned differently to its predecessor. The entrance dignified with a stone porch, is now in the centre of No. 3 instead of at the side and the visitor finds a hall on his right, where a lift . . . whisks him to the upper floors.[68]

Externally the houses appeared much as before, altered by the addition of four plain pilasters placed between the windows. These offices were to remain unchanged until the major rebuilding and extension of 1955.

Developments on the Continent

Before the war, Price Waterhouse had regularly performed work throughout the Continent (audits, for example, were undertaken for Van den Berghs in Rotterdam, Brussels, Cleves and at various places in Denmark, for the Asiatic Petroleum Co. at Baku, Russia, two oil companies in Rumania, the Danish Gas Co. in Copenhagen and for other clients in France, Germany and Austria) but had not resulted in the opening of an office there. The First World War was indirectly respons- ible for changing this situation. Margarine was a staple item of diet in Britain and though it was manufactured by Van den Berghs and Jurgens in Holland, the vegetable oil which it required was refined in Cleves from nuts and seeds shipped from Bremen.[69] Both were from German territory. The British government agreed to permit the raw materials to be sent direct to Holland, a neutral territory, provided that the Dutch severed all links with their German plant. Price Waterhouse were given the task of monitoring manufacture by Van den Berghs, and Martin Farlow & Co. performed the same role in relation to Jurgens.[70] This control task fell to Charles Evans of the London staff, later to become a European partner. He had spent most of the summer of 1914 on the audit of Van den Berghs in London and had come to know the family owners. The firm obtained his discharge from the Artists Rifles and sent him to Rotterdam in August 1914 where he remained for a further four and a half years. In 1915 B. Gaastra, a Certified Public Accountant, seconded to London from New York, also transferred to Holland to monitor R.S. Stokvis en Zonen and the import of methyl. He was soon joined by W.M. McKinnon, on loan from Toronto, employed on control work for the cotton industry in the Enschede district. However, Gaastra, being of Dutch origin, felt uneasy at his position and returned to England to be replaced in 1916 by M.C. Spencer.

Spencer was appointed to oversee all control work in Holland, excluding that for oils and fats. He rented premises in Rotterdam in his own name and these eventually became Price Waterhouse's first Con- tinental office. As his practice developed, Spencer was called upon by the British authorities to investigate businesses suspected of trading with the enemy. By 1918 control and government work had reached such proportions that eighteen members of staff were employed in Holland.[71]

In the event, the formal announcement of the establishment of an office in Rotterdam was delayed until October 1919. The new branch was opened at Coolsingel 15c (Standard Bank Building) in conjunction with W.B. Peat & Co. under the style Price, Waterhouse, Peat & Co. and came under the authority of R.W. Ramsden, the resident manager.[72]

Holland was not the only territory that Price Waterhouse entered during the war years. In 1916 McKinnon was sent to Paris on the Lloyds Bank audit and once there attracted an increasing number of referrals. He lived at the Hotel Lotti in Rue de Castiglione and eventually rented a second room there to serve as an office. The business expanded further and in April 1917 premises were taken at 2 Rue Edward VII, which were subsequently to become the headquarters of the Continental Firm.[73]

In the summer of 1916 G.D.H. Pidcock of the London staff and B. Gaastra travelled to Russia and in July opened an office at 16 Gogol Street, Petrograd. This, too, was a joint enterprise with Peats and the new partnership was to be called Price, Waterhouse, Peat & Co.[74] They were not the first firm of UK accountants to practise in Russia since Deloittes had established premises at St Petersburg and Moscow in 1913.[75] British companies had major contracts for the supply of plant and machinery but industrialisation had proceeded slowly. When the revolution of 1917 brought these ventures to a premature end, Pidcock and Gaastra escaped to Norway on a British cruiser, leaving the firm's books and petty cash behind.[76]

6

The Interwar Years

Were the figures faked? Surely not! That would be too difficult, in the face of the accountants. If Soames [Forsyte] had faith, it was in chartered accountants. Sandis and Jevon were tip-top people. It couldn't be that!

John Galsworthy, *A Modern Comedy*

The profession of accountancy ... is a very distinguished, very honourable, and a very essential profession in the commercial affairs of the country. Great trust must be reposed on the skill and judgement and honour of accountants.

Mr Justice Wright in his charge to the jury
during the case of the Royal Mail Steam Packet Co.[1]

For Price Waterhouse the interwar period was characterised by mixed fortunes, which did not always march in step with those of the nation as a whole. The twenties, while the economy struggled to regain pre-war outputs and profits, were years of impressive growth for the firm. The slump of 1920–21 scarcely touched Price Waterhouse, buttressed as it was by income from overseas, principally America. A host of new audit clients flowed from the preparation of prospectuses for those businesses seeking public listing and other investigations brought to the firm by the dynamic and prominent Sir Gilbert Garnsey. Partly as a result of his enthusiasm for expansion, Price Waterhouse had come within a signature of merging with W.B. Peat & Co., an arrangement which, if it had come to fruition, would have placed the amalgamated partnership beyond the reach of its closest rivals. The major financial trial of the twenties was that of Clarence Hatry, the company promoter, who had forged corporation scrip certificates to finance acquisitions in the steel industry. Garnsey, to whom he confessed, was entrusted with the complicated inquiry and liquidation. Paradoxically, the most newsworthy City case of the thirties saw H.J. Morland, a partner of Price Waterhouse, accused of approving misleading accounts. The Royal Mail trial brought about his acquittal, but the firm and the profession were wounded. The consistent growth of the twenties was not matched in the following decade even after the recovery of 1933. This, in great part, resulted from the sudden death of Garnsey only a few days before he was due to become senior partner. Wyon continued in office for a further six years having already served fifteen as executive head of the firm. Although technically sound, Wyon lacked inspiration and imagination. Without the drive and enthusiasm generated by Garnsey, the cautious, conservative policies pursued by Wyon led to stagnation and the firm's fee income declined in real terms. While Price Waterhouse entered the Second World War a larger and more profitable firm than in 1918, there was a sense in which its prospects had been brighter at the beginning of the interwar period than at the close. Unresolved problems of leadership, a reluctance to promote younger men of ability and a need for a coherent strategy were issues which the conflict held in abeyance, ready to awaken once the war had come to an end in 1945.

Partnership Changes

Wyon had succeeded to the senior partnership in 1916 and was to hold the post until his death in 1937. However, it had not been planned in that way. Sir Gilbert Garnsey, hard-working, highly intelligent and ambitious, was the dynamic force in the firm, exercising a growing influence on its management from the latter part of the First World War. While Controller of Munitions Accounts Garnsey met leading politicians such as Churchill, and demonstrated to senior civil servants that he was an exceptionally able administrator with considerable financial expertise. As a result, he was continually in demand to serve upon government committees and investigations. These included: the Demobilisation Board, the Munitions Council for the liquidation of contracts, the Ministry of Health committee for Housing, the committee on the Accounts of Aerodrome Works (all four in 1919), the Metropolitan Water Board (1920), the Lawrence committee into Administration of Accounting for Army Expenditure (1922), the Treasury committee on the Accounting Methods of Government Departments, the Board of

Trade committee on the Assurance Companies Acts and the Court of Inquiry into the Remuneration of Doctors under the National Health Insurance Acts (the last three all in 1924). In 1925 Garnsey was appointed a member of the Government Food Council and in 1930 served as Chairman of the Marketing and Distributing Consumable Commodities Committee of the Economic Advisory Council. In 1931 he became chairman of the British Industries Fairs Sites and Buildings committee.[2]

This formidable public work drew Garnsey to the attention of the financial press and the business community – a development which he seems to have encouraged. He was conscious of his public image, as Sir Nicholas Waterhouse recalled.[3] During the Hatry trial 'one of the illustrated papers', wrote Waterhouse, had included

> a large portrait inscribed as 'Sir Gilbert Garnsey the Wizard of Accountancy'. Unfortunately there had been an error in the make-up of the paper, the face being that of Hatry ... This greatly incensed the Wizard who wanted to demand a published apology and I only made things worse by my attempt to appease him by pointing out that anyhow Hatry was much the better looking of the two and that therefore the mistake might be taken as a compliment.[4]

Garnsey was almost without rival in the City as an accountant of popular esteem. Only Lord Plender and Sir William McLintock were as prominent in the press. They captured the imagination and attracted comment to an extent rarely emulated by accountants subsequently. Garnsey, for example, had lengthy obituaries in all the major newspapers and was honoured with epithets such as 'master of figures',[5] 'unusual "man of destiny" ',[6] and 'financial doctor of industry'.[7] *The Star* even went so far as to suggest that his belief in the occult lay at the foundation of his mathematical prowess and quoted Garnsey as saying:

> Successful men cannot always say why they do certain things ... They do these really because they must. There are things that it is not granted to man to know. I believe that the elements play a larger part than we realise.[8]

The network of connections that Garnsey established between government, industry and commerce, together with his high public profile, led to Price Waterhouse being appointed to a succession of investigations, reconstructions and flotations. These included companies such as the Marconi Wireless Telegraph Co., Farrow's Bank, Armstrong, Whitworth & Co., Spillers' Milling and Associated Industries, and William Beardmore & Co.[9] Often an audit appointment would follow work on a company's prospectus and reorganisation. Special assignments generated, as a rule, a single but substantial fee, while the audit produced a lower but recurring source of income. These complementary tasks, Tull, a partner, suggested, were crucial to the success of the firm in the twenties.[10] Sir Nicholas Waterhouse also recognised Garnsey's influence:

> The way that he attracted much important work to the firm was so stimulating that one day (with Arnold Bennett's latest novel in mind) I alluded to him at a partners' meeting as 'The Card'[11] but he himself had read the novel and for obvious reasons rather resented this nickname.[12]

Staff often found that it was 'an inspiring experience' to work for Garnsey. Southall, then a qualified audit clerk, recollected:

> He compelled the best out of me. 'What use are you to me, Southall, unless you can do it as well as I could?' He could be exacting, partly no doubt because he suffered from insomnia and other health problems; but he could be considerate too and it was thought that he had worked hard to improve the status and remuneration of the managers.[13]

[Sir] Thomas Robson, one of the talented managers who regularly worked for Garnsey, wrote that the latter was a 'task master' who drove himself and his assistants 'very hard indeed':

> GFG had no compunction in sending for a man at 11 am on a Friday and telling him to get to Manchester that evening, clear up what was to be done on some accounts and be back to see him with the draft at 11 am on Monday. And on the Monday GFG could be too busy to see the man who had complied with this order and worked night and day to do so. Both GFG and Howarth [a manager] had the gift of choosing their men and trusting them by delegation of responsibility for the work allocated to them.[14]

From the retirement of Edwin Waterhouse in 1907, the principle of length of service had always governed succession to the senior partnership. Garnsey (admitted to the partnership in 1913), stood no immediate chance of executive authority as Halsey (1900), Waterhouse (1906), W.C. Sneath (1907) and Morland (1907) had been partners for longer. Nevertheless, his claim for recognition was strong. According to Tull, Garnsey put pressure upon Wyon to relinquish some of his shares in the partnership,[15] and when the 1929 deed was drawn up, it was agreed that Garnsey should move up to second place (his interest in the firm's capital being increased to 20 per cent). Further, it was arranged that on 1 July 1932 Wyon would retire to become a consultant and Garnsey would assume the senior partnership.[16] However, on 26 June, five days before the transition of power was to be effected, he and his wife had been entertaining Thomas Howarth (who was to be admitted to the partnership on the same day that Garnsey was to have become the chief executive) at their country home, 'Saint Hill', at East Grinstead, Sussex when Garnsey collapsed and died of a haemorrhage of the lungs. Two years earlier, after a severe attack of bronchitis, Garnsey had moved to the country from his Hampstead home. He had been found unfit for military service which suggests that his health had been weak from an early age. A brilliant career ended just when its greatest potential was to have been realised. As Sir Nicholas Waterhouse recalled, Garnsey had been offered an attractive post at the Treasury, and toyed with the idea of entering politics, but decided to remain with Price Waterhouse where he felt his talents could find most immediate fulfilment.

Sir Gilbert Garnsey possessed an outstanding accountancy talent. He had a keen mathematical brain and, according to one obituary, could 'quote imposing lists of figures and complicated accounts off-hand when the occasion arose'.[17] His grasp of theoretical issues was equally acute and he was one of the advocates of consolidated accounts, publishing his views as early as 1923. Garnsey exhibited a great thirst for work and new ideas. While at the Ministry of Munitions he regularly remained at his desk until midnight. His zeal for endeavour was not diminished in peacetime when he undertook a succession of assignments for the government and a number of special investigations for industry. These earned him the epithet of 'business doctor'. Even when on holiday he telephoned the office every day, and his premature death may have been hastened by over-exertion and stress.[18] His estate was valued at £151,466 gross,[19] a substantial sum by the standards of the time.

The unexpected and sudden demise of Garnsey enabled Wyon to recover the senior partnership, a post he retained until 1937. Little evidence has survived to tell how the two men had dealt with each other. Differences in their personalities and policies (Garnsey, for example, was a prime mover in the attempt to merge with W.B. Peat & Co., while Wyon was implacably opposed to any union) suggest that it may have been a tense and awkward relationship.

During the twenties Sir Albert Wyon had revealed himself an unimaginative conservative who resisted change at every turn. He, as senior partner, had scuppered the advanced negotiations with Peats for an amalgamated practice (p. 139). According to S.H. Mearns, a partner in Whinney, Smith & Whinney, Wyon also resisted reform of company legislation despite growing pressure from shareholders, the press and some far-sighted accountants. He was reported as describing the 1929 Companies Act as 'expressed in washerwoman's English – and a washerwoman who washes on a Sunday afternoon at that'.[20]

Wyon himself wrote very little, confining his literary excursions to a short pamphlet entitled *The Intelligent Auditing of Detail*, which was published by Price Waterhouse in the wake of the Royal Mail case. In this he revealed a methodical, orderly mind devoid of liveliness or the capacity to inspire. In one passage Wyon tersely observed:

> I have heard the auditing of detail described as 'ticking' or 'donkey work'. Such phrases are very misleading ... Intelligent auditing of detail needs continuous alertness of mind, which again needs the exercise of will power, particularly when work involves continuous repetition of a simple process.[21]

He had earlier been more forthright in *The Accountant* when discussing the nature of partnership organisation. Wyon was perhaps justifying his opposition to the aborted merger with Peats when he argued against large firms and for a restriction on the number of offices:

> What methods assure to a large accounting organisation, composed for the most part of salaried employees, the same sense of professional responsibility as that attainable by an individual practitioner or small group of practitioners working together as partners? ... It has sometimes been said in criticism of large firms that, while the ethics of the senior partners and of the head offices are a pattern for smaller firms to follow, the same cannot always be said of their

branch offices ... It may be admitted that conditions may arise under which such criticism would be justified.[22]

He appears, therefore, to have been an advocate of small partnerships limited both in numbers and territorially. Such restrictions, Wyon believed, would 'secure uniformity of standards and the preservation of traditions, ideals and a high sense of responsibility'.[23]

Sir Laurence Halsey, who succeeded Wyon as senior partner, recalled that when he joined Price Waterhouse in the early 1890s

> the chief articled clerk was at that time Albert Wyon, two or three years my senior. He was notable even then for the thoroughness and orderliness of all his work and one always felt pretty safe in following closely in his footsteps even if one could not imitate the neatness with which he worked and recorded his results.[24]

However, the qualities which made Wyon an exemplary chief articled clerk did not fit so well with the role of senior partner. Eric Southall, who joined Price Waterhouse in 1921 as a newly qualified member of staff, had the opportunity to observe Wyon as leader; he was, Southall wrote,

> an unimpressive, but benevolent-looking figure, dressed in black clothes of an old-fashioned cut. There was a story that a new lift-man had taken him straight up to the audit room supposing him to be a rather shabby member of the staff, only to be told that if this happened again he would be dismissed. Unquestionably, he was a very able accountant of great experience, with a clear mind, indefatigable in his attention to the work in hand and of unflinching rectitude. He was a member of the Liberal Club but in some ways extremely conservative ... I think one could regard AWW as a man whose youthful ability had not been ripened by experience. He did not strike me as a wise man who could give good advice outside his speciality.[25]

Staff generally found Wyon unapproachable. Even junior partners 'looked with some anxiety' at him,[26] and stories were told of his irritability. On one occasion a hapless clerk presented a file of papers with the retaining pin pointing downwards, and thus likely to scratch the desktop. Wyon hurled the papers across the room scattering them over the carpet to discourage this from happening again.[27] When George

Scheu, a porter, took coals around to the partners' offices in the afternoons, Wyon would brusquely say 'only one [lump]'.[28] Wyon was responsible for insisting that the dark green railings outside No. 3 Frederick's Place were regularly polished. Something of the formality of the office was contained in an oft-quoted joke: Wyon had on one occasion wished to see a long-serving but junior audit clerk, so the latter was summoned by one of the commissionaires, a former NCO, who found the hapless individual in the basement toilet of Frederick's Place. On being told that 'Sir Albert Wyon wishes to see you with the utmost urgency', the clerk was reported to have replied, 'Well send him in immediately'.

With Garnsey dead, Wyon was able to retain executive authority, in part because Waterhouse and Halsey, the two most senior partners, were not ambitious men. Wyon continued in office for a further six years until his own death, aged sixty-eight. These were his least successful years and represented, for Price Waterhouse, at best, a missed opportunity. A younger man of vigour and enthusiasm might, for example, have been introduced at a time when the economy was recovering rapidly. F.S. Tull, a partner perhaps at the time embittered by illness, wrote forcefully of Wyon's latter years:

> Far more serious to my mind is the sort of life, according to credible accounts, AWW was leading before he died. He should have retired so as not to sully the firm's name if that was his idea of a life. Instead of which, after GFG's [Garnsey's] death (who I verily believe would have forced him to retire for the reason given had he lived) he was allowed to purchase additional goodwill which GFG had forced him to relinquish, and go on leading the firm.[29]

The 'sort of life' to which Tull referred was not fully revealed, though contemporaries observed that Wyon, a bachelor, had a liking for chorus girls.

Wyon was a man of ingrained habit. 'It was rumoured,' recalled Southall, 'that every year he took holidays in company with his brother and brother's wife, one in Kent and the other to the Lake District.'[30] The brother was William Wyon, who had joined the staff of Price Waterhouse in May 1916 and remained with the firm for almost twenty years, leaving in May 1935.[31] Sir Albert Wyon's love of the Lake District appears to have been heartfelt, and in 1926 he gave the National Trust a capital sum to acquire the upper part of Ennerdale that lies below the 1,500-ft contour and east of the footpath between Scarth Gap and Black Sail pass.[32]

Sir Albert Wyon died on 1 December 1937. His estate was valued at £277,992. He gave a portrait of himself by Sir William Llewellyn to the ICAEW, and his house, 41 Hamilton Terrace, St John's Wood, was left to his niece. It was perhaps inevitable that comparisons should have been drawn with Sir Gilbert Garnsey. While the latter attracted public acclaim, Wyon preferred anonymity. Garnsey sought to expand and develop the firm, Wyon resisted growth and change. Garnsey was an inspiring leader who selected able men, entrusted them with responsibility and encouraged the development of talent, Wyon had few disciples among his colleagues. Garnsey had a wide circle of friends and contacts, Wyon had virtually no interests or connections beyond his professional involvements. It was, therefore, a cruel irony that Garnsey should have died at the height of his powers, while Wyon continued in office long after he had given his best. Wyon proved, in fact, to have held the longest term as senior partner, retaining the office for twenty-one years.

Wyon was succeeded as senior partner by Sir Laurence Halsey. Having been admitted to the firm in 1900, he was the longest serving of the partners and, in the absence of any other obvious competitor, was elected on this basis to executive authority. An obituary described him as being of

> a modest and retiring nature, but all who knew him, and there were many, were impressed by his charm, his sincerity ... He had a particularly marked capacity for evoking the affection of younger men and of encouraging their development; newcomers to his office often remarked that he was as courteous to a shy recruit to the staff as he was to an important client.[33]

The succession of Halsey may in part have been a reaction to the brusque and uninspiring personality of Wyon. Southall recalled that Halsey possessed

> an artistic side. I believe he collected watercolours. In his room there was an antique wooden desk and cupboards to hold papers in light-coloured wood with inlay along the edges. No other partner had so personal a room.[34]

When he retired in 1945 there was some rivalry among the partners to occupy Halsey's beautiful office.[35]

Halsey was a consensus leader. His courtesy and natural modesty enabled the partners to develop in their own individual ways. He did not seek to push the firm forward but attempted to maintain the status quo – particularly during the war years when the firm was desperately short-staffed. Aged sixty-six when he accepted the senior partnership, his appointment was not designed to introduce radical new policies. His contribution was perhaps to have restored the quiet, gentlemanly and respectable image that Price Waterhouse so cherished, and which had become somewhat tarnished during Wyon's latter years.

The interwar period saw eleven new partners: W.P. Rocke (1922), A.E. Jones (1926), F.S. Tull (1926), W.E. Seatree (1926), W. Harrison (1929), T. Howarth (1932), F.E. Welch (1934), T.B. Robson (1934), G.E. Richards (1939), and two partners from the US Firm: W.B. Campbell, who was admitted in 1926, and whose place, when he died in 1934, was taken by I.G. Pattinson. Their appointment maintained the cross-partnership arrangement with the US Firm and did not, therefore, materially affect the operation of the UK practice. Sir Arthur Lowes Dickinson and W.P. Rocke retired in 1923 and 1939 respectively. As a result, when a new partnership deed was drawn up in July 1939, there were eleven partners based in the City of London, including Halsey as senior partner, together with G.O. May (based in New York), I.G. Pattinson (Los Angeles) and W.E. Seatree (Paris).[36] Sir Nicholas Waterhouse, having been admitted to the firm in 1906, was the longest-serving partner and acknowledged as Halsey's successor. The capital of Price Waterhouse totalled £152,250, of which the largest contributions were from Waterhouse (£19,500), Jones (£19,500), Spencer (£18,750), Tull (£18,750) and Harrison (£16,500). That Halsey contributed only £9,750 suggested that his involvement in the firm was part-time, akin perhaps to a non-executive chairman of a major company.

It is possible that by 1933 Price Waterhouse had reached the natural limits of the partnership as set by Wyon. There were eleven partners (the legal maximum was twenty) and he refused to admit more. All partners had to be expert in auditing, which prevented specialists, such as Seed in taxation, from being promoted. Wyon was opposed to the opening of branch offices and those that existed were all run by managers – Monkhouse, Goddard & Co., in essence, the Newcastle office, being the only exception. Wyon was also, as the events of 1920–21 involving W.B. Peat & Co. demonstrated, implacably opposed to merger with any other City practice. Given these embargoes on the size, nature and territory of the partnership, it is difficult to envisage how any further growth might have occurred.

The Wyon legacy, however, was not simply to place a brake upon expansion. He had failed to deal with a major and potentially damaging problem of management. By 1939 Sir Laurence Halsey, then senior partner, was sixty-eight; Sir Nicholas Waterhouse, his successor, was sixty-two; the two most recent admissions to the partnership were Robson, aged thirty-eight, in 1934, and Richards, aged forty-three, in 1939. The partnership was becoming elderly – it had a mean age in the upper fifties. The war years were to compound the problem as those in office were asked to continue beyond normal retirement age, and there was, in effect, only one further admission. No organisational mechanism existed within the firm to allow young men of talent to rise through the ranks more swiftly. During the late thirties the consequences of the partnership's age-structure were dormant; they were to be concealed by the Second World War, but would emerge with potentially devastating consequences in the 1950s.

It may perhaps be significant that of the nine London-based partners admitted during the interwar period only two (A.E. Jones and W.P. Rocke) had served articles with Price Waterhouse. Tull had trained with Jackson, Pixley, Browning, Husey & Co., Seatree with James Watson of Carlisle, Harrison with Monkhouse, Goddard & Co., Howarth with N. Nicholson in Preston, Welch with Greaves & Armstrong at Newcastle, Robson with Sisson & Allden also of Newcastle and Richards with Mellors, Basden & Mellors.[37] This, in part, was a reflection of the ability of Price Waterhouse to attract talented accountants from the provinces, but was also evidence that training, both before and after qualification, did not occupy a high priority in the firm's culture.

With the continued expansion of Price Waterhouse it was decided in October 1936 to introduce an element of formality into the firm's organisation. Until then partners met every morning on an *ad hoc* basis to discuss pressing business; there was no structure to these gatherings which, so long as the partnership remained of limited size, dealt adequately with matters as they arose. On 9 October 1936 the first official 'Partners' Meeting' was held, attended by Tull, Harrison, Jones and Waterhouse, who presumably served as chairman.[38] The minutes were handwritten on a single sheet of foolscap paper. Initially most of the matters discussed were of a routine and uncontroversial nature, such as the allocation of work to audit clerks, the length of holidays for those serving in the Territorial Army and the purchase of office equipment. During 1938 the committee began to gather on a more regular basis, around six times a year. The first set of typed minutes appeared in April 1938.[39] Nevertheless, in the period up to the Second World War, the Partners' Meeting did not address policy issues or consider strategic changes of direction; it was a body set up to deal with tactical changes and, in effect, to promote the smooth operation of existing procedures.

Development of the Practice

The interwar years were notoriously difficult times for British industry. The deep depression of 1920–21 was followed by a gradual recovery that collapsed in 1929 into a more prolonged slump from which the nation emerged during the mid-thirties. Yet to a remarkable extent Price Waterhouse (Table 5, see Appendix) appears to have escaped the worst effects of these harsh economic circumstances. Disrupted by the First World War, the firm made a rapid recovery, its fee income more than doubled, from £102,398 in 1918 to £207,970 in 1922; when expressed in real terms this was nearly a threefold rise. Total profits increased from £72,638 in 1918 to £138,051 in 1922 (by 178 per cent in real terms). Price Waterhouse had been cushioned against economic collapse at home by income from overseas. In 1920 this contributed 41 per cent of total profits compared with 18 per cent in 1914 (Table 6, see Appendix). Growth continued at a steady rate throughout the remainder of the twenties, and by 1930 the firm's fee income had topped £300,000 for the first time in its history. This sustained progress (Figure 9) undoubtedly allowed Price Waterhouse to retain its position as one of the leading firms in Britain. Only Peat Marwick Mitchell & Co. and Deloitte, Plender, Griffiths & Co. were of comparable size in the City; Cooper Brothers & Co., Whinney, Smith & Whinney and Turquand, Youngs & Co., all three eminent practices, were smaller.

The harsh slump of 1929–32 did not prevent Price Waterhouse from continuing to expand, its fees growing impressively in real terms. From

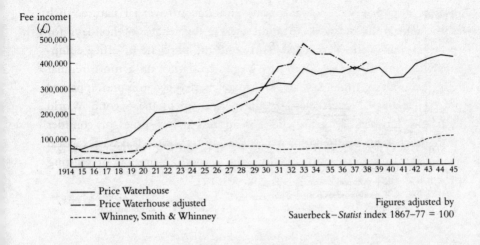

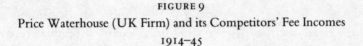

FIGURE 9
Price Waterhouse (UK Firm) and its Competitors' Fee Incomes
1914–45

1934 until the outbreak of war, a period of general economic recovery, the firm stagnated, its turnover reaching a plateau of around £360,000 per annum. Fees fell in real terms between 1933 and 1938. The likely explanation was that the firm had reached the limits of its capacity and that Wyon refused to allow the partnership to grow. In these circumstances the firm found its resources fully employed, and without Garnsey's inspiration and example there was not the same urgency to seek new work.

As regards profits (Table 6, see Appendix) a similar picture to that for fee income emerged. A rapid recovery followed the return to peace in 1918 with a rise from £72,638 to £138,051 by 1922. Progressive growth increased profits to £201,446 in 1930 and these continued to advance, reaching a peak of £237,305 in 1931. Henceforth they stabilised at around £225,000 for the remainder of the decade.

During the late 1920s and early 1930s Price Waterhouse was arguably the largest and possibly the most prominent practice in the City and, by implication, in Britain. In real terms the peak in fees achieved in 1933 was not to be surpassed by the firm until 1956, and the profits earned in 1933 were not overtaken in real terms until 1963. Staff numbers totalled 409 in 1939 and this figure was not to be exceeded until 1957. This

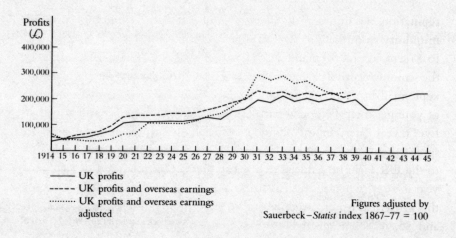

FIGURE IO

Price Waterhouse (UK Firm) Profits 1914–45

remarkable record of enterprise and growth resulted in the main from the influence of Sir Gilbert Garnsey. His high public profile, coupled with his widespread network of contacts in business, government and the civil service, attracted a variety of important assignments. Able young accountants were drawn to Price Waterhouse as its reputation flowered. Within the firm Garnsey was an inspirational leader whose talent and contribution were undeniable. His death in 1932 was crucially responsible for the period of stagnation and very gradual decline which was to follow.

The percentage contribution of overseas partnerships to UK profits fell progressively in the interwar period, declining from a peak of 41 per cent in 1920 (when the US Firm generated £34,482 or 27 per cent) to around 10 per cent in 1939. To a large extent this trend reflected a reduction in the profits transferred from America. From the figures it appears that the US Firm suggested a new arrangement in 1933 which substantially reduced the percentage of their profits payable to the UK partnership. In part, this was a response to the depression which had swept across America. Although *Fortune* magazine had described Price Waterhouse as 'easily the world's foremost accounting firm in size, in reputation, in number of clients',[40] these features could not provide immunity from the effects of slump. Profits fell from $2,131,800 in 1930 to $1,210,900 in 1932 and $1,031,700 in 1933.[41] William B. Campbell, the senior executive partner of the US Firm, decided that the partnership, kept small by May and rapidly ageing, required an immediate infusion of younger men. Five new partners were admitted in 1933 and a further five a year later. In this context of a falling surplus and the need to spread the profits more thinly, the US Firm was pressing that payments to the UK Firm be reduced. Although the US Firm enjoyed a successful year in 1937 (when profits rose to $2,136,452 and fees reached $3,200,580) this growth was not sustained and in 1939 these figures were $1,132,156 and $2,896,800 respectively.[42] By comparison, contributions from the European and South American Firms remained remarkably stable throughout the thirties but were small in relation to the business as a whole.

In the absence of day books, it has proved impossible to say which areas of work generated the principal source of fees for Price Waterhouse. Whinney, Smith & Whinney, a smaller City practice, earned 67 per cent of its turnover in the thirties from auditing and had earned over 25 per cent of its fees during the twenties from liquidations and bankruptcies.[43] Given that Price Waterhouse did not have such a tradition of insolvency work, it was likely that the bulk of the firm's fees derived from auditing. Speaking in 1938, Sir Nicholas Waterhouse observed that the 'growth in audit work has been the main source of increase in the opportunities of business for professional accountants'.[44]

The audit clients of Price Waterhouse fell into three main categories during the interwar period: railway companies, manufacturing and financial institutions. The first amounted to some of the largest assignments, and the technicalities that came with them had led to a Railway Department being formed. In 1923 in order to eliminate the duplication of lines and to revive profitability, the nation's railway companies were amalgamated into four main groups. Price Waterhouse became auditor to three of the four – the London Midland & Scottish, London & North Eastern and Southern Railway – though these remained joint appointments. In 1938 this work occupied thirteen full-time members of staff.[45] The manager responsible for supervising railway audits was a Mr Searle, who in 1929 celebrated fifty years with Price Waterhouse. 'He dressed smartly in a black coat,' recalled Southall, 'he wore formal ties in which nestled a gold tie-pin which had belonged to Edwin Waterhouse, a gift from the widow.'[46] The volume of work generated by these three mammoth companies, its spread across the country and the 'wide variation in book-keeping methods',[47] encouraged the creation of the only specialist audit department within the firm. The LMS audit, for example, demanded between 700 and 1,000 hours per annum in the late thirties, while the decision by the Southern not to reappoint a third joint auditor in 1938 resulted in Price Waterhouse taking on an estimated further 800 hours.[48] The average time spent by the Newcastle office and Scottish staff on the LNER audit between 1934 and 1937 was 2,500 hours per annum.[49] Sir Albert Wyon had taken over much of the railway work originally performed by Edwin Waterhouse and on his death in 1937 was responsible for the audits of the LNER, Southern Railway and the Railway Clearing House.[50] W.P. Rocke, a partner in Price Waterhouse from 1921, had joined the firm from the Railway Clearing House and 'it was said ... always had a piece of blackboard chalk at his bedside, so that if he had a fresh idea in the night he could write it on the dressing table mirror'.[51] Sir Nicholas Waterhouse had audited the LMS by virtue of its having subsumed the LNWR to which he had been appointed in succession to his father.

The second group of audit clients comprised major manufacturing enterprises. By the end of the thirties these included Westinghouse Brake & Signal Co., Armstrong, Whitworth & Co., Beecham, Beyer, Peacock & Co., Consett Iron Co., Courtaulds, Harland & Wolff, Hawker Siddeley, Imperial Chemical Industries, Unilever and Vickers-Armstrong. From the light or processing industries Price Waterhouse had gained as audit clients Freeman, Hardy & Willis, Peek, Frean & Co., Huntley & Palmers, Coca-Cola, Kellogg & Co., Kodak and Reckitt & Colman.[52]

Thirdly, Price Waterhouse had assembled a list of important financial institutions, most of which were based in the City. These included Bankers Investment Trust, Barclays Bank, Eagle Star Insurance Co., Equity & Law Life Assurance Society, Legal & General Assurance Society, Lloyds Bank and Westminster Bank. Tradition dictated that major organisations should have joint auditors (inherited from the days when two shareholders were elected to report on the published balance sheet), so that Price Waterhouse shared many of these appointments with other City firms. Barclays Bank (Dominion Colonial and Overseas), for example, was shared between Price Waterhouse, Peat & Co., Deloitte, Plender, Griffiths & Co. and Cooper Brothers & Co. Sir Gilbert Garnsey and Sir Harry Peat were joint auditors of the Bank of British West Africa and the London & North Eastern Railway, while Sir Nicholas Waterhouse and Sir Harry Peat together audited the National Provincial Bank.[53] Joint appointments began to disappear after 1945 (though Price Waterhouse retained both Unilever and ICI as such until the 1980s) and were a feature of an era when accountancy firms viewed themselves primarily as professional practitioners rather than competing commercial enterprises. The joint audit was viewed as a safeguard to the shareholder at a time when accountancy firms were comparatively small in relation to their major clients. The leading practices tended to maintain a spirit of comradeship and co-operation at a time when economic vicissitudes could have made competition ruinous.

Investigations, reconstructions and other special appointments were important for Price Waterhouse. Such single assignments often carried a higher hourly charge and could, in the long run, lead to an audit. Garnsey was a master in attracting this work. [Sir] Thomas Robson recalled that during the twenties Garnsey had gained

> a reputation as a 'doctor of industry', being called on to act in receiverships such as that of a South Wales ship-owning concern . . . or to make investigations of other firms in difficulties. He also got a large proportion of the prospectus investigations which were available. Many of the large companies in difficulty were large groups with subsidiary companies, among them the Armstrong Whitworth armaments and shipbuilding group (audited by PW & Co. in Newcastle), Marconi Wireless Telegraph Co. (audited by Cooper Brothers) and Wm. Beardmore & Co. Ltd., Glasgow steelmakers and shipbuilders (audited by a Glasgow firm) . . . About the end of 1928 GFG was asked to see if a scheme could be devised to assist Richard Thomas & Co., a group of steelmakers and colliery owners in South Wales and Lincolnshire.[54]

In 1926, for example, Armstrong Whitworth found themselves in a financial crisis and the Bank of England, to which they were indebted, appointed James Frater Taylor,[55] an industrialist, to investigate. He, in turn, enlisted the help of Garnsey, and the two issued a report which resulted in an amalgamation with Vickers.[56] In 1920–21 Garnsey as auditor of both Lloyds Bank and Fox, Fowler & Co., a country bank with branches in the West Country, arranged the 'complicated and delicate business' of their merger.[57] Robson also recalled how the acquisition of the Manchester-based Hulton group of newspapers by Sir William Berry (later Lord Camrose) and his brother, Gomer (later Lord Kemsley), had involved Price Waterhouse, who were appointed to determine a purchase price. The takeover led to the formation of Allied Newspapers which, in turn, brought the firm substantial audit, tax and investigation work as the group acquired other publications.[58]

In 1938 J. & J. Colman, already a client, entered into negotiations with Reckitt & Son of Hull. Robson was given the task of advising the former on the merger and Price Waterhouse were appointed joint auditors of the new company, Reckitt & Colman.[59] The joint appointment to audit Imperial Chemical Industries on its formation in 1926 was a major acquisition.

Tax work assumed a greater proportion of the firm's assignments after the First World War. The twenties were much taken up with the settlement of claims for Excess Profits Duty. Often, as Tull recalled, large sums were involved. The firm represented one shipping line, which had initially itself negotiated with the Inland Revenue. Price Waterhouse were able to recover £250,000, receiving 20,000 guineas for their services.[60] Once these claims were settled the firm's tax department was principally involved with sorting out the tax liability of their audit clients, and, to a lesser extent, with the management of the personal affairs of wealthy individuals.[61] The department, which numbered ten in 1930, was headed by a Quaker, H.E. Seed, who had joined Price Waterhouse in 1918. Seed had started life in the Post Office but then served his articles as an incorporated accountant, latterly with J.H. Ward in Preston, and qualified in 1913.[62] Although Seed was promoted to manager in 1921, despite his ability he could never be admitted to the partnership as an incorporated accountant. Accordingly in 1928 he was articled to W.B. Campbell and in 1933 qualified as a chartered accountant. He wrote several text-books, including *Inspector and Accountant, A Discussion on Mutual Relations* (1928), lectured, and served on the ICAEW's Taxation and Financial Relations Committee from its foundation in 1944; subsequently he chaired the Taxation sub-committee. Seed never became a partner in Price Waterhouse, excluded by the firm's rule that only general practitioners, rather than specialists, could be admitted. By 1939 the tax department numbered twenty-two, including three managers, Seed, Culling and Mackinnon.[63]

One further specialism developed in the interwar period – systems work. In 1919 Albert Cathles, an Edinburgh chartered accountant, was recruited from the Ministry of Munitions where he had been Deputy Director of Factory Accounting.[64] He had been selected by Garnsey who brought him to Price Waterhouse as a costings and systems expert.[65] Although Cathles was a manager, the Systems Department remained small, undertaking specific tasks probably for existing audit clients. Cathles retired because of ill health early in the Second World War and was succeeded by Eric Green.

Proposed Merger with W.B. Peat & Co.

Early in the summer of 1920 Sir Gilbert Garnsey and Sir William Peat engaged in negotiations which were intended to lead to the amalgamation of their respective firms. The idea was not a new one. In January 1915 a meeting had been held between Sir William Peat and four Price Waterhouse partners (Fowler, Wyon, Dickinson and Waterhouse). They discussed the possibility of setting up a partnership between the two firms to conduct 'business carried on outside the United Kingdom'.[66] There was already a joint firm in Egypt and another was shortly to be established for Russia. It was agreed that 'any further offices opened in any part of the world outside Great Britain should be opened on this same joint plan'.[67] Tentative discussions followed on the possibility of sharing their UK branch offices, all being 'treated and considered as joint offices of both firms',[68] though this was postponed as it was believed that it might be confusing to clients.

In October 1919 the two firms set up a joint partnership to open an office in Rotterdam.[69] Sir Harry Peat was a personal friend of Sir Nicholas Waterhouse and cordial relations had arisen between the families. Although not established in the City until 1868, W.B. Peat & Co. had grown rapidly and was beginning to challenge Price Waterhouse: in 1926, for example, their respective fee incomes were £210,000 and £234,216. A union would have brought a measure of geographical synergy both within the UK and abroad. While Price Waterhouse had branch offices in Plymouth, Liverpool and Newcastle, Peats had spread much wider and opened premises in Middlesbrough, Barrow-in-Furness, York, Cardiff, Swansea, Leeds, Darlington, Birmingham, Sheffield, Glasgow, Manchester and Nottingham.[70] On the other hand, the latter were poorly represented in America and Canada following the end of their agreement with Marwick Mitchell in 1919.[71] There were also similarities in their client lists, and the firms shared a number of joint audits: the National Provincial Bank, Standard Bank of South Africa, a subsidiary of Barclays Bank, Bank of British West Africa and the Metropolitan District Railway, while after 1923 the London & North Eastern and Southern Railway audits were undertaken jointly.[72]

No documentary evidence survives to relate who inspired the merger talks or from which side they originated. Sir Gilbert Garnsey was crucially involved at an early stage in negotiations with Sir Harry Peat. His adventurous spirit and drive to push Price Waterhouse forward may have initiated the proposals. By July 1920 it was certain that discussions had reached an advanced stage. They were, for example, considering the question of special fees which might be regarded as entirely personal to Sir William Peat.[73] In attempting to reach an equitable settlement Peats were concerned that the calculation of an average fee (as a measure of size) should not be taken over too great an historical period in view of their recent rapid growth. The partners of Price Waterhouse then voted on the issue of amalgamation 'in principle'; six concurred (Halsey, Waterhouse, Spencer, Garnsey, Sneath and Dickinson) and three (Wyon, Price and Morland) objected.[74] Sir Albert Wyon, as senior partner, was mandated to write to Sir William Peat on 9 July to report the decision:

> We are prepared to agree in principle to a complete amalgamation
> forthwith of the two firms on the basis of the average profits for the
> five years ending in 1920, subject to our arriving at a satisfactory
> agreement on details, many of which might better be called in view
> of their importance 'secondary principles'.[75]

Peat replied three days later to assent and to suggest that he and Sir Harry Peat, his son, should join Dickinson and Garnsey as a special committee to implement the scheme. This body proposed that a new, merged partnership be established as from 1 October 1920 to run for a period of four years. The profits of the two firms were to be pooled and divided according to agreed percentages. A management committee, comprising two partners from each firm together with the senior partners or senior partner, would handle the practical matters of the business such as salaries, office organisation, allocation of work and supervision of branch offices.[76]

Negotiations continued throughout the year. In October Sir Harry Peat observed to Wyon

> I feel confident that if our amalgamation does not go through a spirit of rivalry and competition will be engendered between our firms ... We are bound to protect our interests in the North in view of your purchase of the business of Monkhouse, Goddard & Co., and this rivalry may easily develop into a feeling of bitterness and mistrust ... Therefore I do feel that complete amalgamation is and always has been in my mind the natural and inevitable corollary of our co-operation abroad.[77]

Peat was here referring to two agreements, both concluded in October, to set up joint partnerships: one on the Continent to run their Rotterdam and Paris offices and the other in South America based at Buenos Aires. The revised heads of agreement passed through many drafts[78] but were finally reviewed by Slaughter & May on 17 December.[79] Copies were circulated to the partners of the two firms for ratification. Sir Harry Peat wrote to Dickinson on 29 December to report that the document had been 'unanimously approved' by his partnership.[80] A few changes followed and Peats concurred with the 'final agreement' on 7 January 1921.[81] A week later Sir Harry wrote to inform Price Waterhouse that 'Sir William and all the London partners have signed the agreement and I am sending around the signatures of Nancarrow, McBain, Forster and Granger. I hope to return the two copies fully signed in a day or two.'[82] Yet at this final hour the merger collapsed and no signatures were forthcoming from the Price Waterhouse partners.

Until recently no reason could be discovered to explain the abrupt termination. However, a draft letter written in pencil by Sir Albert Wyon has provided the answer. It is addressed to Sir William Peat and outlines clearly his objections to the union:

> You are aware, of course, that the proposal for amalgamation has never appealed to me and my views are shared by others of my partners. Our views ... have tended to become stronger rather than the reverse during the progress of the discussions.

It is quite undoubted then that if the two firms come together there will not be unanimity with regard to the wisdom of the step taken, nor that singleness of aim which in matters of importance are so essential to the successful conduct of a partnership . . .[83]

Wyon had passed the draft to Sir Laurence Halsey for comments, and the latter wrote:

W.B.P [eat] is well aware already that you don't like the scheme in any form; he is also aware that we are anything but unanimous on the subject . . . All we have to tell him in effect is that some of our partners are, we believe, about to enter into an engagement which they won't keep.[84]

Halsey added that he felt obliged to stand by the agreement 'unless I was prepared with some proposal adequate to meet such a breach of faith as is implied in breaking away now for any other reason than a failure to agree on reasonable secondary principles'.[85]

Although Wyon and Halsey both referred to a lack of unanimity within the partnership, the vote had been overwhelmingly in favour, six for the union and three against.[86] It seems, therefore, that Wyon, as senior partner, refused to sign the merger document, thus bringing matters to an end. The two firms continued to operate joint arrangements overseas but Peats, who needed representation in North America, revived their relationship with Marwick Mitchell and joined them in partnership in January 1925. This action stifled once and for all the resurrection of the scheme as the US Firm of Price Waterhouse would not have tolerated any involvement with a domestic rival.

Had the amalgamation come to pass, it would have created an impressively large firm. Its fee income would have been around £500,000 (a sum not achieved by Price Waterhouse until 1947), this at a time when the fees of a City rival, Whinney, Smith & Whinney, totalled £60–70,000 per annum.[87] The combined partnership would have numbered eighteen. It would have possessed a truly national network of offices in Britain, and a growing overseas representation. Deloittes, their nearest rivals, had seven partners in 1919, and only eight in 1939.[88] The combined firm of Price Waterhouse–W.B. Peat would, therefore, have been almost three times the size of their nearest rival. It had been a scheme of imagination and great promise, undoubtedly taken up by Garnsey, supported by Dickinson, but wrecked almost single-handedly by Wyon, with some support from F.S. Price, Morland and latterly Halsey. Although Wyon had given lack of unanimity as the reason for not ratifying the union, he had other grounds for opposing the arrangement. He believed that the enlarged partnership, located in several offices, some at a distance from London, would have undermined a professional spirit; it would, too, have weakened his personal authority and demanded the introduction of a formal management structure.

The Hatry Case

In 1929 a scandal erupted which shocked the City and was to have important repercussions on the issue of company disclosure and legislation. Clarence Hatry was a successful promoter and financier of businesses who in 1927 had established Austin Friars Trust as the key element in a complicated network of investment and industrial enterprises. He set about creating manufacturing groups and devised an ambitious scheme to take over the United Steel Companies and United Strip & Bar Mills and to restructure them as Steel Industries of Great Britain, which would then be floated on the London Stock Exchange.[89] However, the acquisition required Austin Friars Trust to find over £8 million. Earlier, Hatry had entered the municipal loan business, establishing Corporation & General Securities in 1926 to supply funds to local authorities. Faced with the collapse of his steel venture Hatry decided to borrow on the basis of forged corporation scrip certificates (for the Borough of Swindon, City of Gloucester and Corporation of Wakefield), supposedly held by Corporation & General Securities. The certificates did not need to be presented for registration and could be redeemed when the steel combine was floated. Hatry purchased the two steel companies in 1929 but was then faced by a collapse in share prices. He tried to shore up the value of shares in his own businesses (such as Photomaton and Associated Automatic Machine Corporation) by buying them himself but soon exhausted his capital.

Faced with financial ruin and the knowledge that an inquiry could reveal forged local authority scrip certificates, Hatry and his three remaining directors travelled on 19 September 1929 to 3 Frederick's

Place where they asked to see Sir Gilbert Garnsey, who was currently conducting an investigation into Austin Friars Trust on behalf of its bankers. Hatry confessed to Garnsey who contacted the Governor of the Bank of England and his client banks and suggested to Hatry that he should surrender himself to the police.[90] The following day Hatry and his colleagues visited the Director of Public Prosecutions, Sir Archibald Bodkin.[91] In his confession, Hatry took virtually all the blame for the entire fraud, a statement which led to his prison sentence of fourteen years.

After Garnsey had heard Hatry's story he called T.B. Robson, an able and newly promoted manager, into his room. He instructed Robson to prepare a report on the financial state of the Hatry group by the beginning of December and added that 'he would leave me without interference to get on with it (a promise which he scrupulously kept) but that this assignment would have a very significant effect on my own future relationship with him and the firm'.[92] Briefed thus, Robson and half a dozen staff moved into Hatry's offices where for the next two months they worked exceptionally hard attempting to unravel the complex financial nature of the group. Robson recalled that in November

> we were doing a 12 hour day including all day on Saturdays. Sunday 1st December was a 22 hour day and all-night work was needed in order that I might present my findings to G.F.G. on Monday 2nd. I remember that at midnight on December 1st I had to tell one of the team to go home as he was literally asleep on his feet.[93]

They discovered that losses on the collapse totalled £13.6 million and the forged securities had a face value of £3.75 million.

At the trial, held at the Old Bailey in January 1930,[94] Garnsey was a key witness for the prosecution. Robson attended to assist him with the evidence. Garnsey, he wrote, 'gave a masterly display of clarity and fairness . . . and never overstated the extent of the crime but confined himself to facts and did not allow himself to express opinions on motives which had actuated the defendants'.[95]

Although he expected his staff to work hard, Garnsey was not unappreciative. The team all received salary increases and Tinling, the senior, was promoted to manager. Robson himself was given the maximum increment and was told that thereafter any further raise would have to come from profit sharing.[96]

Following the investigation and trial, five of Hatry's companies were put into liquidation and Price Waterhouse was entrusted with their winding-up, a task which took ten years to complete. The scale of the fraud and its repercussions again opened the issue of how much information companies were legally required to disclose. The law had been recently revised by the 1928 Companies Act which came into force in 1929 through consolidating legislation. As a result companies were required to publish a balance sheet containing a summary of the authorised share capital, issued share capital, liabilities and assets, to state how the values of fixed assets had been calculated, and to present a profit and loss account at the annual general meeting.[97] Given the nature of the Hatry fraud it is unlikely that the limited provisions of the 1929 Act, had they been applied from the formation of Austin Friars in 1926, would have alerted shareholders or bankers to the group's parlous financial state at an earlier date. As the official history of the ICAEW observed: 'Excellent though the 1929 Act was so far as it went, accountants did not have to wait long before having it painfully brought home to them that it did not go far enough.'[98] The event in question was the trial surrounding the financial statements and prospectus issued by the Royal Mail Steam Packet Co.

The Royal Mail Case

The case of the Royal Mail Steam Packet Co., which opened in July 1931, proved to be a *cause célèbre* in the City's history, attracting considerable attention and controversy in the business world. Price Waterhouse were involved because through their partner, Harold Morland, they were auditors of the holding company and a number of its principal subsidiaries, including Harland & Wolff (from 1900), Elder Dempster, and the White Star and Union-Castle Lines.

The Crown brought a joint prosecution against the chairman of the Royal Mail group, Lord Kylsant, and Morland under the terms of the 1861 Larceny Act, claiming that they had published a balance sheet for 1926 in a form that was capable of misleading shareholders as to the true trading position of the group. In addition, Kylsant alone was accused of having issued a prospectus in June 1928 which distorted the financial state of the Royal Mail Co. Although the facts of the case were relatively straightforward, the circumstances leading to the prosecution were tangled in the extreme.

The Royal Mail group was, in fact, a vast enterprise and quite the largest shipping business in Britain at a time when this was a key activity in the economy. By 1930 it comprised 140 subsidiary companies with total liabilities of £120 million and a fleet tonnage of 2.6 million tons.[99] However, the manner in which it had been assembled by Lord Kylsant (using cross-shareholdings and paper transactions) resulted in few, apart from the government, appreciating just how substantial its operations had become. At the trial the court was asked to consider only the Royal Mail Steam Packet Co. and six of its wholly owned subsidiaries (whose liabilities totalled a mere £25 million) as there was a fear that full disclosure of its holdings could precipitate a major financial crisis in a context of general depression.

In order to understand how the group had fallen into such a parlous financial state, it is necessary to examine the events of the mid-twenties. Appointed chairman of the Royal Mail Co. in 1903, Owen Philipps, Baron Kylsant, set about establishing almost autocratic control of the enterprise. This he had achieved by 1918. However, post-war depression produced a collapse in freight rates which, in turn, undermined the profitability of the Royal Mail Co. Yet by the opening months of 1926 it seemed to many that the worst of the slump might be over. Freight rates began to recover and it appeared that an era of prosperity might be about to dawn. With this hope in mind, Kylsant published a set of healthy looking accounts in May 1927. A profit of £478,563 was announced and an ordinary dividend of 4 per cent declared. The result was to inspire optimism in the press, the *Shipbuilding and Shipping Record* commenting that 'stockholders can regard the outlook with confidence in the ability of the Royal Mail Steam Packet Co. to develop their vast shipping undertaking on sound and progressive lines'.[100] Alas, this judgement was far from the truth. Unknown to the financial press, the shareholders or even some of the directors, the books of accounts had revealed a trading loss of £507,104. As early as October 1926 Kylsant had been considering a contingency plan to cover an estimated deficit of £1.3 million by transferring sums from reserves and taking a £200,000 bonus from Nelson Steam Navigation Co., a wholly owned subsidiary.

In the event, he made the balance sheet seem respectable by a transfer into the profit and loss account of £550,000 from the Excess Profits Duty reserve and a further £175,000 from the income tax reserve.[101] The only movement recorded in the published accounts was the injection of £150,000 from the general reserve fund. The profit and loss account had also been swollen by the receipt of £151,000 from several subsidiaries and of £44,000 from the Pacific Steam Navigation Co. settled by a transfer to Royal Mail of 60,000 £1 shares in the Argentine Steam Navigation Co.

At a meeting held to approve the accounts to 31 December 1925, McArthur, the manager responsible for the audit, drew Morland's attention to the fact that there were large transfers from Excess Profits Duty and Income Tax reserves and suggested that this should be indicated. Without discussion with Kylsant or his fellow partners, Morland agreed and wrote 'adjustment of taxation reserves' alongside the entry for 'dividends on shares in allied and other companies' in the profit and loss account. This procedure he repeated in 1926 and 1927.[102]

Perhaps no great harm would have ensued had the nation's economic fortunes risen and the company returned to profitability. Nevertheless, the complex and concealed nature of the group's structure made it virtually impossible for any external assessor to judge its viability in the short term, and this fact enabled Kylsant to take further opportunities to disguise its financial predicament. In 1927, in order to declare a dividend of 5 per cent and publish a profit of £737,293 (when in fact there had been a surplus of a mere £6,064, and even this was only achieved by reducing the allowance for depreciation), Kylsant paid £300,000 from a subsidiary, Nelson Steam Navigation Co., to the Royal Mail Co., this sum being financed by the Royal Mail purchasing one million £1 ordinary shares in Nelson Steam Navigation Co. at par. This and other internal transactions boosted the profits of the Royal Mail Co. by £550,000. To an outsider, even one with professional expertise, it would have appeared, therefore, that the Royal Mail group was successful with sound profits and regular dividends being generated by the principal companies within the mighty enterprise. Furthermore, the accounts were audited by a reputable and highly respected firm of accountants.

Matters continued to deteriorate for the Royal Mail group. The accounts for 1928 showed a profit of £457,216 (reinforced by a transfer of £350,000 from secret reserves, £268,200 in dividends from subsidiaries and a further cut in the allowance for depreciation) which in fact concealed a true trading loss of £290,326.[103] The ratio of share to loan capital was 1 to 2.6 and since much of their short-term loan capital was to be repaid over the next eight years this required a cash flow in favour of the group in the region of £10 million per annum; the figure for 1928 had been estimated at a mere £5 million.

The deep-seated financial instability of the Royal Mail group began to emerge only in 1929 when Harland & Wolff, one of its principal subsidiaries, approached the Trade Facilities Act Advisory Committee (TFA) to request that a five-year moratorium be placed on their loan of £1,194,676 from the Midland Bank. Their application was rejected. When the annual instalment of £298,669 was due in May 1929, the bank received only £100,000. The TFA and the Treasury, uncertain as to how to proceed, consulted Morland as the group's auditor. Basing his opinion on the strength revealed by the published accounts, he concluded that there was no need for the Midland Bank to grant an extension on the loan.[104]

In July 1929 a public dispute arose between Kylsant and his elder brother, Viscount St Davids, a trustee of the 4½ and 5 per cent stocks. The latter suggested that the auditor's amendments in the 1928 accounts required further investigation. He asked to interview Morland but his request was refused. By September 1929 the share price of the Royal Mail group had begun to slide as former directors voiced concerns over its overall soundness. In January 1930, for example, Arthur Cook, a former managing director of Lamport & Holt, had complained to Morland that 'there are now no assets corresponding to the ordinary capital and the 6½ per cent preference shares and the 6 per cent preference shares are barely covered'.[105]

Rumours that the Royal Mail group was in serious difficulties occurred at an awkward time for the Treasury. As we have seen, Clarence Hatry had been arrested in September 1929 on charges of fraud. This had contributed to a further deterioration in sterling and to the bank rate rising to 6½ per cent on 27 September. Neither the government nor the City could afford a second major scandal.

In October Kylsant approached Sir William Plender, senior partner of Deloitte Plender Griffiths & Co. and chairman of the TFA Committee, to report that the group could pay the instalments on the Midland Bank loan but could not pay the £1,805,804 owed by three subsidiaries. He added that although dividends of over £500,000 had been declared in 1928–9, there was no money even in reserve accounts to meet loan liabilities. As far as contingent liabilities were concerned Kylsant argued that they could be covered by the asset values of vessels belonging to the group. Plender pointed out not only that such assets were an inappropriate means of meeting liquid liabilities but that given the depressed state of trade they would be realised at only a fraction of their purchase price. Kylsant attempted to justify his belief in the soundness of the group as a whole by announcing in September 1929 that he had commissioned Price Waterhouse to prepare a consolidated balance sheet.[106] However, as events were to prove, the auditors' report was to be of little value, since Kylsant had withheld from them much vital information.

In December 1929 Price Waterhouse informed Kylsant that the cash flow for the entire group would amount to only £3.4 million. As this sum would not cover debenture interest payments (estimated at £5 million), he agreed to waive preference and ordinary share dividends of the Royal Mail Co. This convinced Plender that the group must undergo an independent investigation and, after discussions with Philip Snowden, Chancellor of the Exchequer, it was agreed that Sir William McLintock, the distinguished City accountant, should be appointed to undertake the task.[107] In March 1930 McLintock reported on losses in a number of subsidiaries dating back to 1926 and estimated that the group's current liabilities totalled around £30 million.[108] Depression and excess tonnage in the shipping industry made it unlikely that these debts could be settled in the short term. Accordingly, Montagu Norman, governor of the Bank of England, suggested that the enterprise be placed into receivership.[109] Kylsant fought on. He instructed Sir Gilbert Garnsey to frame a reconstruction scheme.

In the meantime, Plender had been shaken by McLintock's findings. Plender had no sympathy with Kylsant's methods and was saddened that Morland, a colleague on the TFA Committee, had failed to provide a more forthright view of the group. In a speech delivered to the Leicester Society of Chartered Accountants on 14 March 1930 he warned that

> auditors run grave risks if they do not take reasonable care to satisfy themselves that a balance sheet showed a true and correct view of the state of a company's affairs as shown by the books and contained a correct record of the company's transactions for the period

covered by the audit. An auditor did not accept implicitly information . . . offered him by directors or officers.[110]

On 31 March 1930 Garnsey presented his report to Kylsant. As the
gravity of the situation became increasingly apparent to the government,
Sir Norman Fisher, permanent secretary to the Treasury and head of the
Civil Service, wrote to Kylsant for a copy of the Price Waterhouse
report. This recommended a 'series of surgical operations', including
Kylsant's immediate retirement as chairman,[111] and a scheme for the
fusion of virtually all the group's constituent companies together with
an issue of prior lien debentures of no less than £10 million to clear its
indebtedness. Neither Plender nor McLintock thought this a practical
proposition as the report appeared to have overlooked current liabilities
in respect of shipbuilding commitments to the value of £4 million and
failed to address the financial plight of Harland & Wolff and David
Colville & Sons. Unless these facts were disclosed to shareholders and
creditors, McLintock argued, 'I cannot see any prospect – even a remote
one – of a scheme on these lines being carried through, and even if it
were I do not think it offers any final solution to the troubles of the
group'.[112] Garnsey, as McLintock now realised, had not been given
the freedom of access to the group's records that he himself had obtained and had also been denied an opportunity to study the Treasury's
files.

A confrontation could no longer be avoided. Kylsant was summoned
to the Treasury on 14 May 1930. Accompanied by Sir John Craig,
chairman and managing director of David Colville & Sons, Sir Albert
Wyon and Mr James of Price Waterhouse, he was greeted by Plender
and McLintock, together with Fisher, Hopkins and Bamford representing
the government. It was impressed upon Kylsant that the immediate
problem was the group's short-term debts and that he should consult his
bankers whom Plender believed to be unaware of the true position.
Wyon, who learned for the first time of the Treasury's attitude and of
the real position of the group, urged Kylsant to call a meeting of
creditors at once. In the event, the representatives of the five clearing
banks rejected Kylsant's scheme. As a result it was agreed to set up a
committee of inquiry, which would include McLintock, to propose a
solution to the group's financial predicament.[113] While this was underway, Walter Runciman MP, Brigadier Arthur Maxwell, managing

partner of Glyn Mills & Co., and McLintock were appointed voting trustees and in effect took executive control from Kylsant for the running of the group.

Thus, by the summer of 1930 it appeared as if a great crisis had been averted. The true position of the Royal Mail group had been determined and concerted action was underway to reconstruct the enterprise. Kylsant nursed the notion that he would be allowed to resume control once the companies had been restructured, but in November it was made clear to him that his return to power was unacceptable. Early in 1931 matters took a new and worrying course. Viscount St Davids, whose animosity towards his brother persisted, objected publicly to the rescue plan being assembled by the voting trustees, and asked for an explanation as to why the audit system had failed to warn shareholders of the true nature of the group's profit and loss allocations.[114] Questions were raised in the Commons and in response to political pressure Sir William Jowitt, the Attorney-General, instructed that a prosecution be brought.

On 13 May 1931 Detective Inspector George Stubbings handed summonses to both Kylsant and Morland.[115] The charges were that the former had published false statements of the Royal Mail's accounts in 1926 and 1927 and that Morland had aided or advised him on their publication. The trial at the Old Bailey between 20 and 30 July was one of the most celebrated of the interwar years. Sir William Jowitt led the prosecution, while Sir Patrick Hastings served as leading counsel for Morland and Sir John Simon led for Kylsant.

The key witness, however, was Lord Plender. The doyen of his profession, in 1929–30 he had served a second term as president of the ICAEW, and as senior partner of Deloitte, Plender & Griffiths was a leading practitioner; a year earlier he had been the first accountant to receive a peerage. His evidence, therefore, was of crucial importance. As Sir Patrick Hastings recalled

> Lord Plender himself was the first witness called before the jury, and his evidence for the prosecution was merely formal. It was upon his cross-examination that everything depended. I never re-member to have approached a cross-examination with more anxiety.[116]

It was essential that Plender confirm that Morland's actions were proper and that the term 'including adjustment of taxation reserves' be deemed adequate to cover the presentation of the balance sheet.[117] Hastings knew that Plender's judgement would probably decide the case.[118] Accordingly he had attempted to forestall the cross-examination by obtaining permission from the Attorney-General to interview Plender before the trial. A questionnaire was submitted to him which, in effect, sought his approval of Morland's actions.[119] In one of his answers Plender observed:

> It is not unusual in the case of a company enjoying exceptional prosperity to set aside to inner reserves sums which are in excess of normal earnings which sums may be used in lean years to supplement profits; but the circumstances and facts of each case must determine whether or not this disclosure should be made or the amount stated. This disclosure is largely a matter of judgement.[120]

Hastings took the precaution of displaying prominently on his desk in court the reports of companies which Plender had himself audited, reports which contained 'words substantially similar to those complained of in the present case'.[121] These presumably would have included the balance sheet of the Union-Castle Steamship Co., a member of the Royal Mail group, and audited by Deloitte, Plender, Griffiths & Co.[122] In the event, Plender agreed that the use of secret reserves was common practice and indeed allowable under the terms of the 1929 Companies Act.[123] Given the size of the Royal Mail group, the number of transfers made, its trading losses and the overall complexity of the case, the prosecution should perhaps have re-examined Plender to ask whether its circumstances were different from those envisaged in the cross-examination.[124] But the failure to put these questions weakened its case and allowed the defence to take the initiative.

Sir William McLintock, the original investigator and now a voting trustee responsible for the running and reconstruction of the group, was the second prosecution witness. He described the parlous state of the group as revealed by his inquiry, but said that he had been reluctant to speak out largely because of his fears about the effect of the trial on the fate of the group and because he knew that the accountancy profession was also under close scrutiny. Simon and Hastings were able to plead that the secret transfer of hidden reserves was commonplace in large companies, particularly in the shipping industry where it was an accepted method of ironing out the effect of cyclical variations.

Two expert witnesses were also called by the defence to reinforce the probity of Morland's actions. H.L.H. Hill, then president of the ICAEW, commented that the transfers from excess profits duty and income tax reserves were 'properly brought in', and remarked of Morland's qualification 'adjustment to taxation reserves' that 'I think the phrase used is quite suitable'.[125] Secondly, Brian O.D. Manning, a partner in Messrs Cole, Bond & Co., when asked whether he would have signed the 1926 and 1927 accounts, replied 'I should'.[126] In other words, the four accountant witnesses (two of whom had been called by the prosecution) agreed that Morland's behaviour was both legal and within the bounds of accepted practice.

At this point it was intended that Sir Gilbert Garnsey be called as a further witness for the defence. Garnsey had, as he wrote in a letter to May, 'given up all my other work and concentrated my efforts on the investigation of the facts of this case'.[127] Subsequently Morland spoke 'with great appreciation of G.F.G.'s brilliant work on his defence'.[128] Garnsey was responsible for discovering how often the words 'adjustment of taxation reserves' were used by other accountants (and by whom) in similar circumstances, for negotiating with the various professional bodies and for establishing the true facts surrounding the transfers from the Excess Profits Duty reserve. The sums disclosed in 1926 and 1927 were estimates, coming as they did from a hybrid account headed 'Sundry Balances, Accounts not closed and Debts owing',[129] but 'nearly two weeks' of inquiry revealed that the transfers were 'almost exactly correct: the figure for 1926 should have been £551,022 instead of £550,000', while the £232,787 was for 1927 an 'exact figure'.[130] Garnsey was not called into the witness box because the defence counsel was planning to cross-examine him on the issue of the prospectus in order to incriminate Kylsant. Morland had been on holiday in Cornwall when the 1928 debenture prospectus was discussed at Price Waterhouse, and it was reported that Garnsey had validated the document on the grounds that an improvement in the trade cycle would bring the Royal Mail group back into financial health.[131]

It was the turn of Morland to be cross-examined. As he entered the witness box, Hastings recalled,

> anything less fraudulent in appearance it would be impossible to imagine ... He treated any allegation made against him with supreme indifference, and regarded his accusers almost with good-natured contempt.[132]

His attitude and the inadequate state of existing legislation are illustrated by the following interchange:

> JOWITT: Do you think that when an ordinary, intelligent member of the public or shareholders . . . looked carefully through the accounts for 1926 and 1927 he would have a true picture of the company's position?
>
> MORLAND: The balance sheet gave him a perfectly true picture of the company's position. . .
>
> JOWITT: It is very important for a shareholder to know . . . what current earnings his company is making?
>
> MORLAND: I do not see why.
>
> JOWITT: Do you agree that one of the most material circumstances which every shareholder has a right to know is the earning capacity of the company?
>
> MORLAND: Of course, I do not agree with that.[133]

Later Jowitt asked whether the shareholders, if they had realised at the time what the true position of the company was and how it had behaved between 1921 and 1927, would have been seriously disturbed. This was an important question to which Morland replied:

> That is not a very easy question to answer; I should doubt if they would. The chief thing a shareholder wants is regular dividends, and that he had all the time.[134]

Sir Patrick Hastings later observed that Morland's personal conviction of his innocence was 'a little trying' as he 'absolutely declined to recognise the very grave position with which he was faced'.[135] 'Moreover,' he wrote,

> being a devotedly religious man, he was convinced that a divine interference would necessarily decide the issue, a view which, although no doubt satisfactory to him, was a little trying to his harassed and even exasperated legal advisers.[136]

After deliberating for about three hours the jury acquitted both Morland and Kylsant on the charge of publishing false statements, although the latter was pronounced guilty of issuing a false prospectus and received a lenient sentence of twelve months in prison. Public opinion thought this unjust and The Economist concluded that 'if he was guilty then most of the chairmen of large public companies would today be in custody'.[137] The press was overwhelmingly sympathetic to Morland, and *The Times* observed 'the verdict was what the evidence plainly required', while the *Daily Telegraph* concluded 'the case against Morland was obviously worthless and ought never to have been taken to court'.[138] In waiving their fee, as was then accepted practice between professional firms, Slaughter & May, the firm's solicitors stated that they believed that Morland had been unfairly treated.[139]

Victory in the case had in part been won by the care and thought which had gone into the collection and presentation of the evidence. In legal circles the documents for the defence became known as the 'rainbow brief'[140] because they had been bound and annotated in seven volumes each with a different colour.[141] Hastings could draw upon his material with ease using a colour-coded chart, while the prosecution was not so well prepared. This organisational advantage may in part have resulted from Garnsey's involvement, and it set a precedent for later trials where complicated factual issues were involved.

The effect of the trial on Morland was severe. Sir Nicholas Waterhouse, who sat in the courtroom as an observer, thought that some of his unsatisfactory answers derived from him being '*too* honest . . . and it was also partly due to his great anxiety to say nothing which might to his own advantage incriminate Kylsant'. Waterhouse, who knew him well, had suggested that his high intelligence had encouraged him to be 'bone lazy'.[142] It was perhaps true that Morland should have been more vigilant than he had been, but his honesty was clearly established. During the proceedings he had assumed a mask of coolness to the extent that it almost resembled 'apathy',[143] and when Waterhouse asked him how he coped, Morland replied, 'Well, they treated Christ much worse for much less so why should I bother.'[144] It was reported that in the early evening, while the jury were considering their verdict, Mrs Morland rang the court to inquire whether her husband would be late for dinner.[145] The solicitor who took the call, under the stress of uncertain outcome, answered, 'Yes, madam, I should think about 12 months late.' Under the terms of the 1929 partnership deed Morland was due to retire in June 1932, aged sixty-three, and he duly left the firm as agreed.[146] His last ten months with the firm, however, were not happy ones. It was reported that some partners, in the belief that he had committed the cardinal sin of having failed to consult others when matters had become contentious and potentially damaging to the firm, refused to speak to him.[147]

Harold McArthur, the manager who assisted Morland with the audit, believed that his own prospects had been blighted (though as an incorporated accountant he could never have become a partner)[148] and left Price Waterhouse in June 1932 a month before the trial.[149] McArthur had joined the Liverpool office in 1912, transferred to London in March 1919, and had taken charge of the Royal Mail audit on qualifying in 1921. He thought that Morland had been insufficiently explicit in his description of the transfer and had found him an awkward partner, not open to persuasion, though this judgement may have been clouded by the events which prompted his resignation.[150]

Following the case, Thomson McLintock were entrusted with the reconstruction of the Royal Mail group. Price Waterhouse retained the audits of the Royal Mail Steam Packet Co., Harland & Wolff, Elder Dempster & Co., Lamport & Holt, White Star Line, Oceanic Steam Navigation Co. and Coast Lines. A.E. Jones took partner responsibility on Morland's retirement in 1932.[151]

The affair provoked much criticism of both the 1929 Companies Act and of the training offered to accountants. In 1933 Carr–Saunders and Wilson in their study of the professions asked whether

> the accountant's professional ethics are adequate to his responsibilities, and if his education is such as to fit him for the varied and highly skilled duties which he is called upon to perform.[152]

They also criticised the failure of the legislature to keep pace with developments in business:

> In recent years the increasing size of the typical company, and the increasing application of accounting methods to trading operations have profoundly affected both the relations between the shareholders and the board, and the actual . . . relations between the board and the auditors. Nevertheless, the law has remained in all important respects unchanged.[153]

Nevertheless, as de Paula remarked in the sixth edition of his *Principles of Auditing*, also published in 1933,

> there is no single event in my memory which has made so profound an impression upon the accountancy world and . . . is destined to

influence accountancy practice in a marked degree ... The attitude
of auditors as regards secret reserves is being challenged; the whole
subject therefore is one which merits serious consideration and upon
which some form of uniform practice should be adopted by the
profession.[154]

Once the case was over, undisclosed transfers from secret reserves
continued to be made and the practice was permitted for banking,
shipping and insurance companies. The change which occurred after
1931 was that although the amount of the transfer from secret reserves
could be concealed, the fact that such a transfer had been made was to be
disclosed. The ICAEW resolutely opposed any legislative change, arguing that new laws would result in auditors being 'reduced to mere
automata, to obey audit programmes laid down by statutes'.[155] Yet the
decision by the ICAEW to encourage accountants to work towards
improved reporting standards was not accompanied by explicit guidelines
as to what constituted best practice. As a result substantial change was
delayed until the passing of the 1948 Companies Act.

Perhaps the final irony in the whole saga is that a recent analysis of the
accounts of the Royal Mail group has demonstrated that the importance
of transfers from secret reserves to disguise poor returns was exaggerated
at the trial.[156] There was no doubt that the company set aside substantial
sums during the First World War (partly by introducing excessive
depreciation charges), but these funds were not, in fact, the principal
means of enhancing profits in the period 1922–7. Rather, a healthy
surplus largely resulted from the failure to disclose income from non-
trading sources (such as an income tax reserve set up in 1915–21 and
sums received from dividend payments).[157] Whatever the device that
Kylsant may have employed to distort the true trading results of the
group, the company legislation of 1907 and 1929 remained deficient in
revealing such actions.

Consolidation and Other Accountancy Themes

The issues which lay at the heart of the Royal Mail case – how groups
of companies should arrange their balance sheets and how much information should be conveyed to the public – had been live since the end of

the First World War. Mergers both before and during the hostilities had created large industrial and commercial organisations. These were not, in general, single entities but typically would comprise a holding company surrounded by a host of subsidiaries, which to all the world appeared as independent beings. By 1923, for example, Guest, Keen & Nettlefolds, a holding company with its own manufacturing capacity, also governed a considerable number of subsidiaries, including John Lysaght, Joseph Sankey & Sons, F.W. Cotterill, John Garrington & Sons, Bayliss, Jones & Bayliss, Cwmbran Collieries, Meiros Collieries, D. Davis & Sons and the Consolidated Cambrian. Although the ownership of these satellites was never concealed and each published its own accounts, the investor had no means of telling how the group as a whole earned its profits. For example, funds might have been transferred from a few highly successful subsidiaries to the parent company to preserve an illusion of profitability, or, as in the case of the Royal Mail, transfers from a secret reserve, set up during the war, might be employed to similar effect. No provision existed in the 1907 Companies Act to compel major industrial enterprises to provide details of their holdings.

Sir Gilbert Garnsey was one of the first accountants in Britain to appreciate the limitations of the existing legislation and to call for reform of reporting procedures. In December 1922 he read a paper, entitled 'Holding Companies and their Published Accounts', to London members of the ICAEW, and published the text shortly afterwards. He observed that the 'legal balance sheet' did not give 'shareholders the information to which they are entitled. It fails to recognise the practical nature of the relationship existing between the holding company and its subsidiaries'.[158] Accordingly, Garnsey recommended the simultaneous publication of a

> consolidated balance sheet of the whole undertaking amalgamating the assets and liabilities of all the subsidiaries with those of the holding company and a consolidated profit and loss account embracing the profits and losses of all the companies.[159]

Although consolidated accounts of this kind were virtually non-existent in Britain, they had won widespread acceptance in America, where, as Garnsey wrote, the consolidated balance sheet is now almost universally adopted by companies whose interest in subsidiary companies form any considerable proportion of their total assets. The practice began to spread at the time of the movement for consolidations about the end of the last century – a movement which culminated in the formation of the United States Steel Corporation in 1901. The consolidated balance sheet issued by that company has become in a large measure a standard for public corporations in that country.[160]

The US Firm of Price Waterhouse were, of course, the auditors in question and this suggested that Garnsey's views were greatly influenced by contacts with America. Nevertheless, a review in *The Accountant* described Garnsey's paper as 'the first serious examination given to the subject on this side of the Atlantic'.[161]

Although he continued to press his case, Garnsey encountered widespread opposition in the profession.[162] A fellow critic was Sir Josiah Stamp, then company secretary at Nobel Industries, who in 1922 had produced the first consolidated balance sheet for that group covering forty wholly-owned and thirty-five majority-owned subsidiaries. In 1925 Garnsey chaired a lunch of London members of the ICAEW at which Sir Josiah spoke in favour of consolidation but, rather surprisingly, stopped short from advocating legislative change:

I am not pleading for legal action. It will grow by the establishment of the best as practice, and the best is not necessarily what is oldest until it is shaken up by some abuse in a law court . . . [163]

In the face of concerted opposition to change, Garnsey, too, adopted a similar approach in the second edition of his study:

I cannot find myself in agreement with those who urge that legislation is necessary to compel a holding company to publish additional information . . . I am of the opinion that it's not legislation that we want but rather education . . .[164]

Consolidation, as Garnsey recorded, was gradually filtering into British financial reporting:

most of the large insurance companies of this country prepare nothing but consolidated balance sheets, while some large commercial enterprises such as Agricultural & General Engineers Ltd, Crosse

& Blackwell Ltd, Meadow Dairy Co. Ltd, Nobel Industries Ltd . . .
publish consolidated balance sheets by way of supplementary
information.[165]

Nevertheless, both the profession and industry remained largely unrecept-
ive to these ideas. Various explanations have been offered. Garnsey
himself thought that it was a problem of management: '[they] are not at
all imbued with the desire of giving their shareholders as much information as possible'.[166] A psychological barrier may have arisen in the early
twentieth century, according to R.H. Parker, which prevented British
accountants, who saw themselves as the progenitors of the American
profession, from adopting technical advances pioneered across the
Atlantic.[167]

In the event, it was, as Sir Josiah Stamp had predicted, 'abuse in a law
court' which raised the issue to one of national concern. First, the Hatry
trial and then the Royal Mail case highlighted the deficiencies of existing
legislation. Although neither case brought about any immediate change,
the publicity surrounding them discouraged groups from making transfers from secret reserves without full disclosure. These cases also accelerated the pace at which consolidation was introduced. In 1934 much
attention was given to the group accounts of the Dunlop Rubber Co.
which had been assembled on a consolidated basis by their chief
accountant, F.R.M. de Paula.[168] These included a clearly compiled
statement of profit for the year, showing how the amount available for
dividend had been calculated. The tradition within Price Waterhouse of
writing on the subject was taken up after Garnsey's death by T.B.
Robson, who had helped to revise the third edition of *Holding Companies*
(1937).[169] Five years later Robson brought out his own study, entitled
The Construction of Consolidated Accounts, in which he remarked:

> the special aim in preparing consolidated accounts is to provide
> statements which shall reflect the position and earnings of a hold-
> ing company group, viewed not as a series of separate entities but
> as an economic unit, the underlying theory being that such a group
> is in effect one business carried on in several branches or
> departments.[170]

Such however was the strength of opposition within sections of the
profession and industry that the principles discussed by both Garnsey

and Robson were not enshrined in law until the passing of the 1948 Companies Act.

Branch Offices

In January 1932 a Committee on Local Offices, comprising Garnsey, Price, Rocke, Jones and Tull, was set up to consider the question of branches in the UK.[171] To date Price Waterhouse had established only four offices outside London: Liverpool in 1904, Newcastle in 1912 (consolidated in 1920 by the merger with the local firm of Monkhouse, Goddard & Co.), Plymouth in 1914 and Leeds in 1928. In addition, the firm had informal representation in the provinces. From the early thirties, for example, the liquidation of large colliery interests in South Wales had necessitated the employment of a small staff in Cardiff under the supervision of W.E. Jones who used the premises of a client as his headquarters. As there was sufficient work in the region to occupy two qualified men and a junior, it was recommended that an office be opened. In March 1932 two rooms were taken in the National Provincial Bank building, Cardiff Docks.[172] Jones remained as manager in charge until he departed to work for the D.M. Evans Bevan group in December 1936. V.C. Woods, who had worked for Price Waterhouse in South America, took his place as manager in January 1937.

In 1924 J.O. Collett[173] was sent to Yorkshire to assist a number of woollen manufacturers in settling their claims for Excess Profits Duty. This proved a time-consuming task and also resulted in the firm acquiring a number of local audits which Collett undertook with the assistance of staff sent from London. Finding that he was based almost permanently in Leeds, it was agreed that Collett should open an office in the city. In April 1928 a room was taken in Lloyds Bank, Greek Street Chambers. The practice expanded rapidly, employing five at the end of its first year, rising to sixteen in 1938 and thirty-one in 1948.[174] By the time of their survey of offices in 1932 the committee were able to conclude that, with a fee income of £10,000 and profit of £6,200, the Leeds office had proved to be 'an unqualified success'.[175] Collett had joined the firm in August 1918 and worked his way to the level of manager by application and natural ability.[176] However, his path to partnership was blocked first because he never qualified as a chartered accountant and secondly because of the firm's rule that partners had to be based in London.

The Liverpool office, in the National Bank Building, James Street, employing twelve staff, and with a turnover of £6,800 generating profits of £1,440 was not as viable as the Leeds concern. The lower rate of return may in part have been occasioned by its broader catchment area. In 1930–31 24,927 hours were worked of which 15,572 (62 per cent) were for shipping companies in Liverpool and a further 2,916 (12 per cent) for local clients, while 5,591 hours (23 per cent) were accounted for activities in Manchester and 848 (3 per cent) in Glasgow.[177] The question of opening an office in Manchester was considered and the partnership concluded that the time seemed 'opportune':

> There are signs that the depression in the cotton industry is passing the same way as in the Yorkshire woollen industry. Further, there is the prospect of the new work in connection with the textile machinists merger and also in connection with the Renold and Coventry chain merger. Our opportunities in each of those directions would be much more favourable were we represented on the spot.[178]

Accordingly, J.M. Horsley was transferred from London on 1 April 1932 to open the Manchester office, in the Lloyds Bank Building, King Street, which was then placed under the overall supervision of J.O. Collett. When Searle retired as manager in charge of Liverpool, that office also came under his authority. The London partners had considerable confidence in Collett concluding that

> he has powers of organisation, driving force and personality; creates a good impression upon and soon gains the confidence of clients and succeeds in imbuing his staff with his own spirit of enthusiasm thereby getting the best out of them.[179]

It was not until September 1939, when L.H. Norman was transferred from London to replace Horsley, that Manchester and Liverpool were granted autonomy from Leeds to be run by their respective managers.[180]

The Glasgow office, the first to be opened by Price Waterhouse in Scotland, arose from the needs of the LMS railway audit. In October 1937 Sir Nicholas Waterhouse, who had overall responsibility for the work, reported that arrangements had been concluded with the railway company for Price Waterhouse to take rooms in their office building, but a brass plate was not to be placed on the front door 'as we do not hold out that we have an office in Glasgow'.[181]

In February 1939 W. Harrison and T. Howarth were delegated to investigate the possibility of setting up an office in Birmingham.[182] In view of the threat of war and the wisdom of dispersing the firm's records and work, it was decided in October to establish a base in that city. G.B. Pollard, who had recently returned to Britain from the Continental Firm's Berlin office, was appointed manager-in-charge.[183]

The Newcastle office of Price Waterhouse was in part the product of a merger with the local firm of Monkhouse, Goddard & Co. (see below). Unlike other branches, it was the only regional office which had partners – this fact reflecting its size and origins. On the formation of the merged firm in 1920, the first partners were J.H. Armstrong, Thomas Harrison, Norman Harrison, J.B. Swan and T.P. Parmeter, together with W.F. King from the London office.[184]

Monkhouse, Goddard & Co. had been founded in 1868 by George B. Monkhouse and soon became one of Newcastle's leading practices.[185] Monkhouse, who had originally trained in Messrs Backhouses' Bank at Darlington,[186] joined Frederick Robertson Goddard, who, aged twenty-one, had just completed his articles with Gillespie, Swithinbank & Co. Monkhouse was described by a contemporary as being of 'an intensely nervous temperament but underlying his outward appearance of irritability, there was . . . a store of good nature and large-heartedness'.[187] The business grew swiftly in both Newcastle and Cleveland. In 1882, however, Monkhouse decided to move to London where he opened an office, becoming in the same year a Council member of the ICAEW. The premature death of Goddard in 1891 resulted in the senior partnership passing to J.H. Armstrong, son of William Armstrong, a mining engineer. Under his leadership the firm built up an extensive audit clientele of colliery and electrical undertakings.[188] Branch offices were opened in London (under the style of Armstrong, Harrison, Swan & Co.)[189] and in Carlisle. Staff also made regular visits to the Continent in connection with the interests of Armstrong Whitworth.

The Newcastle merger appears to have been a success with the smaller Price Waterhouse practice being absorbed within the Monkhouse,

Goddard organisation, now renamed Price Waterhouse. The partnership suffered considerably in the early thirties as the depression was particularly severe in the north east. Yet in 1932 they began to take a more optimistic view:

> on any trade revival taking place, it was the opinion of the Newcastle partners that the practice there would quickly reap the benefit as we had practically no competitors. Peats appear to have made no impression in Newcastle and their presence was not felt by us . . . It was pointed out that the London partners had a large sum invested in Newcastle business . . . The results of the last three years represented a return of only nine per cent on the total amount invested.[190]

The Newcastle office, as distinct from the UK branches opened by Price Waterhouse, created its own unique problems. Being a partnership, which was in part the product of a formerly independent firm, there was a natural desire to maintain a higher level of autonomy than elsewhere. By 1932 this distinction was apparent and Garnsey observed that

> there was a general feeling in London that the Newcastle practice was becoming rather isolated in the sense that there was not much close co-operation between the London and Newcastle partners . . . It was the intention that regular half-yearly or other periodical meetings should be held.[191]

Despite this attempt to forge closer links, the Newcastle firm remained somewhat detached from the rest of the UK partnership until its progressive integration during the 1960s.

In terms of profits the Newcastle practice was about one-tenth the size of the UK Firm (Table 13, see Appendix). Between 1934 and 1939 its profits were never less than £19,136 (1935) and reached a maximum of £22,476 in 1938.[192] When a new partnership deed was drawn up in 1939, the Newcastle firm comprised, in order of seniority, three partners: W.F. King, T.P. Parmeter and J.M.S. Coates.[193] The latter, having served in the First World War and completed his articles, joined Monkhouse, Goddard & Co. a year before they merged with Price Waterhouse.[194] His determination and ability brought him promotion and in 1924, at the age of thirty-three, Coates was admitted to the partnership.[195]

Frederick's Place: Routines and Character

By the 1930s Price Waterhouse had taken over the remaining parts of No. 2 Frederick's Place, and had progressively occupied No. 1, the corner house, formerly used by E. Winterbotham, a solicitor.[196] The entrance hall was panelled and the building furnished throughout in oak and mahogany.[197] Partners' rooms had leather upholstered chairs, and, as Southall recalled,

> held rows of black boxes with the name of a client painted in white letters . . . There was no display of modern art in the corridors and what pictures there were tended to be steel engravings of buildings in the City, some with a little colour.[198]

Although the firm had spread through several buildings, it had not yet achieved a size where staff would not know each other by name. A family atmosphere with overtones of a gentleman's club prevailed.

Routines remained relatively straightforward and unvarying. Hours were from 9.30 a.m. to 5.30 p.m. Monday to Friday, and from 9.30 a.m. to 1 p.m. on Saturdays.[199] Staff engaged on audits were required to report every Monday and Friday morning. They queued in the hallway to inform the most junior partner (who was entrusted with the 'book' which recorded work in progress) of their activities. Otherwise audit staff spent little time at Frederick's Place, being for the most part at the premises of the firm's clients. As a result the office was principally occupied by the partners and specialist staff (such as those engaged on taxation, estates and share registrations) together with their attendant administrators, typists and comptometer operators.

Most members of the audit staff were not attached to any particular partner, manager or client (with the exception of those engaged upon railway or insurance work). This 'fluidity', according to Southall,

> was very beneficial; it spread different points of view, widened outlooks and eased personal relations.[200]

W.E. Parker, then an articled clerk, recalled the variety of audit work:

> To begin with, I spent a week at the Foundling Hospital . . . a week at the Brompton Hospital . . . three days at the Hearts of Oak

Benefit Society in Tottenham Court Road and three weeks at Dunn's hat factory in Camden Town. One never knew where one was going to be sent next; it might be anywhere in Britain ... My first out-of-London job was not long in coming ... I was sent over to Belfast for six weeks to join the dozen or so PW men who were working on the accounts of Harland & Wolff.[201]

A feature of the interwar period was the gradual mechanisation of office routines. Typewriters had been introduced at Price Waterhouse in the early 1900s and progressively replaced script for letters, reports and even financial records. In February 1938 the firm purchased a second-hand Addressograph for £85 with which they were reported as being 'very satisfied'. Reliable calculating machines had been mass-produced in America from the 1870s, and in 1922 a comptometer was devised which could automatically multiply and divide.[202] It is not certain when Price Waterhouse purchased their first comptometers though it appears to have been in the mid-1930s. Perhaps intending to extend this early mechanisation, the London office sought to evaluate the efficiency of the machines being used in Leeds and Newcastle. A report in 1936 concluded that

each machine plus operator would be equal to about three juniors, or say 1½ semi-senior assistants. It is quite possible that an intelligent girl with a machine might easily, from the point of view of fee earning, become equivalent of at least one junior.[203]

It was envisaged that the comptometer could be used for casting and checking stocks and wages considerably faster and so allow more time for detailed verification. J.O. Collett was reported as having discovered a large defalcation at ICI's Billingham works by examining wage records with the help of a comptometer.

No detailed record of staff numbers was kept throughout the interwar period. However, in December 1936 M.C. Spencer analysed employees by length of service.[204] He discovered that out of a total of 383 around 180 (47 per cent) had been with Price Waterhouse for more than ten years. Of the remainder, 109 had more than three years' service (28 per cent). This represented a remarkable example of continuity. Nevertheless, employees changed jobs less often than today, and moving between professional firms as a way of gaining promotion was not favourably regarded.

The absence of records makes it impossible to know where staff came from, their social background or education. However, there were few graduates in the firm, because many chose to serve articles rather than opt for a university course. After the First World War, as Southall recalled, it was decided to recruit only qualified seniors as auditors and this may have narrowed the class from which the firm drew its employees. Many of the articled clerks seem to have been from public schools and W.E. Parker, who joined the firm in 1926 on leaving Winchester, found himself among kindred spirits:

> I am bound to confess that things were rather more enjoyable when I found myself working with fellow-Wykehamists. There were a number of these, among them Claude Ashton ... a chap called Brown ... and an older Wykehamist, Thring, who was no athlete but a most charming companion.[205]

Articled clerks had paid a substantial premium (500 guineas) in order to train at Price Waterhouse and received no salary. They, recalled Parker, 'were rightly treated as a privileged class'.[206]

During the latter part of the nineteenth century and the interwar period Price Waterhouse became a training ground for ambitious and able accountants. Many joined, either after qualification or as articled clerks, to gain experience before moving to posts in industry, to a partnership in another firm, to set up on their own account or to work abroad. The following examples illustrate this trend. Harold Barton and Basil Mayhew left Price Waterhouse in December 1907 to set up in practice; Henry Savill served five years of articles before joining his father's partnership, A. Savill & Sons; R.F.W. Fincham joined the Law Guarantee Society after three years' service; E.C.N. Palmer, having served his articles with Sir Laurence Halsey, became a director of Huntley & Palmers; while A.G. West, S.S. North and J.G. Gibson all entered partnerships.[207]

In the interwar period it was not uncommon for members of the audit staff to be recruited by clients needing accountancy personnel. R.A. Kinnes, for example, left Price Waterhouse in 1935 to become chief accountant at Courtaulds. In 1938–9 several of the directors there had raised the issue of breaking down the organisation into specific operating companies, linked together by a central holding company with overall control of policy and finance. Kinnes persevered with this objective and in 1943 asked Price Waterhouse to prepare a report. Despite the firm's favourable verdict, the idea was shelved until Kinnes' persistent pressure secured its approval in January 1947.[208]

7

Price Waterhouse Abroad

By 1918 Price Waterhouse had begun a territorial expansion which was ultimately to lead to the creation of an international network of offices. Partnerships had already been established in America (from 1899), Cairo (1907), Buenos Aires (1913) and four locations in Canada (1914).[1] In addition the firm had entered into an agency arrangement in 1896 with Davey Flack & Co. in Australia. The First World War had drawn Price Waterhouse to the Continent and premises were set up in Rotterdam in 1914, Petrograd in 1916 (though closed in the following year) and Paris in 1917. Some of these overseas enterprises involved collaboration with W.B. Peat & Co., notably the Egyptian Firm (partnership jointly from 1911) and the Russian venture,[2] while the formal opening of the Rotterdam office in 1919 at Coolsingel 15c (Standard Bank Building) was a joint activity under the style Price, Waterhouse, Peat & Co.[3] This territorial expansion had not, however, been undertaken in a spirit of imperial conquest but rather in an attempt to serve existing or new clients as the latter developed in new regions. It had been a reactive, not a proactive, process. The progressive growth of businesses across national boundaries accelerated this trend during the interwar period, drawing Price Waterhouse into the Continent and to the Dominions.

Development of the Practice

Initially, the two Continental offices, Rotterdam and Paris, remained branches of the UK Firm and were supervised by managers rather than partners. As the volume of referred business increased, particularly from America, it was decided that a more substantial organisation was required. In view of the arrangement which already existed in Egypt with W.B. Peat & Co. and the recent merger talks, a joint Continental Firm was established in October 1920 under the style Price, Waterhouse, Peat

& Co.[4] W.E. Seatree, hitherto a partner in the US Firm of Price Waterhouse, was elected to the partnership together with W.M. McKinnon, who recently had been appointed as Price Waterhouse's resident partner in Paris, and with R.W. Ramsden, then manager in charge of the Rotterdam office. In the event McKinnon was not included in the deed of 14 March 1921 (effective from 1 July 1920) having withdrawn from the venture.[5] The first meeting of partners and managers was held on 7 January 1922 at the firm's Brussels office, 19 Rue de la Chancellerie. Seatree took the chair and A.E. Jones (representing the UK Firm) attended; G.H. Evans – 'laid up with influenza' – was unable to be present.[6]

In March 1921 Seatree moved the Paris office, headquarters of the Continental Firm, to larger premises at 47 Avenue de l'Opéra.[7] Originally occupying only the third floor this accommodation had become overcrowded by 1935 and new premises were sought. Agreement could not be reached with Chase Bank to occupy their premises in the Rue Cambon, and their landlords at Avenue de l'Opéra allowed them to take the fourth floor as well as half of the fifth.[8] The firm remained there until 1973.[9]

When W.B. Peat & Co. decided to merge their UK firm with the American practice of Marwick Mitchell in 1924, it was necessary to terminate the joint partnership with Price Waterhouse since the latter already had a Paris office. Henceforth the Continental Firm was known simply as Price Waterhouse & Co. Even so, the two firms continued to act together in South America, India, Egypt and South Africa.[10]

William Ernest Seatree served as the first senior partner of the Continental Firm. Born at Penrith, he was educated at St Bees School in Whitehaven. He may have been a son or close relative of George Seatree, a corn dealer in Penrith, who from the 1870s pioneered many of the famous rock climbs in the Lake District.[11] George Seatree's experiences, published under the title *Lakeland Memories*,[12] reveal a tough and adventurous personality undaunted by challenge. W.E. Seatree was articled to James Watson of Carlisle and qualified in 1899. Two years later he applied for a post in the American Firm of Price Waterhouse. Initially he worked in New York where his ability and determination attracted the attention of May; in July 1906, at the age of twenty-nine, Seatree was admitted to the partnership. He had also qualified as a Certified Public Accountant and taken American citizenship. Following his promotion Seatree transferred to the Chicago office.[13] There he wrote a pamphlet entitled *Relation of the Auditor to the Valuation of Inventories*[14] which relied heavily on English case law for its evidence.

During the First World War Seatree was released by the US Firm to take accounting responsibility for the accounts of the Canadian YMCA in Paris. His ability in organising this task brought him not only a special commendation from General Pershing, commander of the American forces in Europe, but official recognition by the French government.[15] When the hostilities ceased, Seatree went back to America but his love of French culture and of the individual nature of work there, led him to return to the Continent.[16] Pollard, who himself was to become senior partner of the European Firm (as it was renamed after 1945), described Seatree as a 'forceful personality' who 'displayed many contradictory traits':

> He was autocratic yet fundamentally kind and considerate, highly intelligent yet quite unable to acquire a grasp of any foreign language, shrewd yet spontaneous. He had a marked business acumen yet was always motivated by the highest ideals of accountancy. Fundamentally he was an individualist who would not be squeezed into conventional patterns ... His use of English though sometimes unorthodox, was always vivid and rarely failed to make the impact he sought. He had a passion for the use of capital letters for his nouns, especially in report writing. Indeed, this peculiarity was once brought up at a partners' meeting but he dismissed the matter by asserting that 'no general rules can be laid down'.[17]

Marcel Contil, who worked in the Paris concern during the twenties, recalled that the office was 'under the dictatorship of Mr Seatree with his boundless vitality and professional abilities. He terrified the staff who did not know him well but he had a sense of humour.'[18]

Seatree was unusual among Price Waterhouse partners of the interwar period because he had been divorced at a time when legal separation was considered almost shocking. This was, in part, a reflection of the different culture existing in France and America but also revealed something of Seatree's 'forceful personality'. Tull, when expressing his general criticisms in 1946, thought it 'intolerable' that the senior partner of the Continental Firm should be divorced and believed that he should have retired.[19] This, too, reinforces Pollard's judgement that Seatree was a man of individual character.

A small office had been opened in Brussels shortly after the end of the war, and in November 1921 Thomas Lowe Ferguson, who had been on the Paris staff since January 1920 and who had a Belgian wife, was appointed as manager in charge there.[20] An office was established at Bucharest in December 1923 by Frederick Thompson chiefly to handle work arising from the Shell and Phoenix Oil companies. Thompson had served his articles with Monkhouse, Goddard & Co. before joining Price Waterhouse in 1915, transferring to Rotterdam four years later.[21]

The character of work on the Continent was quite different from that in Britain and, as a result, attracted different personalities. While the duties performed by qualified staff in London were for the most part dominated by auditing, that is regular and recurring assignments according to set standards, the accountant in Italy, Germany or France could not expect such uniformity in his practice. There were fewer regulations on the Continent and greater room for accounting manoeuvre. In France, for example, the standing of the profession was comparatively low and often audits were performed by unqualified staff, the procedure itself being of a superficial nature. However, parent companies in the UK and America increasingly required that financial reporting on their overseas' operations conform to their national regulations and this entailed much reorganisation and investigative work. By 1919, for example, twenty-one of the largest 200 companies in the UK had overseas subsidiaries; by 1930 the number had risen to sixty-two and by 1948 to seventy-three.[22] Since these figures recorded only incorporated enterprises and excluded branches of UK registered businesses, they understated the extent of British commercial involvement abroad. Special assignments were as common as audits and these could involve a degree of ingenuity in coping with problems of language, the peculiarities of an unfamiliar business and local regulations. For the young, recently qualified accountant several years in the Continental Firm represented an adventure, an opportunity to travel and fewer constraints than in the London office. For many the lifestyle had a compelling quality and they continued to work on the Continent, occasionally moving to different cities, only returning to Britain for holidays or to retire.

Price Waterhouse were not alone in following this territorial expansion. Whinney, Smith & Whinney and Brown, Fleming & Murray set up a joint partnership, Whinney Murray, to handle their Continental and

Middle Eastern operations, opening offices in Paris and Antwerp (1920), Berlin (1924), Hamburg (1925) and Warsaw (1934). Similarly Deloittes established offices in Paris (1920), Rome (1923), Brussels and Antwerp (1924), Milan (1927) and with Binder, Hamlyn & Co. in Vienna and Berlin (1924).[23]

A rare portrayal of what it was like to be employed in an accountancy firm was provided by Bruce Marshall, an Edinburgh chartered accountant who had worked in the Paris office of a major firm (possibly Peat Marwick Mitchell) during the twenties.[24] Set in 1933–4, his novel *The Bank Audit*, written from the standpoint of a member of staff with no immediate prospects of partnership, offers an insight into the attitudes and behaviour of audit clerks and managers:

> Tarbolton was the managing clerk, overworked, intelligent and industrious, and Sir Eric Stugby Wharton, [the senior partner of the UK Firm] had heard about him; but he knew nothing about the audit clerks who worked under Tarbolton . . . it was not in the interest of the local partners to let the London partners know too much about the excellence of their subordinates.[25]

A slight recession occurred in the fortunes of the Continental Firm in 1923 after the French occupation of the Ruhr had precipitated the runaway inflation of the mark. In November 1923 G.O. May wrote to Sir Albert Wyon to suggest that 'some new arrangement' should be found for handling the great volume of referred work undertaken in Germany; this, he observed, had attained 'such proportions' that 'our own reputation and connections were deeply involved'.[26] Such assignments, which were later to be managed by the Berlin office, included Brown, Harriman & Co. Inc., German Credit & Investment Corporation, L.C. Smith & Corona Typewriter Co. and Wm. R. Warner & Co.[27] The inflation of 1923–4 was being brought under control following the publication of the Dawes Plan. In June 1924 the issue of setting up in Germany was discussed by the partners. It was reported that Turquand, Youngs & Co. were considering establishing an office in Berlin and Ramsden added

> that it was becoming increasingly difficult, owing to constantly changing circumstances, to keep track of the German Tax Laws, and it would therefore be desirable, if and when the question of a representative in Berlin came to be discussed, to have someone with

a legal mind coupled with a sufficiently good knowledge of German . . .[28]

It was unanimously agreed that the time had arrived to open an office in Berlin, and also in Madrid.[29] As a result, Ramsden transferred from Rotterdam as the resident partner and was joined by J.W.F. Neill as the manager. H.O. Norris Helmsley, an English chartered accountant who had joined the US Firm before the war and who had served in France, had been persuaded by Seatree to leave Pittsburgh for Paris; he, too, moved to Germany and became a Berlin partner in 1925.[30] Seatree consistently encouraged members of the UK and US practices to join the Continental Firm as a way of reinforcing links between the three, particularly as the last relied on much referred work from Britain and America.

The German practice of Price Waterhouse grew rapidly. In December 1932, for example, it was reported that the firm there was 'in need of further English staff and it was decided that . . . the offices there should take on some of the temporary staff that were employed in Paris during the last busy season'.[31] Apart from the regular examination of the accounts of British and American subsidiaries, investigations were undertaken into major German companies seeking finance through dollar bond issues on the US market. An extensive clientele was acquired following work for an international electric lamp pool. Under the terms of the Dawes Plan the Reparations Commission in Paris was replaced by an Agent General for Reparations Payments with offices in Berlin, and Price Waterhouse became the organisation's auditors. Additional offices were opened in Düsseldorf in 1927 to manage important audits connected with the financing of the Ruhr steel industry, and at Hamburg in 1928. The latter closed in 1934 largely because a number of its leading clients had transferred their headquarters to Berlin.[32]

Until 1931 German companies were not legally required to have their accounts audited. In that year a new act made the annual audit binding for every public corporation or *Aktiengesellschaft*, and the work was to be performed by a professional accountant (*Wirtschaftsprüfer*) or a firm whose partners held this qualification. With the transfer of Ramsden to Paris, the two partners in Berlin were Hemsley and Neill, neither of whom had served articles in Germany.[33] After much negotiation with the authorities they were both admitted as Wirtschaftsprüfer on the basis of an oral examination.[34] The Berlin office not only handled work within Germany but, because of its territorial position, supervised assignments in Austria, Hungary, Czechoslovakia, Poland, the Baltic States and the Saar, though in 1934 control of Vienna and Budapest passed to the Paris office.

Richard Cuthbert Duffill, who had joined the Berlin office of Price Waterhouse shortly after it was established, was of such interest to Paul Theroux, the travel writer, that he recalled having met him on the Orient-Express between Paris and Istanbul. Duffill, an accomplished linguist had worked for the Inter-Allied Plebiscite Commission from 1919 being based at Allenstein, Klagenfurt and then Berlin. After about ten years with the Continental Firm he resigned in 1935, returning to England to become chief accountant to an American film company. Theroux speculated that he had been gathering information for the British secret service and was on the point of being discovered. When he left Europe Duffill was, as photographs showed, a 'very stylish dresser – waistcoat, plus-fours, cashmere overcoat, homburg, stick pin'.[35] Whether Duffill was in fact involved in espionage remains conjecture, though it is likely that a few expatriate accountants, whose duties took them around the Continent, were indeed engaged in intelligence-gathering as war threatened.

During the early twenties there was a rising volume of work undertaken in Italy. In particular Harold Edwards spent a lot of time on referred work for Vickers-Armstrong in Pozzuoli, near Naples.[36] Hence, an office was opened in Via Silvio Pellico, Milan, in November 1926 with Ralph Grut as the resident manager. Thompson took charge in March 1928 and was admitted to the partnership two years later, a reflection of the volume of business conducted in Italy. The investigations required by the financing of Italian public utilities and industrial concerns on the US stock market, together with a major banking scandal, earned substantial fees for the firm. These included reports upon Montecatini, Pirelli, Isotta Fraschini, Breda and Ercole Marelli – all situated in Milan, Società Idroelettrica Piemontese in Turin, the Terni group in Genoa, Società Adriatica de Elettricità in Venice and Cosulich in Trieste. As in the UK, such assignments would sometimes be followed by the firm's appointment on an annual basis. In March 1929 a base with a small resident staff was established in Genoa, which quickly developed when the New Jersey oil audits were acquired a few years later.

Two major bank assignments were undertaken in these early years. The first, in 1929, concerned the Banca Italo-Britannica, an Italian bank formed by a consortium of British bankers, which had run into difficulties following irregular transactions effected by the two senior executives. A lengthy inquiry ensued which resulted in a liquidation. An investigation was also undertaken into the affairs of the Banca d'America e d'Italia, which covered the period 1930–1 and initially required some forty members of staff.[37]

The Milan office proved to be a rewarding training ground for newly qualified accountants. The ingenuity and resourcefulness with which local accounts were sometimes prepared introduced junior staff to the full rigours of practical business. Coincidentally, the first three post-war senior partners of the European Firm of Price Waterhouse had each served a lengthy period in Italy.

Price Waterhouse had undertaken work in Switzerland for some years before the establishment of their Zürich office in May 1937. In the previous year Evans and Edwards had been entrusted with the task of compiling a feasibility report on 'the possibility of domiciling the Continental Firm in Switzerland and the establishment of a Swiss Firm'.[38] They concluded that both were desirable and that Zürich was preferable to Basle, Berne or Geneva as the site for their office.[39] The first representative of the firm was J.H. Watts, who was married to a Swiss national. Using a room in his apartment for the storage of files and to accommodate his secretary, he set up a base in 1933 intended simply as an outpost of the Paris office.[40] Among his most important clients were BIS, Lloyds Bank, NCR, Lumina AG (now Shell Switzerland), Standard Oil and Aluminiumwerke. In October 1935 it was decided to file 'an application, in the name of the French firm, for permission to act as bank auditor',[41] though the question as to whether this might involve the opening of an office was held in abeyance. This was, in part, a response to a new federal law for banks and savings associations which required that a list of recognised auditors be drawn up. Price Waterhouse were included in the thirteen appointed, the only international firm so to be recognised.[42]

In September 1936, when the annual workload in the country had reached 6,000 hours of which about 3,500 were in the neighbourhood of Zürich, Seatree decided it was time to establish a formal office.[43] Ramsden transferred from Paris to take charge of the permanent staff of five. The office, registered with the Swiss authorities in June 1937 and located at Talstrasse 9, was soon given responsibility for those countries in Europe where Price Waterhouse had no representation – Austria, Spain, Portugal, Yugoslavia, Greece, Bulgaria and Turkey, the so-called 'neutral territories'. Morocco and the North African states were, however, treated as the preserve of the Paris office. The practice grew at such a rate that by the end of 1937 the Zürich staff had risen to fifteen (ten qualified auditors and five administrative and secretarial employees). In March 1938 authorisation to perform bank audits was transferred from the Paris office to the Swiss Firm.[44]

The Continental Firm achieved a considerable measure of commercial success during the interwar period (Table 7, see Appendix). The fee income had grown steadily in the twenties as new offices were opened and staff numbers rose from seventy-five in 1922 to 202 by 1930. A new partnership deed signed in that year saw the admission of W.G. Eden, T.L. Ferguson, J.W.F. Neill and F. Thompson, thereby doubling its strength.[45] The practice continued to expand, reaching a peak in 1938 when it comprised nine partners and around 250 staff (about half of whom were accounted for by the French and German Firms) located in nine offices – Paris, Brussels, Berlin, Düsseldorf, Rotterdam, Milan, Bucharest, Stockholm and Zürich.[46] The majority of the staff were expatriates and around half the total were British chartered accountants, though Berlin office had only 30 per cent so qualified. In December 1938, expressing concern at their declining proportion, Seatree ruled that their numbers should not be allowed 'to fall below 50 per cent unless local laws and conditions made this minimum impossible of attainment'.[47]

The accounts for the Continental Firm for the nine months to 31 March 1936 revealed that Germany was the most profitable partnership (with a surplus of 322,778 Swiss francs) followed by France (268,115), Belgium (93,552), Holland (68,768), Italy (43,602), Sweden (37,061) and Romania (21,273), while Switzerland and the neutral territories contributed 14,735.[48]

Following the admission of Willem Voors in 1934, T.W. Webster became a partner in July 1935 and Harold Edwards followed three years later.[49] Edwards had been a manager in the Paris office where he specialised in tax work;[50] this fact almost prevented him from being promoted in a firm which revered the generalist. However, as Thompson observed,

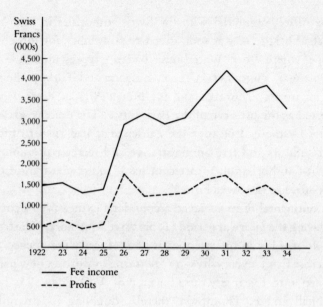

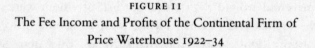

FIGURE II

The Fee Income and Profits of the Continental Firm of
Price Waterhouse 1922–34

Edwards has brains and good manners and presents well . . . Also he
has the courage of his convictions and will make an active and
useful collaborator . . . I am sorry that he has been sunk in a
specialised job.[51]

The Continental Firm had grown almost without design or structure
since its inception. It responded to the demands of clients and the market
by opening offices and establishing partnerships as needs and opportunities arose. In 1938 when the Continental Firm comprised a substantial
organisation in its own right, there were signs that this loose confedera-
tion, run by the dictatorial Seatree, was encountering difficulties. However, the partners seemed unprepared. Charles Evans, a partner in Paris,
wrote to May and Waterhouse:

As to the general organisation of the firm and the questions affecting
its future – this is a wide subject. Operating as we do in about two
dozen countries with a very great variety of governments, peoples,

laws, languages, accounting standards, financial, monetary and social conditions, one can do little more than live day to day and deal with problems as they arise – 'cross over bridges when we come to them'.[52]

Ferguson, based in Brussels, had no clearer notion of how the firm might develop:

the Continental organisation does not possess any one individual who would be capable of guiding the destiny of the firm with anything like the wisdom and authority of Mr Seatree. It consequently looks to me as if . . . the tendency must inevitably be to develop along broader lines.[53]

No solution was found to the problems posed by the success of the Continental Firm, partly because the events of 1939 rendered the question obsolete. Within the space of a year every office (with the exception of Stockholm and Zürich, located in neutral territories) had closed and their British staff been evacuated to the UK or America.

The Kreuger Fraud

In January 1932 Price Waterhouse received instructions from the International Telephone & Telegraph Corporation (ITTC) to examine the accounts of the L.M. Ericsson Telephone Company of Sweden, which then belonged to Ivar Kreuger. Born in Sweden and an engineer by training, Kreuger had entered into partnership with Toll as building contractors. Together they had won the prestigious contracts to construct the Swedish Olympic Stadium (1912) and the Stockholm town hall. Kreuger, who through his father had contacts with the country's match industry, organised a merger between two leading groups in 1917 to create the Swedish Match Co., of which he then became managing director.[54] During the 1920s Swedish Match expanded rapidly, concluding production agreements with a number of governments. These often included loans and the Swedish Match group became an international credit institution. The reputation of Kreuger grew with that of his companies. However, the boom ended with the New York stock exchange crash in October 1929 and two years later rumours spread that

Kreuger had difficulty in meeting all his financial commitments. He had acquired substantial interests in other industries including L.M. Ericsson in an attempt to build up a monopoly in European telephone companies. In New York, the International Telephone and Telegraph Corporation (ITTC) expressed an interest in Ericsson and in May 1931 Kreuger, hard pressed for funds, crossed the Atlantic to negotiate the sale of a majority shareholding in return for cash.[55] Having given him an advance payment of eleven million dollars, the completion of the deal was subject to an audit of Ericsson's affairs. In preliminary discussions an Ericsson official disclosed to E.R. Niemela, a manager in Price Waterhouse New York, and G.F. Chinlund, controller of ITTC, that about 27.5 million Swedish kroner listed as 'cash' actually consisted of claims against Kreuger companies.[56] This led ITTC to demand the return of their deposit. In March 1932 Kreuger, aware that his fraud was on the point of being exposed, committed suicide in his Paris apartment on Avenue Victor Emmanuel. Realising that his illegal financial dealings were of a complex interrelated nature, the Swedish government appointed a six-man investigative commission, and they in turn instructed Price Waterhouse to make an examination of the entire Kreuger & Toll group from 1918.

A preliminary report by the firm was read at the Riksdag in Stockholm on 5 April 1932. This concluded that the Kreuger & Toll accounts for 1930 had grossly misrepresented the true financial position of the company.[57] The full investigation took seven months to complete and required the assembly of a team gathered from the various Continental offices and London. Seatree, as senior partner, travelled to Stockholm to take charge of the inquiry, while Thompson, Neill and Webster also played a major part. G.O. May took an active role in negotiations with creditors. The final report, issued in November 1932, revealed fraud on a grand scale and an overall deficiency of many hundred million kroner. For example, Kreuger had borrowed money on the security of fictitious match concessions, forged Italian government bonds, pledged German government bonds turned over as collateral for loans, and appropriated large sums from his five principal companies, some of which were used to acquire unsubscribed portions of his own capital issues and to bolster up declining dividends.[58]

The Kreuger affair became an international *cause célèbre*. The frauds had survived undetected for so long because of the lax state of company law which allowed Kreuger to maintain a high level of secrecy around the group's affairs. In January 1933, G.O. May testified to the United States Banking and Currency Sub-Committee, observing that

> the Kreuger & Toll frauds could not have been concealed if either the audits of the companies had been co-ordinated under a single control, or if the audits, though not so co-ordinated, had been carried out in all cases with a proper honesty, efficiency and independence.[59]

As a result of the investigation, new corporate legislation was framed in Sweden though it was not adopted until 1944 and did not become operative for a further four years.

To Price Waterhouse the affair brought much kudos and considerable commercial reward. Seatree was made Commander of the Order of Vasa, second class,[60] and the firm were appointed joint auditors of the Swedish Match Co. and its principal subsidiaries.

In November 1932 the firm petitioned the King of Sweden for permission to open an office in Stockholm.[61] In view of the work they had undertaken on the Kreuger fraud, the request to 'carry on an auditing business' was granted and Price Waterhouse became the first foreign firm to enter the country in this way.[62] The Stockholm office was opened at Kungsgatan 30 in March 1933 and Thompson was appointed partner in charge. Ironically, only five years earlier Sir Gilbert Garnsey had pressed Seatree to open a Stockholm office to handle the accounts of Electrolux and the Skefco Ball Bearing Co.,[63] but the latter was unimpressed and had argued:

> as a matter of broad policy, we are not anxious to have a number of small offices which are unprofitable and ... we are at present burdened with one of this character, viz. Bucharest. As you also know neither here nor in America have we ever descended to 'touting' for work in any city ... and I should not care to start in Stockholm.[64]

Apart from the Swedish Match Co., Price Waterhouse gained several other important audits including L.M. Ericsson[65] and Aug Stenman AB, Eskilstuna, a manufacturer of screws and fasteners, acquired by Guest Keen & Nettlefolds in 1930.[66] The majority of the work, however, was referred from overseas and included assignments for Esso and Shell, and for other film companies such as Columbia, Fox and Metro-Goldwyn-Mayer.

Relations with the US Firm

The formal exchange of staff between America and Britain had been discussed by G.O. May and A.L. Dickinson early in 1914 (p. 96) though implementation of the scheme had been prevented by the outbreak of war. In January 1929 G.O. May again raised the matter. It appeared that the US Firm were acutely short of 'really competent men' and were 'faced with the alternative of refusing business or running the risk of trouble through using unsatisfactory staff'.[67] Given that the US Firm were making a substantial contribution to the UK partnership's profits, May suggested that it 'might be an opportune time to give effect to the idea that some of your promising men ought to have American experience'.[68] Accordingly, in that year Adams, Forrest, Pawlyn and Hauxwell crossed the Atlantic to work in New York.[69] A total of nineteen London staff were sent on exchange between 1929 and 1938, while six Americans came to the City in 1936–7.

Not only did the scheme maintain links between the two firms but it also provided the respective practices with an insight into each other's methods of working and attitudes. T.B. Robson, who was seconded to the New York office for five months in 1933[70] recalled that the exchange had not been planned adequately:

> I did get a few assignments but had a general feeling of frustration and conviction that a programme ought to have been worked out beforehand so as to make the visit really beneficial in the technical respects ... But the visit was invaluable in the personal contacts which I made.[71]

W.E. Parker, who followed him in 1934, had previously been involved in an investigation of the reporting policies endorsed by the UK and US partnerships. May had been convinced by the Royal Mail case that 'the firm and the profession in Britain were miles behind the times and miles behind the Americans'. He then persuaded the London partners to put me [Parker] at his disposal for a study to be conducted simultaneously in London and New York of the standards of disclosure in accounts for which (a) PW and (b) other firms were responsible ... His instructions were to take the published accounts of 50 major British companies, 25 PW clients and 25 others, and be as critical of them as I liked. The parallel study of 50 American companies was to be done in New York office by his own son, Oliver May ... Several of the London partners were not too pleased with some of the things I had had to say about accounts for which they had been responsible. Perhaps for that very reason George May was pleased with the result.[72]

As has been suggested, the dramatic reduction in the contribution made by the US Firm to the profits of the UK partnership (Table 6, see Appendix) in 1933 implies that a new agreement had been concluded. It was no longer possible to view the US practice as an offshoot of London. By the mid-thirties the American Firm had more partners and offices than the UK Firm. The majority of its qualified staff were American nationals who had received their training in the United States and had no natural allegiance to Britain. The American Firm of Price Waterhouse had come of age and saw itself as the equal of its progenitor. The relationship between the two was now one of mutual partnership.

G.O. May, tiring of the administrative duties attached to the post of senior executive partner and wishing to devote more time to writing and lecturing, approached Sterrett, his colleague, for advice. The latter suggested that resignation would allow 'an opportunity for a younger man to assume broader responsibilities'.[73] He proposed William B. Campbell, describing him as 'an exceptional man'[74] possessing 'ability of an outstanding order'.[75] May was duly succeeded by Campbell on 1 January 1927 but remained a partner until 1940.[76]

India, South Africa and South America

In July 1920 Price Waterhouse concluded an agreement with W.B. Peat & Co. whereby they acquired a 50 per cent share in the latter's Indian firm.[77] In 1916 Peats had obtained a capital holding in Meugens, King & Simpson, a practice based in Calcutta and Cawnpore,[78] whereupon the style was changed to Meugens, Peat & Co. After 1920 it became Price,

Waterhouse, Peat & Co. The new partnership arrangement increased the amount of work undertaken by Price Waterhouse in the subcontinent. In 1921, for example, A.L. Dickinson accompanied by Cathles and W. Wright, spent many months investigating the accounting systems of various Indian railway companies.[79] Spencer made an extensive tour of India in 1923 to review the organisation of Price, Waterhouse, Peat & Co. and its business in general. Eventually the original partners were replaced by qualified staff from London: W.J. Younie, for example, was admitted in 1924 and in 1935 succeeded Law as the resident senior partner.

A second overseas partnership was formed in 1920 when Price Waterhouse and Peats agreed to act jointly in South Africa. Under the same style of Price, Waterhouse, Peat & Co. an office was opened at Standard Bank Chambers, Johannesburg, at the end of the year, with F.B. Gibbins from Peats' London headquarters in charge.[80] Initially the practice was slow to develop and in 1924 a merger with the Pretoria firm of Dougall, Lance & Hewitt followed.[81] Visiting Johannesburg and Pretoria in 1930, F.S. Price reported that the joint business

> in South Africa is a small one, the total fees amounting to only about £10,000 per annum but there seem good prospects of progress being made although it may not be very rapid . . . I judged that Mr Gibbins is well known to leading businessmen and he had quite a good reputation as an accountant.[82]

Johannesburg was the headquarters of the firm, with its two partners and a complement of fourteen including articled clerks and typists, while the Pretoria office had nine members of staff.[83]

In South America Price Waterhouse had established offices in Buenos Aires and Valparaiso before the First World War and acted as agents there for Peats. In 1915 the US partners decided that they wanted a greater level of involvement in the South American Firm and it was agreed that Richard Wilson, a manager in New York, should travel to Brazil in order to open an office in Rio de Janeiro.[84] Wilson arrived in October but after a few months accepted a post as a commercial accountant in an Argentine company and went to live in Buenos Aires.[85] In the same year it was arranged that Peats should be allowed to join the partnership and from January 1916 the style was altered to Price, Waterhouse & W.B. Peat.

In 1919–20 Sir Arthur Lowes Dickinson made an extensive visit to South America. He returned via New York where Dickinson wrote a forty-seven-page report which concluded

> It would have been better if instead of starting our own business in South America we had made arrangements with existing firms there to work for us on agency terms ... But having started the business we must go through with it and make a success whatever time and money it may cost. A firm cannot admit failure.[86]

As a result he recommended that a merger be concluded with Touche, Faller & Co. a well-established Buenos Aires practice. The union was effected in July 1921 and the combined firm was called Price Waterhouse, Faller & Co. despite the fact that W.B. Peat & Co. remained members of the partnership. This was because Touche, Faller & Co. was notably larger than the Price Waterhouse Peat firm, and Albert Faller, a popular and exceptionally able accountant, was a key figure. This dynamic and intelligent leader was described as being

> a dapper little man, always very well dressed, a strict disciplinarian, very just and fair in all his dealings, very well liked by staff and clients – people talked of Faller twenty years after he left Buenos Aires.[87]

He became senior partner of the merged firm and brought to the organisation offices in Buenos Aires, Rosario and Montevideo together with a staff which totalled fifty-four.

In September 1929 G.O. May and A.E. Jones, a partner in the UK Firm, left England for Buenos Aires on the MV *Alcantara*.[88] Their task was not only to review the various practices in South America but to find a successor for Faller who was due to retire in 1930. Their nominated successor was John J. Waite, an English chartered accountant who had worked in the Buenos Aires office of Deloittes from 1913 to 1918 when he took the prestigious post as chief accountant to the Argentine Great South Railway. Identifying his talent, Faller had recruited him directly into the partnership in 1929. It was agreed that Faller should retire in October 1929 and Waite should take over as the senior partner. In November 1935 the firm's style reverted to Price, Waterhouse, Peat & Co.[89] Visiting South America in 1936, F.S. Price reported that the practice's net annual profits currently totalled £48,500 and concluded that our own business has been put on a firmer and surer foundation during these few years and ... this is largely due to Mr Waite's wise decisions that certain aims of policy and organisation are essential and to his pertinacity in working assiduously until those aims have been realised.[90]

In Australia Price Waterhouse had established an agency arrangement with Flack & Flack but this had been discontinued after a difference of professional opinion with the US Firm.[91] In 1920 the latter raised the question of re-establishing links with the Australian firm, and it appears that a second agency agreement was concluded. In 1936 the UK partners discussed the possibility of a merger[92] but in the following year postponed the scheme on the grounds that 'Australia is rather a long way for us to become too intimately connected'.[93]

8

Price Waterhouse in the Second World War

> There will be time to audit
> The accounts later, there will be sunlight later
> And the equation will come out at last.
> Louis MacNeice, from *Autumn Journal* XXIV (1939)[1]

With memories of the First World War still vivid in many people's minds, the outbreak of hostilities in September 1939 was hardly greeted with the exuberant patriotism of August 1914; the mood was rather one of release from tension, fearful determination and grim resignation.[2] The character of the Second World War was different from the outset. Both conscription and a national register of occupations had been introduced a couple of days before the conflict began. Although rationing had not been considered necessary until the last year of the First World War, Chamberlain's government resorted to this expedient by January 1940. As it became clear that this would be a lengthy and genuinely world-wide conflict so state controls broadened. Never before had the government taken such far-reaching powers to intervene throughout the economy, regulating output, prices, wages and the distribution of goods. Among those civil servants and officials employed to administer and monitor these policies, account-ants played a crucial part. As a reserved occupation, they were recruited in large numbers to perform these duties, while those that remained in private practice often found themselves assisting clients affected by new wartime regulations governing production and taxation. While account-ants, as individuals, found themselves in great demand as the state's financial instruments, their firms, including Price Waterhouse, were subject to general economic disruption. For them loss of staff to the forces and government departments and the need to disperse client services were some of the most tangible effects of Britain going to war with Germany.

The Impact of War

In the uneasy peace of the late thirties, many young accountants had joined the Territorials and were therefore partially prepared for the conflict ahead.[3] Despite their profession being designated a 'reserved occupation' (for qualified men of twenty-five years and over and those of any age with ten years' experience),[4] many exempted accountants volunteered for active duties. In September 1939, just after war broke out, seventy-three members of Price Waterhouse staff were engaged in full-time military or other service.[5] Although Price Waterhouse could not deny their young men's patriotic wish to enlist, the manpower shortages that had been created led the partners to recommend that employees

> remain in their present positions in order that the business of the firm might be carried on and that such assistance might be given to the government as might be called for. It was considered particularly important that all key men should be retained and it was thought not impossible that efforts might be made later to withdraw certain men from national service to make use of their abilities in other directions.[6]

This pattern of behaviour was repeated in the firm's overseas offices where so many of the professional staff were expatriates. In December 1939 the South American practice reported that 'although the war has only been in progress some three months . . . we have already lost not less than 30 per cent of our audit staff in national service'.[7]

In these circumstances of grave shortages it was understandable that a letter was sent to all members of staff serving in the armed forces pointing out that the outbreak of hostilities had necessitated 'the cessation of your services to the firm' and ended any entitlement to pay. An offer was made to consider the reinstatement of employees when peace was restored.[8] Given the tradition established in the First World War of guaranteeing jobs and of granting allowances to those with dependants, this letter was insensitive and caused widespread 'hard feelings'[9] among Price Waterhouse men in the services. Its harshness was in contrast to the firm's customary gentlemanly behaviour, and can be seen as an aberration prompted by fears of staff shortages, falling revenue and increasing expenditure. A change of heart resulted in the firm sending an annual Christmas bonus to those on national service as a recognition of 'our very real interest in their welfare'.[10] In addition, Price Waterhouse sent food parcels to staff in the front line. This generosity may have been inspired by the US and Canadian Firms which sent similar gifts and even suits of clothes to their colleagues in the UK. In October 1944, as the hostilities drew to a close, Robson and Richards prepared a list of those staff in the forces with their pre-war salary and a recommendation of the amount they should receive on reinstatement.[11]

It has not proved possible to record how many members of Price Waterhouse enlisted. A survey conducted in 1951 reported that 155 employees had served in the forces but these included many who had joined the firm after 1945.[12] A war memorial, commissioned from the architect F.H. Shann, listed nineteen individuals who had been killed in the conflict. They included the following relatives of partners: A.R. Dickinson, G.B. Faller, A.E. Howarth and R.N. Waterhouse.[13] Also commemorated was H.L. Cousins, who had joined Price Waterhouse in 1937 having qualified in Barrow in Furness with R.F. Miller & Co. He enlisted in the RAF in May 1940 but was killed shortly after having qualified as a pilot, though his son, whom he never saw, subsequently joined the firm and became a partner in 1975.

The novelist Paul Scott, commissioned into the Royal Indian Army Service Corps in 1943, put his accountancy skills to good effect. Although he had yet to qualify, his work for C.T. Payne, a sole practitioner at Regent's Arcade House, had brought him wide experience of auditing small businesses. His unit was entrusted with the supply requirements of the 19th Division as it advanced through Burma to Mandalay. Scott described the work as

> fascinating, inglorious, but memorable . . . working out how many parachutes you needed to drop a jeep successfully – or a canoe, feather-weight, plus two or three chaps who were going to reassemble it on the ground and paddle up a creek to disaster or opposite.[14]

Air supply companies were in essence industrial units with a uniformed management and labour force. General Slim compared them with the mail order department of a great department store, supplying plain and fancy goods with promptitude and exactness.[15]

From 1943 Price Waterhouse conducted an annual survey of staff numbers, and this included a retrospective calculation for 1939. The latter revealed that London office then had 11 partners, 23 managers and

276 professional staff (253 audit, 20 tax and 3 liquidators), together with 99 ancillary employees – a total of 409. This census revealed the full impact of the war; London office had been reduced by over 100 in 1943 to 306 and had diminished further to 288 by 1945. The audit staff suffered most, the total declining from 253 in 1939 to 153 in 1943 and 140 in 1945. Numbers of partners and managers remained largely constant (being elderly or in a reserved occupation they were not called up), while the specialist and ancillary staff were maintained at their pre-war levels. It took Price Waterhouse over a decade to recover its manpower, and not until 1957 was the 1939 total surpassed.

While many members of staff continued to serve as soldiers, sailors or airmen for the duration of the war, leaving their accounting skills in abeyance, a number were recalled in order that their professional expertise could be utilised. Stanley Duncan, for example, later to become senior partner, having joined the Territorial Army in 1938, found himself performing the duties of a Royal Army Service Corps driver, ferrying staff officers around London. As a qualified man, he rightly believed that his talents were not being employed to their best effect and agreed to the suggestion from Price Waterhouse that he should leave the forces in order to work as chief accountant to A.V. Roe, a Manchester subsidiary of the firm's client, Hawker Siddeley.[16] Since Roe manufactured Anson aircraft and Duncan developed a batch costing system there it may be concluded that he made a greater contribution to the war effort than had he remained as an RASC driver.

Staff were not only lost to the military; others were seconded to work for the government. W.E. Parker, for example, who had joined the firm in 1926 from Winchester College, qualified in 1931 and was promoted to manager in 1937.[17] Having joined the Territorial Army in May 1939, Parker was commissioned into the 1st/5th Battalion of the Essex Regiment.[18] In the spring of 1940 while on exercise in Northumberland, he received a telegram summoning him to report to the Board of Trade in Whitehall.[19] Having been interviewed and offered a post Parker debated whether to accept:

> Having taken the plunge of forsaking my profession to become a soldier, it seemed to me to be all wrong that I should return to a desk job in civilian life. How could I desert my battalion, leaving them to go off and fight and probably be killed while I sat in Whitehall . . . On the other hand I had no doubt that I was a much

more competent accountant than I should ever be a soldier . . . I finally decided that, as it was intended to be only a short-term assignment, I had better take it on.[20]

Once at the Board of Trade, Parker was instructed to recruit a team of ten accountants to implement the controls for the supply of textiles for civilian use. He was also to devise a scheme for the rationing of clothes. In the event the team was entrusted with the control of virtually all non-food consumer goods which necessitated a tenfold increase in his staff:

> We moved into the Automobile Association's building in Coventry Street and there set about administering . . . the Limitation of Supplies (Miscellaneous) Order 1940 . . . With now nearly 100 accountants to train, guide and direct I was very heavily occupied indeed, but I had some able senior men among them (several from PW's European Firm, which had been driven out of most of the Continental countries).[21]

In 1941 Parker transferred from the Accountants Division to general administrative duties with the Board of Trade at the rank of assistant secretary and remained in this post until October 1945.[22] There Parker had to address general issues thrown up by rationing and control:

> how to prevent traders from concentrating on the higher priced goods when they had only a limited quantity to sell; how to prevent costs and therefore prices from rising as factories on civilian production suffered a diminishing output; how to make sure there was no under-employment in those factories; how indeed to release whole factories for war production; above all, how to make certain that there would be enough supplies to meet the clothing ration, unexpectedly strained as it was . . . by the supplementary rations which had been given to the miners and others.[23]

Solutions to these problems required a 'rash of new controls', including the 'Utility' scheme for textiles and garments (involving the allocation of raw materials to the production of a limited range of clothes for which minimum quality specifications were set), the introduction of maximum prices for Utility clothes, a national production budget based upon multiplying up the output of Marks & Spencer, and schemes for concentrating manufacturing in particular factories.

Accountants had been asked either to advise the government or to implement its interventionist policies from the outset. In 1938, when substantial contracts were being offered to aircraft manufacturers in an attempt to hasten the pace of rearmament, it was suspected that companies were earning excessively high profits.[24] Accordingly the Air Ministry asked Lord Plender to examine their published accounts, his report leading to a new agreement based upon fixed profits paid on actual costs. In August 1939 Sir Francis Freemantle MP wrote to Sir Laurence Halsey as senior partner of Price Waterhouse to request that the firm volunteer to assist the Ministry of Supply in the audit of businesses engaged on munitions work.[25]

Many of the partners of Price Waterhouse, though not seconded for government service, did, nevertheless, find themselves undertaking part-time jobs for the state. Sir Nicholas Waterhouse served as chairman of the panel set up by the Ministry of Supply to advise on the selection of accountants or accountancy firms to implement the controls made necessary by government contracts and rationing.[26]

Often accountants were propelled into positions of great responsibility. Lord Benson recalled how he had been seconded from the Grenadier Guards to be Director of Factories (Accounts) at the Ministry of Supply. His authority on accounting matters extended to some forty-one factories many of which had only rudimentary financial controls and reporting procedures. He took an autocratic line:

> From a given date I ordered all the factories to suspend all their existing cash records and to start afresh on the basis of the manual restriction on cash. They were not permitted to buy or use any stationery or books except those specified in the manual. Returns had to be submitted to me monthly . . . In due course I dealt with stores and wages in the same way and at the end made some radical changes in the costing procedures . . . I spent about 10 months on the job altogether and during the time reduced the staff employed in the factories on financial records by about 900.[27]

Disruption to Routines and Offices

The staff problem was at its most acute in the initial phase of the war when young qualified staff and articled clerks departed almost en masse. The introduction of the reserved occupation scheme and the firm's attempts to recall employees helped to ease the situation. The Blitz had destroyed many small offices in the City throwing large numbers of experienced clerks and book-keepers out of work. During the winter of 1940–41 Robson recruited some of these as temporary staff, though many, having proved their value, remained after the hostilities had ended.[28] In addition a review of procedures was undertaken. Robson urged, for example, that

> as much interim work as possible be taken up in the autumn, that programmes be again reviewed to see to what extent detailed work could be reduced and suggested that consideration should be given to surrender of work which did not show a margin over approximate cost.[29]

This was the first war in which civilians were directly involved in the conflict. In the autumn of 1940 the decision by the German high command to bomb London into submission brought Price Waterhouse and its office staff into the firing line. This involved the firm taking a novel policy decision:

> It was agreed that time lost through air raid warnings and other delays should normally be charged to the client on whose work the clerk was engaged. If material, a note of the total should be made on the time summary.[30]

The comments of clients who were footing the bill for the consequences of Hitler's blitz have not been recorded. The bombing offensive of 1940 caused an alteration to office routines. Staff were encouraged to arrive earlier than 9.30 a.m., restrict their luncheon break by bringing sandwiches and were permitted to depart at 4.30 p.m., if necessary, and Saturday working was abandoned.[31] The reduction in hours did

> not apply to audit staff working outside and efforts are to be made by the staff by limiting the lunch interval, coming early and taking work home to make up at least 41 chargeable hours per week.[32]

Given the manpower shortages, this reduction to the working week was, in fact, more serious than it seemed. It was calculated that a loss of six hours per member of staff would produce a cumulative total of 2,000 hours per week even with the recruitment of additional men.[33]

Despite the shortages of manpower and general disruption caused by the war, Price Waterhouse attempted to uphold the standards and routines of peacetime. The character of this work was recalled by Stanley Duncan who rejoined the firm as a manager after secondment to A.V. Roe:

> A report I was involved with was for Philip Hill, the issuing house, on Odeon Cinemas. They were thinking of floating the company ... I took a team up to Birmingham and we were there for many months ... this was a very prolonged assignment as each cinema was a separate company and the bookkeeping for the cinemas was very rudimentary ... It was here I met a very good, but forceful accountant, John Davis, who eventually became managing director and then chairman of Ranks. About the best thing we did for Philip Hill's was to show them that the profits of Odeon Cinemas really came from the sale of ice-creams and chocolates ... rather than from the films or cinema takings.[34]

The threat of widescale bombing, never a practical proposition in 1914–18, caused the partners of Price Waterhouse to consider a policy of decentralisation. In September 1939, fearing an aerial attack on London, they raised the idea of opening an office in the Midlands, 'to deal with work in that part of the country, to which the records of such jobs and the necessary taxation and typing staff could be moved, together with certain of the audit staff'.[35] A report presented by three partners, Jones, Robson and Howarth, concluded that an office should be opened in Birmingham as soon as possible. They also recommended that G.B. Pollard, a manager recently evacuated from Berlin, be placed in charge and that a small staff be assembled: six qualified men, two tax specialists, two typists and an office boy. The dispersal of London office was to be held in abeyance though it was suggested that 'in the event of an air raid in the daytime care should be taken that partners and managers should not all congregate in the same shelter'.[36] The Blitz, which saw London bombed every night between 7 September and 2 November 1940, in fact left Price Waterhouse's premises untouched. Thereafter the Germans continued to attack the capital in a sporadic way. On Sunday 11 May 1941 a 'basket' of incendiaries fell in the Cheapside–Old Jewry area causing a major conflagration. Damage to the offices in Frederick's Place was limited to broken windows, burnt frames and soiled furniture.[37] However, this served as a warning and in June 1941 it was decided to seek premises in the Highgate area because of its 'transport facilities [Northern Line] and being less densely populated than other areas within easy reach of the City'.[38] Accordingly, the firm agreed to rent 'Shenley', 22 Shepherd's Hill, Highgate, as alternative accommodation at £175 per annum, though the renovation of this large house to make it suitable as an office was estimated at £500–750.[39] It was eventually occupied by the estates, tax and liquidation departments and a typing pool, and was used for the storage of business records. Price Waterhouse staff occupied the building until the summer of 1945 when it reverted to a private residence.[40]

London suffered relatively little further damage until June 1944 when the first flying bomb hit the capital. A new evacuation followed and by the end of July nearly 1.5 million people had departed. Although the V1 flying bombs had been counteracted effectively by September they were followed by the V2 rocket against which there was no sure defence. In August the partners again considered moving from the City in the event of heightened enemy action,[41] and by September some of the firm's 'essential records' and the share registers of clients were transferred.[42]

At about 8 p.m. on Friday 6 October 1944 a bomb fell in Old Jewry, the blast wrecking No.1 Frederick's Place. The structure was considered unstable and subsequently had to be demolished. In addition the explosion destroyed a number of partitions and interior fittings in Nos. 2 and 3 though temporary repairs enabled these offices to continue functioning.[43] Fortunately, no lives were lost and damage to working papers had been limited by the rule that all documents should be stored in safes or filing cabinets.[44] Members of staff volunteered on the Sunday to clear the debris and on 12 October a notice of thanks was put up. All those who had assisted, with the exception of managers, were paid a bonus of £10, with an additional £10 to those who had been firewatching that evening.[45] The reconstruction of No. 1 Frederick's Place was delayed by post-war building restrictions and it was not until 21 January 1955 that the foundation stone for a new structure was laid by Sir Nicholas Waterhouse.

Shortages and rationing encouraged further changes in procedures. In order to save on paper, secretaries were instructed to type letters extending over one page with single spacing.[46] In 1940 the comma between 'Price' and 'Waterhouse' in the firm's style was dropped as being a superfluous survival from an earlier age, and a columnist in a national newspaper joked that this was a further economy measure designed to save ink.

As in the 1914–18 war, shortages led to inflation and the cost of basic commodities rose dramatically. Aware that 'the goodwill of the firm is dependent on the contentment of the staff' and that both Peats and

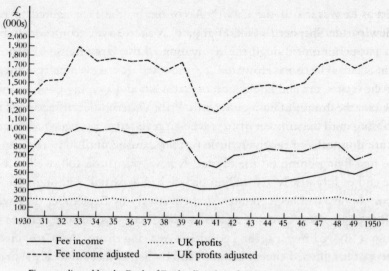

£
(000s)

Fee income ········ UK profits
----- Fee income adjusted ——·— UK profits adjusted

Figures adjusted by the Bank of England's index of consumer prices,
January 1974 = 100

FIGURE 12

Price Waterhouse (UK Firm) Fee Income and Profits 1930–50

McLintocks had granted special payments,[47] Price Waterhouse decided
to award a 'war bonus' in the summer of 1941.[48] It was decided to make
a general increment of 10 per cent, and a basic supplement of 10 shillings
a week was awarded from 1 July.[49]

As Table 8 (see Appendix) demonstrates the war years were of little
financial benefit to Price Waterhouse. Both fee income and profits fell in
real terms from 1939 to reach a trough in 1941 when disruption and staff
shortages were at their height. A gentle recovery followed but was not
sufficient to lift the firm above its performance for 1939. Not until 1947
were fees exceeded in real terms and profits did not recover until 1960.

Partnership Changes

In May 1941 F.E. Welch, who had been admitted to the partnership in
1934, died of a heart attack while in the office.[50] Although he was not
replaced immediately, W.E. Parker, then a manager seconded to the
Board of Trade, was informed that a partnership 'was open to him as

soon as he was in a position to return to the firm'.[51] Accordingly, when a new partnership deed was drawn up in May 1943 the firm consisted of ten partners resident in the UK (Halsey, Waterhouse, Price, Spencer, Jones, Tull, Harrison, Howarth, Robson and Richards), together with three overseas members, May, Seatree and Pattinson.[52]

Concern about the state of the partnership had led the firm to instruct Robson and Richards to write a report on its organising principles and future prospects.[53] A key statement was that

> the firm seeks to maintain its strength by recruiting its partners
> from tried members of its staff, chosen as suitable by reason of their
> character and ability rather than because of their financial
> resources.[54]

The increase in taxation occasioned by the war had reduced the margin of income available for capital purposes to an extent that any new partner would have found his initial capital and goodwill payments prohibitively high.[55] In addition the hostilities had exercised an adverse effect upon the firm's profitability, thereby reducing any new partner's potential income. As Robson and Richards observed in September 1941 the problem was becoming urgent as only 'two of the present partners have not reached their fiftieth year, whilst four partners, who between them own 38.5 per cent of the firm's capital, have passed their sixtieth years'.[56] Taking the shares of recently deceased partners into account, over 45 per cent of the capital would require purchasers in the relatively near future. To reduce the financial burden on any new partner, they recommended that goodwill payments be spread over ten years and the cash capital contribution paid over three years.[57] Retiring partners could not, of course, receive a capital sum for goodwill as before but were appointed as consultants and were paid a percentage of profits for an agreed term.[58] This proposed scheme was subsequently modified so that incoming partners did not have to pay for goodwill and retiring partners received nothing for it, the quid pro quo being the receipt of a pension in the form of a share of profits. These amendments cleared the way for the admission of younger men though they did not tackle the questions of their selection and training.

However, with so many younger men away in the forces or on government service, it was concluded that the firm was likely to become top-heavy in terms of age, and that there would be insufficient talented managers with the experience needed to assume the responsibilities of partnership. Consequently, in July 1942, it was agreed that a number of new managers should be created:

> Some might therefore be promoted now without detriment to the position of men now serving with the forces who . . . on their return to the office might also be looked upon as eventually suitable for partnership . . . It was finally agreed . . . that between now and the end of the year . . . that Duncan, Falkner, Theodore Waterhouse and Jack Price should have their names put on the [managers'] board . . .[59]

With the intention of guaranteeing the introduction of younger men it was proposed in September 1943 that Parker should be invited to join the partnership from 1 July 1944 and serve as an honorary partner until his release from the Board of Trade could be secured. L.H. Norman, then manager in charge of Manchester, who had served his articles with Wm. Cutcliffe, Knill & Co. of Exeter and joined Price Waterhouse in 1930,[60] was also offered a partnership as from July, but since it was policy that partners should not supervise branch offices, he had to return to London to take up this position.[61] A vote was also taken on the admission of Seed, a tax manager, to the partnership. Opposition arose about 'the inadvisability of appointing a specialist as a general partner' and because the majority in favour was so narrow, the matter was left in abeyance.[62]

With the war in Europe drawing to a close, Halsey felt that it was time for him to retire, and he departed from Price Waterhouse on 30 June 1945 after fifty-five years' service.[63] He was succeeded by Sir Nicholas Waterhouse, the longest serving of the partners, who, in view of his established position with clients, his name and ICAEW connections (president in 1928–9), had been the senior partner designate for many years. In Newcastle, W.F. King announced in March 1940 that he was keen to retire. His place as senior partner was taken by Parmeter, and Kellet was admitted to maintain the number at three.

Thus the need to appoint new men was pressing, but few were perceived as having both ability and experience. Parker, on rejoining the firm in the summer of 1945 after five years at the Board of Trade, believed that adversity had encouraged an atmosphere of insularity:

It seemed to me that Price Waterhouse had become too wrapped up in its own affairs. I could not escape the feeling that my senior colleagues and those of my contemporaries who had chosen to stay (protected from compulsory call-up because they were in a 'reserved occupation') had come to look on Price Waterhouse as the be-all and end-all of existence . . . I did not dare to reveal that in 1943, when the scope of the Schedule of Reserved Occupations was being cut down in order to release more people for the armed forces, I had put up a memorandum in the Board of Trade advocating that audits under the Companies Act should for the time being be suspended so that more manpower could be released from the accountancy profession. The risk of some fraud in company accounts seemed to me a small risk to take in comparison with the fate which would be ours if we lost the war.[64]

Parker discovered 'an appalling shortage of staff (not helped by the fact that many of those who had left at the start of the war chose not to come back), tiredness and discontent and low morale among those who had stayed with the firm'.[65] Although there had been an attempt to maintain contact with former members of staff in the forces, a more active approach to personnel management had been needed. The somewhat passive gentlemanly stance adopted by the partners, so successful in peacetime when the supply of staff exceeded the demand, proved deficient in an economy characterised by shortages. An elderly partnership failed to adapt to circumstances in a way that maintained a spirit of enthusiasm and enterprise. The post-war period for Price Waterhouse did not, therefore, proceed from a propitious base. To a great extent the problems of the late thirties had been magnified, rather than resolved, by the extended conflict.

The Role of Women

By 1939 single women had become established within Price Waterhouse as secretaries and typists but were not accepted as articled clerks (although the ICAEW opened its doors to them in 1924) or as audit clerks. Desperate shortages forced the firm to change its policy and in April 1940 it was agreed that qualified women could be engaged as audit clerks with the proviso that their appointment be solely for the duration of the war.[66] A number of the experienced clerks taken on in the winter of 1940–1 were women. In March 1944 the partners debated whether the firm should accept female articled clerks but decided against such a change.[67] Although some professions and businesses admitted women in considerable numbers (by October 1944, 48 per cent of the non-industrial Civil Service was female),[68] this was not true of Price Waterhouse or indeed of accountants as a whole and the firm retained its rule that female employees had to leave on marriage. There was much prejudice and the contribution of women, even when employed in reserved occupations, was not fully recognised. Price Waterhouse had difficulty in keeping some of its female staff as the government would not accept that they performed valuable work as accountants:

> In dealing with the male side of the profession, the Ministry of Labour recognises that because of the importance of the profession's war effort it must be allowed to retain the men necessary for its performance. In dealing with the women problem there seems to be no recognition that those whose work is a substitution for, or complementary to, that of the men are performing work of national importance.[69]

Although there was a considerable increase in the work opportunities open to women during the Second World War, accountancy continued to be a male-dominated profession. Price Waterhouse was no exception. The partnership remained exclusively male, and women could find jobs only as secretaries, comptometer operators and, more rarely, as audit clerks.

Taxation

As in the First World War, tax became a major instrument of the government's fiscal policy and, as a result, brought considerable employment for accountants. On the outbreak of hostilities a 60 per cent excess profits tax was imposed but this did not unduly impress public opinion.[70] In May 1940 an increase to 100 per cent met with popular approval. Income tax was raised from 5s 6d in the pound in 1938–9 to 7s and climbed to 10s in 1941 (with an additional surtax of 9s 6d for the highest incomes) where it remained until 1946, so that tax receipts rose from

£392 million in 1939 to over £1,310 million by the end of the war, despite restrictions and rationing.[71] In 1940 a new tax was introduced by the Purchase Tax (Commencement) Order which was levied on most consumer goods.

The upshot of this legislation was that accountants specialising in tax work found themselves more busily employed than ever before. This, too, presented staffing difficulties at Price Waterhouse during 1940.[72] Because of the growing complexity of the subject, the ICAEW established a Taxation and Financial Relations Committee in 1942 under the chairmanship of Sir Harold Barton. A forerunner of the present Technical Advisory Committee, it drew up the first recommendations on accounting principles in an attempt to apprise members of new laws and to a limited extent to standardise procedures.[73]

The European Firm: Temporary Suspension

The enforced shutting down of the Continental Firm had been a progressive affair occasioned, in the main, by the territorial advances of Nazi Germany. Aware of the growing political tensions the partnership had assumed a neutral stance from the outset. In July 1938, for example, two members of the Paris office staff, Ellerington and Kennerley, were disciplined for their involvement with the 'British Volunteer Corps' on the grounds that 'it is inconsistent with our status as an international Firm of Accountants'.[74]

The partnership most affected was of course the German, and this was the most profitable element in the Continental practice.[75] A temporary evacuation of British staff in August 1938 had preceded the Munich conference between Chamberlain and Hitler, but, as relations between the nations deteriorated, J.W.F. Neill, the senior partner in Germany, together with other prominent British residents, was expelled in May 1939. Neill travelled to Holland where he took charge of the Rotterdam office, leaving there for America in May 1939. He then qualified as a Certified Public Accountant, and his subsequent admission to the US Firm caused some resentment among his former colleagues.[76] At the time of Neill's departure the German Firm had eighty-six members of staff, of whom sixty-six were German, sixteen British, one Dutch, one American, one Swiss and one Nansen (a stateless person issued with a passport by the League of Nations).[77] Annual fees to June 1938 totalled 1,028,000 marks, and gross profits stood at around 65 per cent of this figure. It was concluded that the partnership could only continue if a nucleus of British staff remained but it was becoming increasingly difficult for them to practise. They had been prevented from undertaking certain audits by the new restrictions imposed by the German government with regard to the admission of foreigners into certain works and offices.[78] In August 1939, when these regulations had been extended to all companies, it became clear that the firm could no longer serve as auditors.[79] Fees from this work were estimated to be about a quarter of the total, and their loss would render the Düsseldorf office unprofitable. It was closed and the remaining business transferred to Berlin. Later in the month, when it had become clear that Hitler intended to invade Poland (whose independence Britain and France had guaranteed), the entire expatriate staff departed, most within twenty-four hours, leaving their household possessions behind.[80] William Voors, a partner and a Dutch national, remained behind to safeguard the firm's assets, and put two senior German employees in charge of the Berlin and Düsseldorf offices before himself leaving for Holland.

The outbreak of war in September 1939 was the signal for Price Waterhouse offices in Holland, Rumania, Belgium and Italy to close and expatriate staff to make their way to the UK. Despite this disruption Seatree attempted to keep the Paris office alive. France had not yet been invaded and he, as a US national, was not directly implicated by the conflict. At the time of the German invasion in the spring of 1940 the Paris office had an audit staff of forty.[81] In June British nationals were told that they were at liberty to depart and they made their way to the Channel ports. Seatree wished to remain and in July wrote to New York to ask whether any American nationals would be willing to transfer to Paris to join him and such French staff as could be mustered.[82] However, the progressive interference of the German authorities made it impossible to continue and on 31 July he told New York of his decision to close the office.

Seatree travelled to New York via Lisbon, where he was visited by Ferguson, who had been partner-in-charge of the Brussels office.[83] The latter observed that Seatree had experienced 'a very difficult time in occupied France', and as a result looked far from well and in need of a rest. Indeed, I felt intensely sorry for him as he seems to have taken the blow harder than any of us. Furthermore, his worries were greatly increased by a sudden illness that overtook his wife shortly after our arrival.[84]

The psychological impact of being driven from home and the partnership which he had created and led for twenty years, had a profound effect upon Seatree, and appeared to have destroyed his faith in the organisation.

The German military authorities occupied 47 Avenue de l'Opéra, paid the rent, collected outstanding accounts and deposited a considerable sum in the firm's Paris bank account before they, in turn, were forced to evacuate the city. The Gestapo had seized many of Price Waterhouse's private documents, but the office was otherwise preserved intact, the names of partners remaining on the doors of their rooms.[85]

The German invasion of Holland on 10 May 1940 saw the destruction of the Rotterdam office, although Van der Burg, a Dutch-qualified accountant, was able to carry on some of the firm's business in his own name, operating initially from his home.[86] He was joined by Voors who practised there and in Belgium without using the Price Waterhouse name until September 1944. The work of an independent accountant in occupied territories presented complicated problems. Most of Voors' clients in the Low Countries were British or American-owned and therefore under the control of the German Custodian of Enemy Property, who appointed administrators to liquidate or manage the businesses. They also had instructions to test the political feelings of staff, which resulted in auditors being given lectures in Nazi philosophy. Following the Liberation of Holland in May 1945, Voors obtained permission to re-establish a Price Waterhouse office in several rooms in Unilever House, Museumplein, Rotterdam.[87]

While many of the younger staff who returned to the UK during 1939 enlisted in the forces or could be offered employment at London office, the partners could not be accommodated so easily. Ferguson was encouraged to accept the offer of a post in New York or Canada; Edwards took responsibility for looking after continental matters and kept in touch with the two surviving offices in Zürich and Stockholm, while it was suggested to Evans and Webster that they find wartime posts in industry or government.[88] Seatree, the senior partner, as a

naturalised American citizen and having originally come from the US
Firm, returned to New York in October 1940, served for two years as
special adviser to Donald Nelson, chairman of the War Production
Board, and subsequently became controller of the Smaller War Plants
Corporation.

With the Continental Firm placed in a state of abeyance, in May 1942
Seatree prepared a memorandum on its future. G.O. May, as the US
partner entrusted with liaison with Britain, sent a copy to London three
days later. A key proposal concerned the winding-up of the partnership:

> [given] the many uncertainties regarding the future, and the difficult-
> ies of re-establishing the business, it is advisable to liquidate the
> Continental firm by mutual consent at the earliest practical
> moment.[89]

The partners, they argued, should retire; Ferguson should join either the
US or Canadian Firms, and 'Evans, Webster and Edwards should make
the best arrangements they can for themselves'.[90]

Not surprisingly, the Continental partners chose to resist this challenge
and won the support of the UK Firm.[91] The three threatened men
drafted a reply which argued that the 'international reputation' of Price
Waterhouse would suffer should this strategy be implemented:

> We feel an obligation to ... clients to preserve its Continental
> organisation in being so as to be in a position not only to resume
> normal business, but to be able to assist them in the task of
> straightening out their Continental affairs in the post-war period.[92]

They also alluded to the personal loss that they would suffer:

> We should perhaps remark that we all three move in circles in
> London where we are known to be partners in the firm and have
> considered it essential to maintain such reasonable standard as is
> consonant with this position.[93]

G.O. May was asked to reply to the Continental partners who were
being supported by London. With an ironical touch he dealt with the
question of their personal remuneration:

> Since all three of you think that I am in error about standards of
> living in England and that your financial requirements are, in fact,
> affected by the need of living in a manner consonant with your

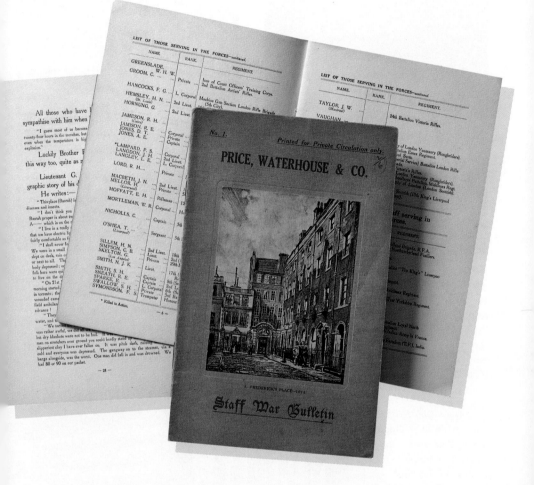

39. *Staff War Bulletins* from the First World War showing an illustration of Frederick's Place.

40. (*Above left*) No. 3 Frederick's Place under reconstruction in 1915–16. Price Waterhouse vacated the building while the work was carried out. (*Guildhall Library*)

41. (*Above right*) A 1960s photograph of 16 Gogol Street, Petrograd, where Price Waterhouse established their first Russian office in 1916. It closed in the following year with the overthrow of the Tsar.

42. (*Right*) Gresham College, situated at the junction of Basinghall and Gresham Streets, and occupied by Price Waterhouse in 1915–16 as temporary offices. (*Ecclesiological Society*)

43. (*Left*) Sir Gilbert Garnsey, described in the press as 'the wizard of figures' or as a 'financial doctor of industry'. Admitted to the partnership in 1913, and senior partner elect at the time of his death, he was the outstanding accountant of his generation.

44. (*Below left*) Sir Laurence Halsey at his desk in Frederick's Place with an Adam fireplace behind. His office was described as the most beautifully decorated of all the partners' rooms and was coveted after his retirement.

45. (*Below right*) W.P. Rocke, admitted to the partnership in 1922, having joined the firm from the Railway Clearing House.

LONDON
NEWCASTLE
LIVERPOOL
PLYMOUTH

CAIRO
ALEXANDRIA

PARIS
ROTTERDAM
BRUSSELS

JOHANNESBURG
CALCUTTA
CAWNPORE

BUENOS AIRES
ROSARIO
MONTEVIDEO
RIO DE JANEIRO
SAO PAULO
VALPARAISO
ORURO

MONTREAL
TORONTO
WINNIPEG
VANCOUVER

MEXICO CITY

SAN FRANC
LOS ANGELES
SEATTLE
PORTLAND
PITTSBURG
MILWAUKEE
CLEVELAND

NEW YORK
CHICAGO
ST LOUIS
DETROIT
BOSTON
PROVIDENCE
PHILADELPHIA

8/3
GE.

PRICE, WATERHOUSE & C?

SIR ALBERT WYON, K.B.E.

SIR A. LOWES DICKINSON,
SIR LAURENCE HALSEY, K.B.E.
SIR NICHOLAS WATERHOUSE, K.B.E.
SIR GILBERT GARNSEY, K.B.E.
G.O. MAY (BRITISH-BORN AMERICAN)

W.C. SNEATH,
H.J. MORLAND,
F.S. PRICE,
M.C. SPENCER,
W.P. ROCKE.

Telephone: CITY 4694 (4 LINES)

Telegrams: "ACCOUNTANTS, STOCK, LONDON"

Cablegrams: "PRICEWATER" ALL OFFICES.

3, FREDERICK'S PLACE,
OLD JEWRY,
LONDON, E.C.2.

27th October, 1922.

46. (*Above*) A letterhead dating from 1920, which listed the five knights of Frederick's Place.

47. (*Left*) F.S. Tull, admitted to the partnership in 1926 and forced to retire in 1949 because of a peptic ulcer.

48. (*Below*) Clarence Hatry, who confessed his fraudulent business activities to Sir Gilbert Garnsey in 1929. (*Hulton Picture Library*)

49. Harold John Morland, admitted to the partnership in 1907 and auditor of the Royal Mail Steam Packet Co.

50. Lord Kylsant leaving his London home on the morning of the judge's summing up in the Royal Mail case. (*Hulton Picture Library*)

51. The profit and loss account for the Royal Mail Steam Packet Co. showing the pencilled note 'adjustment to taxation reserves' added by Morland in 1926.

THE ROYAL MAIL STEAM PACKET COMPANY.

Dr.	PROFIT AND		

FOR THE YEAR ENDED

			£ s. d.
TO INTEREST:—			
On 4½% Debenture Stock	£63,000 0 0		
On 5% ditto	£155,000 0 0		
		218,000 0 0	
INTEREST AND DISCOUNT		63,219 8 6	
DIVIDENDS:—			
5% on Preference Stock		45,000 0 0	
6½% on Cum. Preference Stock	...	188,500 0 0	
BALANCE in favour of the Company:—			
2½% Dividend paid in November, 1925, on Ordinary Stock ...	£100,000 0 0		
Proposed to be paid:—			
3% on Ordinary Stock	£150,000 0 0		
	£250,000 0 0		
Balance to be carried forward	£144,956 13 4	394,956 13 4	
		£909,676 1 10	

ROYAL MAIL HOUSE, MOORGATE, LONDON, E.C. 2.
May, 1926.

LOSS ACCOUNT		Cr.

31ST DECEMBER, 1925.

		£ s. d.
By BALANCE FROM 1924 ...	£340,527 15 5	
Less		
Dividend paid in June, 1925	£200,000 0 0	140,527 15 5
BALANCE FOR THE YEAR; including Dividends on shares in Allied and other Companies, *less* Depreciation of Fleet, etc.	£731,103 7 8	*adjustment Taxation*
RENTS OF PROPERTIES	£37,646 1 9	
TRANSFER FEES ...	£398 17 0	769,148 6 5
		£909,676 1 10

52. (*Above*) Greek Street,
Leeds (*c.* 1940), where Price
Waterhouse occupied
premises at Greek Street
Chambers from 1928.
(*Leeds City Libraries*)

53. (*Right*) Lloyd's Bank
building in King Street,
Manchester, where in 1932
J.M. Horsley opened Price
Waterhouse's first office in
the city, photographed in
1953. (*Manchester Public
Libraries*)

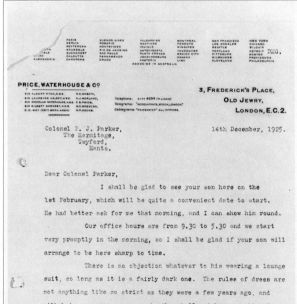

PRICE, WATERHOUSE & Co

Colonel F. J. Parker,
The Hermitage,
Twyford,
Hants.

14th December, 1925.

Dear Colonel Parker,

I shall be glad to see your son here on the 1st February, which will be quite a convenient date to start. He had better ask for me that morning, and I can show him round.

Our office hours are from 9.30 to 5.30 and we start very promptly in the morning, so I shall be glad if your son will arrange to be here sharp to time.

There is no objection whatever to his wearing a lounge suit, so long as it is a fairly dark one. The rules of dress are not anything like so strict as they were a few years ago, and silk hats are never worn now by the staff. A lounge suit and bowler will be quite all right.

Yours very truly,

54. (*Above*) The offices of the Scottish Provident Institution (*left*) in which Monkhouse Goddard & Co. took premises and which subsequently became the Newcastle office of Price Waterhouse. (*Newcastle City Libraries*)

55. (*Left*) A letter to Colonel F.J. Parker, father of W.E. Parker, dated 14 December 1925, about his son's articles.

56. A portrait of Sir Albert Wyon (1869–1937) by Sir William Llewellyn (1858–1941).

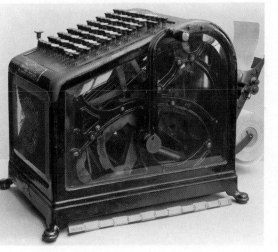

57. (*Top*) A dinner for the staff of Howard Smith Thompson & Co. held at the White Horse, Edmund Street, Birmingham, in December 1938.

58. (*Middle left*) A Duplex comptometer with nine columns for £. s. d., dating from *c.* 1927. (*Science Museum*)

59. (*Middle right*) A Burroughs adding machine, *c.* 1926. (*Science Museum*)

60. (*Left*) An earlier Burroughs adding machine, *c.* 1913 (*Science Museum*)

61. (*Above*) A portrait of William Ernest Seatree, the first senior partner of the Continental Firm, commissioned in 1932.

62. (*Right*) The Paris office and headquarters of the Continental Firm at 47 Avenue de l'Opéra (entrance beneath the Aer Lingus sign) occupied from 1921 to 1973 with an interval during the war years.

63. G.O. May, admitted to the US Firm in 1902 and senior partner from 1911, a high profile and publicly active accountant. He was sometimes referred to as 'GOM' or the 'Grand Old Man'.

64. 56 Pine Street, New York, headquarters of the US Firm, photographed in July 1927.

65. William B. Campbell, elected senior executive partner in succession to May in 1927.

66. (*Above*) Sir Nicholas Waterhouse, who succeeded to the senior partnership in June 1945. A man of charm, good sense and humility, he was an avuncular leader.

67. (*Right*) A letter written in September 1939 just after the outbreak of war to staff serving in the forces curtailing their employment with the firm. It caused much ill feeling which Price Waterhouse sought to assuage over the next six years. The annotations are by W.E. Parker.

The PW letter which caused 'hard feelings' among many members of the staff who had joined the Forces.

PRICE, WATERHOUSE & Co.

3, FREDERICK'S PLACE
OLD JEWRY
LONDON, E.C.2

W.E. Parker Esq.,
Bentfield End,
STANSTED,
Essex.

Answered 1/9/39.

14th September, 1939.

My underlining WEP.

Dear Sir/~~Madam~~,

The outbreak of hostilities, involving as it does the cessation of your services to the firm, brings up the question of your position and remuneration.

You will doubtless appreciate that the war conditions present a serious problem to professional firms. In common with other firms we have ourselves been giving close consideration to the matter.

It is of course our intention that if it is in any way possible we shall on the termination of hostilities reinstate on the staff all who have had to leave us to undertake National Service.

As regards remuneration, the opening of hostilities coincided with the payment of monthly salaries for the month of August, and members of the staff called up would therefore not in general be entitled to pay after that date.

Whilst we wish as a firm to give assistance so far as we can reasonably do so, you will realise that in view of the large numbers of our staff who have gone it will not be possible to do more than give assistance of a limited character in special cases where there are financial difficulties. If you desire your case to be considered in this connection will you please submit full particulars of your position and circumstances as soon as possible in order that we may advise you what we are able to do.

Will you, in any case, give us a note of the permanent address to which communications should be sent in the event of our wishing to get in touch with you.

Yours faithfully,

Price Waterhouse & Co

Christmas 1940.

With Kind Remembrances
and all Good Wishes
for Christmas and the New Year
from
the Staff of P. W. & Co.

5. Fredericks Place.
Old Jewry. London. E.C. 2.

68. A Christmas card sent to Price Waterhouse staff serving in the armed forces in December 1940.

69. A march-past by the Civil Service Home Guard at Horse Guards Parade in 1943.

70. (*Above*) Bomb damage to No. 1
Frederick's Place at the junction of Old Jewry
in October 1944.

71. (*Right*) Clearing up the debris from the
bombing.

72. Damage to No. 1 was extensive and the structure had to be demolished.

73. P.F. Brundage, a graduate of Harvard Business School and formerly in charge of the firm's Boston office, held the senior partnership of the US Firm from 1944 to 1954.

74. A.E. Jones, admitted to the firm in 1926 and a possible candidate for the senior partnership but for his untimely death.

75. No. 1 Frederick's Place as rebuilt after war damage.

position as partners in the Continental Firm, I, of course, accept your statement . . .[94]

May then outlined the reasons for the US Firm's wish to liquidate the Continental Firm:

> I believe the war will be a long one and that it has already had a profound effect on the system of international investment on which our international organisation rested. In particular, the position of British capital and hence of British accounting has been most adversely affected. There may be a demand for international accounting organisations on the Continent, but if so, I think it is likely to be for organisations of a different type and with a new outlook.[95]

In part the dispute over the future of the Continental Firm reflected growing differences between the US and UK Firms for, as May added,

> Looking at the matter more narrowly from the standpoint of the American Firm, forces were at work even before the war which were making necessary changes in its relation to the international organisation. Moreover, the path of American accounting development has been steadily diverging from the British path, along which it went for many years.[96]

Accordingly May pressed the argument that the Continental Firm be dissolved.

The London partners maintained their ground and wrote to New York in November 1942 that it was 'unnecessary and might be very disadvantageous to the future of the firm on the Continent if definite action was taken at the present time involving dissolution or liquidation of the firm'.[97] Negotiations between the two partnerships continued as Edwards, Webster and Evans enlisted the support of their former colleagues. In September 1942 Thompson wrote from Stockholm to support their case:

> If the war ends, as we who live a little nearer to it than our American friends believe it is going to end (and that reasonably early and not in the six or seven years as Sir Maurice Hankey predicted) we have a large ready-made practice to step into. Our

trouble will not be how to get work but how to get competent staff
to do it.[98]

Initially both Ferguson and Seatree were in accord with the American
proposals,[99] but the London partners argued their case forcefully and by
May 1943 Seatree was reported as having changed his mind. As the
senior partner and one who held some influence over the American
partnership, his defection had been crucial in preserving the Continental
Firm. It was then agreed that the existing deeds, which were due to
terminate at 30 June 1943, would continue.[100] It was further established
that once the Allies had regained the territories under enemy occupation,
a new partnership was to be formed for a period of three years to 'carry
on the whole of the Continental business'.[101] Seatree was to remain as
senior partner, and Ramsden (Zürich) and Thompson (Stockholm) were
to function in their existing posts.

Being situated in neutral territories, the Zürich and Stockholm offices
were able to continue in operation but both were disrupted by the loss
of staff who chose to return home when Britain entered the conflict.
The Zürich office set up an accounting system for the British military
internment camp in Switzerland, and acted as a communications centre
for Price Waterhouse staff spread throughout Europe.[102] In addition, the
firm took on special audit work for Swiss companies or individuals who,
due to a lack of evidence which explicitly cleared them of involvement,
had found themselves included on the Allied Powers' black lists. Reports
by Price Waterhouse helped to remove trading embargoes which had
arisen without sufficient investigation.[103]

A depleted Stockholm office found much of its practice curtailed by
the German occupation of Denmark and Norway in April 1940, and by
the loss of two audits for Swedish armaments manufacturers.[104] Work in
Finland also had to be terminated from the autumn of 1942 when entry
permits were withdrawn, following Britain's declaration of war in June
1941. In Sweden itself the practice did not lose much work, the principal
clients continuing to be the Swedish Match Co., the oil companies (Esso,
Shell and Gulf) and American film makers. Some assignments were
undertaken for Unilever, and in the case of Bowater and Gillette, Price
Waterhouse replaced foreign auditors who were unable to visit the
country because of the hostilities.[105] The Stockholm office numbered
about a dozen in 1945, much the same size as in 1939. When Thompson

succeeded Seatree as senior partner in November 1945 he moved to Paris and C.H. Evans took charge of the Swedish practice.

Following the Allied landings in France and the reoccupation of Paris in August 1944, Evans prepared a memorandum for consideration by Jones and Spencer on the reopening of the firm's office there. He concluded that prospects for work fully justified such a course of action. This was agreed by the UK partners and Evans, who was then employed by the Ministry of Supply,[106] prepared himself for a transfer as soon as the war permitted.[107] Evans, Edwards and Webster, with the support of the UK Firm, were keen to re-establish the French practice but they encountered reluctance on the part of Seatree and Ferguson. Spencer suggested that the hesitancy of the latter was the product of 'living a life removed from the constant dangers and impacts of war' leading to a different 'view of present and future conditions'.[108] He advocated a rapid return to business as 'our clients everywhere are calling for our assistance on the Continent and anxiously enquiring whether our offices are re-opening'.[109]

In the event the French practice was officially reborn on 1 March 1945 using local staff.[110] The office at 47 Avenue de l'Opéra, formerly occupied by the German Custodian of Enemy Property and the audit section of the German Military Governor of Paris, had been taken over by a French government department, the Domaines de la Seine.[111] Several rooms were rented from the latter and a number of former staff were re-engaged.[112] Work soon followed for the US Army Exchange Service, Canadian War Services and American Red Cross, while several former clients approached Evans to offer assignments, so that he was able to conclude in his report of March 1945 that 'there is no reason to suppose that there will be any lack of work'.[113]

The International Firm

The extended discussions over the future of the Continental Firm brought a positive gain: this was the realisation that some formal organisation was required to co-ordinate the activities of the various Price Waterhouse partnerships around the world. The formal retirement of G.O. May from the UK Firm in 1940 and the interruption caused by the war to the exchange scheme had, for example, resulted in a greatly reduced level of contact between the American and UK practices.[114] A formal intervention was required to prevent further separation. Accordingly, in July 1945 a contingent of US partners came to London to discuss the possibility of creating 'a single international unit' that would act as an umbrella organisation resolving differences between the various national firms.[115] It was concluded that

> the present very abnormal circumstances, arising from the chaos of the past six years, have offered an opportunity which might never occur again, for putting our international house in order and for preparing the scheme which ... seems to have had such a large measure of enthusiastic approval by our American and other overseas friends.[116]

The scheme had originally been devised by [Sir] Thomas Robson early in the summer of 1945 and had been enthusiastically adopted by Jones. It followed a request from the US Firm that the existing arrangement whereby the former contributed to the UK's profits (Table 6, see Appendix) be revised. It appeared, therefore, that links between the two practices were subject to stress and might with the retirement of May from the US partnership weaken still further. When a three-man team arrived from America (P.F. Brundage, the senior partner, J. Moresby-White, and J.W.F. Neill), it was proposed that an international firm be founded and that it be composed of two partners from the US and UK Firms and one from each of the other overseas partnerships. Each member would contribute an agreed proportion of its profits to a pool and annual meetings would be held alternately in London and New York. The delegates greeted the plan enthusiastically and it was arranged that Robson and Jones would travel to America later in the year to ratify its terms. Crossing to Baltimore in a BOAC flying boat in September 1945, they journeyed to New York where the heads of agreement were drawn up.[117] There Jones became unwell and had to postpone a planned visit to South America. He delayed his return to Britain. On arrival he was immediately admitted to Guy's Hospital but died on 14 December aged only sixty. Formally established on 9 March 1946, the International Firm was registered as a partnership subject to English law. The original members were Waterhouse and Robson representing the UK, Brundage and Inglis for the US, H.G. Norman for Canada and W.E. Seatree for the Continental Firm. Later in the year the Australian Firm joined the organisation and in 1948 Evatt & Co., of Malaya and Singapore, was admitted to strengthen the representation of Price Waterhouse in the Far East.

The formation of the International Firm brought to an end the system by which the US partnership contributed to the UK's profits. Henceforth, the only payments were to the new organisation. Robson recalled that discussions at these early meetings were 'frank and forthright and the representatives of the member firms participated freely'.[118] The International Firm allowed the senior partners of the various national groupings to get to know each other, thereby facilitating the transfer of ideas. This, in turn, led to improved professional standards, regular exchanges of staff and closer co-operation on the audit of multinational corporations. It was the first organisation of its kind set up by accountants and the major competitors of Price Waterhouse were soon to follow suit.

9

Crisis and Change

The accountants, the fastest growing profession in Britain, stand to
the world of corporate business much as the lawyer stood to the
nineteenth century world of rich men's property. They are the
priesthood of industry.

Anthony Sampson, *The Anatomy of Britain*[1]

On 30 June 1950 Price Waterhouse celebrated its centenary with a
dinner held at the Grosvenor House Hotel in Park Lane.[2] Partners and
staff were entertained by the comedian Tommy Trinder and by Jack
and Daphne Barker, while Sir Nicholas Waterhouse, as senior partner,
gave the key address. It was an appropriate choice of speaker as Waterhouse was one of the few who could recall having met 'the original
"Sammy" Price',[3] and it was a reflection of the firm's continuity that the
senior partner, one hundred years on, could vividly recount stories about
the founder.

Although Price Waterhouse had many achievements to record in
1950, there was little margin for complacency. Other practices, notably
Peat Marwick Mitchell, Cooper Brothers and Whinney, Smith &
Whinney were advancing steadily in the post-war economy. The pressure for sustained growth in order to keep pace with rival firms forced
Price Waterhouse to re-examine many of its established policies during
the fifties and early sixties. A radical innovation was the decision to admit
specialist partners – initially in tax and systems (renamed management
consultancy) – ending the tradition that all members of the partnership
should be 'generalist', or able to offer expertise in auditing. The second
significant change was the introduction of a strategy for territorial
expansion based on acquisition or merger. Implemented in 1963,
it involved amalgamation with provincial practices in Bristol and
Birmingham, soon to be followed by others in Leicester and Nottingham. This brought to an end the policy of internally generated

geographical growth; hitherto almost all of Price Waterhouse's offices had been opened *de novo* without reference to existing local services. This new direction also introduced the notion that not all partners would be based in London. Although the Newcastle office had several partners, they had not been accorded the status and authority of those based in the capital. The vacuum created in 1959 by the retirement of J.M.S. Coates, the senior partner there, and the need to strengthen the Newcastle Firm had forced Price Waterhouse to consider the subordinate position of their provincial offices. A levelling process was now under way as part of the drive towards the creation of a truly national partnership.

As Price Waterhouse grew in size so it became necessary to consider its working and structure. A service company was set up to deal with staff matters, including pay, and to manage the increasing number of properties. As the firm became too complex to be managed by the partners meeting on an *ad hoc* basis every morning, it was decided to introduce a formal organisational hierarchy involving a network of functional committees.

Thus, it was in the post-war years that a few key decisions were taken, though their effect was delayed largely until the late sixties and seventies. In terms of fee income, profits, numbers of partners and staff, range of services and geographical spread, the Price Waterhouse of 1965 was still recognisably similar to that of 1945. That the pace of change had not quickened appreciably can largely be attributed to the senior partners who ran the firm. Neither Robson nor Richards sought innovation. Both, in their different ways, attempted to maintain standards of conduct, technical excellence and professional integrity. Neither saw themselves as businessmen or as men who were running a commercial enterprise for profit. They were, of course, concerned to generate a healthy surplus but would have seen this as the natural outcome of a well run practice.

Having slipped from the unchallenged heights it had occupied in the 1920s under Sir Gilbert Garnsey, Price Waterhouse began a concerted attempt to recover its position in terms of commercial success and peer recognition. The policies introduced in the 1950s and 1960s would, in part, determine whether the firm was to decline into the ranks of the medium-sized practices or would hold its own among the profession's leaders.

Changes to the Partnership

A crisis in the upper ranks of Price Waterhouse coincided with the end of the Second World War. Although Parker and Norman had been offered partnerships from July 1944, the resignation of Halsey in June 1945 and the impending retirement of Price made it essential that new partners be introduced to an already depleted firm. The situation was soon to deteriorate further: Tull's perforated ulcer caused him to resign, while Harrison too was a sick man.[4] This left only Waterhouse, Spencer, Howarth, Robson, Richards, Parker and Norman.[5] In December 1945 a partners' meeting agreed that the admission of two further members was 'essential' and a committee comprising Spencer, Robson and Richards was set up to consider candidates.[6] They recommended that S.M. Duncan and D.E. Darker be offered partnerships from January 1946.[7] Darker had served his articles with J.W. Hinks & Co., a Birmingham firm, and after qualifying joined Price Waterhouse in January 1930. His career in the partnership proved shortlived: a heart attack in 1952 brought about his death in the following year. Duncan had served his articles with Harry White & Co., a sole practitioner in Nottingham, and won first place in the 1931 final examinations. He moved to London to join Price Waterhouse in February 1932 and became a manager in July 1942.[8]

When Price finally retired in May 1946, C.R. Culling was introduced,[9] thereby bringing the effective partner strength of the firm to twelve.[10] Eric Green was also found to be of 'partnership calibre' but his qualification as an Incorporated Accountant would have prevented the firm from calling themselves 'Chartered Accountants' should he be admitted.[11] Accordingly, he was encouraged to serve articles and sit the chartered examinations, which he passed. Sadly, however, he died shortly after hearing the result; some believed that the strain of working as a senior audit manager and at the same time preparing for examinations had contributed to his premature demise. Further admissions included A.C. Falkner in 1948 and, following the retirement of Tull and Spencer in June 1949, H.M. Angus in July 1950. Falkner, having taken a degree in mathematics, had qualified with the London firm of Charles W. Rooke & Co. Seeking better prospects he applied to Price Waterhouse in 1927 and was offered a position by Jones, an acquaintance of his father.[12]

Angus had been educated in Aberdeen and served his apprenticeship there with James Milne & Co. before entering Price Waterhouse in 1935, where he was promoted to manager in January 1946. Both, in a sense, were typical Price Waterhouse partners. Each had qualified with a smaller firm but being able and ambitious had moved to a prestigious City practice where they remained. Price Waterhouse selected its partners solely from the ranks of its managers; the idea of introducing a candidate from another firm was unthinkable.

The admission of C.H. Nicholson to the partnership in 1951 brought the numbers back to twelve.[13] Their average age was forty-nine though this was an inflated figure because Sir Nicholas Waterhouse was then seventy-four.

In January 1946, no doubt motivated by his own serious illness, Tull, a partner since 1926, voiced his fears about the future of Price Waterhouse in a letter to Sir Nicholas Waterhouse, then senior partner:

> we had good material, trained by GFG [Garnsey]. We have it now but we have sadly lacked two things (1) leadership (2) the failure to promote and give more responsibility to younger men of character and ability. Ours is a strenuous and exacting profession and to my mind is essentially a young man's job. After 60, with few exceptions, a man is getting past the energy and drive [that] the professional duties exact of one.[14]

The criticisms voiced by Tull produced no immediate changes, though they appear to have sowed seeds of doubt in Waterhouse's mind. In February 1951, during a stay at the Grand Hotel in Eastbourne, he found time to reflect on the fortunes of Price Waterhouse. Aged seventy-three, a partner for forty-five years and senior partner since 1945, he was akin to a non-executive chairman. His experience, name and the absence of an alternative successor on whom the other partners could agree kept him in office. He conveyed his thoughts on the future of the firm in a letter to his colleagues:

> I feel very strongly that, in spite of the enormous relief now afforded to us by the excellent, and sometimes rather over worked, managing clerks, there are not enough partners to do real justice to our practice. Five years before I myself became a partner [in 1906], there were *five* very active partners supervising a staff of only about 80, and now with five times the number of staff, the number of

partners is little more than doubled, and the loss of W.H. [Harrison] has made the position worse.[15]

Waterhouse, therefore, suggested that one extra partner be admitted immediately, and a further one or two more in 'the fairly near future'.[16] He alluded to the difficulty the firm had experienced in selecting individuals, and it appears from his comments that the partners had fallen into the insular trap of looking for perfection:

> It is seldom, if ever, that a man emerges who is 100 per cent suitable and there is always the fear that selection may be premature and that someone perhaps more suitable will present himself a little later on. On the other hand, delay may mean that the right man is passed over with the result he either leaves us to improve his prospects or patriotically stays on with us for many years during which he may see some of his juniors become his boss.[17]

An overly critical attitude may have arisen because the partners felt the standing of Price Waterhouse within the profession was under threat. Since the death of Garnsey the firm had stagnated in terms of commercial success and popular esteem. It was perhaps thought that further advance would be achieved only if men of the highest calibre were admitted, with the result that it was almost impossible to agree on a particular candidate's abilities and potential.

Perhaps as a result of agitation by Waterhouse a special committee was assembled in December 1952 under his chairmanship to debate the vexed question of the partnership. Consisting of Robson, Richards, Parker, Norman, Falkner, Angus and Nicholson, it debated for one and a half hours but could come to no agreement about the need for additional partners and how many should be admitted. Only one new member was proposed – T.R.T. Bucknill. The matter was raised again in May 1953 when Parker argued, with 'most of the "post-war genera-tion" of partners' supporting him, that 'it is imperative that two addi-tional partners should be recruited within the next twelve months'. The urgency arose because, as Parker noted, Waterhouse, Howarth, Robson and Richards were all likely to retire within the next nine years.[18] Nevertheless, resistance to change won the day and admissions continued at an inordinately slow rate. The 1954 Committee recommended E.D. McMillan to the partnership.[19] He was followed by A.B. Lucas and

M.R. Harris in 1956[20], M.A. Coates in 1959, G.A. Cherry in 1960 and A. Wilson in 1961.

However, despite the recognition that there was a problem in admitting new partners, no radical change occurred either to the selection process or to the numbers during the 1950s. The first major attempt to revise the firm's policy occurred in 1960 when Parker argued that Price Waterhouse should admit specialist partners. The idea was not a new one. As early as June 1945 Jones had suggested creating 'special' partners to overcome the shortage.[21] Richards was resolutely opposed to the innovation as he believed that it would dilute the status of those already admitted. There was little support for the proposal. Hence auditing expertise was still required of every partner in the firm. Before Culling, a tax manager, could be promoted he was forced to return to audit work to refresh his knowledge in this area, although once he had become a partner he reverted to tax. The old argument that a client would expect a partner to be fully conversant with every aspect of their business continued to prevail.

As a result, specialists within Price Waterhouse knew that they could never progress beyond manager and some were tempted to join other City firms where the ranks of partnership would be open to them. Parker believed that there was a basic injustice in the system and that two tax managers, D.O. Bailey and A.M. Inglis, should be admitted. His proposal, submitted in July 1960, was circulated to the partnership for comments. Nine votes were in favour of one or both being made partners, five against and one undecided.[22] In essence, the younger partners were in favour, the opposition being mobilised by Richards, an arch conservative. The case against the admission of specialists rested on the fact that this would introduce an element of 'divided responsibility', and that it would not improve the 'flow of work within the firm'.

Duncan was among those advocating the introduction of specialists. He believed that the future development of the firm depended upon its 'attaining a reputation for outstanding services additional to those of auditing'. Since business and the professions were becoming increasingly complex, he suggested that clients would seek ever more expert opinions which could be provided only by specialists who, in view of this demand, would seek requisite rewards. In such a context there was a danger that Price Waterhouse would fall behind more progressive firms.

Thomas Howarth, senior partner at the time of the decision, supported the change in principle. With a majority in favour of the new policy the matter was referred to the 1960–61 Committee which in its report of April 1961 recommended the admission of specialist partners.[23] In May it was resolved that Bailey and Inglis along with L.W. Shaw, who was in charge of the systems department, be offered partnerships.

As regards the leadership of the firm, Sir Nicholas Waterhouse continued as senior partner until 1960 when at the age of eighty-two he took an overdue retirement.[24] Today, given the pressures of modern business, it would be unthinkable that someone in their eighties could hold the senior partnership of a major accountancy firm. In his latter years Waterhouse was, of course, a figurehead leader and real authority lay with the longest-serving partners, Howarth, Robson and Richards. Waterhouse himself had not wished to remain in office for such a period. In September 1955, for example, having reached his seventy-eighth birthday, he wrote to Robson to offer his resignation.[25] The latter resisted, arguing that 'his presence with us is useful'.[26] He wished him to continue until eighty, and to encourage Waterhouse to stay was prepared to place on record 'that he is not expected to do more than be an advisory partner . . . and not expected to attend the office except when he wishes to come'.[27] In the event, Robson was able to persuade both Waterhouse and his fellow partners that the former should stay on for a further five years.

While there were clearly advantages from having a respected and well-known figurehead leader of the firm, Robson also had his own motives for this strategy. With Waterhouse in place it was Robson who was entrusted with much of the daily management of the firm and who acted as its principal representative on the Council of the ICAEW. Had Waterhouse retired sooner, the senior partnership would have passed to Thomas Howarth, a ponderous, heavily built man, who had served a longer term than Robson, having been admitted in 1932. Although an able accountant, Howarth suffered from deafness, a disability which interfered with the conduct of meetings. By 1955 he was sixty-three years old and, with no rule compelling retirement at a particular age, could have held the post for many years. Robson, who chaired the 1960 Committee, negotiated both that Sir Nicholas Waterhouse would retire on 30 June 1960 and that Howarth would depart in June 1961.[28] The senior partnership of Howarth was, therefore, in the nature of a twelve-month interregnum, and it is unlikely that Robson surrendered much authority to him during this period. Howarth was, of course, more active than Waterhouse had been latterly, and regularly chaired partnership meetings.

On his retirement in June 1960, Waterhouse was the longest serving member of Price Waterhouse. He had joined the firm as an articled clerk in 1899 and had thus completed sixty-one years' service, fifty-four of these as a partner. The personification of the English gentleman, Waterhouse was liked and admired by many. Robson observed at his death:

> When difficult points were under discussion he was accustomed to wait until others had made their points, sometimes with greater heat than reason, and then with unfailing charm and brevity to prick the balloon of their rhetoric with the pin of humour and common sense ... He never pretended to a deep knowledge of accountancy, but members of his firm's staff who took him at his own valuation soon found themselves ashamed when his apparently simple but searching questions confronted them with their ignorance ... His readiness to forgive was a stimulus to them to strive for better things; he had a unique capacity for evoking affection from old and young alike.[29]

Waterhouse was a shining example of the idea that a person's contribution to the workplace need be made not solely in terms of long hours, ambition, drive and exceptional intelligence. He was, in many respects, the very opposite of Garnsey. Waterhouse had passed his finals by the slimmest of margins (a fact which led him to remark that he had secured his goal with the 'minimum of effort'); he had to a large extent inherited his partnership from his father (an election which he described as 'nepotism');[30] he admired Morland for being 'bone lazy',[31] and had himself been castigated for a lack of interest and commitment.[32] And yet his fellow partners respected him. Robson repeatedly requested Waterhouse to extend the term of his senior partnership. What, then, were the qualities which were so endearing and that proved so valuable? Robson mentioned his 'common sense', 'charm' and a 'readiness to forgive'. In fact, Waterhouse was an avuncular figure from whom partners and staff could seek reassurance and encouragement. He had a capacity for self-deprecation and his puckish humour could often defuse a tense situation. It was reported, for example, that while on a pre-war visit to Germany,

Waterhouse had urged his chauffeur, Jebbitt, to steal a Nazi sign which he could then display at the entrance to his Surrey farm. His generosity of spirit was evinced during the 1930s when he offered financial support to Wyndham Lewis, the writer and artist.[33] But above all, he personified the Price Waterhouse ethic. Bearing the Waterhouse name, in direct descent from Edwin, he manifested the qualities of a gentleman: honesty, reliability, modesty, an absence of show or ostentation, reserve and probity. So long as Sir Nicholas Waterhouse was senior partner it was felt that the reputation of the firm remained intact.

Waterhouse had one enduring and absorbing interest, philately. He had begun buying stamps in the 1880s, building up a general collection which he sold in 1914 in order to specialise in nineteenth-century stamps from the United States.[34] This first American collection was sold in 1924 so that he could purchase a house in Swan Walk, Chelsea. It realised over £14,000 in spite of his retaining a nucleus to form a second collection. Around 1930 this too was disposed of in order that Waterhouse could buy a thirteenth-century farmhouse, Norwood Farm, at Effingham in Surrey.[35] A third collection was then begun and this, amounting to fifteen volumes, he finally sold at auction in June 1955.[36] Waterhouse revealed considerable acumen and some authority in these ventures. At the 1936 Philatelic Exhibition in New York he was awarded the gold medal of honour for the best collection of US stamps held outside America.

Nicholas Waterhouse married Audrey Lewin in August 1903 in Abinger Church, near her home, 'Parkhurst', close to Edwin Waterhouse's residence, 'Feldemore'.[37] She died in 1945, and eight years later Waterhouse married his housekeeper, Louise How. Waterhouse explained his decision to Mrs Robson:

> I think that you realise what my 42 years of married life were to me and the desolation that came on me eight years ago, but I am not one who can face living alone and 'Tim', though only 46, is such an old friend of ours and has so devotedly looked after me ... that I am more than thankful that she is now to become my wife.[38]

There were no children from either union, and his estate was valued at £291,396 on his death in December 1964.

His ultimate successor, Robson, was born in 1896 and took a degree in history at Durham University before serving his articles with the

Newcastle firm of Sisson & Allden. In the 1922 finals of the ICAEW he was placed second and awarded the W.B. Peat gold medal. Seeking broader experience and greater remuneration, he joined Price Waterhouse in October 1923 at a salary of £250 per annum. He, like Howarth, had been selected by Garnsey as a talented and competent practitioner who had proved himself in demanding assignments. Reward came in the form of promotion to manager and ultimately to the partnership. Admitted in 1934, Robson eventually became the most experienced of its members. In addition, he had served as president of the ICAEW in 1952–3 and continued to sit on its Council. A respected and able professional, Robson was a natural choice as leader of the firm. Indeed, in 1946 Tull had argued that Robson, as 'a man of character and ability whom I think everyone respects' should have been offered the senior partnership 'at once'.[39] Now at the age of sixty-five he had his chance. The problem of promotion by length of service was that leaders tended to be elderly and it could be argued that Robson's achievements would have been greater had he been appointed fifteen years earlier as Tull had suggested.

Although Robson had proved himself to be a theoretician and draftsman of great ability, he remained a cautious and conservative technocrat. Staff sometimes found him cold and his reserved manner did not make him approachable. Although polite and correct, Robson did little to encourage younger men of talent and the most junior partners had to struggle to find a voice in the organisation.

Robson, like many of the senior partners of Price Waterhouse, was a freemason. In 1922, at the age of twenty-one, he had been initiated into the Achilles University Lodge at Newcastle. Robson transferred to the University of Durham Lodge in London where he became senior warden and the master in 1933, remaining a mason until 1970.[40] His predecessor, Howarth, had been initiated into Lodge No.2308 in 1924, and in December 1932 joined the Chartered Accountants Lodge, resigning in 1961. However, W.E. Parker, who followed Robson as senior partner, was not a mason.

The partnership that Robson inherited and led could be divided into two principal groups: those with whom most authority rested and who adopted a traditional outlook, and the younger members who took a reformist stance. The former included Robson himself, Richards, Norman, Falkner, Angus and Nicholson, and the latter comprised Bucknill, Harris, McMillan, Coates, Cherry and Wilson. Parker and

Duncan, although established figures, were both of a reformist disposition. Led initially by the able Richard Bucknill, the junior partners began to press Robson and his senior colleagues.[41] Bucknill, an old Etonian of private means, could afford to be more outspoken than the others and his obvious talent had marked him out as a potential senior partner of the future.[42] Having served as a captain with the Royal Corps of Signals during the war,[43] he returned to Price Waterhouse in 1946 to complete his articles.[44] He achieved second place in the final examination of that year. It was an incalculable loss to the firm when Bucknill died in 1965 of systemic lupus erythematosus, a rare disease of the auto-immune system for which there is no known cure. Aged only forty-seven, he had appeared to possess the talent, ambition, energy and imagination to make an outstanding leader.[45]

Bucknill and his fellow junior partners complained that the workload was unevenly distributed: the most prestigious and manageable audits were held in terms of seniority, while the newer partners were entrusted with the growing number of administrative roles that the firm generated. They also asked to be given a greater voice in policy-making as at that time important decisions were delegated to small committees. Supported by McMillan and Harris, Bucknill approached Robson with various suggestions for reform. These resulted in the setting up of a special committee chaired by Duncan and including Angus, Bucknill and Harris which reported within a month and produced around ninety recommendations for improving the management of the firm.[46] Although the Executive Committee was to tone down its contents, it was the first manifestation of a process of change that would eventually revolutionise the character and size of the partnership.

One enduring and negative feature of the fifties and early sixties was the rift which occurred between two of the firm's most senior partners – Robson and Richards. They were individuals of different temperament, outlook and abilities and this generated a damaging rivalry which absorbed much of the partnership's time and energy. G.E. Richards had been articled to Mellors, Basden & Mellors in Nottingham in 1914 and his training was interrupted by military service with the Green Howards.[47] As a young officer in the trenches he was wounded twice and the bullet removed from his lung and the uniform jacket which he was wearing at the time were among his prized souvenirs. What effect the terrors of the war had upon him can only be imagined but they may have toughened his manner and made him less sympathetic to others. On demobilisation he returned to accountancy, passing his finals in November 1919, and joined Price Waterhouse in October 1920. Appointed a manager in 1932, he was admitted to the partnership in July 1939 shortly before the outbreak of war and, as the most junior partner, was entrusted with staff matters, holding this post until 1946. By this time Richards, who enjoyed administration, had also taken responsibility for the firm's property, fixtures and office machinery. He purchased new typewriters and a multilith duplicating system which dramatically improved the quality of documents sent to clients. From the mid-1950s he took responsibility for the rebuilding of No. 1 Frederick's Place, playing a considerable part in the design and planning of the interior. He also wrote the first history of the firm, whose publication coincided with its centenary celebrations.

Although sharp-witted and pragmatic,[48] Richards could be coarse and abrupt. He also harboured grudges.[49] He made enemies and blocked several managers' promotion to partner.[50] He was opposed to the admission of specialists and the expansion of the practice and generally resisted innovation. He had little interest in auditing and left the daily management of his clients' affairs to his managers, notably Tinling.[51] By the mid-sixties he had alienated most of the partnership with the exception of Angus and Nicholson. It was thought that Robson remained in office until his seventies in order to prevent Richards from succeeding to the senior partnership, and introduced a rule that no partner could continue beyond seventy in order to force him to retire.

In the event, both Richards and Robson retired in the summer of 1966. Although bullying on occasions, Richards could be kind and generous to those he trusted.[52] By increasingly concentrating upon administrative matters and neglecting the audit side of his duties, Richards may in some respects have wasted his talents and was perhaps envious of Robson who had built a sound reputation as a practitioner and theoretician within the firm and the ICAEW.

There were eight further admissions sanctioned during the period of Robson's senior partnership. A.H. Chapman and T.R. Watts joined in 1963, and J.B. Sewell in 1965. In 1966 no fewer than five new partners were introduced: P.L. Ainger and C.I. Brown in January, and J.H. Bowman, W.G. Carter and J.L. Read at the customary time in October. This unprecedented expansion had been inspired in part by the

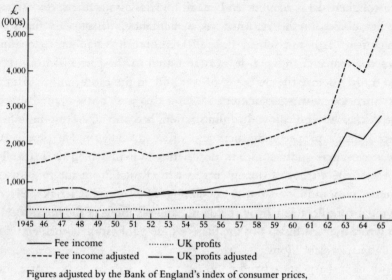

£
(000s)

Fee income
Fee income adjusted
UK profits
UK profits adjusted

Figures adjusted by the Bank of England's index of consumer prices,
January 1974 = 100

FIGURE 13

Price Waterhouse (UK Firm) Fee Income and Profits 1945–65

death of Bucknill and the impending retirement of Robson, and also by
the belated acknowledgement that younger men were desperately
needed.[53]

Nature of the Firm: Fees and Profits

Price Waterhouse experienced steady rather than spectacular growth
during the fifties and early sixties (Table 9, see Appendix). In monetary
terms its fee income rose from £422,994 in 1945 to £1,456,674 in 1962
– an increase of 244 per cent. However, if these figures are adjusted for
the effects of inflation the gain was 88 per cent. A similar pattern
presented itself for profits; these rose from £224,041 in 1945 to £527,527
in 1962, an increment of 135 per cent but in real terms this represented a
gain of only 28 per cent. However, the much slower growth rate
revealed by profits in contrast to fees reflected a general trend. In 1945
profits were about 53 per cent of income, a similar proportion to that of
the interwar period and before. By 1955 this percentage had dropped to

41, by 1960 it was 37 and in 1962 it fell to 36. This declining proportion was not the result of growing inefficiencies, but of the changed character of the firm. As early as 1949 the rising requirements of working capital were recognised. Costs per chargeable hour increased by 1s 4d between 1942 and 1948 and rose still further with the introduction of a luncheon ticket scheme and salary increments.[54] Price Waterhouse raised fees in response to these greater overheads, but not sufficiently to maintain profit margins. At a regular managers' meeting held in February 1951 to discuss problems within the firm it was concluded that the requirements of the 1948 Companies Act had produced lengthier audits which, together with higher salaries, had raised costs and thereby narrowed any potential surplus.[55] Further, they believed that the scope for increasing fees was limited. They concluded that the

> average all-in rate for normal jobs should be at least 15s [75p] per hour compared with 10s [50p] pre-war . . . On jobs with an unduly high proportion of partners' or managers' time 15s is quite inadequate. 21s [£1.05p] for managers' own work was a fair pre-war rate.[56]

In general, Price Waterhouse found itself facing the problem of rising overheads as the firm grew in size and widened the scope of its practice. The need, for example, to train its articled clerks and qualified staff was an escalating source of expenditure in the post-war period since higher standards of teaching were required to enable candidates to pass ever more rigorous examinations.

Staff and Articled Clerks

Another measure of the changing fortunes of Price Waterhouse may be provided by staff numbers. In 1900 there were five partners and eighty-six employees; by September 1950 the twelve London and three New-castle partners were responsible for 544 members of staff, including thirty managers.[57] The extent to which the development of the firm was hampered by the Second World War is revealed by Tables 10 and 11 (see Appendix). London office, with 409 partners and staff in 1939 found itself reduced to 288 by 1945. Recovery was predictably slow in a post-war economy of full employment and in which demand outstripped

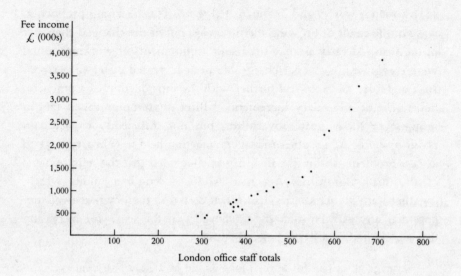

FIGURE 14
Price Waterhouse (UK Firm) Fee Income and Staff Totals in
London Office 1939–67

supply. It was easier to recruit staff in the provinces; there were, for
example, more working outside the capital in 1945 than there had been
in 1939 though this was in part due to a policy of decentralisation. Even
demobilisation did not enable the firm to restore its establishment and it
was not until 1956 that London office attained its pre-war staffing level
of 409, a figure that was overtaken in 1957 (423). The recruitment of
qualified audit staff proved so difficult throughout the late forties and
early fifties that the number for 1939 (253) was not surpassed until 1960
(280). These problems endured despite a progressive rise in the numbers
of chartered accountants (13,332 in 1945, increasing to 18,772 by 1955
and 20,124 in 1957).[58] The major City firms now competed for staff by
offering higher salaries. Even by 1954 Price Waterhouse had failed to
secure 'an adequate margin for contingencies on the ordinary audit
work, let alone for the further development of systems work and similar
specialist technique'.[59] The situation was eased, however, by a low
turnover of staff; in 1953, for example, only fifty-one (9.2 per cent), out
of a total UK workforce of 552, had to be replaced.[60]

In 1962 Bucknill presented a report from the staff committee which concluded that although adequate numbers of audit staff had been recruited for both London and most of the provincial offices, there was a 'shortage of applicants of above average ability' and a 'high proportion of staff were relatively inexperienced'.[61] Because of a relatively rapid turnover, it was decided to devise incentives to 'encourage the promising members of the staff to stay longer with the firm'.[62] The new grade of 'Assistant Manager' was introduced from July 1963, and two years later a 'progressive training programme extending over several years' was developed.[63]

The ratio of managers to professional staff improved marginally after the war. In 1939 it was one to twelve; in 1945 it fell to one to 7.6, probably because partners and managers, being in a reserved occupation, were almost entirely retained by the firm, while the younger, unqualified and part-qualified men generally chose to serve in the forces. On their return the ratio climbed back towards pre-war levels. By 1950 the proportion had risen to one manager to 9.9 professional staff; in 1955 it was one to 8.3 and in 1959 one to 10.1. The ratio of partner to professional staff followed a similar trend over the same period. In 1939 it was one to 27.2, falling to 16.5 in 1945; it rose to 23.7 in 1950 and then fell to 19.9 in 1955, climbing again to 22.2 in 1959.

In terms of staff numbers, both tax and liquidation work remained subsidiary to audit. The number of those employed on taxation never grew beyond the low twenties during the fifties, and only two were engaged on insolvency assignments. A systems department (MCS) was set up in 1955 with two members of staff, which rapidly expanded to twelve by 1958.

The dominance of London office was clear. In 1953, for example, of 464 staff, only 101 were located in the provinces (excluding the Newcastle practice). These were divided between the following regional centres: Birmingham seventeen, Manchester twenty, Glasgow seven, Plymouth ten, Liverpool ten, Cardiff eight and Leeds twenty-nine. In 1939 London office employed 89.5 per cent of all UK staff (not including Newcastle), a proportion which fell only slightly after the war: 1945 83.5, 1950 79.5, 1955 79.0 and 79.2 in 1959.

A breakdown of staff by location conducted in June 1964 (Table 12, see Appendix) revealed that London office had 57 per cent of the UK Firm. The ratio of managers and assistant managers to professional staff had not altered greatly from the previous decade (one to 8.2) and that for partners (one to 19.7) was again little altered.

Further change in the ratios of partners and managers to professional staff occurred throughout the seventies and eighties. In 1970 the relationship between partners and all other fee-earning staff (including managers and students) fell progressively from one to 19.1, to 17.8 in 1975, 16.1 in 1980, 12.3 in 1985 and 10.8 in 1989. The ratio of managers and assistant managers to fee-earning staff (including students) also improved from 7.6 in 1970 to 4.1 in 1975, 3.6 in 1980, 2.9 in 1985 and 2.4 in 1989.

The late fifties and sixties (Table 9, see Appendix) were a period of sustained, if unspectacular, expansion for the UK Firm of Price Waterhouse. Between 1957 and 1962 the practice generated growth internally at an average of around 5 per cent annually. A more rapid increase in staff numbers followed mergers with regional practices. That with Hudson, Smith Briggs & Co. in Bristol helped to boost the total for 1963 by 15.7 per cent. In the following year Howard Smith Thompson & Co. of Birmingham joined Price Waterhouse and the total percentage increase was 14.4. In 1966 the merger with Mellors, Basden & Mellors of Nottingham produced a growth rate of 18.0 per cent, while that with Bolton, Bullivant & Co. of Leicester in 1969 was less significant, causing a rise of only 6.1 per cent.

Until 1939 jobs at Price Waterhouse were not advertised. Staff were engaged on the basis of a personal introduction. However, with the post-war rise in manpower demands this informal method of recruitment could no longer suffice. In 1964 shortages were such that the larger offices outside London experienced 'great difficulty in obtaining newly qualified men and one or two report that they have had no answers to their advertisements'.[64]

Initially, the demand for places as articled clerks outstripped supply. Because the 1948 Companies Act restricted the total number of partners to twenty and ICAEW regulations determined that each partner should supervise no more than four clerks, the firm was constrained in the numbers it could engage. In 1946 it was decided that articled clerks be offered positions only if they 'were connected with clients or other friends of the partners'.[65] The wisdom of such a restrictive approach was soon questioned. In December 1947 the staff committee was granted permission to make exceptions and consider offering articles to managers and staff who had not qualified as chartered accountants.[66] Entry was, of course, severely limited by income, as a premium of 500 guineas was payable on engagement. Although largely recouped in the form of annual bonuses, this financial requirement effectively restricted articles to the upper-middle class. In January 1952 Price Waterhouse decided to abandon the system and in future to grant all articled clerks 'a flat rate allowance of £100 per annum'[67] and they were also eligible for a bonus every six months.

From the late nineteenth century to the interwar period, the education of articled clerks had been largely unstructured and informal. Individuals paid for their own tuition through correspondence courses, such as those offered by H. Foulks Lynch,[68] involving study in the evenings and weekends. Parker addressed the firm's articled clerks in 1958 to explain the nature of their training:

> Price Waterhouse & Co. differs from a school or university whose primary function is that of education of its pupils. Our primary function . . . is to serve the commercial community . . . it would not be right or good professional training for you to take the attitude . . . that service under articles is nothing more than a means of getting your qualification . . . It is not the firm's policy to interfere too much in pupils' tuition arrangements. We take the view that primarily the examinations are *your* affair; *our* responsibility is to see that by the time you have passed them you have not had insufficient practical experience to fit you for what is a practical, not an academic, qualification.[69]

The supervision of clerks had been an *ad hoc* matter and depended upon the interest and involvement of the partner in question. The increasing complexity of company legislation and the examinations set by the ICAEW encouraged firms to take a more formal role. In September 1946 A.C. Falkner, a manager, was instructed to oversee the training of clerks and obtain progress reports from their tutors.[70] Price Waterhouse agreed to pay their subscriptions to the London Students Society. Nevertheless, the largely *laissez-faire* attitude of Price Waterhouse did not generate academic success. 'A particularly dismal report' from Foulks Lynch on the progress of the firm's articled clerks prompted an investigation of pass rates at the first attempt and this showed that only 52 per cent of the firm's candidates were successful in comparison with the overall figure of 60 per cent. However, Price Waterhouse were 'satisfied' with the results in the final examination for which the percentages were

71 and 55 respectively.[71] A meeting was held with two Barton, Mayhew partners, a firm with conspicuous examination successes, and it was concluded that a greater level of internal supervision was required.

With the growth in the size of the firm, there were signs that the 'family atmosphere' was beginning to dissipate. Because the entire London staff could no longer be accommodated within No. 3 Frederick's Place, it was agreed in March 1948 to lease 2,000 sq.ft of offices in Maypole House, Finsbury Square, at an annual rental of £1,500.[72] Additional premises were obtained at Armour House in May 1948 and occupied by the registration department. In 1954 the firm obtained permission to reconstruct No. 1 Frederick's Place, an improvement which had been delayed by building restrictions.[73] By acquiring a lease on the land behind the original structure, it became possible to erect offices on a larger scale. Designed by the architect C.W. Kempton assisted by Richards, the building was completed in 1958.[74]

The Organisation and Structure of the Firm

In March 1961 Duncan circulated a preliminary draft on the establishment of a wholly-owned service company to manage the business aspects of Price Waterhouse. In part the need for such an administrative device had arisen because of the rising requirements for working capital. Debtors and work in progress had increased in value from £280,000 in June 1955 to £562,000 by June 1961.[75] The proposed service company could either employ all the staff (professional or others) or only certain groups, such as administrative, tax and secretarial, and it could own the premises (London and elsewhere) and undertake to supply the firm with offices and other facilities.[76] The company, whether limited or unlimited, would be formed with sufficient capital to acquire all the firm's offices and their contents, and this, Duncan suggested, would then be held entirely by the pension fund. All but the pension fund proposition was accepted and ownership of the service company was passed to the UK partnership. When established, it was probably the first organisation of its kind adopted by a major City accounting practice.

By 1964 it was clear that Price Waterhouse could no longer be run by a small group of partners who met every morning to discuss business. Its territory and the range of services had grown to the point where a more complex formal structure was needed. Two organisational plans were introduced, one for the firm as a whole and one for London office. As a result of this reorganisation, sovereignty was vested in the UK partnership which, in turn, delegated specific functions to four key committees: executive, national staff, standing and technical. The Executive Committee was set up as a policy-forming body empowered to appoint partners to particular posts, create committees and determine their terms of reference, and to make recommendations for admission to the partnership. Its five members were to be the senior partner, the chairman of the Standing Committee and three partners, one from outside London – Robson, Duncan, Angus, Parker and W.L. Barrows.[77] The National Staff Committee was charged with the pressing problem of recruitment not only in the capital but also in the regions and the particular difficulty of finding qualified personnel of the required calibre. The Standing Committee was 'to keep under continuous consideration all aspects of the firm's practice, including its organisation and development, professional techniques, training of staff and financial matters',[78] and its members were Duncan (chairman), Bucknill, Harris, P.W. Barrows, A. Copley and C. Collett. At its second meeting in April 1964 the Executive defined for the technical committee its terms of reference:

> to keep under review the technical aspects of the firm's professional work, including its methods of auditing, the forms of audit, prospectus and other reports and the attitudes to problems of accounting treatment and presentation.[79]

In August 1964 Duncan prepared a note to the Executive Committee on the administrative duties of the partners and in doing so produced the first organisational charts of the UK Firm (Figure 15, p. 230).

When specialist partners were admitted in May 1961, it was agreed that provincial offices should also have partners rather than managers to run them.[80] There were seven: Birmingham, Bristol, Glasgow, Leeds, Liverpool, Manchester and Newcastle – though the last had its own partnership. Within London office, the senior partner had executive authority. Because of its size, several specialist departments had been created (tax, management consultancy, liquidation, secretarial, transfer audit and estates) and a staff committee supervised training and recruitment.[81] Although by no means as sophisticated as today's structure, this represented a novel attempt to tackle growing organisational problems.

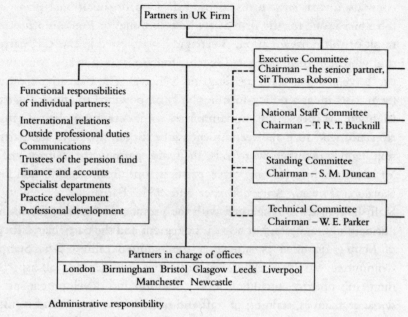

```
┌─────────────────┐
│ Partners in UK Firm │
└─────────────────┘
```

Functional responsibilities
of individual partners:

International relations
Outside professional duties
Communications
Trustees of the pension fund
Finance and accounts
Specialist departments
Practice development
Professional development

Executive Committee
Chairman – the senior partner,
Sir Thomas Robson

National Staff Committee
Chairman – T. R. T. Bucknill

Standing Committee
Chairman – S. M. Duncan

Technical Committee
Chairman – W. E. Parker

Partners in charge of offices
London Birmingham Bristol Glasgow Leeds Liverpool
Manchester Newcastle

——— Administrative responsibility
- - - Consultative and advisory relationship

FIGURE 15

Price Waterhouse (UK Firm) Organisational Chart August 1964

As the firm continued to expand and acquired more offices throughout the UK it became important to improve formal communications. In October 1964 the Standing Committee agreed to the introduction of a partners' newsletter, which would include general and technical matters, and once this means of spreading information had proved itself, it was proposed to issue a staff newsletter as well. The volume of specialist literature had become sufficiently large to justify the appointment of a librarian for London office in November 1964.[82]

It had also become essential that a formal system be devised for the payment of allowances on retirement. In June 1950 it was announced to staff:

> For many years it has been the firm's practice to grant pensions to members of the staff when they retire. These arrangements have been voluntary. We have now constituted, with effect from 1st July

1948, a non-contributory superannuation fund, into which ...
we shall pay each year a sum equal to 5 per cent ... of the
remuneration (not exceeding £1,500) paid to each eligible member
of the staff.[83]

Staff could expect to receive an annual pension amounting to one-
eightieth of their salary multiplied by the number of years' service. It
applied to all over the age of twenty-five and was payable to women at
sixty and to men at sixty-five.[84] With the continued growth in the size
of the firm, the pension fund expanded commensurately, and today
is valued at over £225 million.

In July 1947 Sir Nicholas Waterhouse proposed that the firm acquire
'Feldemore', Edwin Waterhouse's former country home at Holmbury
St Mary, as a hostel for staff, 'particularly for recruits from the provinces
who would have difficulty in finding accommodation in London'.[85] The
suggestion was considered by the Staff Committee but, probably in
view of the expense, was not implemented.

Clients and Services

The return of a Labour government in July 1945 resulted in the
implementation of a series of nationalisation proposals. In 1946 the
Bank of England, Cable and Wireless and Civil Aviation Acts, together
with the Coal Industry Nationalisation Act, were passed. [Sir] Thomas
Robson served as a member of the Central Valuation Board for the
Coal Industry which sought to determine appropriate levels of compensation for owners whose mines had been taken into public ownership.[86]
For approximately five months during 1948, this work occupied Robson
four days a week.[87] Although coal nationalisation had brought a prestigious assignment to London office it had potentially disastrous
consequences for the Newcastle partnership where a number of mine
owners were important clients.[88] J.M.S. Coates was responsible for
negotiating the compensation due to these families and, more
importantly, advised them when it came to investing these sums in land.
In this way he managed to keep them as long-term clients.

When the railway companies were nationalised in 1947 and combined
as British Railways, separate auditors were appointed to each of the four

regions. Robson together with Sir Harry Peat became joint auditors of Eastern Region and Price Waterhouse also served as co-ordinating auditors for all four regions. The firm was disappointed when it failed to obtain reappointment to the Southern or Midlands Regions, Sir Nicholas Waterhouse having audited their predecessors the Southern Railway and the LMS. Deloittes, long-standing auditors of the Great Western Railway, were appointed to Western Region. In 1963, after the network had been considerably pruned, the Minister of Transport decided that British Railways should have a sole auditor, and this assignment was lost to Peat Marwick Mitchell. However, the suspension of Price Waterhouse's historic railway connection was to prove temporary as in 1986 they became auditors to British Rail.

Because of its historical inheritance and the entrepreneurial skills of Garnsey it was said that Price Waterhouse had one of the most impressive audit practices in the City. A sense of its range and scale was provided by a summary drawn up in 1946 of each partner's principal clients:

> N.E. *Waterhouse*: Bank of New Zealand, Duchy of Cornwall, London Midland & Scottish Railway, National Provincial Bank, Royal Exchange Assurance, Southern Railway, Westminster Abbey, Siemens Brothers & Co., Fishmongers' Company, Mercers' Company.
>
> M.C. *Spencer*: Associated Biscuit Manufacturers (Huntley & Palmers), Barclays Bank, Goodyear Tyre & Rubber Co. (Great Britain), Lever Brothers & Unilever, Van den Berghs & Jurgens.
>
> F.S. *Tull*: Lloyds Bank, Halifax Building Society, Kemsley Newspapers.
>
> W. *Harrison*: Harrisons & Crosfield, Imperial Chemical Industries, Legal & General, Pinewood Studios.
>
> T. *Howarth*: Beecham Group, Hawker Siddeley Aircraft Co., Vickers-Armstrong.
>
> T.B. *Robson*: Courtaulds, Gas Light & Coke Co., Horrockses, Crewdson & Co., Harland & Wolff, London & North Eastern Railway, John Lewis & Co., Westinghouse Brake & Signal Co.
>
> W.E. *Parker*: British Medical Association, Cambridge University, RKO Radio Pictures, Shell Petroleum Co., United Artists Corporation, Warner Bros. Pictures.[89]

This list demonstrates the success that Price Waterhouse had achieved in winning the audits of many of the nation's leading enterprises.

The creation of larger business units by nationalisation had its parallel in the private sector. For the most part British industry grew in the fifties and sixties by merger, so that major manufacturing companies typically increased the number of their subsidiaries. Take-overs occurred both within the UK and abroad, so that the territorial bases of these groups also expanded. Once incorporated within the organisation, the acquired company's audit would normally pass to the firm appointed by the group as a whole. Thus, by being associated with a few major businesses, an accountancy practice would gain important new clients without undue effort.

The attempted take-over of Courtaulds by ICI in 1961 illustrates these developments in practice. Courtaulds did not relish the idea of being acquired by ICI and resisted the bid.[90] They called upon Baring Bros., the merchant bankers, and Binder, Hamlyn & Co., chartered accountants, to advise them; they would perhaps have chosen Price Waterhouse, their auditors, but the firm was placed in an invidious position being, in addition, joint auditors of ICI. Anthony Burney of Binder, Hamlyn demonstrated that Courtaulds' potential earnings were much greater than the ICI terms implied and in another memorandum outlined a possible reorganisation of the group which would separate trade investments from manufacturing divisions.[91] These strong financial arguments were material in enabling Courtaulds to ward off ICI's take-over bid. Ironically, had it succeeded the audit would probably have remained with Price Waterhouse as Courtaulds would have become a subsidiary of ICI.

However, as businesses themselves became larger and expanded over a wider geographical area, they demanded that their professional advisers offer commensurate services. Thus the nature of client demand provided much of the explanation for Price Waterhouse's merger with local firms in Bristol and Birmingham during 1963, and for their diversification into specialist areas such as management consultancy and taxation.

Between 1957 and 1963 Price Waterhouse calculated that 158 new audit assignments had arisen because an existing client had acquired a company and a further 460 had followed because an existing client had set up a subsidiary.[92] These represented 13.2 and 38.5 per cent of the total respectively. In other words, over half of new audits arose because established clients were themselves growing either internally or by take-over.

A further area of development for Price Waterhouse occurred within one of their specialisms – the Systems Department. In April 1963 the Standing Committee conducted a review of its activities in order to assess its future development.[93] At that time it comprised one partner, L.W. Shaw, and nineteen qualified staff. The Standing Committee discovered that its activities were concentrated within five principal areas and that these were considerably narrower than the services offered by independent management consultants. They comprised: periodic reviews of management organisation; advice on the form and content of statistical information (management accounts) provided to the board and other levels of management to evaluate and control the undertaking; reviews of administrative systems; advice on the organisation of office procedures; and proposals for mechanising accounting procedures and the use of computers. The Committee recommended that the Systems Department continue to focus upon these core services, and could only diversify into other areas which were 'within the scope of the firm as practising accountants'. However, they were not granted the freedom, for example, to attempt to offer advice on production problems, marketing and sales policies or time studies. Such work would necessitate the employment of specialists, such as engineers, and such a 'development would give rise to fundamental problems for the firm and for the accountancy profession'. Nevertheless, to recognise the widened scope of the department's role it was agreed that henceforth it should be called Management Consultancy Services (MCS).

A survey of new work conducted between 1957 and 1963 revealed that of the 131 new assignments performed by the Systems Department ninety-five of them (72.5 per cent) were for existing audit clients.[94] An analysis of work by type over the six years to December 1966 showed that 178 (45.3 per cent) out of a total of 393 assignments were advising clients on financial and accounting organisation and procedures,[95] and that this work was distributed widely across all forms of industry and commerce. Advice on computers and systems analysis was still embryonic and represented a mere 11.7 per cent.

Company Legislation

During the thirties a growing body of popular and professional opinion had been campaigning for more far-reaching company legislation and for greater guidance from the ICAEW as it had become clear that unscrupulous businesses were being granted too wide a margin for legitimate reporting. To date the ICAEW had been reluctant to intervene further. They continued to believe that their role should be restricted to disciplining members who breached recognised rules and ethics. The notion that they should offer guidance on technical matters was seen as an infringement of the professional's autonomy, but this view was finally overturned in 1941 when pressure from members resulted in the formation of the Taxation and Financial Relations Committee.[96] In an atmosphere of greater state intervention, the government at last took heed of the long-standing criticisms of the 1929 Companies Act and in 1943 the President of the Board of Trade appointed a committee under Mr Justice Cohen to report and make recommendations.[97] It was composed of lawyers, businessmen, politicians and one accountant, Russell Kettle of Deloittes. Memoranda were submitted by the major professional bodies and by F.R.M. de Paula as chairman of the ICAEW's Taxation and Financial Relations Committee.[98] The Association of Certified and Corporate Accountants observed that 'under the law as it stands, as long as the balance sheet is mechanically accurate, it can be as obscure and uninformative as the directors may find expedient'.[99] Robson, a member of the ICAEW's sub-committee dealing with holding companies and an author on the subject, played a large part in drafting their submission, and was subsequently called with Sir Harold Howitt to give oral evidence.[100] The most radical proposals were submitted by *The Economist* and included a standard form of accounts which required a fully itemised trading and profit and loss account. The Hatry and Royal Mail cases had contributed to this major change in public opinion. Confidentiality had been a watchword of the Greene Committee, reporting in 1926; now, the 'fullest practicable disclosure' was the objective identified by Cohen and his colleagues.[101]

The presentation of the Cohen Committee report in 1945 was warmly welcomed by business, the professions and politicians. Because of the backlog of work in the Commons it was decided to introduce the Bill directly to the Lords and Kettle, assisted by Robson, was responsible for advising the parliamentary draftsmen on technical issues. The major changes introduced by the 1948 Companies Act were: group accounts, usually in the form of a consolidated balance sheet and profit and loss account, were to be published; both documents were to be circulated to shareholders prior to the AGM and then filed with the Registrar; the scope of the audit report was to be expanded to cover the profit and loss account and the group accounts; henceforth the auditor would be required to state whether the accounts represented a 'true and fair view' rather than the old 'true and correct' one; and transfers to or from reserves were to be fully disclosed. The committee had also identified a comprehensive range of headings for disclosure in the balance sheet and put forward a more modest list for the profit and loss account. To prevent holding companies from concealing some financial information by operating through wholly-owned subsidiaries, the freedom enjoyed by private companies from the filing requirements was withdrawn, except for those with no corporate shareholders.[102]

Another novel feature was the definition of those qualified to perform audits. Members of the English and Irish Institutes and the three Scottish Societies of Chartered Accountants, the Society of Incorporated Accountants and Auditors, together with the Association of Certified and Corporate Accountants were alone deemed fit to undertake such commissions.[103]

Following the introduction of this legislation, Price Waterhouse contacted the partners of its associated firms to ask them to retire from directorships of companies as this would disqualify them as potential auditors.[104] Partners in Price Waterhouse itself had long since resigned from boards in view of the conflict of interest that might arise. As Sir Thomas Robson was to observe in *The Accountant*, the effect of mounting regulatory legislation was to undermine the freedom of action available to each practitioner.[105] The ICAEW refused to countenance the promulgation of 'a formal written code' and argued that

> a sense of personal responsibility and a highly developed conscience
> are much more important; and, indeed that membership of a
> profession implies the obligation to have such a sense and such a
> conscience.[106]

Robson was perhaps typical of other senior chartered accountants in rejecting the suggestion that there might be 'an all-embracing list of regulations'. He preferred to rely upon the 'integrity and high moral character' of the professional and his 'balanced judgement' and 'independent mind'. In an era of growing competitiveness, and when the state was increasingly encouraged to modify the behaviour of the market, Robson was likely to be fighting a rearguard action.

Regional Expansion

Until 1963 Price Waterhouse had resolutely opposed any plans to grant autonomy to its provincial offices. Only in Newcastle, where a merger with an established local firm had taken place, were partners permitted, and these were excluded from direct participation in the London Firm. The other provincial offices – Leeds, Manchester, Cardiff, Birmingham, Liverpool and Plymouth – were all supervised by managers. As a result most of their clients and all the major assignments remained the responsibility of a partner in London. This structure was probably unique to Price Waterhouse among the leading City firms: Cooper Brothers, Whinney, Smith & Whinney, Peat Marwick Mitchell and other practices all appointed partners to run their branch offices. Indeed, in the late sixties when firms reached the limits of the twenty-partner rule imposed by partnership legislation, it was considered useful to have additional firms elsewhere to which new members could be introduced although for all practical purposes they worked in London.

Accountancy firms expanded territorially throughout the UK in two ways. Either they acquired smaller provincial practices in those towns where they had several major clients (as in the case of Turquand, Youngs & Co., Barton, Mayhew & Co. or Whinney, Smith & Whinney)[107] or, as in the case of Price Waterhouse, they established their own offices without reference to existing local firms. The reason for pursuing this second strategy was so that clients could retain a personal contact with a partner who, according to the firm's policy, had to be based in London. Peats, by contrast, had followed a different approach. By 1926 they had set up eighteen offices in the UK,[108] each responsible for a region and each under the control of one or a few autonomous partners. As a result Peats had a devolved management structure with forty-six partners[109] in the late fifties at a time when Price Waterhouse had about half that number.

In the early sixties, once it had become clear that the general growth in the scale and complexity of business required accountancy firms to offer commensurate geographical and technical services, Price Waterhouse abandoned its policy of having a London-based partnership. During 1962 Robson was mandated to write to Howard Smith Thompson in Birmingham and Hudson Smith Briggs & Co. in Bristol to inquire whether each would be prepared to consider some form of association.[110] From the standpoint of Price Waterhouse, such mergers would provide not only a broader territorial coverage but also a direct input into an established regionally based practice. Furthermore, the provincial firm would gain the prestige and specialist services of a major City practice thereby defending themselves against the potential loss of their largest and most valuable clients. Extensive negotiations followed and in 1963 both practices agreed to a merger.

Price Waterhouse had already opened an office in Birmingham in 1939, partly in an attempt to disperse the London practice. Having established itself during the war, the practice grew in the post-war years under the supervision of Douglas Sandry, a tax manager who had been transferred there from Manchester in 1951.[111] Most of the work took the form of relatively large audits (including Armstrong Whitworth, Hawker Siddeley, Goodyear Tyre Co. and British Thompson Houston) which were ultimately controlled by a London partner. Little work arose for local business.[112] A merger with a Birmingham practice would, therefore, have integrated Price Waterhouse more securely in the region. After the amalgamation Howard Smith Thompson & Co. changed its name to Price Waterhouse and in March 1964 the two offices were moved into one building, in accordance with the firm's new policy on regional partners. Also to give him parity with the Howard Smith Thompson members, Sandry was admitted to the partnership. Howard Smith Thompson & Co. had a staff of 115 compared with the twenty that made up the Price Waterhouse office.[113] The former also had a small London office which was closed and its work and personnel integrated within Frederick's Place.[114]

Howard Smith Thompson & Co. had been founded in 1867 by Howard S. Smith, son of Brook Smith, a prominent Birmingham factor and merchant. Articled to Carter & Co.,[115] he became a clerk in the borough treasurer's office in 1866 and, when he narrowly failed to be elected to that post, decided to set up on his own account. Under his guidance the firm became one of the leading practices in Birmingham, concentrating on the audit of collieries, manufacturing enterprises (including Archibald Kenrick) and steelworks. The standing of the firm was such that Neville Chamberlain worked there to gain experience of financial matters.[116] Howard Smith, son of the founder, joined the partnership and in 1923 a merger with O.W. Thompson resulted in a change of style. The informal connections which existed between the two firms had been assisted because [Sir] Hugo Huntington-Whiteley, a partner in Howard Smith Thompson, had formerly been a manager in the London office of Price Waterhouse and maintained his contacts there. In addition, a mutual involvement in the ICAEW helped as W.L. Barrows, later to be senior partner of Howard Smith Thompson, served as president of the Institute in 1958–9, an office which [Sir] Thomas Robson had held in 1952–3.

The second important merger, completed by September 1963,[117] was with an established provincial firm, Hudson Smith Briggs & Co., a Bristol practice which could trace its foundation to 1846.[118]

These two events confirmed that Price Waterhouse was henceforth working towards a truly national partnership and a series of amalgamations followed in the late sixties and seventies. In July 1964, the Executive Committee concluded that

> it would be to the benefit of the UK practice to be represented in Nottingham and Leicester, that this representation might best be achieved as regards Nottingham by a complete association with a local firm and that Mellors, Basden & Mellors was the best choice of the local firms.[119]

In other words Price Waterhouse were now actively seeking associations with existing firms rather than attempting to establish their own circumscribed base without local assistance.

The post-war years had witnessed one further development in the traditional means of territorial expansion. Although Price Waterhouse staff had been based in Glasgow since 1937, they had worked almost exclusively on the LMS audit and were located in the railway company's offices in Buchanan Street, next to the station.[120] The loss of the audit, following nationalisation in 1947, forced Price Waterhouse to reconsider the nature of their Scottish operations. The need to have representation there and a volume of referred audit work (including the Clyde branches of Harland & Wolff, Clyde Portland Cement Co., a subsidiary of Tunnel Portland, Robert Brown, a subsidiary of Seagrams of Montreal, BOCM, a Unilever company, and Seedhill Finishing Co., a subsidiary of William Hollins)[121] encouraged the firm to open a branch office in 1949. Situated at 38 Bath Street, it was placed under the supervision of

W.B. Morrison, a manager, transferred from London.[122] As with the other Price Waterhouse branch offices, reports were despatched weekly to the partner nominated to take professional responsibility for the audits, in this case Darker and subsequently Angus. In 1959 the firm sought new premises at 144 West George Street, remaining there until 1967 when larger offices were occupied in St Andrew House, 141 West Nile Street. During the sixties locally based clients were attracted and included Alexander Findlay & Co., Shaw & McInnes, Keir & Cawder (Engineers), Irvine Knitters and Queen of Scots Knitwear.[123] By December 1970 the Glasgow staff totalled thirty-five.

By 1946 the Leeds office, managed by J.O. Collett, comprised fifteen qualified staff. In 1932 it had moved from its original premises in Greek Street Chambers to the Legal & General Building at 7 South Parade.[124] Unlike Glasgow, it had little referred work from offices other than London, concentrating upon local audit and tax assignments. Among its principal clients were the Burton Group, Hepworth Ceramics Group, Rowntree Mackintosh and Stylo Shoes, while referred work included ICI at Billingham, Batchelors Foods, Reckitt & Colman and Rank Leisure.[125] In accord with Price Waterhouse policy all its professional activities were subjected to partner review in London. As Sandry recalled of the Birmingham office in this period: 'we were not encouraged to seek new work, and we were not allowed to take any on without prior sanction from London'.[126]

The Newcastle office remained the major exception. With its own partnership it was not subject to the constant supervision of London, and had in J.M.S. Coates a leader of authority, ability and determination. He had succeeded to the senior partnership in 1940 and ran the office almost as a separate firm with regard to its local clients, internal management and staff matters.[127] Under the terms of the partnership deed, Newcastle paid Price Waterhouse 'the whole of the net profits' and each of the partners then received 'a sum equivalent to 16 per cent' of this surplus.[128] In all other respects, however, they were granted a high level of autonomy.

Price Waterhouse in Newcastle dominated the city's accountancy profession to an extent that no other London firm had achieved in any provincial town. By sheer force of personality and business acumen, Coates attracted many of Newcastle's industrial and commercial enterprises and secured them as clients. Unlike some Price Waterhouse offices, Newcastle did not rely on referred work from London or the US Firm for its core practice. It was recorded that Coates had

> an intimate social as well as a professional association with many clients. He seemed to possess the knack of establishing without effort on his part what he ... described as a 'friend-cum-client' relationship with hundreds of those who came to him for advice. It was largely on this account that his influence and with it that of the Newcastle Firm grew with the years.[129]

That Coates was a freemason doubtless assisted this process and would also have helped him to win the confidence of clients. Initiated into Northumberland Lodge No.685, Newcastle, in 1928, he served as the master in 1935 and 1936.[130] He subsequently joined the Northumberland Masters Lodge and from 1952 to 1975 served as provincial grand master.

It had long been recognised that the Newcastle Firm behaved almost as an independent practice. The 1951 Committee, for example, concluded that its 'absorption [was] considered desirable in principle but not regarded as a matter for present action'.[131] The strength of Coates' personality, his opposition to interference from London and the particularly regional nature of the practice were no doubt factors leading to this conclusion. The retirement of Coates in 1959, after thirty-five years as a Newcastle partner, was the spur to change. Fifteen of the office's major audits were transferred to London partners, though this had caused disquiet among clients who detected inefficiencies and a division of authority between the two offices. It was recommended that a single partner in London be appointed to supervise these audits and become 'au fait' with the important Newcastle clients.[132] This decision appears to have been governed by the firm's policy that partners should be based solely in the capital; it was overturned in 1961 when this strategy was abandoned. 'Circumstances in Newcastle,' the 1960–1 Committee concluded, 'made the continued admission of resident partners essential to the preservation of the practice and its competitive position in relation to rival firms.'[133] The retirement of Coates, and the vacuum that this created, was the catalyst needed to re-examine the status of the regional offices. T.R. Watts, a London manager, was invited to accept a partnership in the Newcastle Firm from July 1961, though he preferred to remain in the capital where he was made a partner two years later. J.M.S. Coates had hoped that his son Michael, then a manager in

London, would succeed him as senior partner in Newcastle, but the latter, at Robson's wish, was admitted to the partnership in the capital.[134]

Disrupted by bombing in the Second World War, the Plymouth office of Price Waterhouse languished during the fifties and early sixties. It remained limited in size, and in January 1964 the partners decided that the office should close at the end of October.[135]

The Continental Firm Re-established

Following the disagreement with the US Firm, it was established that the Continental practice would be reconstructed as soon as circumstances permitted. The first post-war meeting of the Continental partners was held in Paris from 11 to 15 September 1945.[136] Spencer represented the London Firm but Seatree, who had expressed his intention to return to France as head of the partnership, was too ill to attend, and died shortly afterwards.[137] At a third meeting, assembled in July 1946, it was decided that Ferguson, Thompson and Webster should constitute an executive committee, and they, together with Evans, Ramsden, Edwards and Voors, became the sole proprietors of the capital of the various Continental partnerships.[138] After consulting both the UK and US Firms it was also decided that Thompson, then based in Stockholm, should be offered the senior partnership. He moved to Paris and Evans transferred to Stockholm. Thompson was described by Pollard as 'tough' with 'enormous energy and drive'.[139] He also had an extensive knowledge of European accounting methods having worked in Romania, Italy, France and Sweden. When he retired in 1957, after forty-two years' service with Price Waterhouse, Thompson was acknowledged as having been the chief architect of the Continental Firm's post-war prosperity,[140] but although able Thompson was also dictatorial and had been feared as much as respected by his fellow partners. His departure left an executive vacuum, not filled until the early sixties.[141]

During 1945 Price Waterhouse reopened offices in Paris, Brussels and Rotterdam, to add to those at Zürich and Stockholm which had continued to function throughout the war. At some point between June 1946 and December 1947 the style of the practice was changed to that of European Firm, perhaps to emphasise its new constitution and the attempt to integrate its practice more fully. By December 1947 the reconstituted firm comprised eight partners, four of whom were based in Paris (Thompson, Kerr, Ramsden and Webster), and the other four posted to Stockholm (Evans), Zürich (Edwards), Brussels (Ferguson) and The Hague (Voors).[142] In order to reestablish a practice in Italy, Price Waterhouse acquired IRCA, a Swiss accounting company set up in October 1946 by former employees of the Milan office.[143] This, in turn, led to the opening of the Milan office in February 1948 under the charge of W.P. Earley, who became a partner two years later. In December 1946 it was judged that 'the time had not yet arrived to open an office in Germany and that there was a decided objection to appointing a former German member of our pre-war organisation as an agent'.[144]

The late 1940s proved commercially problematic as nations suffering the cumulative effects of war struggled to return to peacetime economic performance. The Paris office reported in 1949 that 'there is little encouraging news to give of the year's activities' and though 'profits have been maintained, there is little room for enthusiasm'.[145] They experienced 'serious staff difficulties':

> Good men are not easy to find and when we find them, they seem
> disinclined to leave home to come abroad. We have tried repeatedly
> to find suitable French staff with senior qualifications but have been
> unsuccessful.[146]

The Zürich office assumed considerable importance in the immediate post-war years for not only did it supervise work in Italy, it also took responsibility for work performed in Germany and Austria.[147] During this period Voors contacted the Allied occupation authorities in the major German cities with a view to re-establishing the firm there. Such was the disruption in the country that nothing could be organised until 1951 though the volume of German business conducted from elsewhere grew appreciably. In 1950, for example, the Brussels office examined the accounts of Esso AG, Hamburg, and the firm did work for Unilever, Shell, National Cash Register, Tidewater Oil, Coca-Cola and various film companies based in Germany.[148]

With Voors having regained his German accountancy qualification, lost as a result of the war, Price Waterhouse was re-registered as a *Wirtschaftsprüfungsgesellschaft* in Hamburg in 1951. The local firm of

Johann Philippi & Co. GmbH of Frankfurt was acquired and became, in effect, the practice's second office.[149] At this stage the Frankfurt staff was wholly German and Pollard, who had worked in Berlin before the war, was transferred there as a partner to take charge.

The reopening of offices in Hamburg and Frankfurt marked the final phase of the European Firm's reconstruction on the Continent. Romania and the other Eastern European nations in which Price Waterhouse had been active pre-1939 refused to allow members of the practice to return. The legacy of war also endured in other ways and the standard of living in many Continental countries remained low. Even Sweden suffered an acute housing shortage. In Holland, for example, it was difficult to obtain residence permits for British staff and virtually impossible to engage trained Dutch accountants as they would automatically lose their qualification on joining a foreign firm. New international bodies, such as the United Nations, UNESCO and ECA, offered attractive posts to accountants which many accepted and this added to Price Waterhouse's staffing difficulties.[150]

The core of the European Firm's practice in the post-war period was the protection of British and American capital investments through the audit and investigation of subsidiaries based on the Continent. To achieve these ends it employed the standards and procedures current in the UK and United States. Because the accountancy profession had been relatively slow to develop in most Continental nations, there was considerable scope for firms like Price Waterhouse to expand their partnerships. There were, nevertheless, a number of problems inherent in the conduct of the European practice. First, in performing most audits there would be two clients to serve, the British or American parent and the subsidiary governed by domestic laws or regulations. Often, therefore, accounts would have to be reported upon or prepared according to two sets of standards, which could, in turn, lead to conflicting judgements.[151]

Before the Second World War only one partner in the Continental Firm was not British or American – Willem Voors, a Dutch national, who had been admitted in 1934. As locally recruited accountants became increasingly proficient, so they were promoted in greater numbers. By 1970, for instance, eight Continentals (of French, Belgian, Swiss, Swedish and German nationality) had become partners and the trend was for a growing proportion of European nationals to be elected.[152] Moreover, an increasing amount of work arose from within the Continent, rather than being referred from outside, as taxation and management consultancy commissions increased; these, in turn, required a high degree of expertise in local company and tax law.

The fifties and early sixties have been characterised as a period of 'consolidation and steady growth'.[153] In 1955, for example, most of the firm's principal offices reported moderate levels of 'improvement' in both fee income and profits.[154] This was largely the product of new work, the Brussels office, for example, undertaking twenty-six additional assignments, including that for the Belgian textile company, Roos Geerinckx & De Naeyer S.A. Alost.[155] In September 1946 the European Firm had comprised 135 partners and staff (the largest office being Paris with forty-four). By January 1953 it had grown to 225, the respective office totals being Paris (forty-nine), Brussels (twenty-four), The Hague (twenty-four), Stockholm (seventeen), Milan (twenty), Zürich (thirty-eight), Hamburg (twenty-six) and Frankfurt (twenty-seven).[156] Ten years after the reopening of the Paris office in 1945 numbers had recovered to near their pre-war level. There were ten partners: F. Thompson, W. Kerr, J.W. Keenan (all in Paris), H. Edwards (Zürich), T.L. Ferguson (Brussels), W.P. Earley (The Hague), W. Voors (Hamburg), G.B. Pollard (Frankfurt), J.C. Dickinson (Stockholm) and J.A. Anderson (Milan). They were spread over ten recognised offices with resident professionals based in a further six locations.

Representatives had been stationed in Madrid, Barcelona and Lisbon since 1948, and branch offices were opened in these cities in the next six years, a Spanish partnership having been formed in 1951. A Portuguese Firm was set up in 1956 and a branch of the Swiss practice in Copenhagen followed in 1957. Offices were also established in Düsseldorf in 1954 and Rome in December 1955.[157]

There was a radical change in partnership policy in July 1955 when Klas de Vylder was admitted to the Swedish Firm. Hitherto all partners in the European practice contributed capital and were members of the overriding Swiss partnership and of the local partnerships constituted in the various countries. However, de Vylder (and Johann Philippi who in January 1956 became a member of the German Firm based in Frankfurt) was admitted as a 'local' rather than a 'general' partner. The distinction was introduced to allow qualified nationals to become partners but without the expectation that they might be transferred beyond their country of origin. In time, however, this two-fold division was revised, and British qualified staff were initially promoted as local partners, with the award of a general partnership being reserved for those who showed particular merit.

In 1956 Thompson, the senior partner, announced that it was his intention to retire in the following year. He was succeeded by Harold Edwards, who being almost sixty, stipulated that he should not be asked to hold the post for more than four years. Described as 'conservative and intellectual', he resisted change and encouraged the status quo after the strenuous and difficult years Thompson and his colleagues had negotiated in rebuilding the practice. The period 1957 to 1961 saw the European Firm transformed from a medium-sized practice over which a single individual could retain executive authority into one which, by virtue of its size, demanded a more complex form of organisation.

In July 1961 Edwards was succeeded as senior partner by Pollard who in the eight years of his office set about modernising and developing the firm. Pollard who had joined Price Waterhouse in 1929 having qualified with a Lancashire firm, had worked successfully in Milan, Romania and Berlin until the impending war forced him to return to the UK. Having served as resident manager in Birmingham, Pollard was admitted to the European partnership in 1951, when he returned to Germany. Before becoming senior partner, he had headed the Swiss practice and thus had acquired an extensive knowledge of European methods and thinking.

At the time of Pollard's succession the partnership had eighteen members with offices at Paris, The Hague, Brussels, Copenhagen, Stockholm, Hamburg, Frankfurt, Düsseldorf, Zürich, Geneva, Milan, Genoa, Rome, Madrid, Barcelona, Lisbon, Algiers, Casablanca and Tripoli, while there were also bases with resident representatives in Oslo and Helsinki.[158] The only country in Western Europe where the firm had failed to establish premises was Austria, where foreign accountants were excluded by law from setting up in practice, though a considerable amount of work was carried out in Vienna by staff despatched from Zürich.

The pace of growth quickened. In 1960 the overall increase in work created staff shortages which were particularly acute in France, Italy (where assignments were refused) and Switzerland.[159] Four new partners (D.L. Burns, C.B. James, N. Lathom-Sharp and F.H. Vogt) were admitted during 1961.[160] The Paris office now totalled seventy-eight partners and staff, not including the eleven based in Algiers and Casablanca, sixteen in Portugal and twelve in Spain, all of whom were supervised from France.[161] These figures represented an annual growth rate in staff of 18.8 per cent. In the year to June 1962, for example, the Paris office (then the headquarters of the European Firm) took on sixty new clients and undertook numerous investigations of companies being considered for acquisition by British and American interests. Between 1963 and 1964 eight new partners were admitted. A major problem, therefore, was to maintain adequate staffing levels and yet provide opportunities for those seconded from the UK Firm to gain experience on the Continent without necessarily considering a permanent career there.[162]

By 1965 the European Firm had not only been re-established but had far surpassed the levels it had achieved by 1938 – a considerable organisational achievement given that the firm was spread across seventeen nations at a time when communications were principally by letter. Much effort had been directed to establishing a sense of common objectives and purpose. As the partnership remained within manageable limits and was largely composed of expatriates, this had encouraged the creation of a 'family' atmosphere and bi-annual meetings were arranged to foster contacts. However, the pace of change began to quicken and Price Waterhouse's leading position in Europe was about to be challenged by other ambitious firms.

The Quiet Revolution

In the thirty years following the Second World War the contribution of Britain's service sector to GNP, to the balance of payments and as an employer steadily and significantly increased. In 1955, for example, 9.4 million people, representing 40.1 per cent of the total working population of the UK, were employed in manufacturing, while services accounted for 10.7 million, or 45.7 per cent. By 1973 the former had dropped to 7.8 million and the latter risen to 12.5 million, an increase of 17 per cent.[1] In other words economic growth in Britain had been achieved, in part, by an expansion in banking, insurance, distribution and the professions to take the place of a declining industrial base. By growing in absolute size, extending the range of their services and developing their overseas networks, the major accountancy firms played an important part in this dynamic change.

The seventies witnessed the rise of what the accountancy press christened 'The Big Eight' (Arthur Andersen, Arthur Young McClelland Moores, Coopers & Lybrand, Deloitte Haskins & Sells, Ernst & Whinney, Peat Marwick Mitchell, Price Waterhouse and Touche Ross), those firms which by their size were considered distinct from the remainder of the profession. In achieving this dominant position, these large-scale practices managed to avoid both acrimony and unwelcome headline publicity even though the external forces which encouraged these changes and the internal responses to them were both fundamental and far-reaching. Partnerships which had been formally limited to twenty members now numbered in excess of a hundred. Firms which had hitherto been tied across the world in a loose network adopted a single corporate style and sought to introduce common procedures and technical standards. Whereas the leading firms traditionally looked to their respective professional institutes for guidance, now that they had become major business concerns they turned to their own committees and research groups when matters of policy and practice arose. As a key member of the Big Eight, Price Waterhouse played an important part in this movement which in view of its undemonstrative but dramatic character may be termed the 'quiet revolution'.

Partnership Changes

Sir Thomas Robson, who had become senior partner in 1961 aged sixty-five, decided to retire in September 1966. Because of the increasing pressures of running a major accountancy firm Robson had proposed, a few years before his own departure, that partners should be entitled to retire on full consultancy terms at sixty, or on a lower scale if this occurred before, but that they must resign at sixty-five unless requested to continue.[2] When Robson himself left the firm aged seventy-one, it was ruled that G.E. Richards, the longest serving of the partners and, by tradition, next in line to be head of the practice, should also retire. Richards, who had no wish to leave the firm, felt personally wounded by the new regulation and never returned to the office which he had supervised with such zeal for so many years.

With the departure of Richards, the unwritten rule of seniority prevailed and W.E. Parker, who had been admitted to the partnership in 1944, succeeded Robson as head of Price Waterhouse. However, this succession had not been automatic. In January 1965 Robson had canvassed his fellow partners on the best method of choosing a future senior partner. He agreed that:

> a)   Age and length of service are not the most important factors for determining choice, though they enter into the consideration of it.
>
> b)   The object should be to choose the individual who has the highest qualities of character, personality and leadership, whose judgement the partners respect, and in whom they have confidence. He should be a man of high standing in the profession and in the community . . . It is desirable that his age and health and his own personal plans should be such as to give reasonable expectation that his tenure of office will be at least five and preferably five to ten years.[3]

These proposals had been adopted by the Executive Committee, and a 'Sounding Committee' was set up to 'elicit the views of each individual

UK partner as to the partner whom he considers to have the best qualifications'.[4] The committee then had to decide on a single candidate and recommend their adoption at a meeting of the partnership. 'The desirability of avoiding a dispute' was considered an important guideline in order to maintain 'unanimity'. In this way a formal election was avoided in favour of an emerging consensus somewhat in the manner that a new Pope is elected by the college of cardinals.

The growth of the firm and its broader geographical base resulted, as Robson observed, in it being increasingly difficult to find 'a United Kingdom leader acceptable to the partners'. Parker, as the man most likely to win this approval, responded to Robson:

> Looking to the longer future it appears to me that the internal leadership of the firm will increasingly call for the vigour and drive of a comparatively young man (perhaps in his early fifties) whereas the attributes needed for the outward representation of the firm will usually be found in a man of greater age, experience and reputation. We have seen such a duumvirate work well in the period soon after the 1939–1945 War when N.E.W. and T.B.R. were both active and T.B.R. provided the internal leadership while N.E.W. was an excellent senior partner for external purposes and as the holder internally of an elder statesman's watching brief.[5]

Parker was perhaps concerned that he, aged fifty-seven on Robson's retirement, might have been overlooked in favour of a younger man. In the event the Sounding Committee decided that the firm's interests would best be served by recommending an established and trusted figure rather than risk an able but untried junior partner.

Parker had spent all his professional life with the firm, apart from the war years when he was seconded to the Board of Trade.[6] Actively involved in ICAEW affairs (Chairman of the London and District Society of Chartered Accountants in 1956–7 and elected to the Council in 1957, Chairman of the Committee on Education and Training and President in 1967–8), he fell into the traditional mould of senior partners. Educated at Winchester College, he had been articled to F.S. Price in 1926 and qualified in 1931, having obtained honours in the intermediate examination. Proving himself to be an intelligent and able accountant, he became a manager in 1937. Parker was not, however, a radical nor was he perhaps a great strategist or long-term thinker. He was, nevertheless, a man of considerable charm and charisma. He took an interest in people, particularly the young, and was happy to give them their heads and to encourage them. The five new partners admitted in 1966 were candidates strongly supported by Parker and he proved receptive to their ideas. Two of these new partners, Read and Bowman, though very different personalities, formed an informal alliance to raise issues. In order to avoid the impression of collaborating too much, they sat on opposite sides of the square of tables at partnership meetings. Parker never discouraged their constructive criticism.

However, according to Michael Coates, himself subsequently to become senior partner, Parker was reluctant to alter the essential nature of the practice and retained a strong allegiance to the idea that all the partners should be able to gather in a single room on a daily basis to discuss policy in an informal and relaxed manner.[7] Parker, like Robson, believed that the professional ethic was more important for a firm such as Price Waterhouse than mere business considerations. While recognising, of course, that the partnership could survive only so long as it earned profits, he believed that its status relied upon technical excellence and high standards of personal conduct rather than in competing with rivals to win new clients and extending the range of services. Parker himself felt, a view he expressed to Lord Benson, that his lengthy period as understudy to Robson had diminished his enthusiasm for the senior partnership and resulted in his succeeding to executive authority comparatively late.[8] Parker later recalled that he had inherited from Robson

> a firm bursting with talent and energy but vaguely frustrated. My main task was to give it its head. The consequence of doing so was . . . an almost explosive expansion. Concurrently I was anxious also to break away from the rather oligarchic tradition that had hitherto prevailed and to get much wider participation, not just by partners but by staff as well, in the framing of policy and the extensive tasks of administration. In all that I was immensely helped by my colleague, Stanley Duncan, who effectively played the role of 'managing director' to my 'chairman'.[9]

After his retirement from Price Waterhouse, Parker was knighted in 1974 for public services. He had among other achievements been the independent expert called upon to assess the price payable by the government for the aero-engine assets of Rolls-Royce and been chairman of the Local Employment Act's financial committee.[10]

When Parker retired in 1971 the senior partnership passed to Stanley Duncan. The latter had joined Price Waterhouse in 1932 and had been admitted to the firm in 1946; he was the longest serving of its members.[11] However, the emphasis placed on experience was now greatly reduced. Again several partners who were not candidates themselves were empowered to collect opinions and reduce these to a single name on which the partnership could vote by secret ballot. If there was a majority then the recommendation was carried forward. It was an oligarchic procedure by which only a few could run for office and wherein the selection process was not available for scrutiny. Nevertheless, it represented a mid-way stage between succession based primarily on seniority and the electoral college of today's largest partnerships.

In June 1966 Duncan had been appointed executive partner, a post 'with national responsibilities to relieve the senior partner as much as possible of administrative duties'.[12] To some extent it was an understudy role, so that it would have come as no great surprise when, in June 1970, the Sounding Committee recommended Duncan as the next senior partner.[13] Ratification was followed by his appointment as deputy senior partner, a newly created position.

Duncan liked to describe himself as 'a bit of a rebel'.[14] He had been a protagonist of the reforms carried through in Price Waterhouse from the mid-fifties, and had been involved in the creation of the service company, the introduction of specialist partners, the determined recruitment of staff from outside the firm, improved training for articled clerks and the reorganisation of management procedures. Although sixty-one when he became senior partner, Duncan was appointed for a five-year period. He believed that in view of his impending retirement his term of office would be shortened. Given the limitations of time, he decided that his priority should be the structure of the firm rather than its public image. The Industrial Society were consulted and eventually a new framework for the firm was devised.

Duncan, a gentlemanly figure with a disarmingly warm manner (which led to the nickname 'Uncle Stan'), was not an autocratic leader. Although he had a clear vision of what he wanted to achieve, Duncan sought to encourage able lieutenants and then to arrive at a consensus view. He created an atmosphere in which change could evolve rather than driving it through himself against opposition.[15]

Duncan took his retirement in June 1975, a year earlier than planned, in order to take up the important post of chairman of the International Firm.[16] With a view to smoothing the transition of authority, in December 1973 the partnership set up a Sounding Committee (consisting of Fred Chapman, Douglas Sandry and Joe Sewell) to nominate a deputy senior partner by March 1974.[17] Sewell, who had joined Price Waterhouse in 1939 having qualified in Middlesbrough with Chipchase Wood & Co., was an accountant of acknowledged technical expertise and as an active member of the Society of Friends maintained a tradition of nonconformity in the firm. The three duly selected M.A. Coates, appointed with effect from July 1974. Having served in two key positions (director of manpower from 1969 and director of office operations from 1972), Coates was in many respects the natural successor to Duncan.[18] Between 1959 and 1970 his main professional responsibilities were in auditing though he was also involved in investigations and prospectus work. Coates, like Duncan, was appointed senior partner for five years, but was eligible for re-election.

By the spring of 1966 Price Waterhouse had twenty-one partners based in London. The growth of the firm's business, not only in new assignments but also in the expansion of work done for existing audit clients, outstripped the rate at which partners could be admitted. Parker calculated that a further four to five partners were needed for professional and administrative duties simply to cope with the 'existing' workload.[19] In fact, the problem could not be solved simply by selecting and training managers. As Coates subsequently discovered from a survey of professional staff in 1970,

> the number of partner prospects was hardly sufficient to meet the anticipated needs of the firm. The manager prospects appeared to be sufficient in numbers but no account had been taken of the number of existing managers who did not have partnership potential.[20]

In June 1971 Coates again drew attention to the 'shortage of candidates to meet the expected requirements for partners and managers . . . and the unduly high proportion of the manager strength which consists of "career" managers'.[21]

The problem related, therefore, to the internal structure of the firm and its traditional partner ethic. In the thirties and forties it was accepted that the firm should consist of no more than around a dozen partners. These were life appointments and drawn solely from within the ranks of Price Waterhouse. Most professional staff realised that they had little or no chance of ever becoming a partner. Success flowed from high marks in professional examinations, technical excellence and an ability to handle clients. Thus the vast majority of the firm's qualified staff had limited prospects of promotion; they could, if they wished, step up the slow ladder of seniority leading to manager, or use Price Waterhouse as a source of experience and opportunity. Those who had no hope of a partnership but did not seek the path of 'career manager', either sought employment in commerce and industry or joined lesser-known firms. This created three distinct groups: a hard core, in whom commitment to the firm combined with circumscribed ambition, who remained with Price Waterhouse until retirement; secondly, a floating population whose intention was to leave as and when openings emerged; and thirdly, a select body whose talent and good fortune marked them out for the partnership. As a result, there was no system for selecting and nurturing partners, and Price Waterhouse had no established means of recruiting the able for progression to positions of authority. To guarantee a sufficient number of talented accountants ready to assume the responsibility of partner required a major overhaul of recruitment, training and career structure within the firm. Such an innovation could not be effected quickly nor without upsetting established practices and ethics.

In the short term Price Waterhouse attempted to solve the problem by carefully interviewing its professional staff in order to assess all available talent. The rate at which managers and partners were promoted was increased, while the mergers with provincial and specialist practices helped to raise numbers further. By 1970 the UK partnership had reached sixty-five members (Table 15, see Appendix), and it continued to grow at a steady, if not spectacular rate throughout the decade, reaching eighty-seven by 1975 and 134 by 1980.

A major upset occurred in October 1974 when Martin Harris, a partner for eighteen years, resigned to take up the post of Director-General of the Panel of Take-Overs and Mergers. Although Harris gave his wish to explore fresh challenges as his reason for leaving, it was thought by his colleagues that disappointment at not being elected senior partner was a contributory factor.[22] His contribution to Price Waterhouse had been very different to that of Michael Coates. Having performed a substantial amount of investigation work, Harris built up extensive contacts in the City, in government and the ICAEW. As a result, he attracted many new assignments. Unlike Coates, he did not have a great facility for administration, but did have a boyish and enthusiastic manner which endeared him to many younger members of the firm. This was particularly important at a time when the partnership was largely composed of shy introverts. Harris, along with Bucknill, Parker, Read and Wilson, had a more open, relaxed style which made him approachable to both staff and clients. Aided by Tony Bayliss, he played a key role in breaking down the barriers that existed between partners, managers and staff by calling everybody by their christian name at a time when surnames were the usual form. The departure of Harris was a considerable loss as his abilities would have complemented those of Coates.

A further disappointment followed in May 1975 when John Read left the partnership.[23] An able accountant with considerable business acumen, he had joined Price Waterhouse in 1958 having qualified with Northcott, Lyddon & Co. in Plymouth.[24] His promotion within the firm had been rapid, from assistant manager in 1963 to manager a year later and to becoming a partner in 1966. His audit responsibilities included Hawker Siddeley, Esso and Viyella, though he had gained his reputation for investigations, including the Dunlop–Pirelli merger, work for Guardian Properties and the Spillers–French amalgamation. He had been placed in charge of Audit Group 4 in London office, creating, by the force of his personality, something of an élite force, attracting and inspiring younger, talented accountants. They, in turn, found it interesting and stimulating to work for him. Many of these subsequently became partners or held positions of executive authority in Price Waterhouse. His departure, albeit to take the post of financial director of Unigate, came as a shock to the firm. He gave the need for change and fears about the growing size of the partnership as his reasons for leaving,[25] though his colleagues believed that he had been disappointed not to have been elected that year to the Policy Committee.[26] As one of the more ambitious of the firm's younger partners, he had an uneasy relationship with Coates, particularly over the execution of the Southwark Towers project (see p. 271).

Restructuring the Firm

By the spring of 1965 the growth in the scale of Price Waterhouse's audit operations had created the 'urgent need for a review of the firm's organisation'.[27] It had become difficult to implement decisions promptly and to monitor the quality of work, while there was also a sense that the practice had become unwieldy and slow to respond to change.[28] Writing with the benefit of hindsight, Michael Coates believed that

> the firm was on the verge of irreversible decline. The first step in the modernisation of the firm was to establish an element of democracy under which the appointment of the senior partner and of the principal committee which supported him became subject to the vote of all the partners rather than a matter of seniority. Another crucially important decision was to establish a fixed retirement age for partners. These reforms were not easily won, but ... the opportunity existed ... to examine every facet of the firm's internal and external operating procedures and as time went on to relate them to an overall strategic plan.[29]

Accordingly, a review 'of existing resources and an assessment of actual and prospective needs' was ordered.

Early in 1964 a 'group' system of management for London office had been introduced. Five groups (labelled A,B,C,D and E) were formed. Each was based around a team of managers who were engaged upon recurring audits.[30] The aim was to devolve practical responsibility to manager level so that they could control staff requirements and the allocation of work to certain individuals more efficiently. Each group was designed to operate 'as a sort of medium-size practice within the totality of London office'.[31] However, the full administrative ramifications of the scheme had not been envisaged and serious problems soon emerged. Unbalanced workloads between the various groups necessitated the retention of central control over allocations. Managerial responsibilities had not been adequately defined, and it was found that large audits could involve the professional staff of one group combined with managers from another team.[32]

Accordingly, in December 1966 after two years in operation, the group structure was abandoned and London office reverted to 'a system of central allocation of staff to general professional work'.[33] However, the rejection of a devolved organisation proved to be a mistake. London office, by 1966, was simply too large to be managed in such a focused manner. At that time there were forty-seven managers (some of whom were specialists) and 347 professional audit staff (Table 11, see Appendix).

Duncan realised that it was necessary to reassess the problem. He approached John Garnett, director of the Industrial Society, who then addressed a partnership conference at Branksome Towers, Bournemouth.[34] Garnett recommended that this large body of audit staff be broken into teams, each to be no larger than twelve members as this, he argued, was the maximum number that could be properly supervised by a single manager. The teams were assembled into four groups, and a more rigorous attempt was made to define their operating roles, procedures and limits of action. Each group was headed by a partner of seniority; they were respectively Fred Chapman, Tony Bayliss, Colin Brown and John Read.[35] In essence these groups, though reorganised, have remained the essential structure for the management and execution of audit assignments up to the present day.

At much the same time that the firm's mode of operating was being re-examined, the issue of its internal management became important. In January 1966 Parker concluded that 'the growth and heavy accumulation of . . . "non-chargeable" pre-occupations' was such that it was necessary to 'reverse our long-standing policy of spreading these as widely as possible over the London partners'.[36] Hitherto administrative tasks, training, recruitment, technical questions and the financial aspects of the partnership had not been so onerous that they could not be entrusted to audit partners. Parker now recommended that four national committees (finance and general policy, technical, staff and review) be formed to report to the partnership. After discussion the review committee was renamed 'special' and was designed to make recommendations for admissions to the partnership. These bodies were formally adopted by the firm in December 1966.[37]

Not only had the firm outgrown its managerial structure, it had also developed beyond existing financial reporting procedures. When George Carter was appointed finance partner in 1966, he discovered that there were five sets of separate records: for London and the old regional offices, together with books for the firms that Price Waterhouse had merged with in Birmingham, Bristol, Newcastle and Nottingham. All were handwritten to preserve confidentiality. Over the next four years he set about standardising procedures and integrating these into a truly consolidated accounting record.[38] In the 1970s the data was transferred to computer and this permitted the collection of more detailed records about the firm's financial performance, chargeable hours and staffing levels, which, in turn, enabled the executive to be better informed when taking management decisions.[39]

However, continued growth not only in the size of the practice and its geographical spread but also in the range and complexity of services provided required further organisational refinement. In July 1972, Duncan introduced proposals for a new executive structure for the UK Firm. This involved the creation of a Policy Committee (composed of the senior partner and seven influential partners: Bowman, Cherry, Coates, Collett, Harris, Milligan and Wilson), and a redefinition of the management structure. The latter was achieved by the appointment of five 'national directors' each responsible for a specific area of administration, reporting to the senior partners.[40] They comprised: Michael Coates (director of office operations), Martin Harris (director of professional relations), Fred King (director of finance), Jeffery Bowman (director of technical services) and Ernest Barnes (director of UK management consultancy services). Authority was also devolved to the ten regional offices (Birmingham, Bristol, Cardiff, Glasgow, Leeds, Leicester, Liverpool, Manchester, Newcastle and Nottingham) which each had a partner in charge. London office, because of its size, had an executive partner, Tony Cherry, and was subdivided into four audit groups, as well as having specific partners responsible for tax (Eric Bridges), special services (Graham Stacy) and insolvency (Monty Eckman).

In June 1973, Michael Coates presented a report entitled 'The Firm in the Future' to the partnership meeting. His report questioned the very identity and goals of Price Waterhouse. It was a seminal paper; its ideas and proposals were to exercise the firm for the next decade. His researches revealed that

> the financial community still thought that PW is too 'superior', too fussy and not commercial enough. Some partners think we tend to breed introverts . . . There is a general feeling that too few partners are well known outside the firm. There is also a recurring comment that we have a reputation of being uninterested in medium and small sized clients.[41]

It was also concluded that

> excellence rather than size for its own sake should be our goal; nevertheless, it was agreed that a certain size is inescapable to enable us to have a large enough base to provide a full range of external and internal services and in order to be able to attract the cream of young men coming into the profession. In practice this means that

we must aim to be broadly comparable in terms of size with our
major competitors.[42]

The position of Price Waterhouse in the market was considered in a
formal way, perhaps for the first time in its history. It was concluded
that it would be 'hazardous to place too much reliance on the growth of
... existing large clients' and that the firm should concentrate 'on the
lower half of *The Times 1000* list, and on the next 1,000 companies'.[43] A
more positive attitude to practice development was considered desirable,
and was probably necessary if the firm wished to maintain its 'existing
national reputation' as expansion of the client list was the only sure
defence against 'stagnation or decline'.[44] The document was subjected to
much debate and formed the basis for a strategic plan submitted to the
Policy Committee in November 1973.[45] This recommended that in
order to achieve its aims, Price Waterhouse should set an annual growth
rate of 5 per cent in terms of chargeable hours with a minimum of 3 per
cent.[46] The objective should be to double the firm's market share by
1980, with priority being given to the northwest, Yorkshire, Humberside
and the West Midlands.

Growth over the following decade was seen as deriving from an
increased market share at the expense of other firms (and in practice this
proved to be those of medium size); a rapid move to work commanding
'premium rates', such as investigations, tax consultancy and management
consultancy assignments; and, to a lesser extent, by expansion into new
types of work.[47] Projections indicated that an increase in chargeable
hours of less than 3 per cent per annum would not generate sufficient profits to support rising indirect costs of training and accommodation.

As regards regional coverage in Britain, it was concluded that Peats
alone of the UK firms had a comprehensive network (based upon an
established policy of territorial growth). Price Waterhouse was recognised as having a 'commanding' market share only in the northeast (as a
result of the merger with Monkhouse Goddard). Its representation was
considered 'reasonable' in the East Midlands and Yorkshire but deficient
in the West Midlands and northwest, while its market occupation in
Scotland was 'negligible'.[48]

The Statistics of Growth

In terms of fee income (Table 14, see Appendix) the late sixties and early seventies were years of impressive and sustained growth. Turnover rose from £2.8 million in 1965–6 to £14.2 million in 1975 which, even after adjusting for inflation still represented an increase of 126 per cent. Profits also advanced from £919,000 in 1969 to £2,275,000 in 1975, a rise of 71 per cent in real terms. The lower percentage growth for profits was a reflection of the rise in the number of partners and the greater provision made for training, premises and business services within the firm. The ratio between profits and fees had declined since the late nineteenth century when profits commonly represented 75 per cent of turnover; by the late 1960s the proportion was around 20 per cent (Table 14, see Appendix).

How, then, was this dramatic growth financed? If a manufacturing business wishes to expand, it generally requires capital expenditure on buildings, plant and machinery and this is often sufficiently heavy to demand a substantial bank loan or even a share issue. The nature of accountancy and the financial arrangements of the partnership have combined to render these methods either inapplicable or unnecessary. The unlimited nature of the partnership has made resort to the stock market impossible, while the arrangements for the retention of profits resulted in its capital needs remaining within the scope of internally generated funds.

On admission partners have to make a contribution, spread over four years, towards working capital. This is then repayable on retirement. As a partner's share in the profits increases, so additional capital is required. The capital contribution per profit unit remained unchanged from the late 1960s until after the European Combination in 1988, by which time, after taking account of inflation, it had become a relatively small amount. A key barrier to entry was dismantled by Sir Nicholas Waterhouse after the Second World War when he abandoned the system of making payments to retiring partners for their share of the goodwill of the business. Thus, new partners were no longer expected to pay for goodwill.

With the exception of the period when the Newcastle office had a separate partnership, the UK Firm has operated a single profit pool from which partners drew their income. On admission to the firm, a new partner is allocated a number of profit units which then determine the level of his income. Additional units can be granted on the basis of performance and experience. The maximum number of units that can be held by any partner is about three and a half times the allocation of a newly admitted member of the partnership. The single profit pool (in contrast to some practices where there may be several arranged on a geographical division) has created a strong partnership spirit and has facilitated the management of the firm, requiring a single decision when capital expenditure is required. Thus, profits in a partnership have a different character to those in a limited liability company insofar as they represent three elements: first, executive remuneration for the efforts put into the enterprise by the partners; secondly, interest on capital invested by the partners; and thirdly, profit from the ownership of the business.

The other way in which capital contributions from new partners were kept low was the establishment in 1965 of a service company, which was owned by the partnership and which, in turn, owned the fixed assets and a substantial part of the working capital of the firm as well as employing the staff. The service company earned a profit on the tasks which it undertook and it was decided at an early stage that no partner should be credited with his share of these retained funds. This enabled the firm to accumulate substantial assets within the service company which allowed it to finance expansion and also served as a base for borrowings to make up any shortfall in working capital. The assets of the service company were also boosted in 1975 by the sale of the leasehold interest in Frederick's Place, the proceeds from which were retained and provided funds for the firm's investment in Southwark Towers.

During the 1960s and early 1970s Price Waterhouse owed its position in the marketplace to a dominant audit practice. It was estimated in 1968, for example, that the firm audited seventy-nine (or 15.8 per cent of the total number of appointments) of the 500 largest industrial companies in Britain, Peats being second with sixty-four and Deloittes third with forty-seven.[49] Based on data from *The Times 1000* for 1974–5, Price Waterhouse ranked first in the UK with the greatest number of audit appointments from the 500 largest companies together with a group of financial institutions and nationalised industries, ahead of Deloittes, Coopers & Lybrand and Whinney Murray in descending order.[50]

An approximate analysis of the work performed by Price Waterhouse in 1975 can be obtained from the distribution of professional staff (Figure

16, p. 293). Within the UK 83 per cent were involved in auditing, 12 per cent in tax and 4 per cent in management consultancy. By 1984 the proportions had altered to 67.5, 14.6 and 14.1 respectively, with insolvency and other specialist commissions making up the remainder.[51] Although audit contributed around 75 per cent of Price Waterhouse's fee income in the late seventies,[52] the following decade witnessed a dramatic fall in its overall contribution as both tax and management consultancy work increased their share. In 1987–8, for example, the percentages were as follows: audit (41), tax (21), management consultancy (24), corporate reconstruction and insolvency (4) and special investigations (10).[53]

Throughout the sixties Price Waterhouse experienced great difficulty in recruiting professional staff of the calibre they desired. In May 1966 the Staff Committee reported that

> more men are now staying with the smaller firms to which they were articled, after qualification, and we believe that fewer men are interested in the prospects of living and working in the London area than was the case.[54]

As a result, the committee recommended increasing the number of articled clerks trained by the firm. In London they represented only 20 per cent of new employees.[55] In 1968 a report by Peter Ainger on 'Staff Planning' concluded that 'almost every audit manager is carrying too great a burden of professional work' such that they 'cannot be expected to control their jobs or devote sufficient time to planning or administration'. In a context of 'overall staff shortages', he concluded that much 'time is wasted or is ill-spent'.[56] The scarcity of able staff and a growing appreciation of the need to plan in strategic fashion, led to a formal debate at the UK Partners' Meeting in June 1969, chaired by Ernest Barnes. The status and function of the manager was examined in a paper presented by Michael Coates who suggested that the shortage of 'good managers' was a result of a policy failure. He concluded that Price Waterhouse should move

> in the direction of the 'up or out' policy of the United States firm under which, with a limited number of exceptions, a manager who has not reached partnership potential after say five to seven years is 'encouraged' to make his career elsewhere.[57]

In support of his argument Coates quoted a survey of the US Firm, conducted by external management consultants, which revealed that 47 per cent of professional staff reported that their goal was to become a partner; whereas only 7 per cent wished to remain a career manager. Coates believed that the UK Firm had not inspired a similar level of ambition and competitiveness.

In June 1971, presenting the National Staff Committee's report to the partnership, Coates again drew attention to the 'shortage of candidates to meet the expected requirements for partners and managers in future years and the unduly high proportion of the manager strength which consists of "career managers"'.[58] In response to this prompting it was concluded that a major review of staff requirements should be undertaken by Coates, Ainger and Bayliss in order that manpower needs could be planned on a strategic basis.[59] In essence, their plan involved calculating the proportions between each grade of staff assuming a high level of internal promotion; that is the number of articled clerks that might be expected to achieve the assistant manager, manager and partner grades, allowing for examinations, resignations and varied levels of competence. These then had to be co-ordinated within a timetable. How long, for example, did an assistant manager need to acquire the skills and experience of a manager? Those proportions also had to be related to the needs of the UK Firm, and in particular to its projected growth rates. The calculations were complicated and, if inaccurate, could leave the firm stranded with too few staff at certain levels or with a surplus at others. In later years it was estimated that for every hundred students recruited nine would eventually progress to become a partner and that on average this would take twelve years to achieve.[60] The proportions that were devised formed the fundamental basis for the recruitment of articled clerks.

As a result of the manpower report of 1971, Peter Ainger was appointed the firm's first national staff partner. Since Price Waterhouse now sought to supply their professional staff needs from internally trained students, it became increasingly important that they pay close attention to the recruitment of articled clerks. Further if the firm were to maintain its impressive rate of growth, these would have to be attracted in ever rising numbers. Indeed, throughout the seventies and eighties the student intake was cut only once, in 1976 in response to the secondary banking crisis and dramatic increase in oil prices.[61]

In order to respond appropriately to the expansion of the firm's audit business and the even more rapid growth in specialist services, it was essential that Price Waterhouse plan for the efficient recruitment and training of staff. The total UK workforce rose from 1,656 in 1970 to 2,857 in 1980 and to 6,580 in 1989 – growth rates of 73 and 130 per cent respectively. Over the entire twenty-year period, the partnership increased by 512 per cent, though the greatest increment (775 per cent) was in the number of managers; students grew by 329 per cent, practice support staff by 437 per cent and the smallest recorded increase was for 'other fee earning staff' at 112 per cent.

The training department within Price Waterhouse witnessed dramatic change during the decade from 1965. Two years earlier a report by Martin Harris concluded that there was a 'complete void of formal training courses between those for newly qualified accountants . . . and the managers' residential course'.[62] He recommended that both senior audit managers and assistant managers receive specific tuition. In 1966 when these proposals had been effected and the course for new seniors lengthened from two days to one week, it was concluded that

> the high rate of turnover in qualified staff makes it important to try
> to turn new joiners into useful members of the audit staff as
> quickly as possible. The revised and extended course is designed . . .
> to teach the PW method of tackling a medium or large-sized
> audit.[63]

The UK Firm lagged behind its American counterpart as Jeffery Bowman discovered when on exchange there. 'A comprehensive training programme,' he observed,

> is one of the inducements used to attract new staff to the firm. In
> addition, the firm must be able to offer reasonable prospects of
> fairly rapid promotion and indeed the rate of staff turnover makes
> swift promotion necessary; staff members, therefore, require training
> to enable them to occupy positions of responsibility after only
> relatively short periods of experience with the firm.[64]

The rising cost of training articled clerks and qualified staff caused the UK Firm to take due care both in the selection of new recruits and in taking steps to retain them once they had passed their examinations. In order to be able to provide the highest quality teaching, it was decided in

May 1973 to acquire a disused hop warehouse at Chapel Yard, Union Street, Southwark, and to convert it into a modern training centre.[65] This building, completed for occupation in August 1975, was the first of its kind in any UK accountancy firm.[66] It was followed in 1978 by the appointment of Mike Phillips as the first national training partner.

Because the expansion of the firm had been constrained in the early sixties by a shortage of able, qualified staff, it was decided in January 1967 to adopt a more active recruitment policy. A brochure was authorised,[67] and issued in September.[68] At about the same time graduates were actively encouraged to join the firm as articled clerks. The 1964 London intake of twenty-seven had contained only four graduates.[69] In 1965 the firm experimented by raising the proportion to eleven out of twenty-eight partly because the expansion of the universities was greatly increasing their supply and partly because the calibre of non-graduates was 'very disappointing'. By 1967 the Oxford University Appointments Committee was able to report that Price Waterhouse was recruiting around twenty graduates as articled clerks, of whom around six were from their colleges.[70] In June 1968 Price Waterhouse appointed their first 'recruitment officer', Ian Macpherson,[71] who had been employed in industry. This was in response to the conclusion that although the firm was obtaining 'a satisfactory share' of 'the limited number of graduates wishing to make their career in accountancy', this group was a relatively small proportion of those who entered 'commerce and industry'.[72] Macpherson was entrusted with the task of touring the major universities to establish contacts with their appointment boards.[73] A brochure entitled *Facts about your Future with Price Waterhouse & Co.*, dating from around 1972, was addressed exclusively to graduates.[74]

In 1973 Howard Hughes, as London staff partner, approached Dick Shervington, then a manager in MCS, to join the recruitment team, and three years later he became the first non-fee-earning partner. In 1974 when the new policy was in place 142 graduates joined Price Waterhouse, and eight of these were women.[75] The proportion of graduate articled clerks entering the profession rose from a mere 19 per cent in 1969 to 72 per cent ten years later.[76] Today Price Waterhouse normally admits only graduates as students. Over the same period the proportion of female trainees rose from 2 to 22 per cent and is now close to half.[77]

The Growth of Specialist Services

The predominant position held by auditing in the practices of the major City firms was progressively undermined during the seventies as taxation and management consultancy grew in significance. Nineteen sixty-five was the watershed year for taxation. Price Waterhouse conducted a survey of their taxation department's services in that year and concluded that its principal activities were: the preparation of tax computations for companies, individuals, trusts and estates, general advisory work (including businesses which were not audit clients), tax planning and back duty investigations.[78] London office estimated that 75 per cent of their work was the preparation of tax returns for companies; Leeds and Manchester offices had a similar proportion, though Birmingham reckoned that 70 per cent of their activity was on personal tax returns together with estate and trust work.

However, this pattern was to be disturbed by the events of 1965. The budget of that year not only raised levels of taxation (from 7s 9d to 8s 3d at the standard rate) but also increased their complexity. It saw the creation of Corporation Tax, designed to separate companies from individuals, and the introduction of Capital Gains Tax. From Peel's 1842 budget up to 1965 the British tax system had experienced few dramatic changes, and a considerable body of legal experience had been accumulated during the period through countless legal cases fought by individuals and companies against the Inland Revenue. However, the mass of new legislation in 1965, to be complicated further in 1973 by the introduction of Value Added Tax, overtook many of these precedents and created circumstances of 'uncertainty regarding the interpretation and application of fiscal statutes',[79] which, in turn, resulted in professional advisers suddenly finding themselves unable to predict with any certainty the outcome of any dispute with the Revenue. Consequently, negotiations and compromise with the authorities began to displace 'the settlement of disputed points by reference to the law'.[80] On 14 February 1968, under the heading 'Tax Overhaul Needed Say Accountants', *The Daily Express* concluded that 'the massive and complicated amount of government legislation introduced in recent years is bringing our tax system to near breaking point'. W.E. Parker as president of the ICAEW was quoted as saying 'recent measures – such as Capital Gains Tax,

Corporation Tax, the Land Development Levy, and S.E.T. [Selective Employment Tax] – have meant changes on an unprecedented scale'. This drew clients into closer involvement with those accountants or solicitors who acted as their informed intermediaries.

Price Waterhouse were aware that the emphasis on auditing and the historical requirement that all partners be general rather than specialist had hampered the emergence of the tax department, so they were suitably disposed when Michael Carr, senior partner of Sturges, Fraser & Co., approached them in 1970 to suggest a merger. The two firms had been jointly engaged on the flotation of Rentokil Group, Sturges, Fraser being the auditors. Carr was aware that the future for small and medium-sized City practices with audit clients was becoming perilous but was also conscious that Price Waterhouse wished to augment their specialist departments. Both he and his firm had developed an expertise in tax work. The possibility of a merger was initially discussed with Fred Chapman and, having gained the support of Duncan and Coates, concluded in 1971. Carr, together with Colin Duff, were both admitted to the partnership, and the former became the seventh tax partner in Price Waterhouse. Four years later, after the retirement of Inglis and Bailey, Carr was appointed Director of Tax Services and, because of his relatively short service in the firm, was assisted by Chris Collett.

Carr recognised that the market for tax services was broad and largely unexploited and that his first task was to persuade the partnership as a whole that investment in staff was required. He set out to recruit audit managers of high quality and to retrain them (this programme being entrusted to Peter Pullin). Partners in charge of regional offices had to be convinced of the importance of these specialists so that a truly national network of expertise could be established. Once the numbers of partners and staff had been increased it was possible to extend the activities of the department to cover the indirect taxes such as VAT, customs duties, taxes arising on death, personal and expatriate taxes.

In terms of rates of growth, management consultancy has been the most spectacular specialism offered by the major accountancy firms, mirroring the development of specialist services throughout the economy. These practices had their origins in requests from clients to help them reorganise their internal accounting and costing systems. To deal effectively with these problems systems departments were set up by the larger accountancy firms in the immediate post-war years. In order to reflect the size of their management consultancy practice, Price Waterhouse, in May 1966, decided to set up a distinct 'organisation', an unlimited liability company, entitled 'Price Waterhouse Co.', whose share capital was to be owned by the UK partnership. Because some members of the department were specialists, and could for example include engineers or economists, who were ineligible for a partnership, it was decided to appoint directors.[81] Fred King, Ernest Barnes and Bernard Brocks were among the first directors of the new MCS company.

By March 1969 management consultancy totalled forty-five staff in London with a further six in the northwest and two in the Midlands.[82] Growth was to be encouraged and a target of one MCS staff member to every ten auditors was set for the end of 1971. If it were achieved, this would have represented a doubling in the department's size with a disproportionate expansion in the regions. Parker, as senior partner, had some misgivings about the nature of management consultancy, feelings shared by some audit partners; they believed that such activities could become too divorced from the firm's core skills and might raise ethical questions. As a result Parker suggested that the MCS company be renamed to appear as a 'separate organisation', such as 'Price Waterhouse Associates', a style employed in Canada.[83] Barnes, who had succeeded Shaw as head of department, resisted the proposal arguing that there was no advantage to be gained from this change.

After a period of sustained growth the MCS practice encountered difficulties. In March 1971 Barnes reported that the department had traded at a loss for the previous five months.[84] An economy moving into recession had created shortages of work for all consultants.[85] Downturns were experienced more immediately in MCS than in auditing where the effects took longer to permeate. In November a working party of Barnes and Bayliss was appointed to review the activities of the department and to provide recommendations on its future operations.[86] They delivered their report in March 1972. Barnes concluded that the crucial strategic question was whether

> the scope of services should encompass a wide range of specialist disciplines or concentrate to a greater extent on work more directly related to the financial and accounting field ... or whether an intermediate range of services should be offered.[87]

The discussion revealed considerable resistance to the first option. Bayliss observed that 'many audit partners ... had doubts about the standard and direction of MCS services'.[88] In view of these doubts Duncan concluded that the department should reduce the scope of its activities to 'operate as an extension from the audit core of the practice; not as an unrelated service'. Following these decisions, and influenced by the secondary banking crisis, the MCS department contracted into a more cohesive and focused role. However, as Anthony Wilson pointed out in 1973, this left Price Waterhouse with a management consultancy practice with a 'narrower base' than that possessed by its major rivals.[89] This, in turn, prompted a wish to broaden activities in order to compete more effectively for work which might arise from non-audit clients. Opinion within the firm remained divided as to whether such expansion should be countenanced, and by what means.

An event of incalculable consequence to the MCS department had been the death in November 1968 of Len Shaw, the partner in charge.[90] Shaw had joined Price Waterhouse in 1930 on the recommendation of a client,[91] and qualified as an Incorporated Accountant.[92] Inglis, Bailey and Shaw were the first specialists to be admitted to the partnership. Having finished work at Old Jewry, Shaw had crossed the Thames to take his train from London Bridge Station to Orpington.[93] While walking along Tooley Street, he was stopped by two men who demanded his briefcase. One threatened him with a double-barrelled shotgun which then fired. They had asked for £10 and claimed the use of the firearm was an accident.[94] Arriving home alone later that evening after meeting the last train at Orpington Station, Shaw's wife, Mary, heard the news of the killing from journalists laying siege to the family house. The youth who pulled the trigger received a life sentence for murder and his accomplice eleven years for manslaughter.[95]

Although S.L. Price had undertaken some insolvency work in the mid-nineteenth century, Price Waterhouse had never developed a major specialism in this area. The first generation of firms — Turquand, Youngs & Co., Whinney, Smith & Whinney and W.W. Deloitte — had built up much stronger practices in this type of work. Price Waterhouse, by contrast, had concentrated on auditing and as a result undertook only a few insolvency assignments. And, in 1967, as the demand for this type of work rose, the General Committee concluded that the choice lay between doing a minimum of it and equipping the firm to take on this work as a major specialist pre-occupation; and in view of all the existing pressures on the firm's resources it would be wise to try to avoid insolvency work except insofar as it related to voluntary liquidations of the kind which were a formality and to occasional 'constructive' receiverships where we were asked to act with the object of rescuing an ailing business.[96]

Insolvency, therefore, continued to be a low priority department.

In April 1969, Price Waterhouse was approached by Daniel Mahony Taylor & Co., a small London practice, which sought a merger. To Price Waterhouse it was an attractive proposition since the firm would bring with it an established specialism in insolvency work. McNeill, the manager in charge of the liquidation department of Price Waterhouse, was past retirement age and it seemed that Monty Eckman, the Daniel Mahony Taylor partner in charge of insolvency, would be an ideal candidate to succeed him.[97] Negotiations proceeded and an amalgamation of the two firms came into effect on 1 October 1969.[98]

The recruitment of Eckman proved to be an inspired choice; his name and reputation attracted work from the clearing banks and within two years Price Waterhouse was engaged in major insolvency assignments.[99] This aspect of the practice was given a considerable boost by the secondary banking crisis of 1972–3 which generated liquidations that were to last for a further four years. Eckman was admitted to the partnership in 1970 but died suddenly four years later. He was succeeded as head of department by Peter Barrows, a partner in the Birmingham office who had gained some experience of receiverships.

Corporate Image

Although Price Waterhouse had developed a strong sense of its corporate identity and of how it wished to present itself to the external world, active consideration of these issues was limited until the late sixties. In March 1967 it was decided to brief a firm of public relations consultants on how to represent the partnership (albeit in a reactive rather than in a proactive fashion), in particular to the press.[100] A review conducted in the spring of 1970 resulted in the appointment of C.J. Casserley, the City representative of BBDO Public Relations, for a trial period.[101]

During the mid-sixties Price Waterhouse, no doubt under competitive pressures, examined its public image. In September 1963 at a meeting of the International Firm, Stanley Duncan proposed that 'a common style of notepaper' be adopted by all Price Waterhouse partnerships around the world. He had employed the Design Research Unit to produce a number of specimen letterheads,

> having outlined to them the underlying philosophy of the Price Waterhouse Firms, our functions and the image which it seemed to us we wished our notepaper to convey. This we thought should be one of stability and integrity, while at the same time giving the impression that the firm is not insensitive to the changes which are taking place around it and is willing to move with the times.[102]

A clean, modern-looking style, the sans serif Helvetica typeface, was submitted. Agreement was not reached. Duncan raised the matter again in March 1969 with a more limited agenda: that the new notepaper be introduced by the UK Firm alone.[103] It was thought unwise to proceed unilaterally. Again approval was not forthcoming, though the International Firm itself had accepted the innovation, and the UK partnership deferred any changes.[104] As a result it was not until March 1971 that a new style of letterhead and typing layout were introduced, replacing those which had stood from the early 1920s.[105]

One of Price Waterhouse's most important decisions in developing the corporate image was taken in 1970 and involved moving to new purpose-built premises. The design and occupation of Southwark Towers were crucial elements in conveying a dynamic and innovative impression to the public.

Southwark Towers

Having moved to No. 3 Frederick's Place in March 1899, the firm had become greatly overcrowded by the late sixties. The progressive expansion into Nos. 1 and 2 and the rebuilding of the former had created much extra space, while further accommodation had been gained by leasing additional offices in the City. Such incremental growth had created a measure of dislocation and extended lines of communication. A working party into which Michael Coates was co-opted was set up in

March 1968 to consider London premises. It explored the possibility of leasing BP House in Finsbury Square but this was felt 'unsuitable', possibly on grounds of size.[106] Rather than occupy an existing building the working party then considered commissioning their own structure and in the spring of 1969 explored three possible sites, of which the London Bridge Station development appeared to be 'the most promising'.[107] British Rail had designs to rebuild the existing Victorian structures and there was space above the new station for an office block. Planning permission was granted in May 1970[108] and it was decided to consolidate all of the firm's offices in London into a single structure.[109] The firm was helped by the fact that it possessed an office development permit, a valuable asset at the time. The architects, T.P. Bennett & Son, were instructed to design a building of narrow width or block depth because, as with most professional practices, there was only a minimal requirement for open-plan offices.[110] Their colour drawings of the proposed structure were displayed to the partners in November 1970.[111]

The decision to take an equity holding in Southwark Towers, in conjunction with British Rail, had been influenced by the fact that Price Waterhouse possessed an interest in its Frederick's Place premises. It held a long lease from the Mercer's Company which in the property boom of the early 1970s had become worth a considerable sum. Prudently, the value of the lease had never been included in the partnership accounts so that no amounts were credited to partners' capital or current accounts. As a result, new partners joining the firm did not have to make a contribution for the interest in Frederick's Place and later Southwark Towers, while those who were retiring from the partnership did not receive any value for passing it on to the next generation. A similar policy was adopted in relation to the service company set up by Price Waterhouse in 1965. It retained profits each year but no partner was ever credited with a share of those retained funds. This, too, proved to have been a far-sighted policy as it reduced the financial demands on new partners for working capital and provided a valuable asset for the future expansion of the firm.

When the decision was taken to sell the lease on Frederick's Place and to invest the capital in Southwark Towers, it had no cognisance of the property crash of 1973–4. By this time the firm was fully committed to the costs of building Southwark Towers. This led to a serious financial crisis in the following year, and to ease the burden of their expenditure

Jeffery Bowman suggested to Arnold Copley, the finance partner, that the firm acquire a substantial amount of the equipment for the new offices under lease rather than buying it outright.

The architects had been asked to design a building of seventeen storeys.[112] Each floor was to be capable of being subdivided in a variety of ways to provide flexibility for the initial move and to cope with future developments. Under the original timetable the contractors, Sir Robert McAlpine & Sons, were to start work on the foundations in July 1971 and planned to complete the structural framework of the building eighteen months later; a further half year was allowed for the fitting out. In fact, construction did not begin until June 1972 and the completion date was revised to 19 September 1975. Originally all three wings of the tower were to have been of equal height but the Fine Art Commission objected to the design and the decision was taken to raise one of them to nineteen storeys and the others to twenty-two and twenty-four storeys. The total height of the structure was now 327 ft and it comprised 180,000 sq.ft of net office space.[113]

Southwark Towers opened on 1 December 1975 when staff transferred from Frederick's Place and the other satellite premises. As planned, the building incorporated three restaurants, squash courts and a swimming pool. Furnishings were of a high quality and an 'Art Objects Working Party', chaired by Michael Coates, had been assembled to purchase paintings and other works of art. Advised by Thilo von Watzdorf of Sotheby's, they collected on the theme of contemporary British artists. One picture by John Walker, entitled 'Juggernaut IV' (1974) and hung on the staircase between levels one and two, caused particular comment.[114] The elegant terraced offices of Frederick's Place, which outwardly symbolised tradition, reserve, discretion and probity, had been replaced by a purpose-built, eye-catching tower block described by Pevsner as having 'screens of reflecting glass' which 'break up the surfaces and give the building a glittering elegant but secretive face'. Southwark Towers was an outward expression of the firm's professionalism, stability and ambitious approach to business.

The occupation of this new building resulted in Price Waterhouse leaving the City of London for the first time in its history. Yet it remains on the periphery and enjoys a commanding view of its client base across the Thames. It would have been unthinkable for a senior accountancy firm to have practised from offices in Southwark during the interwar period. As partnerships grew and became increasingly internationally orientated with technologically advanced systems of communication, the criteria for location changed. Other firms also left the City: Ernst & Young moved to Lambeth and Arthur Andersen transferred to Surrey Street off the Strand.

Mergers

As in the early sixties, Price Waterhouse pursued a policy of merging with established provincial practices as a way of extending their geographical coverage within the UK. In 1966 an amalgamation was concluded with the Nottingham firm of Mellors, Basden & Mellors. The foundation of the practice dated to 1854 when Robert Mellors was taken into partnership by a Mr Taylor. Subsequently he became a sole practitioner before being joined in 1873 by Duncan F. Basden and later by two of his sons.[115] Robert Mellors was instrumental in founding the Nottingham Society of Chartered Accountants, while T.G. Mellors, his eldest son, served on the ICAEW Council from 1907 and became its president in 1924–5. A later partner, P.F. Granger, also served as president in 1961–2.

In 1898 Mellors, Basden & Mellors were appointed receivers to Ernest T. Hooley, the millionaire company promoter. This, in turn, led to the audit of the Trafford Park Estates Co. in Manchester, which Hooley had owned. This connection brought them the audit of the Ford motor car assembly plant there in 1911, and for the next forty-nine years they were reappointed to audit the English Ford Motor Co. and a number of its European subsidiaries. During the 1950s this audit was carried out jointly with the London office of Price Waterhouse, but in 1960 the American parent acquired the whole share capital of the British subsidiary and the audit was transferred to Coopers & Lybrand.

In May 1969 Price Waterhouse concluded a merger with Bolton, Bullivant & Co., an established Leicester practice.[116] In December 1968 they acknowledged that they needed an office there and that 'the best method to achieve this object would be a link-up with a suitable firm practising in the area'.[117] Such business as Price Waterhouse had there had previously been conducted from London or Nottingham.

In July 1975 an office was established in Southampton following a merger with the local firm of Whittaker Bailey & Co. The latter had been founded in 1863, and had a well-established clientele in the region.[118] Until this amalgamation, clients in the area had been served by either London or Bristol offices. A Price Waterhouse associate firm was also set up on Jersey in July 1975 in association with Norman Allport & Co., with whom the former had a correspondent relationship since January 1974.[119]

The two mergers with London firms during this period were both designed to recruit specialists. The first in 1969 involved Daniel Mahony Taylor & Co., acknowledged insolvency practitioners, and the second Sturges, Fraser & Co. in 1971.[120] The latter, in London and Guildford (later closed), was of interest to Price Waterhouse because of the tax expertise of Carr and his staff and their range of clients.[121]

The Big Eight

During the decade 1965–75 the so-called 'Big Eight' accountancy firms were formed in their essentials and these partnerships stood apart from the remainder of the profession by virtue of their size. An international comparison showed the largest firms to be, in alphabetical order: Arthur Andersen, Arthur Young McClelland Moores, Coopers & Lybrand, Deloitte Haskins & Sells, Ernst & Whinney, Peat Marwick Mitchell, Price Waterhouse and Touche Ross.[122] Within the UK, this phenomenon was to a great extent the product of the disappearance of the majority of the medium-sized firms, which had either been absorbed by the Big Eight or declined in size through the loss of clients. The number of practices having more than three but fewer than twenty clients listed on the Stock Exchange fell from 206 in 1968 to fifty-seven by 1978. Most of this decrease was probably attributable to mergers within accountancy firms rather than the loss of audit clients. The greatest proportion of public company audits was increasingly captured by the twenty largest firms, who in 1948 held 33 per cent of listed audits and by 1979 no less than 68.9 per cent. The top ten firms held 26 per cent of listed companies in 1948 and 56.1 per cent by 1979.[123]

What were the economic forces which compelled so many medium-sized accountancy firms to merge with the larger City-based practices? Generally speaking it was not because their independent and growing

clients deserted them for bigger auditors with wider territorial coverage
and more services (though occasionally this has happened), but because
such clients were themselves absorbed. Groups taking over businesses
either as a subsidiary or as a division inevitably transferred the audit to
their principal firm of auditors. The total number of public companies
quoted on the Stock Exchange declined by 49 per cent between 1948
and 1978 (from 5,978 to 2,955) as a result of liquidation and, more
important, merger.[124] The fortunate auditors of companies growing by
acquisition would themselves reap the benefit – provided that they
expanded in equivalent scale and size and could offer the specialised
services which larger and more complex business structures demanded.
For these reasons the number of accountancy firms with listed audit
clients fell from 1,422 in 1948 to 511 in 1978, a reduction of 64 per cent.
In 1979, for example, the leading twenty firms gained a further forty-
nine audit clients (from a directory of 2,107 quoted companies), representing 2.3 per cent of the whole. In this redistribution the top ten gained an
average of 2.4 clients, the following ten achieved an average gain of 1.9,
while those ranked twenty-one to thirty experienced an average loss of
0.3 listed clients.[125]

Price Waterhouse was, therefore, active in the movement which led
to the polarisation of the profession. In order to serve existing audit
clients adequately and compete effectively with its major competitors it
was forced to merge with medium-sized practices in various locations.
This process, repeated elsewhere, was responsible for the virtual disappearance of the medium-sized accountancy firm.

Company Crises, Legislation and Regulation

In November 1965 Morris Finer QC and Sir Henry Benson, as Board of
Trade inspectors, issued their report into the collapse of Rolls Razor and
its subsidiary Electromatic.[126] They concluded that the accounts submitted for 1960 were in the case of Electromatic 'false and misleading' and
in the case of Rolls Razor 'misleading'.[127] Price Waterhouse had audited
the latter since 1925 and disputed Finer and Benson's judgement on the
grounds that the firm could not have ascertained either the advertising
and purchase tax liabilities or the falsification of stock by normal
methods. It was a complicated situation. Rolls Razor, a company which

had diversified into the manufacture of washing machines, was taken over in 1959 by John Bloom, who was selling cheap twin-tub machines imported in large numbers from Holland. Rolls Razor then began manufacturing his 'Electromatic' machines for which there was a large and rapidly growing demand.[128] By 1963 his competitors had caught up and were producing equally cheap but reliable washing machines. In an attempt to bolster falling sales, Bloom offered low-price holidays and trading stamps. He formed Rolls Tours to handle the Continental holidays and Rolls Rentals to promote the hire of television sets.[129] In 1964 amid resignations from Bloom's boards and speculation about the liquidity of his companies, the directors of Rolls Razor requested the accountants Cork Gully & Co. to investigate, while at the same time the Board of Trade set up their own inquiry. In August Rolls Razor went into liquidation. The inspectors' report was submitted to the Director of Public Prosecutions and in 1969 John Bloom faced trial for fraud. The prosecution experienced the difficulties of presenting a complex financial case to a jury five years after the event. An agreement was reached during the trial by which Bloom pleaded guilty and was sentenced to pay a relatively small fine.[130]

After protracted discussions with Kenneth Cork, the liquidator, and with John Bloom, Price Waterhouse settled a claim against them out of court and the following statement was published:

> The auditors have at all times strenuously denied the allegations of liability and the settlement has been made simply to avoid the extremely lengthy and expensive enquiries which would have had to take place if the matter had gone to court.[131]

An important piece of legislation was enacted in 1967. A committee under Lord Justice Jenkins had been set up in 1959 to report within three years with recommendations on how to revise the law relating to public companies.[132] Its modest proposals resulted in an extension to the minimum disclosure requirements for the profit and loss account and the inclusion of certain items of information in the directors' report, such as numbers of employees and charitable donations. In addition, those private companies which had been exempted from filing annual returns now lost their immunity from public inspection.[133] Yet no sooner had the legislators satisfied themselves that defects in company law had been resolved than a series of take-over bids highlighted further inadequacies.

The first event followed GEC's attempted take-over of its larger rival AEI. In November 1967 the latter forecast a profit of £10 million for the year as part of their unsuccessful defence. When the merger had been completed AEI's accounts for 1967 revealed an actual loss of £4.5 million.[134] Deloitte Plender Griffiths and Price Waterhouse, joint auditors of AEI, were asked by Lord Aldington, the chairman of GEC, to explain how such a discrepancy could have arisen.[135] Their report concluded that 'roughly £5 million of the shortfall [was due] to adverse differences which are matters of fact rather than of judgement, and the balance of some £9.5 million to adjustments which remain substantially matters of judgement'.[136] The press had suggested that the £9.5 million was due to 'the adoption of different accounting methods'. The AEI auditors denied this and argued that it related not to any change in 'method' but to 'the assessment of net realisable value in relation to substantial stocks and incomplete contracts, without any departure from the basic accounting principle'.[137]

The second take-over which raised doubts about the adequacy of the new legislation concerned the bid by Leasco Data Processing Equipment Corporation of New York for Pergamon Press, the scientific publishing house, whose chief executive was then Robert Maxwell. Leasco, under the chairmanship of Saul Steinberg, was involved in management consultancy, shipping containers, insurance and computer services. Wishing to sell his company, Maxwell approached Steinberg to suggest a take-over, and after protracted discussions it was agreed on 18 June 1969 that Leasco would buy the entire issued share capital of Pergamon.[138] Then, having acquired approximately 38 per cent of the latter's shareholding, at a cost of around £9 million, Leasco announced on 21 August that it did not wish to proceed with the merger.[139] Among the reasons for their decision were the position of a Pergamon subsidiary, International Learning Systems Corporation, the trading relationship between Pergamon and Maxwell Scientific Inc. and the composition of the published forecast earnings of Pergamon for 1969. The Take-Over Panel then investigated the matter and concluded that a full Board of Trade inquiry should be set up to shed light on the complicated financial circumstances of the acquisition. Owen Stable QC and Ronald Leach of Peat Marwick Mitchell were the inspectors appointed. Price Waterhouse had already been approached by Wm. Brandt's Sons & Co., the merchant bankers who were looking after the interests of the minority shareholders in Pergamon, to act as 'independent reporting accountants'.[140]

The firm was appointed in September 1969 by the board of Pergamon, while Maxwell was still chairman. At an extraordinary general meeting on 10 October 1969, Maxwell was removed from office and independent directors appointed, while the terms of reference agreed with Price Waterhouse were confirmed. Martin Harris was placed in charge of the investigation, though much of the daily organisation fell to Jeffery Bowman, then a recently admitted partner.

Price Waterhouse was initially reluctant to accept the assignment aware that the investigation was problematic and might involve endless litigation.[141] Only after Maxwell had sent written confirmation that both he and his family trusts would co-operate unconditionally did the firm commit itself. Yet within weeks the undertaking was broken. Maxwell Scientific International (MSI Inc.) claimed, on legal advice, that it could not disclose any documents which would prejudice its defence against suits brought by Leasco. Eight accountants in four teams worked through the Pergamon files in November 1969, while Maxwell himself answered a series of detailed questions. Price Waterhouse then prepared a 'summary of facts' which was presented to Maxwell and his fellow directors so that they could indicate any errors.[142] A final report issued on 21 August 1970 revealed that Pergamon's published profits for the year ended December 1968 (on which the take-over bid had been based) were a gross overstatement.[143] The surplus was £495,000 rather than the £2,104,000 actually reported and included profits from inter-company transactions with private, family-controlled enterprises which Price Waterhouse could not verify. This figure took no account of the losses incurred by International Learning Systems Corporation. Further, the investigators concluded that the net assets of the group at 31 December 1968 should be reduced from £7,034,000 to £4,461,000. According to the detailed Price Waterhouse inquiry Pergamon had actually made a loss during 1968.

Maxwell had forecast that the accounts for the first nine months of 1969 would show profits of around £2.5 million, revising this figure to £2 million in August.[144] When they were published the surplus in fact totalled a mere £29,000 though this was composed of a profit of £360,000 on inter-company transactions with family-controlled enterprises and a loss of £331,000 on normal trading. In addition, this surplus was before writing off the investment in International Learning Systems

Corporation and exceptional items totalling almost £2 million. The deficit on the nine months was £1,991,000.

Maxwell commented that accountancy 'is not the exact science which some of us thought it was'.[145] The Price Waterhouse report effectively ended any ambition that Leasco might have retained to take over Pergamon; there was little reason to bid for a near-bankrupt organisation. Chalmers, Impey & Co., the auditors of Pergamon, were replaced by Cooper Brothers. Price Waterhouse had been offered the appointment by the directors but declined as it might have compromised their independence as investigators. The interim report prepared by the Board of Trade inspectors in June 1971 arrived at the much quoted judgement:

> We regret having to conclude, notwithstanding Mr Maxwell's acknowledged abilities and energies, he is not in our opinion a person who could be relied upon to exercise proper stewardship of a publicly quoted company.[146]

These events stirred up the financial press and inevitably brought adverse comments on the Companies Acts and the profession that was entrusted with their administration. Prominent among the reformists was a Canadian chartered accountant, Professor Edward Stamp, who wrote a sustained critique in *The Times* of 11 September 1969 under the heading 'Auditing the Auditors':

> Medical practice is based upon judgement, but it is also based on principles with a sound theoretical foundation. This is not so in the case of accounting, and most of the accountant's so-called principles are merely descriptions of current, or, even worse, past practice . . . This situation will persist so long as the profession regards principles as merely an attempt to describe what is being done in the best firms . . . The essence of the independence problem is that the auditor is expected to assume the role of a judge while he lacks many of the important attributes of independence which gave authority to the judge in the courts.

Stung by these criticisms and by the GEC-AEI and Pergamon events, in December 1969 the ICAEW published a 'Statement of Intent on Accounting Standards in the 1970s', in which it declared an intention to narrow the areas of difference and variety in accounting practices and to provide a vehicle for the promotion of new accounting standards. In January 1970 an Accounting Standards Steering Committee was set up under the chairmanship of Sir Ronald Leach, the then president of the ICAEW. In the following year it published its first 'Statement of Standard Accounting Practice' (SSAP), on 'Disclosure of Accounting Policies'.[147] Although not having the force of legislation, SSAPs have exercised an important influence on the practice of the profession. In July 1975, for example, the Policy Committee of Price Waterhouse concluded that they 'have the effect of narrowing the choices applicable in giving a true and fair view' and that the firm should only depart from a standard when its application 'would prove misleading'. Adherence was deemed obligatory 'even in those cases where the firm believes the standard to be misguided'.[148]

Two other issues rose in importance during the mid-1970s – inflation and the independence of the auditor. The potentially misleading nature of conventional company accounts in periods of rapid price movements had long been understood in general terms but the need for standardised procedures of adjustment became pressing early in the decade when inflation appeared to be well-established in the short term. To some extent the debate on inflation accounting took up discussions begun twenty years earlier when the expenditure occasioned by the Korean War had led to an upsurge in commodity and other prices but which had never been satisfactorily resolved. A draft proposal, *Accounting for Changes in the Purchasing Power of Money*, published by the Accounting Standards Committee in 1973, indicated that the accounts of 137 major listed companies for 1971 overstated their earnings by an average of 20 per cent. The Committee argued that monetary values subject to attrition from a depreciating currency should be adjusted by the retail price index so that all transactions were converted to year-end constant values – the current purchasing power school of inflation accounting. The issue was particularly pertinent in relation to depreciation and whether this should be calculated on the historical cost or on cost adjusted by the retail price index. The Treasury raised two objections to this method: first, general indices of price movements would not be so precise as to reflect accurately fluctuations in specific businesses. The huge rise in oil prices in 1973–4 had demonstrated that certain values could move wildly out of line with general inflation. Secondly, the government considered that the new accounting convention might encourage further inflation as companies put up prices in advance of expected rises.

With these doubts in mind, the government appointed a committee under Sir Francis Sandilands to report on inflation accounting. Their conclusions, published in 1975, favoured a system of current cost accounting, by which assets were recorded in the balance sheet at their 'value to business'. Plant, equipment and buildings had to be revalued annually, which placed further responsibilities on the auditor. In the event no real agreement was ever reached on the issue of inflation accounting, the matter being settled indirectly by a return to low levels of price and wage movements.

The second major issue of the 1970s concerned the independence of the auditor. There was rising concern that small or medium-sized practices having one or more large clients might be threatened with the loss of audit business unless they compromised their professional standards. The consequences of such pressure upon the biggest firms of accountants would not be so dire commercially, and they could therefore be expected to resist such approaches. In order to protect the auditor the ICAEW introduced a regulation that no practice should have a client which contributed more than 15 per cent of its fee income. This was one further reason why medium-sized firms chose to merge with a larger competitor in that to do so would provide their businesses with greater stability and balance.

The European and International Firms

In October 1975 Nigel Lathom-Sharp, senior partner of the European Firm, was asked to report to the UK Firm's Policy Committee on the development of the Continental practice. He recorded that it had eighty-five partners and 1,500 staff in seventeen nations and thirty offices.[149] Although it had experienced sustained growth over the previous decade Lathom-Sharp believed that there was 'substantial scope for practice development'.[150]

In the immediate post-war years the European Firm had rebuilt itself largely by its own efforts with little assistance from either the UK or US Firms.[151] During the fifties and sixties it worked in the main for American and to a lesser extent British multinationals who had subsidiaries or interests on the Continent, particularly in France and Switzerland. It had little time or scope to gain local national clients as the stock markets played only a minor part in the reconstruction of Europe. In the late sixties and early seventies the volume of work from the United States kept the firm extremely busy. Shortages of staff resulted in assignments being turned down and concerted attempts were made to borrow professionals from other Price Waterhouse firms. Managers, often with a Continental background, were sent from America on a three-year tour and proved to be of considerable value. The European Firm had grown up with a powerful expatriate culture and was initially reluctant to introduce locally qualified accountants to the partnership. However, the need to expand, together with the conspicuous success of some of their rivals who were less wary of engaging nationals, forced the firm to modify its strategy.

Three distinct patterns of development emerged. In nations, such as Italy and Spain, where the national accountancy profession remained embryonic, Price Waterhouse made the greatest progress. It built up a strong local client base and recruited and trained members of the indigenous population as professional staff and partners, supported by expatriates. Secondly, in nations with strong professional bodies, such as Germany, Price Waterhouse was less successful in winning local assignments and limited its activities to referred work. Thirdly, some countries, including France, have tended to resist the incursions of foreign accountancy firms when they have succeeded in building up substantial local client lists. The partnership arrangement was deemed illegal by the French and some accountancy firms were compelled to incorporate under a different name, which in the case of Price Waterhouse was Blanchard Chauveau et Associés.[152]

Just as the UK Firm had built up a range of specialist services during the sixties, so the European Firm followed suit, and on occasion sought to acquire expertise from other partnerships. In 1965, for example, Richard Brooke, a partner based in Hamburg, reported that he had approached L.W. Shaw in London about

> the possibility of transferring a senior systems manager to the European Firm to head the European Systems Organisation ... Shaw had discussed the problem with Robson; they were sympathetic in principle but could not spare one of their senior managers at this time.[153]

In 1963 four of the European Firm's systems staff had attended a two-month training course in London.[154] The largest offices on the Continent, Paris, Frankfurt, Brussels and Milan, remained appreciably smaller than, say, those in London or New York, and did not, therefore, generate comparable economies of scale to allow highly developed support and specialised services.

London periodically loaned staff to the European Firm. In 1963, for example, when the Paris office was particularly stretched:

> Chapman from London gave invaluable assistance over a period of roughly four months, especially with the new Unilever work in France ... From the USA we had the help of White from Philadelphia and Jordan from Detroit ... We were also very pleased to have with us under the exchange scheme Melick from Detroit ... Finally, London again came to our rescue in lending us Bowman for a period of $2\frac{1}{2}$ months. His help was much appreciated in a particularly difficult period.[155]

By the end of 1968 the specialist departments of the European Firm had grown to sufficient size to be considered important in their own right. The management consultancy had twenty-three members of staff at ten locations and plans were laid for an expansion to thirty-six by the following year.[156] It was also believed by Jack Moore, a tax manager in Paris, that the tax department had considerable capacity for growth:

> although international tax planning would continue to be the backbone of the department's work it should move steadily into comprehensive business consultancy as opposed to the traditional and limited area of taxation advice. To achieve this end of integrated and comprehensive services to clients the department would move to forge still closer links with the firm's financial and MAS [management consultancy] know-how ...[157]

In 1969 the senior partnership of the European Firm passed from George Pollard to Richard Brooke, who retained the post until 1975, when, having reached the age of sixty, he decided to retire.[158] Brooke, having joined the organisation in 1949 and been a partner since 1956, was well versed in the Price Waterhouse philosophy and the practical difficulties of operating across the Continent. As a result, he believed in a policy of 'expansion within reason'; growth was carefully considered rather than rapid in nature. By May 1970 the European Firm had risen to 928 partners and staff of whom 661 (71 per cent) were auditors (Table 16, see Appendix). An important feature of this expansion was the progressive recruitment of nationals. In the Swiss partnership, for example, 45 per cent of staff were indigenous by 1970, a figure which had risen to 62 per cent by 1975.[159]

Working with the International Firm, considerable effort was made to raise standards to common levels throughout the practice. This could result in the quality of work demanded by Price Waterhouse being higher than the national legislative requirement.

An important development was the establishment of the Middle Eastern practice. In 1907 Price Waterhouse had opened an office in Cairo, which in 1911 became part of a joint practice with W.B. Peat & Co. This partnership also produced a number of smaller offices in other parts of the Middle East. The sequestration of the Egyptian practice in 1956, following the nationalisation of the Suez Canal by General Nasser, was a serious blow though the full consequences were not appreciated until the dramatic oil price rises of the early 1970s led to the enrichment of the oil-producing states. With its competitors, Price Waterhouse saw a need to establish offices in key cities in order to serve rapidly expanding businesses and, more importantly, to track the major capital movements which were beginning to flow from the Middle East to the leading industrialised nations. International firms were no longer able to set up offices without reference to established local accountants and there was a movement among the Big Eight to forge links with indigenous practices.

In 1971 the European Firm, with financial support from the International Firm, entered into such an association in Iran. As a result of that arrangement Richard Brooke, senior partner of the European Firm, was approached by Talal Abu-Ghazaleh, who operated the largest practice in Kuwait with offshoots in surrounding countries. Brooke strongly recommended to the policy committee of Price Waterhouse International that an association should be established with Talal Abu-Ghazaleh and this was agreed. The original intention was that the European Firm should be responsible for the arrangement and would provide the necessary personnel, but given that they were already overstretched, the UK Firm was asked by Price Waterhouse International to take this role. Charles Bailey from London was transferred to Kuwait to become senior partner of the new Middle East Firm and recruited a small team of partners. In spite of strenuous efforts, it became apparent that the objectives and working methods of Price Waterhouse and Talal Abu-Ghazaleh's practice were incompatible. In 1979 a separation was negotiated. In consequence, the firm was unable to maintain an office in Kuwait and responsibility for other offices was divided between the UK Firm (Bahrain, Qatar and the Emirates) and the US Firm (Egypt and Saudi Arabia). Although opinions may differ, it was probably right to have made a concerted attempt to forge a working relationship with Talal Abu-Ghazaleh, though in the end it proved to be a costly failure. Charles Bailey believed that Michael Coates, who took direct responsibility for the UK Firm's involvement, maintained the connection longer than was justified. The dominating position of the oil-producing states did not endure and the need to have a strong presence in the Middle East, while still important, no longer had the high priority that it once held.

By the early 1970s it had become clear that the international organisation of Price Waterhouse had not kept pace with some of its major competitors. Accordingly, a new non-practising partnership, Price Waterhouse International, was created in 1973, led by John Biegler in America and Stanley Duncan in the UK. It had a decentralised, federal structure, but united all partners across the world in a single legal entity that operated through a general council composed of the senior partners and other representatives of the eighteen constituent firms.[160] Within this assembly a policy committee, comprising six to eight senior partners, was created. Now, Price Waterhouse could claim to have a cohesive global organisation which could set about establishing common practices and standards of client service.[161] Henceforth the International Firm became increasingly active rather than advisory in its dealings.

Stanley Duncan had long believed that the international organisation of Price Waterhouse was an important but neglected vehicle for change. Accordingly, when he became chairman of the restructured organisation in 1975, Duncan gradually built up a full-time headquarters staff in London, composed of partners from member firms responsible for monitoring audit quality control and developing staffing procedures and principles. This was funded by regular levies from the various Price Waterhouse partnerships.

'Quality, Growth and Profitability'

In November 1976 at a meeting of the UK partnership, Michael Coates identified 'quality, growth and profitability' as the three crucial aspects of the firm's practice.[1] Each of these elements was of importance during the difficult economic climate of the late seventies and early eighties. Quality was to prove not simply a desirable attribute, a powerful marketing point, but also a necessity as dissatisfied businesses took an increasingly aggressive line towards their auditors, seeking redress through litigation. The problems created by inflation raised questions about the nature of financial reporting which were never adequately resolved. The rapid expansion generated by the major firms prompted them to undertake vigorous reviews of their practices. In an era of tougher competition, growth was a key ingredient to survival as the structure of the accountancy profession continued to change. The medium-sized firm almost disappeared as a small number of large practices dominated the market for major, listed audit clients. League tables were devised by the financial press, albeit on the basis of estimates, to reflect the rivalry which had emerged between the so-called 'Big Eight'. Finally, profitability remained an enduring feature, though it was, perhaps, viewed in a different light. In the interwar period, accountants would have considered themselves professionals first and businessmen second; by the early eighties the demands of running a large-scale enterprise (the need, for example, to support rising overheads occasioned by the introduction of comprehensive training and recruitment programmes) had compelled the partners to re-evaluate their roles and attitudes.

In the seven years spanned by the senior partnership of Michael Coates, Price Waterhouse was to undergo something of a transformation. First, it grew remarkably in physical terms. The number of partners rose by 85 per cent from 87 in 1975 to 161 in 1982, while the UK staff increased by 46 per cent from 2,079 to 3,025 over the same period.

It moved to modern, purpose-built offices, equipped with the latest information technology. The range of services offered broadened from the traditional base of auditing and taxation. In particular, management consultancy (involving an expanding computer software element) entered a period of rapid growth, while insolvency became established as an important department. In addition, local government work (subsequently leading to privatisation assignments) and a special services department to cater for small or embryonic businesses were of increasing consequence. In part, this broadening of client services was a defensive reaction to a belief that auditing was entering a mature market. It was argued that if the auditor could call upon a further level of expertise he could add greater value to his client's business and therefore increase the effectiveness of the firm's contribution. Further, these services developed in their own right, as skills and knowledge were concentrated within single departments, and enabled these to sell services beyond established audit clients.

However, these commercial gains were not to be achieved without losses. The close-knit family atmosphere which the Frederick's Place office had engendered was dissipated for ever. The size of the new organisation and the tough competitive pressures under which the firm operated destroyed the old gentlemanly sense of community. The professional manner which had characterised the partnership was also threatened by the demands of business – the need to protect audits from rivals, to tender for new assignments and to control costs vigorously. It was a successful, confident and assertive partnership which entered the eighties, but in the process a different Price Waterhouse emerged.

Changes to the Partnership

Michael Coates became senior partner of the UK Firm on 1 July 1975 and held this post until 1982 when he took up the chairmanship of Price Waterhouse's World Firm. No deputy senior partner was appointed to take his place as the constitution of the partnership did not provide for such a post. With the re-election of Jeffery Bowman and Tony Cherry in September 1975, the Policy Committee remained unchanged; it also included Colin Brown, Fred Chapman, Chris Collett, Keith Milligan and Tony Wilson.[2] This was the body which discussed strategy and the general direction which the practice was to take, as it was important that continuity be maintained. Accordingly, the membership of the Policy Committee altered only by degrees. In June 1976 Keith Milligan retired. A partner in Howard Smith & Thompson since 1949, he had been admitted to Price Waterhouse in 1963 at the time of the merger. Together with Collett, he was one of the regional representatives, being partner-in-charge of the Birmingham office. In 1976 Collett was not re-elected to the Policy Committee. His father had run Leeds office from its foundation, and he returned there after working in London for a period, though he was subsequently in charge first of the Newcastle office and then of Nottingham. Having qualified with James Worley & Sons, Colin Brown joined Price Waterhouse in 1958 and became a partner eight years later. As partner-in-charge of London Audit Group 3, he was elected to the Policy Committee in 1974 and served for a further five years.

The two new members were Michael Carr and Tim Hoult. Carr had joined the partnership in 1971 following the merger with Sturges Fraser & Co. and three years later had been appointed Director of Tax Services. Hoult had qualified with Percy F.Ward, a local Newcastle firm, and joined Price Waterhouse in London in 1961 before moving back to Newcastle in the mid-1960s where he became partner-in-charge in 1974. Wilson was currently Director of Communications and External Relations and Cherry served as Director of Office Operations. In 1978 Peter Ainger, as partner-in-charge of London Audit Group 4, was elected to the Policy Committee. In the following year he was appointed Director of Manpower with responsibility for planning the complex recruitment and career progression strategies that the firm needed to maintain its growth.

Fred Chapman and Tony Cherry both retired in June 1979. Chapman had joined the firm in 1946, having qualified with M.S. Bradford & Co. He had been admitted to the partnership in 1963. Cherry, too, entered Price Waterhouse in 1946, and having served the greater part of his articles with Coxon, Bannister & Gothard, had attempted to complete them in various POW camps. He took his finals in January 1944 as a prisoner-of-war, but received no results so he took the examination again in August, only to discover when liberated that he had passed at the first attempt.[3] Having been appointed a manager in 1953, Cherry became a partner in 1960. At one stage, Chapman and Cherry had shared a room with Martin Harris and Michael Coates at the top of No. 5 Frederick's Place and the four of them could be observed from partners' offices opposite in No. 3. As able and ambitious managers, they were often called upon to undertake special assignments such as investigations or prospectus work.[4]

The retirements of Cherry and Chapman in 1979 saw the election of Howard Hughes and Alec Campbell to the Policy Committee. Hughes had been articled to Bryce Hammer & Co. in Liverpool and entered Price Waterhouse in 1960. Admitted to the partnership in 1970, he had served as national staff partner and was currently partner-in-charge of London Audit Group 2. Becoming director of London office in 1982, Hughes was appointed managing partner in 1985. Campbell, who had joined Price Waterhouse in 1957, was based in Glasgow and as partner-in-charge of the Scottish practice provided important regional representation. In 1981 Alan Wheatley, then partner-in-charge of London Audit Group 4, was elected to the Policy Committee, and in 1985 became director of London office.

More than any other individual, Coates was responsible for implementing structural and organisational change at Price Waterhouse, though perhaps most of these changes had been introduced before he became senior partner. He had served for fifteen years on the General Committee and its successor the Policy Committee. In 1972 he had been appointed Director of Office Operations and began much of the planning which was to lead to the creation of an integrated and modern firm. Under the senior partnership of Stanley Duncan much of the investigative and research work was completed and the foundations for growth were laid. With the construction of Southwark Towers, the implementation of recruitment and training schemes, the introduction of a progressive career ladder from student through the manager grades to partner, and the development of the specialist services (in particular MCS, tax, insolvency and local government work), Coates was able to guide the firm through a period of dramatic and sustained expansion. During the seven years of his senior partnership, for example, its fee income rose by 305 per cent from £14.2 million to £57.5 million, while staff numbers increased by 46 per cent from 2,079 in 1975 to 3,025 in 1982. It should not be forgotten, however, that Price Waterhouse's major competitors also grew at rapid rates, and, therefore, that there were macro forces at work in the economy driving this expansion (notably the creation of the international, multi-division organisation). The achievement of Coates was to have created the administrative and structural environment which enabled Price Waterhouse to take full advantage of these trends, and to have encouraged the self-belief to venture into novel areas with confidence.

Coates did, perhaps, exhibit one area of weakness, of which he was conscious. Unlike Read or Harris, he was not a natural manager of people and had not developed an easy rapport with many of the executive team.[5] To compensate for this, in his early years as senior partner he offered every UK partner a two-hour session every two years to discuss the firm's policies as well as personal career opportunities and problems – a considerable undertaking given that numbers had reached 150 or more.[6] In addition, it was believed by some in the partnership that he pursued the association with Talal Abu-Ghazaleh longer than was justified.

Interviewed at the end of his senior partnership, Coates was asked to summarise what he had tried to achieve:

> I was told at school that I had the gift of looking round corners. It would be romantic but untrue to think of this as a sort of sixth sense derived from the Scottish part of my ancestry. I do seem to have an unusually well-developed perception that change is a continuing and inevitable process and that the small trickles of today may become the great torrents of tomorrow. I have had a determination to try to mould the firm to be ready to meet the opportunities – and sometimes the threats – that would surely come.[7]

There have been perhaps three outstanding partners in the history of Price Waterhouse, each responsible for moulding or influencing its development. Edwin Waterhouse took a small City partnership and shaped it into one of the leading practices in the country, while Sir Gilbert Garnsey lifted Price Waterhouse above the heads of its rivals during the 1920s. Michael Coates, by revolutionising the structure and organisation of the firm, enabled Price Waterhouse in the UK to compete with the very best in the world.

In July 1982 Coates was succeeded as senior partner by Jeffery Bowman.[8] Educated at Winchester College and Trinity Hall, Cambridge, where he read law, Bowman joined Price Waterhouse in 1958. Qualifying in 1961, he was admitted to the partnership five years later, a particularly rapid advancement. His expertise and ability brought him early election to the Policy Committee in 1972 and appointment as Director of Technical Services (1973–6) and Director of London office (1979–81).[9] Becoming senior partner at the age of forty-seven made him the youngest man to hold the office in the twentieth century; indeed, only Edwin Waterhouse, senior partner at forty-six, was younger in the history of the firm.

The Development of Professional Services

By the end of the seventies Price Waterhouse became concerned that auditing was assuming the signs of a mature market with excess capacity.[10] In the fifties and sixties when the multinational corporations were created, Price Waterhouse and the other leading firms were able to offer real added value through their audit services as corporations sought to understand their new countries of operation and to control their widespread activities. A UK company, which, for example, might acquire or seek to set up a manufacturing base with distribution points throughout Argentina, could call upon the expertise of Price Waterhouse's South American Firm. By the seventies, however, the ability of accountancy practices to add value to their clients through audit services became more difficult. Major corporations had by now adopted modern organisational methods and improved the quality of their middle management. A study of 100 UK companies revealed that in 1950 only 13 per cent had adopted a multi-divisional structure, whereas by 1960 the proportion was 30 per cent rising by 1970 to 72 per cent.[11] Also, these businesses had introduced accounting systems and controls of much higher quality, thus reducing the need for external input.

From 1973, in order to compensate for the growing competition in auditing and as a way of offering established clients further ways of improving the management of their businesses, Price Waterhouse took an increasing interest in developing their specialist services, notably tax and MCS. In the past both had faced opposition from audit partners and staff; many had been indifferent towards tax, while MCS attracted active hostility on the part of those who believed that it compromised the professional integrity and ethics of the auditor.[12]

Taxation services had traditionally evolved within Price Waterhouse

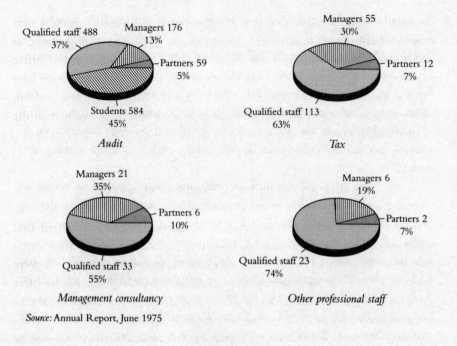

Qualified staff 488
37%

Managers 176
13%

Partners 59
5%

Students 584
45%

Audit

Managers 55
30%

Partners 12
7%

Qualified staff 113
63%

Tax

Managers 21
35%

Partners 6
10%

Qualified staff 33
55%

Management consultancy

Managers 6
19%

Partners 2
7%

Qualified staff 23
74%

Other professional staff

Source: Annual Report, June 1975

FIGURE 16

Price Waterhouse Professional Staff by Occupation 1975

in a reactive, rather than a proactive, fashion. It was not until the end of the seventies that the first proper business plans for tax emerged in the major Price Waterhouse firms. As late as 1975 the practice had only about ten partners (including just one outside London) who were wholly engaged in tax work.[13] Starting from such a comparatively low base, growth was understandably rapid. In 1976, for example, the department generated 218,000 chargeable hours, rising to 274,000 by 1979 and 322,000 in 1980, an increase of 48 per cent over five years.[14] The majority of taxation staff were concerned with corporation tax calculations, while separate groups dealt with customs, VAT, inheritance tax and pensions. Income tax specialists tended to be more often found outside London where they advised smaller businesses. There were also staff concerned with stamp duty and to an increasing extent international tax questions.[15] Although the tax practice undertook a considerable proportion of consultancy work, its ethos and professional attitudes had been closer to auditing than to, say, MCS. This, in part, could be attributed to its tradition of serving audit clients,[16] but was also due to a high proportion of its staff having first qualified as chartered accountants before developing a tax expertise.

Once the tax department had achieved a higher profile and increased representation within Price Waterhouse, it was important to provide it with a structure of its own. To reflect the growing importance of this specialism Carr was elected to the Policy Committee in 1976, though surprisingly, given the substantial contribution of the department to profits, no tax specialist was appointed to the Executive during this period.

In the seventies the greatest opportunities for growth in terms of demand and profitability were presented by management consultancy work.[17] Price Waterhouse had operated a small Systems Department from the 1920s, but it was to be the application of the computer which was to revolutionise the nature of MCS work. In 1963 Price Waterhouse had calculated that sixty machines were employed by clients, a total that had risen rapidly to 275 by 1967.[18] It was calculated that there were around 10,000 computers at work in Western Europe by 1967 and that the number was doubling every two years.[19] By 1970 five important functions had been identified for the office computer: first, its use in undertaking routine clerical tasks, such as invoice writing, mailing and payroll preparation; secondly, data analysis (providing information about stock levels, pricing, sales and costs); thirdly, design work in developing new products; fourthly, facilitating operational decision-making by comparing input data against stored instructions; and fifthly, attempting to predict outcomes through the manipulation of single or multiple variables. By the end of the 1970s the computer was established as a ubiquitous feature of modern business, and with the application of the silicon chip the rate of change in data processing accelerated.[20] Given the investment both in machines and software and the growing applications for computers, businesses increasingly sought professional advice.

The secondary banking crisis and the recession which followed had seen the MCS practice of Price Waterhouse enter a period of retrenchment. This set-back, a serious fall in profitability and a reluctance on the part of audit partners to introduce management consultancy specialists to their clients undermined morale. From 1973 onwards, these problems encouraged MCS to develop international agency funded work in Africa. This new field of activity generated over 50 per cent of the UK department's fees in 1975, 1976 and 1977, restored departmental profitability, allowed recruitment to begin and helped MCS partners and managers to tackle the opportunities of the home market with new confidence. In 1976 the department worked 70,000 chargeable hours, rising to 97,000 by 1979 and 112,000 in 1980, an increase of 60 per cent over five years.[21] Growth was, therefore, steady at around 15–20 per cent per annum throughout the mid- to late seventies. Staff numbers grew accordingly, rising from around sixty in 1975 to 218 by 1982 (Table 17, see Appendix). Although the practice had employed non-accountants (such as engineers and production control experts) from the early sixties, they had remained small in numbers. After 1978 expansion came increasingly from diversification in non-accounting areas in the UK.[22]

Having abandoned software work in the early 1970s, the MCS department set up its own programming group in 1979, hired a number of experienced systems development staff and began the recruitment of graduates. At the same time, K Computer Services, with a managerial and technical staff of thirty-four, was taken over to sell software accounting packages to clients.[23] This acquisition proved commercially unsuccessful and was later sold.[24] Nevertheless, the development of software proved to be an important market and generated considerable growth for the practice.[25]

Ernest Barnes, a chartered accountant who had joined Price Waterhouse in 1955 (having qualified with Hudson Smith Briggs & Co.), succeeded Shaw as head of the MCS practice when Shaw was murdered in 1968 (see p. 269). Barnes had been admitted to the partnership a year earlier and in 1972 was appointed Director of Management Consultancy Services. In the early sixties, with perhaps the exception of Cooper Brothers who had made determined efforts to develop their MCS practice, the major accountancy firms lagged behind the independent consultants such as PA Group, Urwick Orr & Partners, A.I.C and P.E. Group.[26] By the early seventies Price Waterhouse had begun to catch up but fell behind when the secondary banking crisis and a general slump in the demand for MCS services prompted the partnership to order cut backs.[27] The caution displayed by the leading accountancy firms then allowed Arthur Andersen to make inroads into the market, so that by the end of 1973 Price Waterhouse were ranked eighth in terms of staff numbers, behind Coopers & Lybrand, Peat Marwick Mitchell and Arthur Andersen.[28] In 1974 Price Waterhouse introduced their first five-year 'Development Plan' for the MCS practice, which, 'while recognising the fundamental importance of audit clients as a source of MCS work', recorded that

> a primary objective should be to increase the proportion of work done for non-audit clients. The target should be to increase the amount of non-audit client work from the present level . . . about 47 per cent of the total workload in 1972/73 to about 60 per cent (£720,000) by 1979. This target implies a growth rate of about 5 per cent per annum in work from UK audit clients and about 18 per cent per annum in work from overseas clients and from UK non-audit clients.[29]

The success of this strategy, helped initially by work in Africa and by the relative decline of the independent consultants, resulted in Coopers & Lybrand, Arthur Andersen and Price Waterhouse emerging as the three largest practices by the early eighties.

The development of specialist services saw its principal manifestation in the areas of tax and management consultancy, but also expanded into other activities, notably local authority work, insolvency and small business services. Attention was paid to these areas in part because a demand existed in the economy but also because there were usually one or two individuals who, by the nature of the varied assignments performed by Price Waterhouse, had acquired the relevant experience and could now focus wholeheartedly on a specialism. A Local Government department was set up at Birmingham in July 1980 under Tom Walls,[30] who had served his articles with Howard Smith Thompson & Co. and joined Price Waterhouse as a result of the merger in 1963. Becoming a manager in 1969, he was admitted to the partnership in 1973.[31] The specialism had arisen, in part, because of the involvement of Howard Smith Thompson & Co. in local government auditing – in particular the City of Birmingham and Solihull Corporation. This Birmingham firm also audited the City's Water Department and the West Midlands Gas Board. The 1972 Local Government Act, which took effect two years later, allowed authorities to appoint firms of accountants to undertake the entire audit rather than as before to share the task with a district auditor. Price Waterhouse were elected as sole auditors to the City of Birmingham. Walls, who was a manager experienced in this work, had the task of building up a team, under Sir Hugo Huntington-Whiteley Bt as the partner-in-charge. Throughout the late seventies the firm attracted a number of local government and water authority audits, the latter including Anglian, Yorkshire and North West Water.[32]

The election in 1979 of Margaret Thatcher as Prime Minister, with her commitment to privatisation and a reduction of state influence, resulted in a great expansion in local government work during the eighties. Walls had been transferred from Birmingham to be partner-in-charge of Leicester office, but in view of the importance of this specialism returned to Birmingham, where he could supervise major audits such as the City of Birmingham. In time, with a burgeoning programme of privatisation, Price Waterhouse was to set up a Public Sector specialism and Walls moved to London in 1985 to join that department.

Having merged with Daniel Mahony Taylor & Co. largely to recruit Monty Eckman, a noted insolvency practitioner, Price Waterhouse had the expertise to compete for those assignments generated by the secondary banking crisis and recession of 1972–3. The bankruptcies and liquidations which followed from these generated work until the late seventies and saw the number of chargeable hours rise from 47,000 in 1976 to 115,000 in 1980, a five-year increase of 145 per cent.[33] Major appointments at this time included the liquidation of Israel–British Bank (London), the receivership of Triumph Investment Trust and the Guardian Properties Group.[34] The premature death of Eckman in November 1974 resulted in Mark Homan, a manager due to be made a partner in the summer of 1975, being admitted in January, and Peter Barrows, a partner in Birmingham with experience of receiverships, being transferred to London.[35] Homan, like Walls, had served his articles with Howard Smith Thompson & Co. and joined Price Waterhouse by way of merger in 1963. The bulk of insolvency work undertaken by Price Waterhouse was at that time concentrated in the capital. In 1978, however, Price Waterhouse established their first regional insolvency practice, appointing a partner in Newcastle. A second followed in Birmingham three years later. Growth during the eighties was less spectacular than in the mid-seventies, although it did receive a boost from the 1982–3 recession – of an organic nature as expertise was exported from head office to new provincial bases rather than being acquired from outside.

In 1969 a Special Services department had been set up within London office to cope with the needs of emerging smaller businesses.[36] This was, in effect, an institutional response to the changed character of the firm.

Smaller practices in London and many of Price Waterhouse's regional offices undertook this work as a matter of routine. As the firm had expanded in order to focus on work for major businesses, the services it offered and their cost-structure were no longer appropriate for the newer, small-scale enterprise. Yet it was recognised that some of these would grow into the medium-sized, or even major, corporations of the future and that there was therefore considerable business potential in this market. This was an example of well-established skills within the firm being cultivated to create a specialism. If trends were to continue, those well-established skills were likely to have disappeared. Under Graham Stacy, a partner who had joined Price Waterhouse in 1957 having been articled with Walter Smee, Will & Co., and two managers, John Barrett and Howard Hughes, later joined by Chris Ames, it focused on providing advice to the ambitious but small-scale enterprise, often a partnership or a private limited liability company. In part, therefore, its function was to secure the audit of a successful business when it was embryonic but also to make a contribution to its development. By 1975 the Special Services department had three partners and by 1981 had expanded to five. Although Peats, with its decentralised network of regional offices, had a larger small business practice than Price Waterhouse, the latter generated steady growth throughout the eighties. In 1976, when Stacy became Director of Audit Technical Services, Barry Baldwin took charge of the department (later renamed Independent Business Services); Baldwin had joined the Bristol office of Price Waterhouse in 1958, having served his articles with Russell & Mason. Admitted to the partnership in 1969, he transferred to London to head the Special Services department.

Development of the Firm

Having adopted a strategic plan for the size and growth rates of the UK Firm and the career progression of qualified staff, it became essential that Price Waterhouse concentrate an increasing proportion of its energies upon both recruitment and training. In a business where plant and machinery are of comparatively little importance and where the expertise and business skills of its employees are responsible for earning profits, these two areas were perceived as being of crucial significance.

By 1975 the principle of graduate recruitment had been established in Price Waterhouse and Dick Shervington, the first non-fee-earning partner, was touring universities with a team of interviewers. It was important to establish the firm's name and to build up contacts with appointments boards. In general Price Waterhouse did not look specifically for accountancy graduates but preferred to seek those, of whatever discipline, who appeared to have the intellectual capacity to cope with the training, the ability to build relationships and work with a variety of individuals and who had career ambitions.[37] Shervington was joined in 1979 by Keith Bell (admitted to the partnership in 1983), formerly a personnel manager with ICI. As chairman of the Association of Graduate Recruiters, Bell had a measure of public recognition and sat on the boards of the Oxford and Bristol Careers Advisory Services. Thus, as the firm's recruitment department became more sophisticated so the number of graduates entering Price Waterhouse increased. In 1978, for example, the intake was estimated at 285, an increase of 30 per cent on the previous year.[38]

The opening of the London training building in 1975 represented a major step in the education of students and qualified staff. The typical career progression laid down by Price Waterhouse covered a period of twelve years from student to partner admission.[39] The first four years covered qualification and practical experience, followed by two years as an assistant manager; a further two years as a manager led to four years as a senior manager and then progression to partner. It was essential, therefore, if the firm wished to endow staff with the requisite levels of skills and to monitor their progress through these stages that a comprehensive training programme be instituted. A training department based upon a tutorial system had been established in 1968 under Hugh Scott, a manager. Set up at a time when the firm was recruiting a high proportion of qualified staff, it was designed to educate auditors in the methods and systems current in Price Waterhouse. The strategic decision to recruit high quality graduates dramatically altered its focus and created unprecedented demands, which resulted in the commissioning of the Union Street training centre. Mike Phillips was appointed in 1978 as the first full-time Training Partner.[40] From the late seventies the range and number of courses for qualified staff increased, particularly in the senior manager and partner grades.[41]

Price Waterhouse was in the throes of a dramatic transformation. The audit-based, City partnership was developing into a major business organisation, offering a burgeoning range of services and with impressive recruitment and training facilities. It occupied substantial and modern premises. These changes prompted Coates to reconsider the nature of Price Waterhouse's corporate image. Acting through the Policy Committee of Price Waterhouse International, it was agreed that Michael Hallissey and a US partner, Dominic Tarantino, should conduct a review of the presentation of the Price Waterhouse image throughout the world. Hallissey, who had joined the firm in 1964 and been admitted to the partnership in 1974, had just been appointed National Practice Development partner. His report, completed in August 1979, concluded that there was a need for harmonisation and development. He recommended the creation of a corporate identity manual in order to establish the design style for all Price Waterhouse firms. This would then determine the appearance of all letter-headings and memoranda, internal and external publications, and the character of entrance halls and other public areas in Price Waterhouse premises.[42] Following the approval of the Policy Committee of Price Waterhouse International in October 1980, the UK Firm began to implement these proposals. In December it agreed to the removal of '& Co.' from the style as it was no longer seen to serve any 'useful purpose', the change to be effected from July 1981.[43]

Throughout 1980 a study had been conducted on the feasibility of replacing the firm's electric typewriters with word processors. London office alone, it was calculated, generated 1.2 million pages of typescript annually, and the capital cost of computerising this work was estimated at £1.5 million. It was concluded that improvements to the quality of typeface and the greater range of facilities offered by the word processor justified such expenditure. The plan was to have converted all offices in the UK by the end of 1982.[44]

Having raised the standard of the firm's buildings, publications and documentation, and introduced a wider range of professional services, it was considered important to take a more active role in marketing and promoting Price Waterhouse. During the 1970s it had become increasingly apparent that the firm could no longer rely on new clients seeking out Price Waterhouse, attracted by its reputation, and that there was a growing need to defend existing audits from predatory competitors. Price Waterhouse set out to target potential acquisitions, but in recognising that it was more cost-effective to retain a client than to capture a new one, sought to improve relations with key executives and widen the range of services on offer to them.

In July 1980 a marketing department was set up under the supervision of Hallissey.[45] In part the timing of this venture was dictated by the ICAEW which was beginning to relax its rules on promotion. Hitherto chartered accountancy firms were not permitted to issue press releases, and booklets containing professional advice could not be sent without a letter of request and a copy to the current auditors. In 1982 R.G. Wilkes, recently appointed as Director of Communications and External Relations (having been partner-in-charge of Leicester office from 1969), commissioned a public relations consultancy, Good Relations City, to project the image of Price Waterhouse.[46] However, the range of approaches that they and the firm could employ remained limited until October 1984 when the ICAEW allowed accountants to advertise and send direct mail to journalists without prior request.

Throughout the remainder of the 1980s the trend was for a progressive relaxation of restrictions. In January 1985, for example, the quarter-page limit on broadsheet advertisements was lifted and from February 1986 firms were permitted to write direct to potential clients but not to telephone them. In 1986 Price Waterhouse launched its first proper campaign, placing advertisements in business newspapers and journals. It was designed to reposition the firm in the public's mind as business advisers, rather than simply as accountants. As a result it explored the themes of non-audit services, including taxation, management consultancy and recruitment. This was followed in 1989 by a second major campaign designed to target this message at decision makers, chief executives and their support teams. It was based on specific tasks undertaken for clients to illustrate the range of work that Price Waterhouse was now performing.

Accountancy has been in the forefront of the professions in allowing its practitioners to advertise (though important restrictions still apply), while doctors and lawyers remain constrained by much tighter regulations. The current situation is akin to that in America at the turn of the century when A.L. Dickinson successfully targeted future clients with a campaign of leaflets and advertisements. The new freedoms are perhaps a reflection of the increasingly commercial nature of the largest practices and their need to compete across an increasingly wide spectrum.

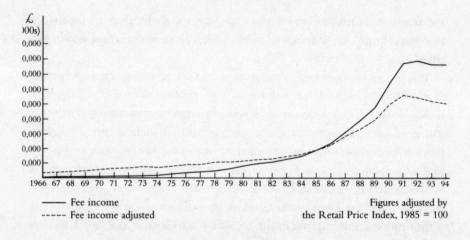

£
)00s)
0,000
0,000
0,000
0,000
0,000
0,000
0,000
0,000
0,000

1966 67 68 69 70 71 72 73 74 75 76 77 78 79 80 81 82 83 84 85 86 87 88 89 90 91 92 93 94

——— Fee income
----- Fee income adjusted

Figures adjusted by
the Retail Price Index, 1985 = 100

FIGURE 17
Price Waterhouse (UK Firm) Fee Income 1966–94

Growth of the Practice

Writing of the major accountancy firms in 1988, Michael Lafferty, a financial journalist, observed that they had been enjoying 'a boom period' and that 1986 had seen 'fee growth of over 20 per cent from eight of the top twenty firms'.[47] In fact, Price Waterhouse had enjoyed growth rates in excess of this for periods during the late seventies and early eighties. In 1976, for example, the firm's fee income increased by 43 per cent, and by 17, 18, 17 and 28 per cent respectively in the four years to 1980. Between 1975 and 1982 Price Waterhouse raised its fee income from £14.2 million to £57.5 million, which represented an increment of 305 per cent. However, the late seventies were a time of high inflation and if the figures are adjusted to take account of price movements then the firm's development, though sustained and substantial, was less dramatic. In real terms Price Waterhouse expanded by 70 per cent between 1975 and 1982, and annual growth rates were more modest – of the order of 2 to 10 per cent.

Over the period 1975–82 total staff numbers grew from 2,079 to 3,025, an increase of 46 per cent (Table 15, see Appendix). There were eighty-seven partners in 1975, a figure which had risen to 161 by 1982, an increment of 85 per cent, which reflected both an improvement to the partner-professional staff ratio (from one to 17.8 falling to one to 13.6) and the need to appoint more specialist and non-fee-earning partners.

The emergence of the so-called 'Big Eight' accountancy firms encouraged the financial press to publish league tables based upon estimates of fee income and partner and staff numbers. Because the major practices still remained partnerships and were not, therefore, legally obliged to publish audited annual statements, the figures on which these comparisons were based did not have the force of verified reports. Nevertheless, as approximations they had some validity. On 3 July 1979, for example, the *Financial Times* ranked Price Waterhouse fifth with a fee income of £21.3 million and a staff of 2,391. The fee income of £32 million given for Peat Marwick Mitchell, placing them as the largest practice, appears to be an accurate figure given statistics provided by the firm.[48] If the figure of £28 million (Table 18, see Appendix) is taken then Price Waterhouse would have ranked third, behind the newly formed Ernst & Whinney.

A league table provided by *The Accountant* in June 1989 suggested, on a fee income basis, that Price Waterhouse ranked third in 1985 behind Peat Marwick Mitchell and Coopers & Lybrand. The quoted figure for Price Waterhouse was £84.9 million though the firm's records show it to have been £94.3 million while the archives of both Peats and Arthur Andersen reveal other discrepancies. Their fee income for 1985 was £98.3 million and £61.0 million respectively, in contrast to the £131.7 million and £47.1 million of the league table. The conclusion to be drawn from the 1985 figures was that the largest firms were ranked much more closely than the financial press imagined. Unfortunately it has not proved possible to obtain comparable statements of fee income from all the major firms for the eighties, in order to construct an accurate picture.

Price Waterhouse had become aware in the early seventies that it was important to collect statistical data and monitor the performance of the firm. In June 1970 Ivor Coats, a corporate planner, was recruited as a manager to oversee the analysis of operating statistics.[49] He was responsible for setting up computer packages to interpret trends in chargeable hours, overheads and direct costs, each broken down between departments. It was on the basis of this data that Michael Coates, as Director of Operations, was able to write his visionary plan 'The Firm in the Future' in 1973. As part of the ongoing strategy to monitor and shape the development of the practice, Leslie Cousins was appointed National Planning partner in 1980.

Quality Control

The theme 'It's a dangerous world' was chosen for the annual meeting of partners in November 1977.[50] Speakers recalled that auditors had been subject to critical comment in the press and were now much more likely to be taken to court by a dissatisfied client. On 14 February 1976, for example, *The Economist*, under the title 'Auditing the Auditors' detailed the recent government inquiries (notably the Sandilands report on inflation accounting), the settlement made by Arthur Young McClelland Moores of £500,000 after Tremlett's acquisition of Tower Assets, and the Board of Trade report into the London and County Securities affair which levelled criticisms at the auditors Harmood Banner. They concluded that 'Britain's auditors are not doing their job', and that it was incumbent on the profession to tighten standards of conduct to prevent the need for further legislation. In view of this public disquiet and indeed to minimise the risk of litigation, Price Waterhouse and the other leading firms reinforced rigorous internal quality checks. The firm had always prided itself on maintaining the highest technical standards, and in this new atmosphere of criticism Price Waterhouse consciously sought to achieve positions of professional probity. When determining the stand it should take on accounting issues, the firm attempted to look beyond the narrow legal form of company law or accounting standards and seek solutions based upon economic substance and common sense.[51] In researching and stating the firm's position a leading role was played by Graham Stacy, Director of Audit Technical Services from 1976. Stacy also served on numerous professional committees including the CCAB Accounting Standards Committee.

A particular issue for the mid- to late seventies was created by high levels of inflation. With price rises in excess of 20 per cent, this could generate significant distortions in balance sheet comparisons. For example, the figures quoted for the purchase cost of plant and machinery could bear little relationship to current costs a year later.[52] Equally, an industrial company employing capital-intensive manufacturing techniques, could show what appeared to be good returns on their investments if expressed in historical costs, but when translated into current figures by means of an index, the figures might show a loss.[53] The debate tended to polarise between those who argued that adjustments ought to be made to account for the general effects of inflation, and those who believed that adjustments ought to be based upon specific price movements for particular assets. In May 1974 the Accounting Standards Committee produced a provisional accounting standard entitled 'Accounting for changes in the purchasing power of money' based on the general indexing approach. In response to this the government appointed a committee under Sir Francis Sandilands which, in September 1975, produced the Sandilands Report on Inflation Accounting which rejected general indexing in favour of a form of specific price adjustments.[54] In November 1976 a committee chaired by Douglas Morpeth and set up by the government produced a report recommending a form of current cost accounting based upon the Sandilands proposals. Although it was well received by the professional bodies, most academics, the Stock Exchange and the government, it was not enthusiastically welcomed by practitioners. Various bodies continued to press for current-cost accounting in the late seventies but no proposal was universally approved. In effect, the issue was settled, albeit by default, by a return to lower levels of inflation during the eighties. So long as government could control price rises, there was little need to abandon historical cost methods.

Price Waterhouse had always sought to be in the vanguard of the movement to improve technical standards not simply by internal pronouncements but also through membership of the ICAEW and its committees. Traditionally the firm had two seats on the Council, having enjoyed a continuous line of representation stretching back to S.L. Price. The involvement of the firm probably reached a peak when [Sir] Thomas Robson became president in 1952–3, though it was felt by some that his continuing commitment during the period of his senior partnership was to the overall detriment of the firm. W.E. Parker, having played a key part in the movement to improve the training of articled clerks, also served as president in 1967–8. Duncan also sat on the Council but under new electoral rules lost his seat before he could stand for the presidency.

By the 1980s it had become apparent that the demands on the senior partners of the major firms were so great that they could no longer combine an active role in the ICAEW with their executive duties. Sir Jeffery Bowman, for example, though a member of the Technical Research Committee and the Council, never stood for the presidency. The larger firms found it necessary to express their opinions through designated partners and Richard Wilkes held this responsibility at Price Waterhouse. He had been elected to the Council in 1969, and became president in the centenary year, 1980–81. Wilkes, having previously been partner-in-charge of Leicester office, then moved to London to serve as Director of Communications and External Relations. A continuing involvement with professional matters led to Wilkes' appointment as president of the International Federation of Accountants in 1987. Price Waterhouse was also represented on the Council of the ICAEW by Tom Watts, the firm's first technical partner. He was involved in many Institute technical committees and played an important role throughout the 1970s in the promulgation and implementation of standards of practice, becoming chairman of the Accounting Standards Committee in 1978. Watts was also the UK profession's representative in Brussels for the development of European Community directives on company law and accounting. Further representation on the Council during the following decade was provided by Chris Hordern, a partner in the Birmingham office, who was elected in 1985 having been president of the Birmingham and West Midlands Society of Chartered Accountants, and subsequently a trustee of the Chartered Accountants Benevolent Association.

Territorial Expansion

By 1975 Price Waterhouse had established twelve regional offices in Britain. They included: Liverpool (opened in 1904), Newcastle (opened in 1912 and greatly developed following the merger with Monkhouse Goddard in 1920), Leeds (1928), Cardiff (1932), Manchester (1932), Birmingham (1939), Bristol (1963), Nottingham (1966), Leicester (1969) and Southampton (1975). The Plymouth office which opened in 1914 had been closed exactly fifty years later. Although staff had been based in Glasgow from 1937 to work on the audit of the LMS, it was not until 1949 that an office had been formally established there. Thus, by the mid-seventies Price Waterhouse had widespread representation in England and Wales. The same could not be said of Scotland where Glasgow attempted to serve the entire country even though, on the basis of staff numbers, it was the smallest office in the UK with thirty-seven in 1974, rising to forty-eight in the following year.[55] This weakness was recognised and in July 1976 an office was opened in Edinburgh at 27 Drumsheugh Gardens.[56] It had been planned to merge with a local practice but all attempts to do so proved unsuccessful.[57] The office came under the overall supervision of Alec Campbell, a partner based at Glasgow since 1970. Campbell headed the Scottish practice from 1976 to 1986, and also served on the firm's Policy Committee from 1979 to 1985. As a response to the development of North Sea oil, Price Waterhouse set up a third Scottish office in 1981 at King's Close, Huntly Street, Aberdeen. Starting from a comparatively low base, the practice in Scotland was able to achieve rapid growth in just over five years. The total number of staff rose from fifty-three in 1976 to ninety-four by 1982, an increase of 77 per cent.[58]

As well as expanding territorially, the firm placed a fresh emphasis on building up the status of regional offices. Traditionally they had been regarded as branches of Price Waterhouse set up to perform basic audit tasks and required to refer important decisions to London. This sense of being second best still lingered in some outposts. One means of unifying the practice was through staff and partner exchanges. In 1980, for example, George Carter, who had been in charge of London Audit Group 1 for six years, transferred to Birmingham, and in 1982 took responsibility for the West Midlands practice.[59] He set about raising the public profile of the firm by setting up seminars for the local business community, and sponsoring a West Midlands Business of the Year Award, with a similar prize for sixth formers. He himself was elected to the councils of the Birmingham Chamber of Industry and Commerce and the region's CBI. This approach has contributed to the growth of Price Waterhouse in Birmingham where its turnover has increased sixfold between 1982 and 1991.

The Pan European Consultancy and the World Firm

In December 1979 Michael Coates was re-elected for a further five years as senior partner and observed that he 'was now almost exactly half-way through his potential term of office'.[60] He also announced that the Policy Committees of the respective UK and European Firms had agreed to the setting up of a 'Project Board' which would prepare a prospectus for an integrated consultancy organisation throughout Europe. Represent-atives from the UK Firm were Tim Hoult, Ernest Barnes and Howard Hughes, while Darwen Templeton was appointed chairman and Tony Thorne was given executive responsibility for the production of the document. Thorne, a chartered engineer who had joined the manage-ment consultancy practice of Price Waterhouse from the British Aircraft Corporation, had been appointed partner-in-charge of London MCS in 1978, and three years later he became chief executive of the Pan European Consultancy. It was intended that the prospectus be available for ratification in the autumn of 1980 and that an integrated consultancy be established by January 1981.[61]

In 1981 the Pan European Consultancy (PEC) was duly supported strongly by the senior partners of its respective firms. The untimely and sudden death in 1984 of Ken Smith, senior partner of the European Firm from 1979, however, was a severe blow to the development of closer relationships between the UK and European Firms as a whole.[62] An exceptionally able leader, Smith had encouraged a closer union with the UK Firm. In fact, the Pan European Consultancy proved a remarkable success. In December 1983 Thorne reported that the four firms' consultancy practices, now operating on an integrated basis, had achieved higher growth rates, greater market penetration and improved levels of profitability.[63] During the first two years of its operation PEC had generated revenue of £25m and its staff numbers had expanded by about 50 per cent to 425. The unification of the consultancy practices had generated the motivation to raise standards in those territories where they had lagged behind. As a result new managers had been appointed and, in some cases, nationals recruited at a senior level.

The clear success and business advantage which had derived from integrating the various management consultancy practices of Price Water-house across Europe encouraged a number of executive partners to push for the forging of closer operating links. However, Smith's successor as senior partner of the European Firm, John Fallon, formerly the technical partner based in The Hague, did not welcome integration, and further fresh organisational changes were delayed until 1987 when Patrick Giffin had taken his place.

While Price Waterhouse International had been restructured under the 1973 agreement and now had its own formal headquarters in London, these changes fell short of attempting to run the various national partnerships as a truly integrated business. As a result, its achievements had been of a technical, rather than of a business or strategic nature.[64] In 1979–80 the US Firm had engaged McKinsey & Co. to conduct a major review of its operations. Some of the insights gained led John Biegler, former senior partner of the US Firm, who had succeeded Duncan as chairman, to conclude that a similar survey could be beneficial to the International Firm. The McKinsey review, entitled 'Realising Worldwide Opportunities' (November 1981), confirmed that Price Waterhouse had lost its global advantage at a time of increasing challenge, was competitively weak in some rising national markets and had an uneven coverage of certain specialist skills across the world.[65]

As a result of these findings, a new organisation, styled Price Waterhouse World Firm, was created in 1982 to take over the duties of the International practice. Michael Coates, who had served only two of the five years of his second term as senior partner of the UK Firm, was elected to be its first chairman. The new body was structured to encourage greater participation by the national partnerships and to increase the focus on global issues. It was managed by a Policy Committee composed of a chairman and eight senior partners of member firms; a Council of Firms comprising the chairman and senior partners of nineteen partnerships; and a Council of Partners which consisted of around one hundred partners selected from across the world to advise the chairman in determining needs and strategies. For the first time partners whose principal task was to serve clients, rather than those with managerial functions, were directly engaged in the international organisation. Among the early projects of the World Firm was the development of distinctive auditing services, global marketing approaches and the strengthening of the MCS practice. In 1984 the World Firm set up a technology centre in Palo Alto, California, intended to identify future information technology needs and assess potential applications within Price Waterhouse firms.

In 1985 a joint study group composed of representatives from the US and UK Firms was appointed to make recommendations for a global strategy. Two years later its results were approved by the World Firm and endorsed by the partners of the various national practices. Thereafter the World Firm set up working groups to develop more specific proposals, producing a new document in 1988 entitled 'Global Strategy for the 1990s: A Call for Action'. In essence it argued for the creation of an effective management body to supervise the national practices and to develop services and monitor personnel throughout the world. Had it been implemented, therefore, it would have represented a shift in executive power towards the international umbrella organisation.[66]

In 1988 Joe Connor, the outgoing senior partner of the US Firm, succeeded Coates as chairman of the World Firm. He encountered resistance to this strategy of centralisation from the member partnerships and a new approach, which recognised both their desire to retain autonomy but also the need to create greater levels of uniformity in audit, tax and consulting services, was introduced.

Epilogue

The paradox of recent events is that they are at once the most interesting but also the most problematical. Their immediacy makes them vitally relevant. Personalities are recognised; facts can be portentous and matters so close to current affairs generally continue to exercise a powerful influence. Yet this very proximity is the enemy of objectivity. Without the distance of time to lend context and establish a balance of emphasis, the commentator finds it difficult to make accurate and verifiable assessments. Although there is an abundance of information available, a lack of distance impedes the sifting process. Details may remain shrouded in the demands of confidentiality. Thus, this epilogue, which considers the Price Waterhouse story during the last decade, does not constitute a true successor to those chapters which have preceded it. Rather, it is cast in the nature of a survey of recent significant events, and one necessarily conducted with less depth and range of research. It sets out to show important trends, and only a historian of the future will be able to judge whether these have been interpreted correctly.

Growth of the Practice

The outstanding feature of Price Waterhouse in the decade from 1982 was its remarkable and sustained rate of growth. The fee income of the UK Firm rose from £57.5 million in 1982 to £395.1 million in 1992, an increase of 587 per cent (Table 18, see Appendix). Even when those figures are adjusted to take account of inflation the scale of the expansion remains significant at 305 per cent. Fee income achieved annual growth rates of between 20 and 30 per cent during the latter part of the eighties.[1] However, these substantial and sustained increases came to an abrupt halt in the year to June 1992,[2] when fees rose by only 2 per cent, which in real terms represented a reduction of 1.7 per cent.

There has always been a strong relationship between fees and staff numbers in accountancy. Rising turnover, therefore, generated a progressive expansion in the numbers of partners and staff in the UK Firm of Price Waterhouse. In 1982 there were 161 partners and 2,864 staff. By 1990 the partnership had increased to 421 and the total number of staff topped 6,500. Throughout this period the partner-professional staff ratio decreased slightly, achieving a figure of one to 10.7 by the end of the eighties.

Recession has always taken longer to affect accountancy firms than business itself. The full force of economic downturn was not apparent at Price Waterhouse until June 1991 when, for the first time in its history, the firm announced 180 redundancies for audit staff, followed in November by a further 150 in management consultancy. The latter, a practice particularly vulnerable in times of economic depression as companies cut back on special assignments, suffered a further 100 redundancies in June 1993.

How, then, did Price Waterhouse earn its fees? Traditionally, it had always held a strong audit practice, which in the interwar period had been the envy of the profession. In 1983 Price Waterhouse had more appointments from the largest 500 companies listed in *The Times 1000* than any other firm, although it was second to Deloitte Haskins & Sells if the top 100 alone were considered.[3] In 1982 2.1 million chargeable hours were worked by the audit department representing 74 per cent of the total – tax with 15 per cent, management consultancy with 7 per cent and insolvency with 4 per cent were all appreciably smaller.[4] By 1987, as the specialist services grew more rapidly, the share of the business attributable to auditing had shown a demonstrable reduction. With 2.7 million chargeable hours, it comprised 65 per cent, while tax with 647,000 (16 per cent) was slightly larger and management consultancy with 616,000 (15 per cent) was noticeably greater.[5] Audit contributed 44 per cent of fee income, tax 20 per cent and management consultancy 22 per cent.

By 1988 the relative importance of auditing had fallen further and represented 41 per cent of fee income; tax had risen to 21 per cent and management consultancy to 24 per cent. Investigation work was now a significant contributor with 10 per cent of turnover.[6] These trends continued into the nineties and in June 1994 the respective totals were: audit 38 per cent, tax 28 per cent, management consultancy 21 per cent and corporate finance 13 per cent.[7]

The slower growth of auditing in favour of specialist services was, therefore, one of the key trends of the eighties and nineties. That this occurred at a time of rapid and sustained increase in fee income suggests that the audit practice was unable to expand as quickly as tax or management consultancy. It is possible to see why this should have been the case. By 1982 Price Waterhouse already held a considerable share of the audit market and, short of merging with a substantial competitor, it was difficult for the firm to add any great number of major clients. Thus, for audit to grow quickly, it relied upon the clients themselves to expand at a faster rate than the economy itself, and this largely through acquisitions. In the context of a declining manufacturing sector and of doubts surrounding the ability of existing financial service clients to make up the difference, this was not considered to be a likely outcome. The shrinkage in the proportion of auditing rather than in absolute size was, therefore, a reflection of macro-economic forces. It is unlikely, in the absence of a merger with another major accountancy firm, that auditing will ever again contribute more than 50 per cent of fee income; whether it continues to fall in importance will depend on the performance of Britain's business sector. If industry and the financial services recover and grow at a rapid rate after the most recent recession, then auditing should regain some lost ground.

How, then, were the various specialist services offered by Price Waterhouse able to grow so rapidly during the eighties? Tax was the oldest of these departments. It combined some of the qualities of both auditing and management consultancy. A high percentage of its clients were also audited by Price Waterhouse so it could rely upon a core of recurring, regular business. Nevertheless, like consultancy, it cannot depend on repeated, legally required assignments, and many of its tasks are of non-standardised nature requiring the application of general principles to novel situations.[8] As it is a highly specialised activity demanding expert opinions, there has been a greater need to recruit qualified staff from outside Price Waterhouse. Whereas the firm's recruitment and training programmes have been designed to supply the firm with its necessary quotas of auditors, around half of the tax partners and managers have joined Price Waterhouse from other organisations.

Rapid and sustained growth by the tax department has been achieved by capturing a greater share of what has been an expanding market for tax services. Why, then, have businesses been increasingly prepared to hand tax matters to consultants? Rising competition has forced corporations to look closely at what can be a major item of expenditure, and one in which important savings can be made. The international character of business has increased the complexity of taxation issues so that it is no longer sufficient for many multinational corporations to understand the regulations of a single nation. Governments themselves compete for revenue and seek to attract foreign investment, increasing the obligation on businesses to have a wider comprehension of tax matters.

As a result of these developments the tax practice in the UK comprised 104 partners and 833 professional staff in June 1990. This represented a remarkable increase over the previous fifteen years, as in 1975 there were only ten tax partners. From 1974 Michael Carr served as Director of Tax Services, and was an example of expertise recruited from outside the firm, having qualified with Sturges, Fraser & Co. in which he subsequently became a partner. However, his successor, as partner-in-charge of the London tax practice from 1985, Ian Vaile, had joined Price Waterhouse on the completion of his articles, rising through the various grades of manager. As the firm became larger and its specialist departments established themselves so it was less likely that skills had to be imported. By 1990 within the European Combination (p.326) there were 187 partners and 1,538 staff engaged in tax work.

While the tax practice often worked closely with audit and developed a not dissimilar culture (influenced by the fact that around half of the tax staff had originally trained as auditors), management consultancy has evolved with a different ethos and operational style. It has no regular and recurring tasks; it exists on the basis of individual and unique assignments. Accordingly, it has been particularly sensitive to cyclical fluctuations. A booming economy would generate far more new work than an auditor would expect to gain, while a slump, equally, would result in proportionately lower levels of activity. Throughout the eighties the management consultancy practice grew at around 25 to 30 per cent in real terms every year,[9] gaining market share from the medium- and small-sized firms and undertaking a number of very large, long-running assignments for organisations such as British Rail, Guinness and Barclays Bank. Largely as a result of internally generated growth, Price Waterhouse became the second-largest management consultancy in the UK (behind Coopers & Lybrand) measured in terms of staff numbers, and this growth was consolidated in 1984, when a merger was completed with Urwick Orr & Partners, a practice which had established a high profile in the sixties and seventies and considerable marketing skills. Originally, MCS relied heavily on assignments from audit clients but this merger, combined with the department's growing reputation, reduced the percentage of internally referred work to around 35 per cent.

As the management consultancy department grew in size and relied to a lesser extent on the audit practice for clients, it developed a distinctive culture. The proportion of chartered accountants fell as it expanded into general consultancy work and information technology. In 1992, for example, out of a total of thirty-two consultancy partners in London only nine were qualified accountants and of these five were chartered. The appointment of Neville Cheadle in 1985 as National Director of Management Consultancy Services in succession to Ernest Barnes reflected this change in emphasis. Cheadle was the first national head of the department not to have qualified as an accountant, having joined Price Waterhouse in 1968 from industry, working for Elliott Automation and Standard Telephones and Cables. However, the trend pre-dated this event as Tony Thorne had become partner-in-charge of London MCS in 1978, having joined Price Waterhouse from a non-accounting background. The need for wide-ranging skills and expertise resulted in extensive recruitment from outside the firm. Consequently, its partners and staff came from a much wider background than the firm's auditors or tax specialists. As most had not trained with Price Waterhouse, they were not steeped in the traditional ethos of the firm. They were more accustomed to moving between organisations, rather than progressing through a single firm. The nature of the work also attracted different personalities and skills. Auditing requires a continuity of commitment and the establishment of an ongoing relationship, whereas consultancy is about a succession of varied assignments, each won by competitive tender. Change and uncertainty are the watchwords of consultancy.[10] It is often pressurised, involving tight schedules, and commonly commands a higher charge rate than auditing, but in periods of recession proves a more risky enterprise.

The differences in the nature of auditing and management consultancy, and the associated personalities that these activities attract, have led to an area of constructive dissonance within the major accountancy firms. Some have argued, particularly in America where SEC regulations have highlighted potential incompatibilities between the two disciplines, that if management consultancy practices continued to expand then they would have to be formally divorced from auditing. A measure of separation had been introduced by Arthur Andersen in 1989 when they established Andersen Consulting as a separately governed body. At Price Waterhouse, the management consultancy department has remained under the umbrella of the UK partnership, though it is operationally divorced to maintain client confidentiality. However, its rapid growth necessitated a move in November 1990 to new offices at Milton Gate, Chiswell Street, about a mile across the Thames from Southwark Towers. Some commentators wondered whether this physical transfer was the precursor to an organisational division. None followed. Recession and redundancy combined to cause the department to take advantage of extra office space at No. 1 London Bridge, and they returned to their earlier location in 1994. Such issues will presumably become more pressing during the next economic boom when consultancy services should be especially active and profitable.

Other specialisms which grew during the eighties included the public sector, corporate finance and insolvency. A Local Government group (which audited local authorities who were increasingly entrusting this work to private sector firms rather than the government district audit service) based in Birmingham had been set up in 1980 and this was followed by a Central Government Services group in London three years later. Most of the early public-sector work was for local authorities but with a Conservative government pledged to introduce business principles to the public sector, and the creation of a central government services group, the scope of public-sector work broadened. By the late eighties, Price Waterhouse was beginning to audit health authorities as well as quangos and colleges of further education, and to undertake extensive management consultancy work in all parts of the public sector.[11]

Out of this public-sector work, Price Waterhouse developed yet another specialism – privatisation. The firm was chosen by the government to undertake these assignments partly because of its acknowledged expertise in local authority and quango auditing but also because it had seconded partners and staff to civil service departments. Ian Mills, for example, a management consultancy partner from 1973 and Director of Central Government Services from 1983 to 1985, took a three-year appointment with the Department of Health and Social Security where he became Director of Finance of the National Health Service. Returning to Price Waterhouse in 1988, he served as Director of UK Business

76. Sir Nicholas Waterhouse (1867–1964) by Middleton Todd (1891–1966).

77. M.C. Spencer, admitted to the partnership in July 1918 and retiring in June 1949.

78. L.H. Norman, admitted to the partnership in July 1944, having run the Manchester office as a manager from 1939.

79. W.E. Parker, admitted to the partnership in 1944, and senior partner on the retirement of Robson in 1966. Seconded to the Board of Trade during the war, he built up extensive contacts in government which were neglected by the firm upon his return.

80. Thomas Howarth, admitted to the firm in 1932, having been a manager especially trusted by Garnsey. He served as a senior partner for a year on the retirement of Waterhouse in 1960.

81. T.R.T. Bucknill, a partner of exceptional talent and independence of mind who died before fulfilling his earlier promise.

82. G.E. Richards, admitted to the partnership in 1939 just before the outbreak of war. As the most junior partner he was entrusted with the administration of the firm, a role which he relished and held until retirement.

83. A cricket match organised by W.E. Parker (*seated third from right*) and held between two Price Waterhouse sides in June 1948. Standing, seventh from the left, is M.R. Harris, later to become an influential partner.

84. A portrait of Sir Thomas Robson (1896–1991) by William Dring (b. 1904).

Ministry of Fuel and Power,
7, Millbank,
London, S.W.1.

7th January, 1948

My dear Parker,

As you know, one of the difficulties of the present petrol situation arises from the existence of a black market in motor spirit, which may be very considerable in extent, and I am setting up as a matter of urgency a small Committee to advise me on the steps that should be taken to bring it under control. I want you to serve on this Committee if you can possibly find the time.

Watkinson has told me how heavily burdened you are and the considerable inconvenience that would be caused to your partners if you take on other work. Nevertheless, I feel that I must press you to give us your help and ask them as a matter of public interest to make it possible for you to do so.

There is a special reason why I must do this. It is vital to have for this enquiry someone with a thorough administrative knowledge of the working of coupon rationing schemes, not merely of their day to day working, but of the way in which machinery is created to safeguard the schemes from evasion, why this method is preferable to that, where risks can be taken and where they must be avoided, and so on. That is precisely the knowledge you gained in creating the machinery for the administration of the Board of Trade controls and rationing schemes, in devising the coupon controls worked in conjunction with the coupon banking scheme that you arranged with Lidbury and the Joint Stock Banks.

I know of no one else with this knowledge and that is why I am so keen that you should take on the job.

All good wishes for 1948

yours sincerely

Hugh Gaitskell

W.E. Parker, Esq., C.B.E.,
Price, Waterhouse & Co.,
3, Frederick's Place,
Austin Friars,
E.C. 2.

85. (*Above*) A request from Hugh Gaitskell, then Minister of Fuel and Power in the Attlee government, that Price Waterhouse assist with a scheme for petrol rationing.

86. (*Left*) The National Bank building, Liverpool, photographed in 1948. It was here during the thirties that Price Waterhouse leased premises for their Liverpool office. (*Liverpool Record Office*)

87. (*Right*) J.M.S. Coates, senior partner of the Newcastle Firm, photographed about the time of his retirement in 1959.

88. (*Below*) W.E. Parker (*seated fifth from left*) at a meeting of the UK partnership at Bournemouth in June 1969. S.M. Duncan is seated on Parker's right.

89. (*Above*) The UK partnership gathered at Bournemouth in June 1970.

90. (*Left*) One of a series of posed photographs taken at Frederick's Place in 1967. This shows John Read, a partner (*third from left*), with George Carter, later to become partner-in-charge of the Birmingham office, looking over his shoulder.

91. (*Above*)
A meeting room at Frederick's Place showing on the left–hand wall photographs of distinguished US partners, and facing the camera portraits of the founding partners.

92. (*Middle*) A group of staff on the new seniors' course being taught by Robert Brooke.

93. (*Below*)
Photographed in 1967, a member of Price Waterhouse's audit team visiting their client, Hawker Siddeley. Behind a new Trident passenger jet is being inspected.

94. S.M. Duncan (b. 1910), who became senior partner in 1971, portrayed by
Ruskin Spear (1911–89).

PRICE WATERHOUSE C°

(an unlimited company)

ORDINARY DIRECTORS
W. E. PARKER
W. L. BARROWS
P. F. GRANGER
S. M. DUNCAN
H. M. ANGUS

EXECUTIVE DIRECTORS
L. W. SHAW
E. W. BARNES
B. J. BROCKS

PRINCIPAL MANAGER
F. H. KING

TELEPHONE: MONARCH 9988
TELEGRAMS: PRICEWATER LONDON EC2
CABLEGRAMS: PRICEWATER

3, FREDERICK'S PLACE
OLD JEWRY
LONDON, E.C.2

P. W. & C°

W. E. PARKER
L. H. NORMAN
S. M. DUNCAN
A. C. FALKNER
H. M. ANGUS
C. H. McMILLAN
E. B. LUCAS
A. R. HARRIS
H. A. COATES

G. A. CHERRY
A. M. INGLIS
D. O. BAILEY
L. W. SHAW
A. WILSON
T. R. WATTS
A. H. CHAPMAN
P. G. BARBER
J. B. SEWELL
P. W. BARROWS

TELEPHONE: MONARCH 9988

3, FREDERICK'S PLACE
OLD JEWRY
LONDON, E.C.2

OFFICES IN GREAT BRITAIN - LONDON, BIRMINGHAM, BRISTOL, CARDIFF, GLASGOW, LEEDS, LIVERPOOL, MANCHESTER, NEWCASTLE, NOTTINGHAM.
ASSOCIATED FIRMS OVERSEAS - UNITED STATES OF AMERICA, THE CARIBBEAN, SOUTH AND CENTRAL AMERICA, CONTINENT OF EUROPE, THE MIDDLE EAST, CANADA.
CONTINENT OF AFRICA, AUSTRALIA, NEW ZEALAND, MALAYSIA, SINGAPORE, INDIA, JAPAN.   CORRESPONDENTS IN - EAST AFRICA, PAKISTAN, HONG KONG, PHILIPPINES.

PRICE WATERHOUSE & C°

W. E. PARKER
L. H. NORMAN
S. M. DUNCAN
A. C. FALKNER
C. H. NICHOLSON
E. D. McMILLAN
A. B. LUCAS
A. R. HARRIS
H. A. COATES

G. A. CHERRY
A. M. INGLIS
D. O. BAILEY
L. W. SHAW
T. R. WATTS
A. H. CHAPMAN
P. G. BARBER
J. B. SEWELL
P. W. BARROWS

OTHER LONDON RESIDENTS
(PARTNERS IN FIRMS OUTSIDE LONDON)
P. L. ANGER
C. I. BROWN
W. G. CARTER

J. L. READ
J. H. BOWMAN

TELEPHONE: MONARCH 9988
TELEGRAMS: PRICEWATER LONDON EC2
CABLEGRAMS: PRICEWATER ALL OFFICES

3, FREDERICK'S PLACE
OLD JEWRY
LONDON, E.C.2

95. A selection of Price Waterhouse letterheads from the mid-sixties.

96. Letterheads from regional offices in the sixties.

OFFICES IN GREAT BRITAIN - LONDON, BIRMINGHAM, BRISTOL, CARDIFF, GLASGOW, LEEDS, LIVERPOOL, MANCHESTER, NEWCASTLE, NOTTINGHAM.
ASSOCIATED FIRMS OVERSEAS - UNITED STATES OF AMERICA, THE CARIBBEAN, SOUTH AND CENTRAL AMERICA, CONTINENT OF EUROPE, THE MIDDLE EAST, CANADA.
CONTINENT OF AFRICA, AUSTRALIA, NEW ZEALAND, MALAYSIA, SINGAPORE, INDIA, JAPAN.   CORRESPONDENTS IN - EAST AFRICA, PAKISTAN, HONG KONG, PHILIPPINES.

PRICE WATERHOUSE & C°

W. E. PARKER
L. H. NORMAN
S. M. DUNCAN
A. C. FALKNER
H. M. ANGUS
C. H. NICHOLSON
E. D. McMILLAN
A. B. LUCAS
A. R. HARRIS

H. A. COATES
G. A. CHERRY
D. O. BAILEY
J. O. HEWIT
L. W. SHAW
A. D. COPLEY
C. COLLETT
R. LOVELY
T. H. MANCLIFFE
J. L. READ

TELEPHONE: NEWCASTLE 28493
TELEGRAMS: PRICEWATER NEWCASTLE UPON TYNE
CABLEGRAMS: PRICEWATER ALL OFFICES

31, MOSLEY STREET
(G.P.O. Box No. 49)
NEWCASTLE UPON TYNE, 1

OFFICES IN GREAT BRITAIN - LONDON, BIRMINGHAM, BRISTOL, CARDIFF, GLASGOW, LEEDS, LIVERPOOL, MANCHESTER, NEWCASTLE, NOTTINGHAM.
ASSOCIATED FIRMS OVERSEAS - UNITED STATES OF AMERICA, THE CARIBBEAN, SOUTH AND CENTRAL AMERICA, CONTINENT OF EUROPE, THE MIDDLE EAST, CANADA.
CONTINENT OF AFRICA, AUSTRALIA, NEW ZEALAND, MALAYSIA, SINGAPORE, INDIA, JAPAN.   CORRESPONDENTS IN - EAST AFRICA, PAKISTAN, HONG KONG, PHILIPPINES.

PRICE WATERHOUSE & C°

W. E. PARKER
L. H. NORMAN
S. M. DUNCAN
A. C. FALKNER
H. M. ANGUS
C. H. NICHOLSON

E. D. McMILLAN
A. B. LUCAS
G. A. CHERRY
D. O. BAILEY
A. M. INGLIS
A. WILSON

RESIDENT PARTNERS
A. L. BARNETT
W. E. DEWONEY

J. D. MARLE
C. F. HARKINS

TELEPHONE: BRISTOL 22108
TELEGRAMS: PRICEWATER BRISTOL 1
CABLEGRAMS: PRICEWATER ALL OFFICES

ST. GILES HOUSE
11, QUAY STREET
BRISTOL, 1

OFFICES IN GREAT BRITAIN - LONDON, BIRMINGHAM, BRISTOL, CARDIFF, GLASGOW, LEEDS, LIVERPOOL, MANCHESTER, NEWCASTLE, NOTTINGHAM.
ASSOCIATED FIRMS OVERSEAS - UNITED STATES OF AMERICA, THE CARIBBEAN, SOUTH AND CENTRAL AMERICA, CONTINENT OF EUROPE, THE MIDDLE EAST, CANADA.
CONTINENT OF AFRICA, AUSTRALIA, NEW ZEALAND, MALAYSIA, SINGAPORE, INDIA, JAPAN.   CORRESPONDENTS IN - EAST AFRICA, PAKISTAN, HONG KONG, PHILIPPINES.

PRICE WATERHOUSE & C°

W. L. BARROWS
D. V. LANCASTER
N. J. MILLIGAN
H. S. HUNTINGTON-WHITELEY

B. H. LARKINS
D. H. SANDRY
E. R. JEYNES

NON-RESIDENT PARTNERS
W. E. PARKER
P. F. GRANGER
S. M. DUNCAN

P. W. BARROWS
P. L. ANGER
C. I. BROWN

TELEPHONE: CENTRAL 5582
TELEGRAMS: PRICEWATER BIRMINGHAM
CABLEGRAMS: PRICEWATER ALL OFFICES

BEAUFORT HOUSE
(P.O. Box 120)
96, NEWHALL STREET
BIRMINGHAM, 3

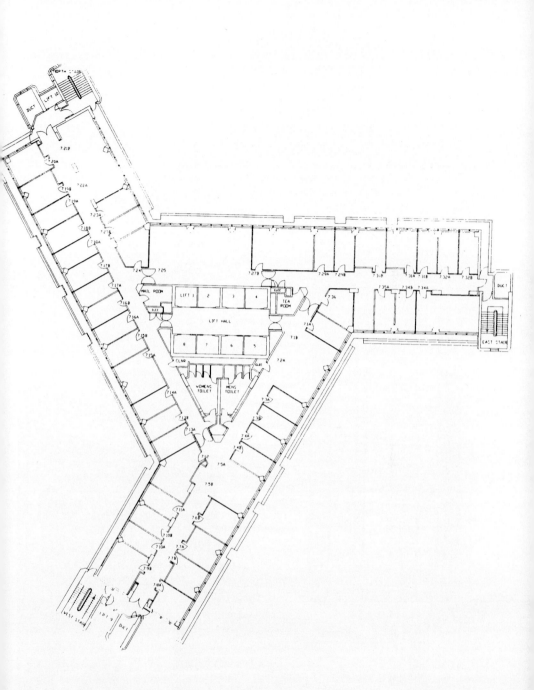

97. A floor plan of Southwark Towers showing the layout of offices in the three wings and central lift shafts.

98. The construction of Southwark Towers beside London Bridge Station well advanced in the spring of 1975. The office block was designed by T.P. Bennett & Son, and Sir Robert McAlpine & Sons were the contractors.

99. (*Above*) A meeting of the
International Firm in
Montreal (*c.* 1971). From left
to right: David Gordon
(South America), Richard
Brooke (senior partner
European Firm), Martin
Harris (London secretary),
T.L. Wilkinson (New York
secretary), W.E. Parker
(senior partner UK Firm),
J.G. Biegler (senior partner
US Firm), Laird Watt (senior
partner Canadian Firm),
F.E. Trigg (senior partner
Australian Firm), George
Young (senior partner South
American Firm),
S.M. Duncan (UK Firm) and
J.E. Connor (US Firm).

100. (*Left*) Michael Coates
photographed in Southwark
Towers.

101. (*Above*) Sir Jeffery Bowman, senior partner of the UK Firm from 1982 to 1991, photographed in the offices of Price Waterhouse at No. 1 London Bridge.

102. (*Right*) An advertisement taken from a campaign mounted by Price Waterhouse in 1989 following the relaxation of Institute regulations.

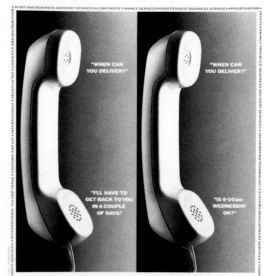

103. M.I. Eckman, a principal figure in Price Waterhouse's insolvency practice; here engaged on the Britten Norman receivership.

104. Ian Brindle, senior partner of the UK Firm from 1991. Joining Price Waterhouse in 1966, he became a partner in 1972 and was director of technical services from 1989.

105. The Edinburgh office of Price Waterhouse situated at 27 Drumsheugh Gardens and occupied from July 1976.

106. Southwark Towers by night.

Development. In 1984 Howard Hyman, on admission to the partnership, was seconded to the Treasury for three years where he worked primarily on privatisation matters. On his return he initially worked as an auditor but in view of the burgeoning programme of selling off nationalised industries was appointed Director of Privatisation Services. In 1982 Price Waterhouse, under the auspices of Alan Wheatley, had been involved with the plans for the privatisation of British Airways, and subsequently worked on the sale of Britoil.[12] This new department under Hyman was responsible for the privatisation schemes for the electricity boards, water authorities, the Rover group and the British Technology Group. Building on this expertise they were able to win assignments abroad and these included Singapore Airport, state enterprises in Hungary, South African Airways, the sale of Skoda to Volkswagen and telecommunications in Guyana.

However, the government's programme of privatisation was of limited duration and it was important to re-employ the skills and expertise acquired in these assignments to work with a greater market life. As a result, Hyman separated the firm's traditional corporate finance assignments from auditing both in London and the regions, establishing a Price Waterhouse Europe network. In essence, the Corporate Finance Department advises businesses on take-overs and mergers; how to find suitable acquisitions, raise the finance and manage the entire operation. It is, therefore, a market-orientated business, rather than a traditional, professional advisory service. While the proportion of UK fee income generated by Corporate Finance remained small, 3 per cent (£13.4 million) in the year ending June 1991, rising to 4 per cent (£16 million) in 1992[13], it made a significant contribution to profits and established a public profile greater than these numbers would suggest.

The revitalisation of the firm's Corporate Recovery and Insolvency Department in the seventies enabled Price Waterhouse to build up a solid reputation for this field of work. Generally the eighties were a quiescent period for insolvency practitioners, a newsworthy exception having been the firm's sequestration of the assets of the National Union of Mineworkers in October 1984. As the recession began to bite in 1990 so the volume of the work grew dramatically. In the year ending June 1991 the department earned £30.6 million which represented 8 per cent of fee income (in contrast to 4 per cent in 1988). In the following year Corporate Recovery and Insolvency increased its turnover by 31 per cent to £40.1 million, which represented 10 per cent of the UK Firm's fees. A notable assignment was the administration of Maxwell Communication Corporation, the first company to be subject simultaneously to Chapter Eleven bankruptcy in the United States and insolvency in Britain, thereby providing legal precedents for co-operation between the two jurisdictions. In February 1993 because of the synergy which exists between Corporate Finance and Corporate Recovery and their counter-cyclical nature, it was announced that the two departments would be merged. This, in turn, brought the UK Firm in line with the organisational pattern adopted elsewhere in the world.

As well as developing the range of specialist services that it offered, Price Waterhouse continued to expand territorially within Britain. In 1983, for example, the firm opened an office in Middlesbrough, a town hitherto served by Newcastle. The increasing concentration of business activity in south-east England led to the setting up of an office in Windsor in 1983, and in Redhill and St Albans in 1988. In 1990 a merger was concluded with the Hull practice of Hodgson Impey. The firm had originally set up in the port in 1880 as Hodgson Harris, expanding to Beverley in 1933. They also opened an office in Grimsby but the Hodgson Impey partners there decided to establish an independent firm. The Hull and Beverley offices comprised twelve partners and 116 staff and their audit clients included Fenner plc, manufacturers of mechanical and power transmission equipment, Dale Electric International, Edmond Holdings, house builders and I.J. Dewhurst, the first supplier to Marks & Spencer.

The progressive expansion of London office and of the specialist and support services which it housed, created unforeseen demands on office space. By the mid-eighties Southwark Towers, which had been opened only a decade before, could no longer cope with the needs of the firm in the capital and a variety of short-lease premises had been taken to accommodate burgeoning departments. So a lease was taken on space in No. 1 London Bridge, beside the Thames and close to Southwark Towers. This was occupied by Price Waterhouse in 1986, providing premises for the management consultancy department, and subsequently the executive function of the European Combination. But even this development was not sufficient and at the end of 1988 part of the head office function, including the firm's mainframe computer and its Systems Department (joined later by its internal accounting department) moved to new premises at Docklands Island Quay, 161 Marsh Wall.

The eighties, therefore, were a decade of strong and sustained growth for Price Waterhouse. Its fee income increased threefold in real terms. Surprisingly, however, this was not the most successful period in the history of the firm. Between 1920 and 1930, turnover rose in real terms by 402 per cent. Sir Gilbert Garnsey had largely been responsible for such a dramatic and continuous improvement in the fortunes of the partnership. Not even Edwin Waterhouse had been able to match these two decades of growth. During his senior partnership the fastest expansion had been achieved between 1889 and 1899 when the firm's fees rose in real terms by 139 per cent.

How, then, can the expansion of the eighties, when fee income was at such high levels, be explained? In a recent paper on the development of Price Waterhouse's world-wide organisation, Michael Hallissey, a partner, has argued that until the eighties this evolution was 'essentially reactive'.[14] This, he argued, was equally the case for tax and management consultancy as it had been for auditing. In responding to situations rather than seeking to alter them, Price Waterhouse were typical of most corporations. The period 'from 1950 to 1973', suggested Hallissey,

> saw a sustained period of economic growth and increasing world trade unprecedented this century. Strong and increasing demand for goods and services does not necessarily encourage innovation, investment in the unusual or strategic self-examination.[15]

The appointment of the management consultants McKinsey to investigate the US Firm in 1979–80, and then their examination of the World Firm in 1981–2, demonstrated that certain members of the executive recognised a need to question and rethink the strategic direction of the business. Although the McKinsey studies were stronger in their analysis of Price Waterhouse's strengths and weaknesses than in recommending new initiatives and how they were to be implemented, they served to introduce the UK partnership to a formal structure for laying down guidelines for decisions and action. In 1982 Jeffery Bowman, as senior partner, agreed that a strategic plan should be prepared. The research was entrusted to the firm's planning department and soundings were taken from partners at their sectional meetings and from the executive team. The results, submitted to the Policy Committee in November 1983, were approved 'wholeheartedly', and the final policy document was then circulated to the partnership for ratification in December.[16]

The text defined strategy as 'a set of guidelines to assist in all decisions and actions'[17] and these, it was argued, 'need not consist of fundamentally new or different ways of serving clients or rendering services . . . [as] a strategy which combined many small but real differentiations . . . can distinguish one firm from another'.[18] The overriding objective of Price Waterhouse was defined as 'to be the best firm',[19] with the following subsidiary goals:

> To provide professionally and financially rewarding careers for all partners and staff
> To contribute to professional and economic developments in the UK
> To enhance our international strength.[20]

These aims were to be achieved by 'outstanding client service'. It was recognised that Price Waterhouse was no longer fundamentally 'an audit-based practice' and that between a third and half of the firm's fee income derived from other sources. The plan recognised the needs of clients to build their businesses and sought to 'exploit new technology' and 'to expand the range of services' offered.[21]

As a way of enhancing the quality of audit and other specialist services, Price Waterhouse initiated a programme of industry specialisation in the early 1980s. The firm had always offered expertise in particular areas (having been pre-eminent in the field of railway auditing from the late nineteenth century) but now sought to concentrate and develop its accumulated skills. With the options of delivering expertise either by professional discipline, by geographical area or by market sector, Price Waterhouse chose the latter as the way of gaining maximum synergy from the cross fertilisation of ideas. Partners from the three core disciplines of audit, tax and management consultancy were allocated to particular industries, such as banking, insurance, building societies, property and energy. Price Waterhouse sought not only to deepen its understanding of over thirty specific sectors, but also to improve the attractiveness of the firm to potential clients.

As regards clients, it was acknowledged that the firm had built up a list of major, blue-chip enterprises 'second to none in the UK'.[22] Work for them formed a dominant part of the UK practice; it was calculated that Price Waterhouse's 100 largest clients accounted for about 50 per cent of its fee income. In addition, a list of the 161 largest audit clients showed that they required 1,856,000 audit hours, which represented 69 per cent of the total.[23] It was recognised that these companies, often expanding by acquisition, were likely 'to grow faster than GDP' and therefore constituted an important, though indirect, source of new work.[24] The protection of the firm's existing share of the audit market was seen, therefore, as a key element in the strategy.

Who, then, were these blue-chip clients? In 1994 Price Waterhouse audited twenty-two of the top 500 major industrial and commercial companies listed in *The Financial Times UK 500*. These were:

Anglian Water	Lloyds Bank
Barclays Bank	Prudential
British Gas	Reckitt & Colman
Caradon	Redland
Courtaulds	Rentokil
De la Rue	Reuters
Eastern [Electricity] Group	Severn Trent
Forte	SmithKline Beecham
Guinness	Tesco
Land Securities	TI Group
Legal & General	Wolseley

Other important audit clients included Scottish Widows, Nationwide and, more recently, Standard Life. The loss of two important assignments in 1986–7 (Unilever and ICI) underlined the importance of the strategy document's stress on safeguarding the firm's established position. Both Unilever and ICI were joint audits which the firm had held over a lengthy period (the latter since its formation in 1926), and which they might have expected to have held. Both corporations wished to appoint a sole auditor and had put the assignment out to competitive tender. These events underlined the fact that auditing could no longer be regarded as a sinecure, and that firms did not henceforth feel inhibited from challenging one another by an unofficial professional code of behaviour.

'People' were also distinguished as an important element in the firm's strategy. 'Neither outstanding client service nor practice development are possible without partners and staff of the highest possible calibre', it recorded.[25] This goal was to be achieved by careful recruitment and by providing career training and motivation for those whom the firm wished to retain. Already a great effort had been devoted to the career structure of professional staff and it was decided that attention needed to be paid to those not engaged in client services. Practice support staff had grown in numbers from 348 in 1970 to 615 in 1980 and totalled 1,795 by 1994 (Table 15, see Appendix) – around 37 per cent of these being secretarial. The number of grades was increased to provide a more attractive career progression and to raise the status of non-fee-earning staff.[26] The introduction of training courses, including those with the Open University, encouraged higher self-confidence and esteem. As this group has felt more valued so turnover in numbers, once unacceptably high, has declined.

Another important cultural shift within Price Waterhouse has been the progressive admission of women within its professional ranks. Rayna Dean, who had been articled to Jeffery Bowman in London and subsequently transferred to the tax department, was the first woman to be admitted to the firm, becoming a partner at Manchester in 1983. Moira Black, who had also been articled to Price Waterhouse, and Pamela Taylor were both admitted in the following year, Black being the first woman partner in London office.[27] Initially it was thought that clients would not find women acceptable, an attitude that was gradually eroded in the seventies and early eighties as the number of female professional staff rose. Today women account for almost 50 per cent of all new students and occupy a similar proportion of the qualified staff ranks. Their representation falls at the higher grades and particularly at the partner-admission level though 12 per cent of tax partners are women, a higher figure than in auditing. In part, this is because some chose to have families, but may also reflect both a male reluctance to surrender authority and the inherent resistance present in many institutions. No woman partner has as yet held a seat on the Policy (now Supervisory) Committee. Doubtless, as the greater proportion of female entrants filters through the hierarchy, the next twenty years will witness important changes in these areas.

What had the strategy document of 1983 and the thinking that went into its formulation achieved for Price Waterhouse? First, it had forced the partnership into a period of self-examination and to consider what its goals and guiding principles should be. Although this may be considered as part of a policy of prudent management, it had, in part, been encouraged by the cultural shift which had occurred within Price Waterhouse during the seventies. It would have been inconceivable that partners would have conducted a survey of their strategy in the fifties. They considered themselves members of a self-regulatory profession which imposed on them obligations of conduct. Their behaviour, and that of their firm, was determined by the rules of the Institute of Chartered Accountants and the inherited traditions of the firm. Just as a barrister or a general practitioner would not at that time have initiated a wide-ranging inquiry into the principles governing the conduct of their chambers or medical practice, an accountant would not have considered these relevant or pertinent questions. Yet by the early eighties Price Waterhouse had been transformed into a major international business and existing professional rules of conduct could no longer cover all its activities nor were they appropriate to all its functions. The partnership itself felt the need for an internally generated statement of aims and principles. As the strategy document itself recorded, these were not limited by time and a continual review of the 'situation, the environment and the competition' was an integral part of the process.[28]

The Structure of the Partnership

An important feature of the strategy devised for Price Waterhouse in 1983 concerned the aim to 'provide the structure and administrative support which will best enable the firm to achieve its objectives'.[29] In March 1985 as part of the ongoing review procedure, it was decided to modify the organisation of the partnership. In essence, this involved the creation of a new executive post, a managing partner, and the appointment of a director of professional services and marketing. The first was designed to reduce the daily burden on the senior partner of monitoring the internal operation of the firm, in order to create more time to see clients, partners and others, or to focus upon strategic questions.[30] The second reflected a growing appreciation of the importance of marketing services and co-ordinating plans for the varied professional activities. The new executive team consisted of Jeffery Bowman as senior partner, Howard Hughes as managing partner and five directors comprising Tim Hoult (professional services and marketing), Alan Wheatley (London office), Peter Ainger (the regions), Chris Collett (finance), and Mike Phillips (manpower).[31] Ernest Barnes was due to retire as Director of Management Consultancy Services and he was to be succeeded by

Neville Cheadle, then partner-in-charge of the London MCS group. This team was restructured in 1988 when it was decided that national direction needed to reflect a combination of service-line responsibilities (audit and business services, tax, MCS and the developing specialisms such as corporate reconstruction and corporate finance) and the geographical location of the partnership, divided as it was between London and the regional offices. The new Executive consisted of a nine-man team under the chairmanship of Howard Hughes as managing partner and comprising Alan Wheatley (London office), Chris Ames (the regions), Tim Hoult (audit), Ian Vaile (tax), Neville Cheadle (MCS), Ian Mills (business development and marketing), Colin Brown (finance) and Mike Phillips (manpower).

The creation, in 1988, of the European Combination (see p.326) with a four-year transitional programme, resulted in Jeffery Bowman being appointed chairman of Price Waterhouse Europe and Patrick Giffin, the senior partner of the European Firm, becoming deputy chairman. There were also two managing partners, one from each of the constituent firms. In order to reduce costs, it was decided to bring together the executive managements of the UK Firm and Price Waterhouse Europe. However, the result was to increase substantially the workloads of these partners as their responsibilities extended to cover Europe as a whole. In 1990, after lengthy consultation, Jeffery Bowman decided that the executives of the UK Firm and Price Waterhouse Europe should be separated. In December of that year a new team was appointed for the UK, freeing the existing Executive to concentrate on pan-European issues directly under Jeffery Bowman.

The new UK Executive included Howard Hughes as managing partner and Alan Wheatley as director of London office. Wheatley had been articled to Norton Slade & Co., joining Price Waterhouse in 1960. He was admitted to the partnership ten years later and his dynamic energy led to his selection as leader of Audit Group 4 in 1978 and director of London office in 1985. Chris Ames provided further continuity, while John Barnsley (director of UK tax services), Ian Brindle (director of UK audit and business services), Eric Hetherington (director of UK management consultancy services) and Geoffrey Johnson (director of operations) all represented new appointments. John Metters, a senior manager with experience of auditing, who in 1964 had joined the firm from university, became partnership secretary in succession to Jim Cook.

As responsibilities were again separated a key managerial issue emerged: whether to appoint a new senior partner for the UK Firm. Jeffery Bowman thought that potential successors had insufficient time to identify and prove themselves and proposed that Howard Hughes surrender his other executive roles in order to concentrate his activities around the position of managing partner. Partners in the UK, who were becoming increasingly concerned about the declining profitability of the practice as the recession began to bite and their ability to influence the management, believed that there should be an election for a new senior partner. Following representations, Jeffery Bowman agreed that there should be a change and that he would henceforth serve as chairman of Price Waterhouse Europe and joint chief executive of the World Firm. In late 1990 the selection process was set in train and in the following spring Ian Brindle, a member of the UK Executive and director of audit and business advisory services, was elected to succeed Jeffery Bowman, who had been knighted in January 1991 for services to the accountancy profession. Educated at Blundells School and Manchester University, Brindle had qualified with Price Waterhouse in 1969. Appointed a manager in 1972 and admitted to the partnership four years later, Brindle became director of technical services in 1989.

Following this succession, Howard Hughes resigned as managing partner of the UK Firm in order to become deputy chairman of Price Waterhouse Europe on the retirement of Patrick Giffin. Two other changes to the UK Executive followed. Chris Ames moved to the European organisation to take up the post of director of operations and his position as director of UK regions passed to Keith Rawcliffe. David Morris, partner-in-charge of the firm's north-west practice and based in Manchester, was appointed director of audit and business advisory services, the post vacated by Brindle. In view of the northern state-school origins of many of the new Executive, the financial press suggested that there had been a cultural shift away from those educated at public schools in the south of England. This was perhaps a coincidence but may imply communally shared attitudes among the new leadership.

Today, therefore, Price Waterhouse in the UK is governed much in the style of a major limited liability company. The partnership as a whole elects the senior partner and he, in turn, selects who should serve on the Executive, which is akin to a board of directors, with each member being given a defined area of functional responsibility. In addition, the Supervisory Committee (formerly called the Policy Committee) monitors the way the Executive runs the business but does not have decision-making powers. Although the financial structure of the partnership may not have changed much over the last century, the way that it is constituted has witnessed major reform.

The territorial growth of the practice and the rise of specialist departments have combined to complicate the practical management of the business. Each regional office, for example, has a partner-in-charge responsible for its executive control. In addition, there will be a number of specialist leaders, in tax, management consultancy, insolvency and so forth, each reporting to him but also to their functional heads in the UK and then subject to strategic decisions made by the European Combination. As in most large multinational enterprises there are inherent problems in reconciling the demands of territory with functional roles.

The European Combination

The most fundamental organisational change of the eighties was the creation of the European Combination. Announced in November 1988, it involved the creation of a single management board for Europe overseeing both the UK and European Firms. It also witnessed the introduction of a structure designed to encourage interdependence and the co-ordination of objectives and services. Sir Jeffery Bowman, who developed a strong personal commitment to the project and had been personally involved in the lengthy and complicated negotiations leading to its formation, was appointed chairman of the management board. Much of the initial planning and negotiation had been conducted by a task force led by Tony Thorne and Marko Rus, and the successful creation of the Combination owed much to their indefatigable efforts. Patrick Giffin, senior partner of the European Firm since 1987, became the deputy chairman. Giffin had served his articles with Price Waterhouse in London, transferring to Geneva in 1959. Admitted to the partnership in 1965, he had worked in both Milan and Paris before becoming partner-in-charge of the French and then the Italian practices. Two joint managing directors were appointed: Howard Hughes and Grant Wilson, the latter being deputy senior partner of the European Firm since 1987 and formerly partner-in-charge of the Spanish practice.

Sir Jeffery Bowman retired as chairman of Price Waterhouse Europe in September 1993 when he was succeeded, following an election, by Jermyn Brooks, a former partner-in-charge of the German practice. Joining the firm in London in 1962, Brooks transferred to the Frankfurt office five years later and became a partner there in 1973. Having also gained a *Wirtschaftsprüfer* qualification, he possessed continental European experience in depth. Interviewed at the time of his appointment, Brooks outlined his goals in the autumn 1993 edition of *PW EuroNews*:

> First the energetic implementation of the strategy we have put a lot of work into defining ... The second area of concentration ... is our people ... The danger is that with an orientation solely to the marketplace and clients, one can give too little attention to key aspects of delivering service, namely having the best people recruited, training them so that they have the relevant skills and can work as effective teams, and ensuring that they enjoy the environment in which they are working.

Each of the existing firms or companies in the European Combination remained in being because of legal and professional requirements, but there was a much greater degree of co-operation and co-ordination in policy-making between these individual practices. The Combination had an estimated fee income of £346 million (SFr 863 million) for the year to 30 June 1988, and had a total of over 500 partners and around 8,000 staff. Price Waterhouse were unique among the major accountancy firms in behaving as an integrated organisation.

The Combination had been inspired by proposals to form a single European market in 1992. It was estimated that Western Europe would have a GNP of around £3,000 billion, creating the biggest market in the world. Price Waterhouse believed it was essential that their organisation and services be arranged so as to compete effectively within this new economic and political community. It proved to have been a far-sighted and significant development. The fee income of Price Waterhouse Europe grew rapidly, rising to SFr 1,513 million for the year ending June 1990, and by a further 33 per cent to SFr 1,933 million in 1994. Although a substantial proportion of this growth derived from the acquisition of new clients (such as Fiat, Alitalia, Perrier, Carlsberg, Christiana Bank and Banco Central/Banco Hispano Americano), there had also been a determined policy to merge with established, national practices. In 1989 Price Waterhouse's French auditing firm, Petiteau Scacchi et Associés, concluded an amalgamation with Befec & Associés (which had more listed clients than any other practice in France), to form the largest audit practice in the country. The united organisation had total fees of Fr 613 million and a professional staff of almost 1,200. Price Waterhouse concluded a merger with the established Danish firm Seier-Petersen in July 1990, bringing clients such as Bang & Olufsen, Bilka, Cheminova and Dansk Super Market.

As part of the same strategy of building up clients and services within the indigenous population, a merger was concluded in September 1989 between Revisuisse and Price Waterhouse Switzerland. The former with 700 partners and staff and a fee income of SFr 77 million was one of the leading Swiss accountancy firms. Although offering a wide range of services, audit was its principal activity generating 41 per cent of turnover. The union had become possible only because the founder shareholders, the Union Bank of Switzerland and Winterthur Insurance Co., agreed to sell their interests to the senior professional staff of Revisuisse. The arrangement dramatically improved the representation of Price Waterhouse in Switzerland since Revisuisse was more than double the size of the firm's existing Swiss practice.

An amalgamation with GRT in Vienna in September 1991 effectively tripled Price Waterhouse's representation in Austria. The importance of Düsseldorf as a key industrial region in Germany was recognised by two mergers with local practices in 1990 and 1991 respectively: FMP & Partner, and Köcke & Partner. A second amalgamation in Sweden was completed in July 1991 with Bångstad, a well-known Stockholm practice. This followed the union with the Gothenburg firm of Olle Falths in 1989 and brought Price Waterhouse's strength in Sweden up to twenty partners and 350 staff. In Finland a merger was concluded with Telomi Oy.

Merger with established national practices perhaps represents the final stage in a lengthy process of integration. Historically the European Firm had been an expatriate organisation reluctant to admit foreign nationals to the partnership. Indeed, two of the senior partners had failed to master any language other than English. During the seventies, as professional standards across the Continent rose and as the firm sought to establish itself within local markets not simply as accountants to overseas parents, so a process of progressive Europeanisation began. Today the organisation is firmly rooted in the cultures and economies of the European Union and has a truly multinational identity.

The creation of Price Waterhouse Europe also proved to have been of major importance following the dissolution of the USSR and the political change which swept through its satellite territories. The firm opened its first East European office of the post-war period in September 1988 in Budapest. It began with just two staff but by 1994 was employing nearly 200. Clients include not simply overseas corporations, but also indigenous public and private sector companies, and the Hungarian government, providing assistance with the drafting of corporate law and privatisation projects. A second office opened in Moscow during 1989, run by two expatriate Russian speakers, one of whom was by training a chartered accountant. Like the office Price Waterhouse had opened in Petrograd in 1916, it has great potential to serve western business keen to invest in this vast emerging market and has won two major audit clients, Gazprom and Avtovaz, makers of Lada cars. Another office was set up in Warsaw, though the Polish practice has been slower to develop due to national instability. Of significance for the future was the opening of offices in Berlin and Prague during the spring of 1990, the latter originally staffed by one expatriate and one Czech national.

In January 1990 the rate of expansion throughout Eastern Europe and the USSR, resulting in five offices by the end of the year, led the management board of Price Waterhouse Europe to create a formal region and appoint Bruce Edwards as partner-in-charge. Just over a year later, in the first edition of *East EuroNews* (spring 1991), Edwards commented that Price Waterhouse's initiatives in Eastern Europe represented a strategic change of direction insofar as the firm had 'led the way into new territory rather than following our clients'. This claim was perhaps somewhat forgetful of the pioneers of the profession who crossed to America and set up practices in frontier townships and, indeed, of the establishment of the Petrograd office in 1916. Since the formation of the East Europe region all the offices there have grown very rapidly.

Abortive Mergers : Deloittes and Arthur Andersen

Concerned to protect and to develop its existing client base Price Waterhouse entered into world-wide merger discussions with Deloitte Haskins & Sells in the spring of 1984. The idea of amalgamating on such a large scale was novel although an impetus to the process had been provided two years before by the McKinsey report on the international organisation and subsequent creation of the Price Waterhouse World Firm, which led to strategic thinking on a global scale and a desire to strengthen transnational organisations. A particular attraction of Deloitte Haskins & Sells was their world-wide client list and their associations in Japan and with SGV in the Philippines. After a period of preliminary investigation, Michael Coates, chairman of the World Firm, began discussions with Deloittes and quickly gained the support of Joseph Connor, senior partner of the US Firm.[32] Although the Big Eight were all familiar with the merger process and had each taken over small or medium-sized practices, none had attempted a union of such scale. In the United States, for example, Deloittes had 8,000 employees in 103 offices, compared with Price Waterhouse's 9,000 staff in ninety offices. In Britain it was estimated in 1983 that Deloittes numbered 2,695 at a time when Price Waterhouse had 2,271 partners and staff; the UK fee incomes of the two firms were each estimated by the *Financial Times* to be around £60 million.[33] The combined organisation would have dwarfed the other Big Six, creating a world-wide firm of exceptional size. However, the negotiations broke down in the summer of 1984 when the Japanese affiliate of Deloittes defected to another firm and it became clear that SGV would not be part of any merger.

However, in the autumn of 1984 the US Firm reopened negotiations with Deloittes and made much progress in a short period of time, and became concerned that the respective UK Firms complete their discussions. By this time Deloittes had appointed a senior partner elect and were taking a more forceful line in the bargaining.

The merger talks gave rise to concern within the profession on both sides of the Atlantic. Members of the smaller accounting firms noted that the Big Eight already audited 94 per cent of the 1,536 companies listed on the New York Stock Exchange, and that a combined Price Waterhouse–Deloitte firm, together with Arthur Andersen, would audit almost half of these.[34] A similar concentration would have arisen in the UK where Price Waterhouse and Deloittes, as established practices from the mid-nineteenth century, had both built up substantial audit bases. In the event, however, both the Department of Justice in America and the British government gave permission for the merger talks to proceed. There was also a fear that these discussions would precipitate a general merger movement within the profession, though, in the event, this did not take place for a further five years.

The negotiations were a matter of great complexity and, given that they had to be conducted in secrecy, placed overwhelming burdens on existing communications. Discussions had to be held at several levels: multi-laterally with Deloittes and at world level; bi-laterally at a national level; and again, multi-laterally between all the Price Waterhouse firms.[35] It was almost inevitable, therefore, that news of the proposed merger leaked to the press, and in August 1984 the *Wall Street Journal* carried the story before most partners in Britain had been told of the plan. As a result, the discussions which had been proceeding in secret were published and the decision-making process was brought forward.

Within Price Waterhouse an elaborate system was set up to seek reactions from clients and partners. It was decided that all the major firms of Price Waterhouse would each vote on the proposal, but that a substantial majority (over 75 per cent in every instance) was required in the case of four (the UK, US, Canada and Australia) before the amalgamation could be ratified. This was designed to protect the international unity of Price Waterhouse in the event of either outcome. Although the votes were never revealed, it was thought that the proposal failed to achieve the necessary majority in two of the four territories. It was clear that the US Firms of both Price Waterhouse and Deloittes had been strongly in favour and were disappointed by the absence of agreement elsewhere.

The UK partnership, in particular, was opposed to the union. Before a formal vote was taken, a majority of the partnership seemed to be unconvinced of the benefits of a merger, though the UK Policy Committee was split roughly in half. Sir Jeffery Bowman, as senior partner, had been closely involved in the negotiations designed to bring this into being, but at the final hour he spoke out against the proposal, much to the acclaim of a partners' meeting called in December 1984 to discuss the issue. It was believed by the minority who favoured the arrangement

that he had sufficient credibility and standing to have swung the partnership had he placed the full weight of his personal reputation behind the
measure.[36] His decision was ultimately influenced by the failure to
achieve any agreement on the Continent where Price Waterhouse operated as a unified firm, while Deloittes had a series of separate partnerships.
No conclusion had been reached on how they would function there
despite the mediations of Michael Coates and David Higginbotham,
senior partner of the Canadian Firm. Sir Jeffery believed that 'chaos'
would ensue and so opposed the union.

The general lack of unity on the issue highlighted the fact that
partners in various firms had different interests, outlooks and objectives.
Partners tended to vote according to how the merger would affect them
in their particular territory rather than based upon its value to the global
organisation. As a result, it was not surprising that the merger gathered
strongest support where the local Price Waterhouse firm expected to
dominate the unified partnership – the United States, South America
and Hong Kong – but ran into greater difficulties where this pattern was
not repeated, as in Britain and Australia.[37] Further, the UK Firm believed
itself to be sufficiently large and resourceful not to need a merger to
generate growth. It was fearful, too, that its powerful, internally based
culture would be diluted, particularly as some partners believed that the
firm had failed to secure sufficient executive posts in the proposed
unified organisation.

The immediate consequence of the aborted discussions was a period of
sterility and difficult relations between some of the member firms of
Price Waterhouse. Consequently, little progress was made during 1985
and 1986 in developing the world-wide organisation. Nevertheless there
were benefits from the negotiations. Senior partners were made acutely
aware of the need for strategic research and planning, and the weaknesses
of the international structure had been made painfully clear. The destruction of the idea that growth could be imported by merger concentrated
minds on considering ways of expanding from within. A new ambition
and resourcefulness developed as it became clear that Price Waterhouse
alone was responsible for its fate.

Having turned down the chance to amalgamate with W.B. Peat &
Co. in 1921 and with Deloitte Haskins & Sells in 1984, it was perhaps
surprising that in 1989 Price Waterhouse entered into a third set of
merger discussions – this time with Arthur Andersen. To some extent

the environment was different. In 1987 Peat Marwick Mitchell had amalgamated with Klynveld Main Goedler, a major European practice, to form KPMG Peat Marwick. The Big Eight were engaged in a period of rationalisation. As a result their number was reduced by two. In May 1989 Ernst & Whinney and Arthur Young McClelland Moores had announced their intention to join together to form Ernst & Young, and discussions were soon to follow between Deloitte Haskins & Sells and Touche Ross. A general feeling existed that new and even larger organisations were in the process of being created and the senior partners of the major firms were engaged in a rash of meetings.

Accordingly, in the summer of 1989 under the initiative of Joe Connor as Chairman of the World Firm, Price Waterhouse and Arthur Andersen gave notice of formal talks, to run for sixty days, to explore the possibility of a merger.[38] Their combined world-wide fee income was estimated at $5,000 million, a sum that would have greatly exceeded their closest competitors – Ernst & Young ($4,244m) and KPMG ($3,900m). The climate of opinion in Price Waterhouse had changed and news of the discussions did not evoke the negative reaction which had arisen in some territories five years before. Although the two firms had contrasting operational styles, each possessed important client bases. An amalgamation, it was argued, would bring together the complementary strengths of Price Waterhouse's international organisation together with its audit and tax practices and Arthur Andersen's management consultancy practice. Yet these were the very issues which caused concern as soon as the talks got underway. Arthur Andersen had evolved a highly centralised international organisation, while Price Waterhouse took pride in a devolved structure. In January 1989 the former's large and vigorous management consultancy practice had become a separate body, Andersen Consulting. This had given the consulting partners greater autonomy and improved their profit-sharing arrangements and they feared that in a unified firm they would lose these recently won advantages. The consulting practice of Arthur Andersen generated around 37 per cent of their fees, in contrast to Price Waterhouse where it accounted for only 19 per cent. Price Waterhouse MCS partners were concerned that they would be dominated by their new Andersen colleagues. Equally, Price Waterhouse audit partners were worried by the impact that Andersen Consulting would have on their clients. Business ties were prohibited by professional rules of conduct and by SEC regulations, yet Andersen

Consulting had important joint ventures with IBM and Hewlett-Packard, both of whom were audited by Price Waterhouse. Should the merger have proceeded, either the joint ventures or the audits would have had to be abandoned.

Although discussions filled the sixty days and were then extended indefinitely, it soon became clear that agreement could not be reached. On 26 September 1989 the two firms announced that the merger talks were at an end.[39] No vote had been taken. Differences in the way the firms funded their retirement plans surfaced in the press as the predominant reason for the termination, but, according to Shaun O'Malley, senior partner of the US Firm, other incompatibilities (particularly those requiring consultancy involvement with audit clients and the dominant role of Andersen Consulting) had proved more troublesome. Mindful that their reluctance over the Deloitte merger had caused ill-feeling within Price Waterhouse, the representatives of the UK or rather European Firm as it had become, were reluctant to be seen as unwilling participants in the negotiations.[40] Although there were reservations, they continued to look for solutions. Eventually the decision to abandon the scheme was unanimous and no residual bitterness arose. Having formed the European Combination only a year before, many partners in the UK not sympathetic to the Arthur Andersen merger considered the exercise to have been a distraction from the important issue of forging closer links throughout Europe and developing the practice there. Although there were further mergers within the profession, notably the union between the UK Firms of Deloittes and Coopers & Lybrand, there appears, for the moment at least, no obvious prospect of Price Waterhouse joining any of its principal competitors. It has a consistent record of rejecting such unions – a product, perhaps, of its own powerful and consistent internal culture.

Troubled Events: Guinness and BCCI

No major institution can be actively involved in public affairs without at some time encountering controversy and its conduct being subject to close scrutiny. In 1983 Price Waterhouse had been appointed auditors of the Guinness Group – having previously provided certain tax services and audited a number of subsidiaries – following changes in the management structure a year before. This rationalisation had been the inspiration of the new chairman, Ernest Saunders. Under his aggressive leadership the Guinness group grew impressively and its share value rose from 49p in 1981 to 120p by 1984. In order to generate further expansion Saunders led the company into a policy of take-overs and appeared to have achieved a considerable coup when in the autumn of 1986 Guinness acquired the Distillers group for £2.8 billion. The latter, one of the largest independent Scottish companies, were major producers of whisky including well-known brand names such as Johnnie Walker, Black & White, Dewars and Haig. For the Price Waterhouse team led by Howard Hughes, this was yet another period of intense activity providing background support for the take-over. It represented a considerable success and the combined Guinness group became the fifteenth largest company listed on the UK Stock Exchange.

During 1986 the Guinness group changed their year-end to 31 December, adding a further three months to the period covered by the annual report. In November two key members of the Price Waterhouse audit team (John Salmon, a partner, and Keith Hamill, then a senior manager) were alerted to several substantial invoices for which there was no clear explanation. They took these to Howard Hughes who, in turn, approached Ernest Saunders. The latter suggested the issue should be discussed at a subsequent meeting a day later, but before this meeting could take place Department of Trade Inspectors arrived to carry out an investigation into the circumstances surrounding the take-over of Distillers. What the Price Waterhouse team of auditors did not realise was that there had been a support operation for the Guinness share price during its contested bid for Distillers. It was subsequently alleged that other industrialists had been contacted in order to purchase Guinness stock to improve its value. As a result of these activities, Ernest Saunders and three others were found guilty at a trial held in 1990 at which Howard Hughes, John Salmon and Keith Hamill were called as prosecution witnesses. At the time of writing, the report from the Department of Trade inquiry has still not been published despite the court cases having run their course. However, in its evidence at the trials Price Waterhouse was able to demonstrate that it had acted professionally throughout and Guinness remains one of the firm's major multinational clients.

The second case was more complex because it involved a bank operating in some seventy countries so that when it was closed by the

Bank of England in July 1991 thousands of depositors around the globe suffered losses. In the summer of 1987 Price Waterhouse had been appointed world-wide auditors of the Bank of Credit and Commerce International (BCCI), and London office took responsibility for the co-ordination of the group audit.[41] For many years the firm in Grand Cayman had been auditors of a major subsidiary, BCCI (Overseas), but the parent company was an audit client of Ernst & Whinney. It appeared that Price Waterhouse had gained a prestigious assignment as BCCI had grown rapidly since its formation in 1972 and seemed to have the potential to become a leading international bank, serving, in the main, developing nations.

At the time that Price Waterhouse accepted the world-wide audit appointment, it was recognised that BCCI had yet to mature as a top-ranking bank. It had expanded quickly and its management and systems of control had not advanced commensurately. In addition, BCCI had a number of large customers with borrowings which were excessive in relation to the bank's capital. However, the board of directors, which included a number of senior European bankers as non-executives, ap-peared committed to change. Following discussions with the Bank of England, it was decided to accept the audit appointment as a challenge which the firm was well-equipped to undertake.

The events of the next three years proved disquieting. Contrary to early expectations, matters did not improve, and during the audit of the 1989 accounts Price Waterhouse became aware of circumstances that cast doubts on the integrity of the BCCI senior management. These concerns were reported to the Bank of England and in April 1990 following complex investigations, BCCI was effectively taken over by the govern-ment of Abu Dhabi, which committed itself to support the group while a programme of reorganisation got underway.

Unfortunately the reforms proceeded too slowly and further inquiries by Price Waterhouse revealed fraud and deception by management on a far greater scale than previously suspected. The outcome was that on 5 July 1991 the Bank of England, acting in agreement with bank super-visors in other countries, closed down BCCI's operations across the world.

This resulted in intense press interest, speculation over the role played by Price Waterhouse and a public demand for an inquiry into the circumstances which had led to the collapse of BCCI. The ability of the firm to respond to questions was severely constrained by the provisions of the 1987 Banking Act which governed the disclosure of communications between the firm and the Bank of England, and by the confidentiality requirements relating to the accounts of BCCI's customers.

Impassioned speculations were fuelled by doubt and rumour, and the role of Price Waterhouse, as world-wide auditor, was called into question. In response to pressure from parliament and the financial press, an independent inquiry into the supervision of BCCI was set up under the chairmanship of Lord Justice Bingham. Although this report, published in October 1992, focused principally on the role of the Bank of England, it also revealed how Price Waterhouse had discovered the extensive fraud and the steps that they had taken to inform the relevant authorities.[42] The Bingham report showed that much of the criticism of the firm had been ill-informed. However, court action had already been initiated in the UK and America. At the time of writing, proceedings in the US have been dismissed but litigation in Britain is expected to continue for many years. Price Waterhouse confidently believes that its defence in these actions will succeed despite the late-twentieth-century trend towards holding auditors responsible whenever a corporate collapse occurs and making them face expensive legal actions regardless of whether or not there is evidence of shortcomings on their part.

Retrospect

In 1982 Good Relations City, a public relations consultancy, conducted a survey of the business community to discover popularly held views about the firm. The results showed that the partnership had several important strengths, notably an established reputation for 'reliability', and 'quality of service' coupled with a 'specialist availability'. It was perceived as possessing an 'impressive client spread' and a deserved 'track record'.[43] Nevertheless, there were criticisms. Some believed that Price Waterhouse was interested only in blue-chip clients and had an impersonal, sometimes arrogant manner, as well as being less approachable than its major competitors.

Both Lord Benson, former senior partner of Coopers & Lybrand, and Sir Ronald Leach, former senior partner of Peats, have remarked upon the high reputation that the firm held in the interwar period.[44] Perhaps it was then that a notion of superiority began. Driven forward by the efforts of Sir Gilbert Garnsey, the firm almost certainly earned the largest fee income in the City and gained one of the highest public profiles, leading Sir Albert Wyon apocryphally to coin the phrase that 'there are accountants and there is Price Waterhouse'. This attitude contributed to a sense of aloofness. Tony Mallinson, senior partner of the solicitors Slaughter & May, recalled that by the fifties there was an air of austerity about the firm and that a sense of great prestige also brought with it a rather staid manner.[45] Throughout this period, Price Waterhouse retained a fundamental respect for propriety, integrity and technical expertise. Its ethos was personified by Sir Thomas Robson, a quiet, gentlemanly figure of great standing within the profession.

Yet by the mid-sixties it had become clear that with the focus on technical excellence, Price Waterhouse was in danger of losing its way. It had not kept pace with the more ambitious and dynamic of its competitors; Cooper Brothers, in particular, were making considerable gains as, too, were Arthur Andersen. If Price Waterhouse wished to retain a position in the upper ranks of the profession, then they had to rethink the guiding principles of the firm. In the competitive atmosphere of the seventies professionalism and probity, though essential, were no longer of themselves sufficient.

In addition, there had been a general decline in the status attached to the leading accountancy firms. During the interwar period Lord Plender of Deloittes, Sir Gilbert Garnsey and Sir William McLintock became public figures and earned reputations for their practices as doctors of industry and financial advisers. After the Second World War the merchant banks assumed these roles at a time when the leaders of the accountancy profession had become preoccupied with technical issues. By the late 1960s this lost ground needed to be recaptured if they were to compete at the highest levels. To lift the status of the firm as part of a general programme of raising self-esteem, Michael Coates encouraged staff to be more ambitious in the goals that they set themselves. When he had rejoined the firm in 1945, Parker had detected low morale and limited objectives and it took several decades to reinstil a spirit of enterprise and confidence.

Because accountancy firms train most of their professional staff rather than attract qualified personnel from outside, improvements in overall capacities and skills require a lengthy timescale. Given the lags occasioned by education and work experience, the graduate recruitment of the late 1960s did not permeate to partner level until the 1980s. The gestation period for change is often lengthy in the qualifying professions.

In general, the last thirty years have witnessed a broadening of attitudes. The self-imposed limitations placed on what assignments the firm would undertake and the type of people that it would recruit have largely been abandoned. In July 1987, for example, Price Waterhouse was appointed to advise the twelve regional electricity companies in England on their flotation on the Stock Exchange. The privatisation of an industry with a turnover in excess of £12 billion and with over 130,000 employees proved a major undertaking. A team of around 150, comprising not only accountants, economists and tax specialists but also engineers and information technology, human resource and treasury specialists, was gathered from within the principal disciplines of Price Waterhouse. Furthermore, in 1991 the firm completed a report for the Home Office to make recommendations on the level of the BBC licence fee. Led by Ian Beesley, a management consultancy partner recruited from the Civil Service, the investigation tackled questions such as the pricing of services and their competition with external markets and measures for monitoring and controlling performance. In 1990 Price Waterhouse assisted British Satellite Broadcasting in their UK launch. Auditors and tax experts were needed to aid management in securing funding in excess of £1.3 billion and in providing a tax-efficient structure for the business.

The wider range of activities undertaken by Price Waterhouse led to the appointment of individuals with varied backgrounds from engineers to civil servants and information technology experts. That innovation, and the growth of the firm's size, has also created a need for the employment of specialists of a different kind: in training, recruitment, public relations and marketing. These changes have wrought major cultural shifts within Price Waterhouse. In the fifties and sixties the firm was dominated by auditors. Taxation was considered an acceptable, albeit subsidiary, activity, while the systems department, or management consultancy as it was later to be called, was viewed by some with hostility and was seen as a threat to professional independence and of dubious value to the business. The growth of the firm's specialist services and their continuing diversity represent a fundamental development in the nature of Price Waterhouse.

The rising admission of women into the firm has exercised an important influence upon its values. Although women have achieved equal representation within the student ranks, at the lower professional grades and in practice-support departments, they have yet to make their full impact in the partnership and particularly within its executive structure. This will doubtless be one of the major trends of the twenty-first century.

Another development of cultural significance has been the progressive recruitment of ethnic minorities. Traditionally Price Waterhouse, and indeed the other major City firms, were staffed by the indigenous white population, and until the 1980s there were no black partners. Accountancy may have lagged behind some other professions, notably medicine, in recognising other racial groups. Today the proportion of ethnic minorities is higher and, although they have achieved representation at partnership level in the European Combination, this is still an evolving process.

A further cultural change of importance for the future has been the formation in 1988 of Price Waterhouse Europe. The combination of the UK and European Firms to create a more unified organisation and the gradual expansion into the former Eastern bloc has opened up opportunities for new growth. Mergers have followed with indigenous firms in Switzerland, Germany, France, Sweden, Denmark and Austria. This reorganisation represents an important shift in managerial focus from the UK to Europe as a whole and reflects the adoption of transnational attitudes. Sir Jeffery Bowman, who presided over many of these developments, believes that this was 'the most fundamental change that has taken place during my career with Price Waterhouse and will be a major advantage to us in the future'.[46]

In response to an increasingly competitive climate, Price Waterhouse undertook a world-wide study in 1992–3 of the market for professional services. It gave a clear indication of clients' needs and the manner of their delivery, and led to the implementation of a major culture change programme. This focused the efforts of the firm and it addressed a number of key issues in staff management and motivation, and the development of business skills. At the same time, significant additional investments were made in new technology to improve the efficiency of work practices and to facilitate both internal and external communications. Although many of these goals have been implicit in the practice since its foundation, this represented a concerted attempt to tailor services more accurately to the demands of the marketplace.

This has been the story of both a professional partnership and a commercial enterprise, focusing on the individuals who led and shaped the firm, and on the clients they served. If a week can be regarded as a long time in politics, then over 140 years in business, earning significant profits throughout and consistently increasing turnover, qualifies as a significant achievement. Most of the City accountancy firms which flourished in the mid-nineteenth century have now disappeared. Distinguished names, such as Quilter, Ball & Co., Turquand Youngs & Co., W.W. Deloitte and Harding, Whinney & Co. no longer survive and the practices which they once represented have been subsumed within larger organisations. Price Waterhouse is almost unique in retaining its style virtually unchanged from the Victorian period to the present day. This is, therefore, a singular history of survival through innovation and growth. What will happen over the next 100 years can be mere speculation but the lesson of the past is that Price Waterhouse will adapt and continue to shape itself to take on the challenges of the twenty-first century.

Notes

Chapter 1

1 Beresford Worthington, *Professional Accountants, An Historical Sketch*, London (1895), pp.1–2.

2 Ibid., p.4.

3 Anthony Sampson, *The Anatomy of Britain*, London (1962), p.466.

4 Mark Stevens, *The Big Eight*, New York (1981), p.8.

5 H. Byerley Thomson, *The Choice of a Profession, A Concise Account and Comparative Review of the English Professions*, London (1857), p.4.

6 Worthington, *Professional Accountants*, p.73.

7 Ibid., p.70.

8 Ibid., p.81.

9 *The Accountant*, Vol.XIII, No.656, 2 July 1887, p.388.

10 Paul Grady (ed.), *Memoirs and Accounting Thought of George O. May*, New York (1962), p.9.

11 Lady Plender (ed.), *Lord Plender, Some Writings and Speeches*, London (1951), p.60.

12 Ibid.

13 Ibid., speech to Royal Grammar School, Newcastle, 16 December 1919, p.104.

14 Detailed biographies of selected senior accountants may be found in the *Dictionary of Business Biography*, Vols.1 to 5 (1984–6), including those of Arthur and Ernest Cooper, W.W. Deloitte, Sir Gilbert Garnsey, Sir Robert Palmer Harding, Sir John Harmood Banner, Sir William Barclay Peat, Lord Plender, William Quilter, William Turquand, Edwin Waterhouse and Frederick Whinney.

15 A.M. Carr-Saunders and P.A. Wilson, *The Professions*, Oxford (1933), p.219.

16 Sir Nicholas E. Waterhouse, 'Matters affecting the Accountancy Profession' in *V Internationaler Prüfungs und Treuhand Kongress*, Berlin (1938), p.160.

17 Carr-Saunders and Wilson, *The Professions*, p.225.

18 Sir Arthur Conan-Doyle, *The Memoirs of Sherlock Holmes*, London (1893), reprinted John Murray (1974), p.190.

19 Charles Dickens, *Little Dorrit*, London (1857), Harmondsworth (1985), p.343.

20 Ibid., p.344.

21 Ibid., pp.347, 462.

22 P.G. Boys, 'Somerset Maugham: Accountant in Bondage' (typescript, February 1989), p.2.

23 Somerset Maugham, *Of Human Bondage*, London (1915), p.238.

24 Ibid.

25 Ibid., p.235.

26 John Galsworthy, *The Man of Property*, London (1906), Harmondsworth (1951), p.243.

27 Emma Lathen, *Accounting for Murder*, New York (1964), Harmondsworth (1967), p.35.

28 Peter Boys, 'What's in a Name', p.100 in *Accountancy*, Vol.103, No.1145, January 1989.

29 *Accountancy*, Vol.103, No.1148, April 1989, pp.118–19.

30 Ibid., Vol.103, No.1156, December 1989, pp.134–5.

31 Ibid., Vol.103, No.1147, March 1989, p.98.

32 [Lord] Henry Benson, *Accounting for Life*, London (1989), Foreword.

Chapter 2

1 Lockhart, *Life of Scott*, Vol.VI, p.223.

2 'Our 125th Anniversary' in *PW Quarterly*, Vol.7, No.1, Spring 1974, p.2.

3 John Steane Price, 'Price Review' (typescript, 1988).

4 R. and P. Jackson and R. Price, 'Bristol Potters and Potteries 1600–1800' in *Journal of Ceramic History*, No.12 (1982), pp.164–5.

5 Letter to E. Jones from T.R. Newell Price, 23 September 1991.

6 *Mathew's Annual Bristol Directory*, 1838, p.157.

7 Ibid., 1833, p.47.

8 PWA, 1/25, letter from E.J.H. Hunt of Tribe, Clarke & Co. to Sir Thomas Robson, 27 August 1964, quoting from a private ledger of Bradley & Barnard, 28 February 1843, p.300.

9 Private ledger of Bradley & Barnard, 23 September 1842.

10 J.B. Mennell, 'The Founding Father of P.W.' (typescript, 10 May 1977).

11 BRO, Burgess Book, Vol.17, 21 September 1799, p.113.

12 Ibid., Vol.20, 4 August 1830, p.232.

13 Letter from T.R. Newell Price, 26 October 1991.

14 *Mathew's Annual Bristol Directory*, 1839, p.62.

15 *PO London Directories*, 1842, p.445; 1844, p.1005; 1847, p.1073.

16 PWA, 1/25, letter from E.J.H. Hart of Tribe, Clarke & Co. to Sir Thomas Robson, 1 September 1964, quoting 'Private Ledger from 1848', p.73.

17 *PO London Directories*, 1849, p.1115; 1861, p.1361.

18 *PO London Directory*, 1849, p.1115.

19 *The Accountant*, Vol.XI, No.527, 10 January 1885, obituary W. Edwards, p.15.

20 *PO London Directory*, 1842, p.759.

21 PWA, 10/17, the *London Gazette*, Vol.1 (1850), p.10.

22 *The Accountant*, Vol.XI, No.527, 10 January 1885, p.15.

23 [Sir Russell Kettle], *Deloitte & Co., 1845–1956*, Oxford (1958), p.9.

24 *PO London Directory*, 1852, pp.717, 937, 1085.

25 PWA, 10/21, handwritten note.

26 H.A. Shannon, 'The Limited Companies of 1866–1883' in E.M. Carus-Wilson, *Essays in Economic History*, Vol.1, London (1954), p.387.

27 Price, 'Price Review', p.14.

28 Edgar Jones (ed.), *The Memoirs of Edwin Waterhouse A Founder of Price Waterhouse*, London (1988), p.82.

29 Price, 'Price Review', p.14.

30 G.E. Richards, 'History of the Firm: The First Fifty Years 1850–1900' (typescript, 1950), p.7.

31 PWA, 2/8, Sir Nicholas Waterhouse, 'Notes of Speeches at the Centenary Dinner of Price Waterhouse & Co. 30 June 1950' (typescript), p.3.

32 Ibid., pp.3–4.

33 [Sir Harold Howitt], *The History of the Institute of Chartered Accountants in England and Wales 1880–1965 and of its former Accountancy Bodies 1870–1880*, London (1966), pp.5, 7.

34 Jones, *Memoirs*, p.81.

35 Ibid.

36 PWA, letter from Mrs J. Knight, Sparkhill, Birmingham, 23 May 1950.

37 *PO London Directories*, 1835, 1836, 1840, 1847.

38 *PO London Directories*, 1848, p.1037; 1851, p.957; 1856, p.1330.

39 *PO London Directory*, 1858, p.1086.

40 For biographies of Edwin Waterhouse see Jones, *Memoirs*, 'Introduction', pp.15–42, *DBB*, Vol.5 London (1986) and J.R. Edwards, 'Edwin Waterhouse', pp.674–8.

41 Thomas Ellison, *The Cotton Trade of Great Britain*, London (1886), pp.195–6; *Gore's Directory of Liverpool and its Environs*, 1841, p.475.

42 H. Hale Bellot, *University College London 1826–1926*, London (1929), pp.170–71.

43 [Edward Fry, ed.], *Theodore Waterhouse 1838–1891, Notes of His Life and Extracts from His Letters and Papers*, London (1894), p.57.

44 Jones, *Memoirs*, p.21.

45 Fry, *Theodore Waterhouse*, p.85.

46 Jones, *Memoirs*, p.68.

47 Ibid.

48 Ibid.

49 E. Cooper, 'Fifty-seven Years in an Accountant's Office' in *ICAEW Proceedings of the Autumnal Meeting . . . October 1921*, London (1921), p.47.

50 Jones, *Memoirs*, p.74.

51 Ibid., p.73.

52 Ibid., p.76; *PO London Directory*, 1865, p.1500.

53 PWA, Diary 1864, 27 February to 7 March.

54 Jones, *Memoirs*, p.77.

55 PWA, Edwin Waterhouse, Letter Book, Vol.I, 3 March 1864–31 July 1871, 4 May 1864, pp.8–10.

56 Ibid., 17 June 1864, pp.15–16.

57 *Manchester Evening News*, No.11,368, 22 August 1905, obituary, p.6; *Manchester Guardian*, No.18,421, 23 August 1905, obituary, p.3.

58 RIBA Library, letter from J. Willey to E. Waterhouse, describing the use of Draughtsmen's Registers, a journal recording changes to clients and proposing a Day Book, 22 February 1865, in Sally Maltby *et al.*, *Alfred Waterhouse 1830–1905*, London (1983), p.16.

59 PWA, Letter Book, Vol.I, 2 April 1864, to Messrs Harmood Banner & Sons, pp.4–5.

60 PWA, Diary 1864, 2 September.

61 Ibid., 3 May, p.8.

62 PWA, Letter Book, Vol.I, 8 July 1864, pp.31–2.

63 Ibid., 28 February 1865, pp.191–3.

64 Dickens, *Little Dorrit*, pp.735–6.

65 Edgar Jones, *Accountancy and the British Economy 1840–1980, The Evolution of Ernst & Whinney*, London (1981), p.47.

66 PWA, Letter Book, Vol.I, 28 June 1864, pp.20–1.

67 Ibid., letter to Edward Burges, 1 July 1864, pp.24–5.

68 Ibid., 9 August 1864, p.44; 13 August 1864, p.47.

69 Ibid., 15 December 1864, p.122.

70 Ibid., letter to J.A. Hallett, 12 April 1865, pp.210–11.

71 Ibid., letter to John Fowler, 25 August 1864, p.53.

72 Michael R. Lane, *The Story of the Steam Plough Works, Fowlers of Leeds*, London (1980), pp.19, 26 and 56–7.

73 Jones, *Memoirs*, p.79.

74 PWA, Letter Book, Vol.I, letters, 22 November 1864, p.98; 23 March 1865, p.202; 30 January 1865, p.167.

75 Ibid., letter to H.C. Gurney, 3 March 1864, p.2.

76 Ibid., letter to W.H. Holyland, 1 March 1865, p.194.

77 Ibid., letter to Henry Plews, 28 March 1865, p.203.

78 Ibid., 22 April 1865, p.214.

79 PWA, 10/25, miscellaneous records.

80 PWA, 10/47, G.E. Richards, 'Price Waterhouse & Co. Partnership Deeds', No.1, 1 May 1865.

81 Jones, *Memoirs*, p.82.

82 Ibid., p.81.

83 [Kettle], *Deloitte & Co.*, p.3.

84 Richard Brown, *A History of Accounting and Accountants*, Edinburgh (1905), p.234.

85 *Census of England and Wales*, Vol.XXVII (1844), Occupation Abstract, p.57; ibid. (1854), p.65; ibid. (1863), Table XIX, p.xliv.

Chapter 3

1 Edgar Jones, *Accountancy and the British Economy 1840–1980, The Evolution of Ernst & Whinney*, London (1981), pp.45–9.

2 J.R. Edwards, *A History of Financial Accounting*, London (1989), p.263.

3 Barbara Weiss, *The Hell of the English, Bankruptcy and the Victorian Novel*, Lewisbury (1986), p.177.

4 Ibid., p.180.

5 *Report from the Select Committee on Limited Liability Acts*, Vol.X (1867), p.463.

6 Edgar Jones (ed.), *The Memoirs of Edwin Waterhouse*, London (1988), p.83.

7 Ibid., pp.91, 94, 89.

8 Barry Supple, *The Royal Exchange Assurance, A History of British Insurance 1720–1970*, Cambridge (1970), p.142.

9 PWA, Letter Book No.2, To George Whiffen from Price, Holyland & Waterhouse, 26 April 1872, p.103.

10 Ibid., E. Waterhouse to Hon P.L. Glyn, 29 November 1871, pp.16–17.

11 Ibid., 5 February 1873, p.64.

12 Jones, *Accountancy*, p.47.

13 James Foreman-Peck, 'The 1856 Companies Act and the Birth and Death of Firms' in Philippe Jobert and Michael Moss (eds.), *The Birth and Death of Companies*, Carnforth (1990), p.40.

14 Robert R. Pennington, *The Principles of Company Law*, London (1959), p.lxxxvii.

15 L.C.B. Gower, *The Principles of Modern Company Law*, London (1957), p.41.

16 Edwards, *Financial Accounting*, p.101.

17 18 & 19 Vict. *c.* 133 Limited Liability Act.

18 T.A. Lee, 'Company Financial Statements: An Essay in Business History 1830–1950' in S.Marriner (ed.), *Business and Businessmen: Studies in Business, Economic and Accountancy History*, Liverpool (1978), p.239.

19 1856 Companies Act, Section 69.

20 Edwards, *Financial Accounting*, p.191.

21 H.A. Shannon, 'The Limited Companies of 1866–1883' in E.M. Carus-Wilson, *Essay in Economic History*, Vol.1, London (1954), p.382.

22 Jones, *Memoirs,* p.83.

23 PRO, Rail 410/13, LNWR Proprietors' Audit Committee Minute Book 1852–1922, printed note, 7 January 1867.

24 Ibid., 21 January 1876, 16 January 1874, 16 February 1882.

25 Ibid., 29 January 1913.

26 PRO, Rail 410/42, LNWR Board Minutes 1911–14, 12 February 1913, item 25179.

27 Edwards, *Financial Accounting*, p.167.

28 *House of Lords Sessional Papers 1849 (12 & 13 Vict.) Vol.XXIX The Audit of Railway Accounts*, q.2237, p.215.

29 Harold Pollins, 'Railway Auditing – A Report of 1867' in *Accounting Research*, Vol.VIII, Cambridge (1957), p.21.

30 PRO, Rail 250/65, Great Western Railway General Meetings of Proprietors, 14 February 1850, pp.166–7.

31 Edwards, *Financial Accounting*, p.118.

32 Ibid., pp.162–3.

33 J.R. Edwards, 'The Origin and Evolution of the Double Account System' in *Abacus*, Vol.21, March 1985, pp.34, 41.

34 Edwards, *Financial Accounting*, p.166.

35 Evidence of William Quilter, *House of Lords Sessional Papers, 1849 (12 & 13 Vict.), Vol.XXIX, The Audit of Railway Accounts*, p.216.

36 Edwards, 'Double Account System', pp.19–43.

37 In November 1905 a proposal was made which to Waterhouse seemed 'to mix up capital and reserve'; he vehemently opposed the suggestion and had it defeated. Jones, *Memoirs*, p.179.

38 *DBB*, Vol.5, p.675.

39 *The Accountant*, Vol.LI, No.2083, 7 November 1914, 'Reminiscences of the Profession in the Pre-Charter Era', p.522.

40 G.R. Hawke, *Railways and Economic Growth in England and Wales 1840–1870*, Oxford (1970), p.262.

41 Jones, *Memoirs*, pp.83–4.

42 Ibid., pp.84–5.

43 PWA, 'Personal Audit Appointments of E.W. at Time of Retirement', 1 January 1906.

44 PWA, Letter Book 1871–87, letter to W.B. Paget from E. Waterhouse, 7 August 1883, pp.338–9.

45 *Bradshaw's Railway Manual and Shareholders' Guide*, London (1869), pp.279, 12.

46 PWA, 'List of Clients and Fee Income 1891–7'.

47 PWA, Letter Book No.2, E. Waterhouse to H.D. Pochin, 10 June 1873, pp.102–3.

48 Jones, *Memoirs*, p.128.

49 PWA, 10/48, Sir Lawrence Halsey, 'Reminiscences' (n.d.), p.2.

50 Ibid., p.131.

51 Humphrey Lloyd, *The Quaker Lloyds in the Industrial Revolution*, London (1972), p.286.

52 PWA, 'List of Clients and Fee Income, 1891–7'.

53 Neil McKendrick, *The Birth of the Foreign & Colonial, The World's First Investment Trust 19 March 1868*, Cambridge (1993), p.33.

54 Jones, *Memoirs*, p.91.

55 Ibid., pp.92–3.

56 PWA, Letter Book No. 2, letter to Edmund Ashworth, 30 November 1871, p.18.

57 Jones, *Memoirs*, pp.104–5.

58 David Cannadine, *Lords and Landlord, The Aristocracy and the Towns 1774–1967*, Leicester (1980), pp.323–4.

59 PWA, 9/27, 'Report by Price Waterhouse', 12 November 1894, p.34.

60 Cannadine, *Lords and Landlord*, p.328.

61 Jones, *Memoirs*, p.109.

62 Jones, *Accountancy*, p.44.

63 PWA, E.W.'s Letter Book No.3, March 1878–December 1886, E. Waterhouse to R.L. Pratt, 30 December 1884, p.198.

64 Jones, *Accountancy*, p.47.

65 Jones, *Memoirs*, p.86.

66 *PO London Directories*, 1869, p.988; 1845, p.421; 1846, p.930; 1865, p.1500; 1852, p.819.

67 PWA, 10/47, Price Waterhouse & Co. partnership deeds.

68 Jones, *Memoirs*, p.86.

69 *PO London Directory*, 1874, p.1025.

70 G.E. Richards, 'History of the Firm: The First Fifty Years 1850–1900' (typescript, 1950), p.5.

71 PWA, letter from William Edwards to Price, Holyland & Waterhouse, 18 March 1871.

72 Ibid.

73 PWA, 10/35, letter to H.G. Norman from G. Martin, Lee & Martin, Halifax, 9 May 1950.

74 PWA, PW & Co. Letter Book January 1871–September 1887, letter to J.A. Mann, 13 September 1880, pp.328–9.

75 PWA, letter from Rupert Sneath to G.E. Richards, 4 April 1950.

76 Ibid.

77 PWA, 10/48, Halsey, 'Reminiscences', p.3.

78 PWA, Senior Partner's Box, letter from F.S. Tull to N.E. Waterhouse, 3 January 1946.

79 *The Accountant*, Vol.LXVI, No.2476, 20 May 1922, obituary, p.702.

80 PWA, 10/39, W.C. Sneath, 'The History of Price Waterhouse & Co.'(typescript, 11 June 1947).

81 Sir Nicholas E.Waterhouse, 'Reminiscences 1877–1960', Part II (typescript, 1961), p.96.

82 Information provided by J.M. Hamill, librarian, United Grand Lodge of England, 12 May 1992.

83 *Chartered Accountants Lodge, Jubilee Meeting*, 3 October 1956.

84 PWA, information from George Sneath.

85 Paul Grady (ed.), *Memoirs and Accounting Thought of George O. May*, New York (1962), p.16.

86 Sir Nicholas E. Waterhouse, 'Fifty Years with Price, Waterhouse & Co.' (typescript, 12 December 1949), p.96.

87 PWA, Eric P. Southall, 'Price Waterhouse & Co. and the Royal Mail Steam Packet Group after the Trial' (typescript, 1983), p.10.

88 Waterhouse, 'Reminiscences', p.3.

89 Grady, *G.O. May*, p.16.

90 PWA, Halsey, 'Reminiscences', p.2.

91 Edwin Waterhouse (ed.), *Extracts from the Journals of Mary Waterhouse 1825–1880*, privately printed, London (1907), 30 April 1879, p.325; 2 August 1879, pp.328–9.

92 PWA, Halsey, 'Reminiscences', p.3; *The Accountant*, Vol.LIV, No.2161, 6 May 1916, obituary, pp.535–6.

93 Waterhouse, 'Fifty Years', p.96.

94 *The Builder*, Vol.IX, No.457, 8 November 1851, obituary, p.709.

95 Waterhouse, 'Fifty Years', p.2.

96 R.F. Hellis, 'Reminiscences of my Early Years with Price Waterhouse & Co.' (n.d.), p.1.

97 *The Accountant*, Vol.CXIII, No.3694, 22 September 1945, obituary, p.146.

98 Richards, 'First Fifty Years', p.8.

99 PWA, Box 168, Salary List Christmas 1894.

100 Ibid., Christmas 1896.

101 Ibid., 1900.

102 *The Accountant*, Vol.XVIII, No.898, 20 February 1892, p.176.

103 Waterhouse, 'Fifty Years', pp.2, 3.

104 Ibid., p.3.

105 Ibid.

106 PWA, Eric P. Southall, 'What it was like to join the staff of Price Waterhouse & Co. in April 1921' (typescript, 1984), p.3.

107 Anthony Trollope, *The Three Clerks*, London (1857), Oxford (1989), p.12.

108 Waterhouse, 'Fifty Years', p.100.

109 Paul Keers, *A Gentleman's Wardrobe*, London (1987), p.33.

110 PWA, Halsey, 'Reminiscences', pp.4–5.

111 W. Somerset Maugham, *Of Human Bondage*, London (1915), London (1937), p.234.

112 Richards, 'First Fifty Years', p.10.

113 PWA, Halsey, 'Reminiscences'.

114 Jones, *Memoirs*, p.207.

115 Cleona Lewis, *America's Stake in International Investments*, Washington DC (1938), p.560.

116 H. Osborne O'Hagan, *Leaves from my Life*, Vol.2, London (1929), p.454.

117 Mira Wilkins, *The History of Foreign Investment in the United States to 1914*, Harvard (1989), p.537.

118 PWA, 1/40, Bob Berger, 'History of Price Waterhouse 1890–1901' (typescript, 1947), p.2; D.G. Allen and K. McDermott, *Accounting for Success, A History of Price Waterhouse in America 1890–1990*, Boston (1993), p.11.

119 Jones, *Memoirs*, p.123.

120 PWA, 10/37, Agreement 11 September 1890; Allen and McDermott, *Accounting for Success*, pp.12–13.

121 PWA, letter to PW New York from PW London, 12 May 1947; see also *The Accountant*, Vol.XXV, No.1267, 18 March 1899, obituary, p.323.

122 PWA, 10/39, Sneath, 'History of P.W. & Co.'.

123 Berger, *History of Price Waterhouse*, XVI, p.1.

124 PWA, Box C10, New York Agency, Statement of Account, 31 December 1890.

125 Ibid., 30 June 1891.

126 PWA, 58/115, letter from PW & Co. to L.D. Jones, 9 January 1891.

127 PWA, letter from J.A. Walker, Secretary of Society of Accountants in Edinburgh, 14 May 1947.

128 PWA, 10/38, letter from W.J. Caesar to PW, 30 September 1890.

129 Ibid.

130 C.W. De Mond, *Price Waterhouse & Co. in America, A History of a Public Accounting Firm*, New York (1951), p.18.

131 Berger, 'History of Price Waterhouse', XV, p.1.

132 PWA, Box C10, American Agency Accounts to 30 June 1893.

133 PWA, 10/40, letter to PW from Winston & Meagher, 16 December 1893.

134 PWA, letter from L.D. Jones to J.G. Fowler, 12 February 1894.

135 PWA, letter from W.J. Caesar to J.G. Fowler, 14 February 1894.

136 Berger, 'History of Price Waterhouse', XI, p.2.

137 M. Wilkins, *The History of Foreign Investment in the United States to 1914*, Cambridge, Massachusetts (1989), p.540.

138 PWA, letter from J.G. Fowler to L.D. Jones, 30 August 1894.

139 PWA, letter from Price Waterhouse to L.D. Jones and W.J. Caesar, 10 October 1894.

140 Berger, 'History of Price Waterhouse', 1, p.7.

141 PWA, Box C10, letter from W.J. Caesar to J.G. Fowler, 17 September 1896.

142 Ibid, p.9; Allen and McDermott, *Accounting for Success*, p.20.

143 PWA, Box C10, letter from W.J. Caesar to PW London, 9 June 1897.

144 Ibid., 7 February 1899.

145 De Mond, *Price Waterhouse & Co. in America*, pp.27–8, 43–5.

146 Berger, 'History of Price Waterhouse', 1, p.12.

147 Ibid., p.13.

148 PWA, Box 58/60, letter from W.J. Caesar to J.G. Fowler, 1 August 1900.

149 Berger, 'History of Price Waterhouse', XVII, p.1.

150 Ibid., p.14.

Chapter 4

1 Lady Plender (ed.), *Lord Plender, Some Writings and Speeches*, London (1951), 'Observations on Half a Century of Business Life in the City' (6 January 1934), p.17.

2 Interview E. Jones with Mr George Scheu, 16 March 1990.

3 PWA, Ms headed 'The suggestion that E.W. should retire from the firm' [n.d.].

4 Ibid.

5 A.C. Falkner, 'Price Waterhouse & Co., History of the United Kingdom Firm, The Second Fifty Years 1900–1950', (1970) p.4.

6 Ibid.

7 Edgar Jones, *Memoirs of Edwin Waterhouse*, London (1988), p.178.

8 PWA, 1/37, Personal Audit appointments of Edwin Waterhouse at 1 January 1906.

9 N.E. Waterhouse, 'Reminiscences 1870–1960', Part II (typescript, 15 February 1952), p.8.

10 Jones, *Memoirs*, p.196.

11 Ibid., pp.200, 204, 207.

12 Waterhouse, 'Reminiscences', p.4.

13 Jones, *Memoirs*, pp.35–9.

14 E.M. Forster, *A Room with a View*, London (1908), Harmondsworth (1978), pp.119–20.

15 Jones, *Memoirs*, pp.34, 146, 157, 164, 166.

16 Ibid., pp.166–7.

17 Waterhouse, 'Reminiscences', p.34.

18 Ibid., p.36.

19 Jones, *Memoirs*, p.181.

20 Sir Nicholas E. Waterhouse, 'Fifty Years with Price Waterhouse & Co.' (typescript, 12 December 1949), p.97.

21 Ibid., p.91.

22 Ibid., p.97.

23 Jones, *Memoirs*, p.207.

24 PWA, 10/45, W.C.Sneath, 'Price Waterhouse & Co., London Office' (typescript, n.d.).

25 *The Accountant*, Vol.CL, No.4657, 21 March 1964, p.369.

26 PWA, 5/11 N.E. Waterhouse, 'William Cecil Sneath' (typescript, n.d.).

27 PWA, Eric P. Southall, 'What it was like to join the staff of Price Waterhouse & Co. in April 1921' (typescript, 1984), p.11.

28 *The Accountant*, Vol.CI, No.3384, 14 October 1939, obituary, p.415.

29 Sir Nicholas Waterhouse, 'Note on H.J.M' (typescript, n.d.).

30 Ibid.

31 PWA, Eric P. Southall, 'Price Waterhouse & Co. and the Royal Mail Steam Packet Group after the Trial' (typescript, 1983), p.9.

32 John Steane Price, 'Price Review' (typescript, 1988), p.53.

33 *The Accountant*, Vol.LXXXVII, No.3004, 2 July 1932, obituary, pp.9–10; *DBB*, Vol.2, London (1985), J.R. Edwards, 'Gilbert Garnsey', pp.487–9.

34 *Wellington Weekly News*, 29 June 1932, obituary.

35 Letter from D. Spinks, Aston Villa Football Club, 31 October 1991.

36 PWA, N.E. Waterhouse, 'G.F.G' (typescript, n.d.).

37 *Evening Standard*, 27 June 1932, obituary.

38 PWA, N.E. Waterhouse to G.E. Richards, 11 February 1955.

39 M.C. Spencer, 'Note on G.F.G' (typescript, n.d.).

40 *Evening News*, 27 June 1932, obituary.

41 *Daily Telegraph*, 28 June 1932, obituary.

42 Typewritten note, 'Liverpool'; Falkner, 'Second Fifty Years', p.10.

43 Ibid., p.11.

44 Lady Plender (ed.), *Lord Plender*, p.52.

45 Paul Grady (ed.), *Memoirs and Accounting Thought of George O. May*, New York (1962), p.21.

46 E.M. Forster, *Goldsworthy Lowes Dickinson*, London (1973), p.2.

47 *The Accountant*, Vol.XCII, No.3144, 9 March 1935, p.345.

48 *DBB*, Vol.2 (1984), J.R. Edwards, 'Sir Arthur Lowes Dickinson', p.103.

49 Note by Sir Nicholas Waterhouse on 'A.L.D'.

50 Grady, *G.O. May*, p.25.

51 George de Mare, 'The Story of the United States Firm' in *PW Quarterly*, Vol.1, No.4, Spring 1969, p.5.

52 Grady, *G.O. May*, pp.21–2.

53 PWA, Box C10, A.L. Dickinson to PW London, 7 December 1901.

54 D.G. Allen and K. McDermott, *Accounting for Success, A History of Price Waterhouse in America 1890–1990*, Harvard Business School Press, Boston (1993), p.31.

55 PWA, Box C10, A.L. Dickinson to PW London, 7 December 1901.

56 Ibid., 12 November 1901.

57 Ibid., 18 April 1902.

58 Ibid., 20 February 1902.

59 Allen and McDermott, *Accounting for Success*, pp.32–3.

60 Ibid., pp.33–4.

61 PWA, Box C10, PW New York to PW London, 6 January 1902.

62 Ibid., 30 October 1902.

63 Allen and McDermott, *Accounting for Success*, p.35.

64 PWA, Box C11, A.L. Dickinson to J.G. Fowler, 10 April 1906.

65 Ibid., 9 February 1906.

66 Ibid., 10 April 1906.

67 Ibid.

68 Ibid.

69 PWA, Box C11, H.W. Wilmott to PW London, 10 April 1906.

70 PWA, Box C11, A.L. Dickinson to J.G. Fowler, 8 June 1906.

71 Allen and McDermott, *Accounting for Success*, p.44.

72 Grady, *G.O. May*, pp.31, 34.

73 De Mare, 'The United States Firm' in *PW Quarterly* Vol.I, No.4, (1969), p.5.

74 Grady, *G.O. May*, pp.31–2.

75 G.E. Richards, 'History of the Firm: The First Fifty Years 1850–1900' (typescript, 1950), p.12.

76 PWA, letter from PW New York to PW London, 30 June 1914.

77 PWA, 1/38, Partnership Agreements – America, 30 June 1901.

78 PWA, Box 3/4, 'Memorandum regarding US Firm History 1901 to 1919' (n.d.), p.2.

79 Ibid., p.5.

80 Grady, *G.O. May*, p.35.

81 PWA, Box 3/4, Correspondence File: US Firm History, letter from G.O. May to A.L. Dickinson, 23 January 1914, p.1.

82 Ibid., pp.1–2.

83 Ibid., letter from A.L. Dickinson to G.O. May, 5 February 1914, p.2.

84 PWA, letter to G.O. May, New York, from PW, London, 13 February 1914.

85 Falkner, 'Second Fifty Years', p.14.

86 PMM, Volume of Announcements, W.B. Peat & Co., 31 December 1910.

87 Ibid., W.B. Peat & Co., 1 December 1907.

88 Falkner, 'Second Fifty Years', p.15.

89 PWA, Box 1/9, F.S. Tull, 'Early Days in South America' (typescript, n.d.), pp.2–6.

90 PWA, 6/13, 'PW Abroad, Australian and New Zealand Firms' (typescript, n.d.).

91 PWA, 7/6, 'Olympic Games 1896/1932'.

92 PWA, 6/13, 'PW Abroad'.

93 PWA, Box 168, Salary List 1900.

94 PWA, 1/27, London Staff, 30 June 1913.

95 B.E.V. Sabine, *A Short History of Taxation*, London (1980), p.123; B.R. Mitchell and P. Deane, *Abstract of British Historical Statistics*, Cambridge (1971), pp.427–8.

96 *The Accountant*, Vol.IX, No.466, 10 November 1883, p.7.

97 Ibid., Vol.X, No.496, 7 June 1884, p.7; No.479, 9 February 1884, p.8.

98 Ibid., Vol.XIII, No.652, 4 June 1887, p.329.

99 Jones, *Memoirs*, p.135.

100 Ibid., p.139.

101 Ibid., p.207.

102 PWA, 1/36, Membership of the ICAEW Council.

103 Jones, *Memoirs*, pp.149–50.

104 J.R. Edwards, *A History of Financial Accounting*, London (1989), p.202.

105 Jones, *Memoirs*, p.177.

106 Edward VII c.50, 1907 Companies Act, Section 21.

107 Edwards, *Financial Accounting*, p.202.

108 Ibid., p.204.

Chapter 5

1 Edgar Jones (ed.), *Memoirs of Edwin Waterhouse*, London (1988), p.207.

2 *Price, Waterhouse & Co., Staff War Bulletin*, No.3 (1916), p.36.

3 Jones, *Memoirs*, p.123.

4 Michael R. Lane, *The Story of the Steam Plough Works, Fowlers of Leeds*, London (1980), pp.7–10, 19, 26.

5 Jones, *Memoirs*, pp.79–80.

6 Ibid., p.207.

7 *The Accountant*, Vol.LIV, No.2161, 6 May 1916, obituary, pp.535–6.

8 PWA, N.E. Waterhouse, 'Reminiscences 1877–1960', Part II (typescript, 1961), pp.68–9.

9 *The Accountant*, Vol.XCVII, No.3288, 11 December 1937, obituary, p.798.

10 Typewritten note prepared by M.C. Spencer, April 1955.

11 Robert Graves, *Goodbye to All That*, London (1929), Harmondsworth (1960), p.120.

12 *The Accountant*, Vol.CXIII, No.3694, 22 September 1945, p.146.

13 Jones, *Memoirs*, p.208.

14 *The Times*, 28 June 1932, obituary.

15 A.C. Falkner, 'Price Waterhouse & Co., History of the United Kingdom Firm, The Second Fifty Years 1900–1950', p.25.

16 R.P.T. Davenport-Hines, 'Sir Mark Webster Jenkinson' in *DBB*, Vol.3, London (1985), p.484.

17 *The Accountant*, Vol.LVIII, No. 2248, 5 January 1918, pp.1, 2.

18 Waterhouse, 'Reminiscences', p.10.

19 Ibid., Part II, p.45.

20 Ibid., p.46.

21 Jones, *Memoirs*, p.208.

22 Ibid., pp.207–8.

23 Waterhouse, 'Reminiscences', pp.49–50.

24 Ibid., p.10.

25 *The Accountant*, Vol.LVIII, No.2271, 15 June 1918, p.428.

26 Ibid., Vol.LVIII, No.2272, 22 June 1918, p.442.

27 Waterhouse, 'Reminiscences', p.10; PWA, 2/19, F.S. Tull 'Longworth Forum', 14 January 1951, p.9.

28 John Keegan, *The Face of Battle*, London (1976), Harmondsworth (1978), pp.220, 221–2.

29 *The Accountant*, Vol.LI, No.2076, 19 September 1914, p.306.

30 Ibid., Vol.LIII, No.2133, 23 October 1915, 'A Recruiting Appeal', p.479.

31 *Price Waterhouse & Co. Staff War Bulletin*, No.1, February 1915, pp.4–6.

32 Siegfried Sassoon, *Memoirs of an Infantry Officer*, London (1965), pp.159–60.

33 Keegan, *Face of Battle*, pp.223, 224.

34 *Staff War Bulletin*, No.1, February 1915, pp.4–5.

35 Ibid., No.3, Christmas 1916, pp.6–9.

36 Keegan, *Face of Battle*, p.226.

37 'The Profession and National Service' in *The Accountant*, Vol.LVI, No.2207, 24 March 1917, p.273.

38 *Staff War Bulletin*, No.3, pp.6–9, 9–10.

39 PWA, 1/27, London Staff, 30 June 1913.

40 *Staff War Bulletin*, No.3, p.14.

41 Ibid., pp.24–5.

42 Ibid., p.1.

43 *The Accountant*, Vol.LVI, No.2202, 17 February 1917, p.159.

44 Ibid., Vol.CXIV, No.3709, 5 January 1946, obituary, p.6.

45 Ibid., Vol.LIV, No.2163, 20 May 1916, p.583.

46 Ibid., Vol.LV, No.2172, 22 July 1916, p.73.

47 Ibid., Vol.LVI, No.2207, 24 March 1917, p.273.

48 Ibid., p.274.

49 *The Accountant*, Vol.LVII, No.2222, 7 July 1917, p.2.

50 PWA, 9/23, Eric P. Southall, 'What it was like to join the staff of Price Waterhouse & Co. in April 1921' (typescript, November 1984), p.4.

51 Ibid.

52 *The Accountant*, Vol.XX, No.1035, 6 October 1894, p.867.

53 Ibid., Vol.XLII, No.1872, 4 June 1910, p.807.

54 Ibid., Vol.XLVII, No.1971, 14 September 1912, p.341.

55 Arthur Marwick, *Women at War 1914–1918*, London (1977), p.167.

56 Ibid., p.162.

57 [Sir Harold Howitt], *The History of the Institute of Chartered Accountants in England and Wales 1880–1965*, London (1966), pp.65–6.

58 Howard W. Robinson, *A History of Accountants in Ireland*, Dublin (1964), p.180.

59 A.A. Garrett, *History of the Society of Incorporated Accountants 1885–1957*, Oxford (1961).

60 Sir Nicholas E. Waterhouse, 'Fifty Years with Price Waterhouse & Co.' (typescript, 12 December 1949), pp.107–8.

61 B.E.V. Sabine, *A Short History of Taxation*, London (1980), p.139.

62 N.A.H. Stacey, *English Accountancy, A Study in Social and Economic History 1800–1954*, London (1954), p.93.

63 Edgar Jones, *A History of GKN, Vol.1, 1759–1918*, London (1987), p.388.

64 Robinson, *Accountants in Ireland*, p.229.

65 *The Accountant*, Vol.CX, No.3626, 3 June 1944, obituary, p.261.

66 Falkner, 'The Second Fifty Years', p.18.

67 *The Accountant*, Vol.LIII, No.2127, 11 September 1915, p.319.

68 *Staff War Bulletin*, No.3, p.39.

69 G.B. Pollard, *A History of Price Waterhouse in Europe 1914–1969*, Norwich (1975), p.16.

70 C.H. Evans 'Vegetable Oil and Prisoners' in *PW Quarterly*, Vol.7, No.2, Summer 1974, p.6.

71 Ibid., p.18.

72 PMM, 'Volume of Announcements', 1 October 1919, p.11.

73 *The Accountant*, Vol.LV, No.2212, 28 April 1917, p.423; Pollard, *PW in Europe*, pp.18–19.

74 PMM, 'Volume of Announcements', August 1916, p.10.

75 [Sir Russell Kettle], *Deloitte & Co., 1845–1956*, Oxford (1958), p.91.

76 Pollard, *PW in Europe*, p.18.

Chapter 6

1 Collin Brooks (ed.), *The Royal Mail Case*, Edinburgh (1933), p.259.

2 Obituaries: *The Times*, 28 June 1932; *Financial Times*, 28 June 1932.

3 PWA, Sir Nicholas Waterhouse, 'G.F.G.' (typewritten memo, n.d.).

4 Ibid.

5 *The Star*, 27 June 1932.

6 *Financial News*, 28 June 1932.

7 *Daily Telegraph*, 28 June 1932.

8 *The Star*, 27 June 1932.

9 *The Accountant*, Vol.LXXXVII, No.13004, 2 July 1932, obituary, pp.9–10.

10 PWA, Senior Partner's Box: letter from F.S. Tull to N.E. Waterhouse, 3 January 1946.

11 Arnold Bennett, *The Card*, London (1911), Harmondsworth (1975).

12 Waterhouse, 'G.F.G.'.

13 PWA, 9/23, Eric P. Southall, 'What it was like to join the staff of Price Waterhouse & Co. in April 1921' (typescript, 1984), p.12.

14 Sir Thomas B. Robson, 'Price Waterhouse and Myself 1923–1966' (typescript, April 1984), p.4.

15 PWA, Senior Partner's Box, Tull to Waterhouse.

16 Robson, 'Price Waterhouse and Myself', p.8.

17 *The Evening News*, 27 June 1932.

18 *The Financial Times*, 28 June 1932.

19 J.R. Edwards, 'Sir Gilbert Francis Garnsey' in *DBB*, Vol.2 (1984), p.489.

20 File 'History of the Firm': letter from S.H. Mearns to G.E. Richards, 13 July 1950.

21 A.W.Wyon, *The Intelligent Auditing of Detail*, London, Price Waterhouse & Co. (1932), p.1.

22 *The Accountant*, Vol.LXXV, No.2696, 7 August 1926, 'The Organisation of Large Accountants' Offices in connection with the Accountant's Responsibility', p.209.

23 Ibid., p.213.

24 PWA, 10/48, Sir Laurence Halsey, 'Reminiscences', (n.d.), p.4.

25 PWA, Southall, 'Staff of Price Waterhouse', pp.7–8.

26 Robson, 'Price Waterhouse and Myself', p.2.

27 Interviews: E. Jones with A.C. Falkner, 6 November 1989; E. Jones with S.M. Duncan, 11 December 1989.

28 Interview E. Jones with George Scheu, 16 March 1990.

29 PWA, Senior Partner's Box, Tull to Waterhouse.

30 PWA, Southall, 'Staff of Price Waterhouse', p.7.

31 PWA, Box C11, Staff Notebook Vol.2 1890–1924, p.227; ibid., Vol.3, p.57.

32 PWA, 11/3, *National Trust Annual Report 1926–27*, p.6.

33 *The Accountant*, Vol.CXIII, No.3694, 22 September 1945, p.146.

34 PWA, Southall, 'Staff of Price Waterhouse', p.9.

35 Interview E. Jones with S.M. Duncan, 1 September 1992.

36 PWA, Articles of Partnership, 31 July 1939.

37 A.C. Falkner, 'Price Waterhouse & Co., History of the United Kingdom Firm, The Second Fifty Years 1900–1950', pp.37–8.

38 PWA, Minutes of Partners' Meetings, October 1936–September 1948, 9 October 1936.

39 Ibid., 8 April 1938.

40 *Fortune*, June 1932, 'Certified Public Accountants', pp.63–6, 95–6, 101–2.

41 D.G. Allen and K. McDermott, *Accounting for Success, A History of Price Waterhouse in America 1890–1990*, Boston (1993), pp.3–7.

42 PWA, 13/3, Profits and Fees of US Firm, 1934–9.

43 Edgar Jones, *Accountancy and the British Economy 1840–1980, The Evolution of Ernst & Whinney*, London (1981), p.99.

44 Sir Nicholas Waterhouse, 'Matters affecting the Accountancy Profession' in *V Internationaler Prüfungs und Treuhand Kongress, Berlin* (1938), pp.162–3.

45 PWA, Executive Committee Folder October 1936–March 1945, memo to N.E.W., 'Suggested Arrangements for the Reorganisation of the Railway Staff', 22 March 1938.

46 PWA, Southall, 'Staff of Price Waterhouse', p.14.

47 PWA, Executive Committee, 'Reorganisation of Railway Staff'.

48 Ibid.

49 Ibid.

50 PWA, Executive Committee Folder October 1936–March 1945, 'List of A.W. Wyon's Audits January–March 1937'.

51 PWA, Southall, 'Staff of Price Waterhouse', p.14.

52 PWA, 'A.W. Wyon's Audits'; 17/10, 'Lists of Clients of Price Waterhouse & Co. in UK Offices' (typescript, November 1946).

53 PMM, 'List of Public Companies Audited by the Firm', p.3.

54 Robson, 'Price Waterhouse and Myself', pp.4–5.

55 John Orbell, 'James Frater Taylor' in *DBB*, Vol.5 (1986), p.460.

56 J.D. Scott, *Vickers, A History*, London (1962), pp.161, 163–6.

57 R.S. Sayers, *Lloyds Bank in the History of English Banking*, Oxford (1957), pp.267–8.

58 Robson, 'Price Waterhouse and Myself', pp.3–4.

59 Ibid., pp.13–14.

60 PWA, 2/19, F.S. Tull, 'Longworth Forum, an address delivered at the Rectory Room, Longworth, 4 January 1957', p.11.

61 Interview E. Jones with A.M. Inglis, 4 February 1992.

62 *The Accountant*, Vol.CXXI, No.3892, 23 July 1949, obituary, p.102.

63 PWA, Executive Committee Folder, H.E. Seed 'Memorandum on Organisation of Tax Work [1939]'.

64 *The Accountant*, Vol.CX, No.3626, 1944, obituary, p.261.

65 PWA, letter from Sir Thomas Robson to R.J. Cornwell, 26 February 1979.

66 PWA, Box 178, 'Memorandum of Conversation between Sir William Peat . . . N.E. Waterhouse on January 6th 1915', p.1.

67 Ibid., p.3.

68 Ibid., pp.5–6.

69 PMM, 'Volume of Announcements', 1 October 1919, p.11.

70 PMM, 'Firms Offices' (typescript, *c.* 1957).

71 'Peat Marwick Mitchell & Co., A Short Outline of its Origins and Growth' (typescript, 1950).

72 'A Short History of the Firm of W.B. Peat & Co.' (typescript, June 1927).

73 Letter from Sir Harry Peat to Sir Gilbert Garnsey, 1 July 1920.

74 PWA, 4/3, memorandum listing voting preferences (n.d.).

75 Letter to Sir William Peat from Sir Albert Wyon, 9 July 1920.

76 PWA, memorandum as amended at conference held 9 September 1920.

77 PWA, draft letter from Sir Harry Peat to Sir Albert Wyon, October 1920.

78 PWA, heads of agreement revised on 29 September 1920, 26 November 1920.

79 PWA, letter to Price Waterhouse from Slaughter and May, 17 December 1920.

80 PWA, 4/3, letter from Sir Harry Peat to Sir Arthur Lowes Dickinson, 29 December 1920.

81 Ibid., 7 January 1921.

82 Ibid., 14 January 1921.

83 PWA, Box 178, envelope marked 'Sir Albert Wyon Private and Confidential'.

84 Ibid., an unsigned note to A.W.W. in Halsey's handwriting.

85 Ibid.

86 PWA, memorandum listing voting preferences.

87 Jones, *Accountancy*, p.265.

88 [Sir Russell Kettle] *Deloitte & Co., 1845–1956*, Oxford (1958), p.xi.

89 P.S. Marley, 'Clarence Hatry' in *Abacus*, Vol.12 (1976), p.54.

90 Robson, 'Price Waterhouse and Myself', p.6.

91 PWA, 2/19, F.S. Tull, 'Address to be delivered at the Rectory Room, Longworth, 4 January 1951 entitled Checks and Cheques, The Accountant's Job', p.34.

92 Robson, 'Price Waterhouse and Myself', p.6.

93 Ibid.

94 *The Times*, 21 January 1930, 'The Hatry Case Opened'.

95 Robson, 'Price Waterhouse and Myself', p.7.

96 Ibid., p.7.

97 J.R. Edwards, *Company Legislation and Changing Patterns of Disclosure in British Company Accounts 1900–1940*, London (1981), p.5.

98 [Sir Harold Howitt], *The History of the Institute of Chartered Accountants in England and Wales 1880–1965*, London (1966), p.75.

99 Edwin Green and Michael Moss, *A Business of National Importance, The Royal Mail Shipping Group 1902–1937*, London (1982), p.3.

100 *Shipbuilding and Shipping Record*, Vol.29, 19 May 1927, pp.563, 572.

101 Green and Moss, *Royal Mail*, p.72.

102 Ibid., p.73.

103 Ibid., p.84.

104 Ibid., pp.85, 86.

105 Ibid., pp.87, 88.

106 Ibid., p.94.

107 Ibid., pp.99–100.

108 PWA, Box 162, 'Sir William McLintock's Report and Appendices' (typescript, 20 March 1930), pp.36–7, 44, 50.

109 Ibid., pp.106–7.

110 Reported in *The Times*, 15 March 1930.

111 Green and Moss, *Royal Mail*, p.109.

112 Ibid., p.113.

113 Ibid., p.117.

114 Ibid., pp.132, 140.

115 PWA, Box 162, *Notes on Proceedings, Central Criminal Court*, p.179.

116 Patrick Hastings, *Cases in Court*, London (1949), p.223.

117 H. Montgomery Hyde, *Sir Patrick Hastings, His Life and Cases*, London (1960), pp.223–4.

118 R.K. Ashton, 'The Royal Mail Case: A Legal Analysis' in *Abacus* Vol.22 (1986), p.9.

119 Hastings, *Cases in Court*, pp.220–21.

120 PWA, Box 162, Vol.G Supplementary Documents, Lord Plender's Statement.

121 Hastings, *Cases in Court*, pp.220–21.

122 PWA, 4/27, Eric P. Southall 'Price Waterhouse and the Royal Mail Steam Packet Group after the Trial' (typescript, 1983), p.10.

123 Brooks, *Royal Mail*, p.39.

124 Ashton, 'Royal Mail', p.9.

125 Ibid., p.190.

126 Ibid., p.177.

127 PWA, Box 163, File 'Correspondence with May and Others', letter from Sir Gilbert Garnsey to G.O. May, 5 August 1931.

128 PWA, Southall, 'Royal Mail', p.10.

129 Ashton, 'Royal Mail', p.11.

130 PWA, Box 163, Garnsey to May, pp.2–3.

131 PWA, Southall, 'Royal Mail', p.8.

132 Hastings, *Cases in Court*, p.226.

133 Ibid., pp.186–7, 189.

134 Ibid., p.189.

135 Ibid., p.217.

136 Ibid.

137 Green and Moss, *Royal Mail*, pp.142–3.

138 PWA, Box 163, Garnsey to May, p.7.

139 Laurie Dennett, *Slaughter and May, A Century in the City*, Cambridge (1989), p.50.

140 Interview E. Jones with F.R. Furber, 1 June 1992.

141 PWA, Box 163, 'Brief for the Defence', p.1.

142 PWA, letter from N.E. Waterhouse to G.O. May, 2 August 1931.

143 Ibid.

144 PWA, note on 'HJH' by Sir Nicholas Waterhouse.

145 PWA, Waterhouse to May.

146 Falkner, 'Second Fifty Years', p.45.

147 Parker, 'For J.P.P.', p.49.

148 Interview E. Jones with F.R. Furber, 1 June 1992.

149 PWA, Box C11, Staff Notebook, Vol.2 (1890–1924), p.198; Vol.3, p.32.

150 Interview E. Jones with F.R. Furber, 1 June 1992.

151 PWA, Southall, 'Royal Mail', pp.1–2.

152 A.M. Carr-Saunders and P.A. Wilson, *The Professions*, Oxford (1933), pp.220–21.

153 Ibid., p.222.

154 F.R.M. de Paula, *Principles of Auditing*, London (1933), Preface.

155 *The Accountant*, Vol.LXXXVI, No.2996, 7 May 1932, p.629.

156 A.J. Arnold, 'Secret Reserves or Special Credits? A Reappraisal of the Reserve and Provision Accounting Policies of the Royal Mail Steam Packet Company, 1915–27' in *Accounting and Business Research*, Vol.21 (1991), pp.203–14.

157 Ibid., pp.205–11.

158 Sir Gilbert Garnsey, *Holding Companies and their Published Accounts*, London (1922), p.15.

159 Ibid., p.10.

160 Ibid., pp.43–4.

161 *The Accountant*, Vol.LXX, No.2563, 19 January 1924, p.118.

162 J. Kitchen and R.H. Parker, *Accounting Thought and Education: Six English Pioneers*, London (1980), p.87.

163 *The Accountant*, Vol.LXXIII, No.2656, 31 October 1925, pp.685–7.

164 Sir Gilbert Garnsey, *Holding Companies and their Published Accounts, Some Further Notes*, London (1926), p.5.

165 Ibid., p.24.

166 Garnsey, *Holding Companies*, (1922), p.45.

167 R.H. Parker, 'Explaining National Differences in Consolidated Accounts' in *Accounting and Business Research*, Summer (1977), p.203.

168 'The Form and Presentation of the Accounts of Holding Companies' in *The Accountant*, Vol.XCI, 15 December 1934, p.853.

169 Robson, 'Price Waterhouse and Myself', p.7.

170 T.B. Robson, *The Construction of Consolidated Accounts*, London (1936), p.4.

171 PWA, Executive Committee, 'Committee on Local Offices', 29 January 1932.

172 Memorandum to G.E. Richards re 'Cardiff Office', 21 March 1955.

173 *Yorkshire Post*, obituary, 28 December 1953.

174 PWA, 'Leeds Office', 29 September 1954.

175 PWA, 'Committee on Local Offices', p.5.

176 PWA, Box C11, Staff Notebook, Vol.2 (1890–1924), p.287.

177 PWA, 'Committee on Local Offices', p.6.

178 Ibid., p.7.

179 Ibid., p.6.

180 PWA, 'Manchester' (n.d.).

181 PWA, Partners' Meeting, 7 October 1937.

182 Ibid., 9 February 1939.

183 Falkner, 'Second Fifty Years', p.63.

184 Ibid., p.32.

185 F.M. Kellett, 'Monkhouse, Goddard & Co. 1868–1920, Some Notes on the History of the Newcastle Firm' (typescript, 1950), pp.1–2.

186 *The Accountant*, Vol.XX, No.1046, 22 December 1894, obituary, p.1127.

187 Ibid., Vol.XXI, No.1048, 5 January 1895, p.11.

188 Ibid., p. 3.

189 *The Accountant*, Vol.XLIV, No.1892, 11 March 1911, p.409.

190 PWA, 'Committee on Local Offices', pp.4–5.

191 Ibid., Appendix 'A', p.1.

192 PWA, 'Record Book P.W. & Co., Newcastle upon Tyne'; Executive Committee, memorandum N.E.W. to W.H. re Newcastle profits, 2 June 1939.

193 PWA, *Articles of Partnership of the Newcastle Partnership* (1939), p.1.

194 *PW Quarterly*, Autumn 1981, p.12.

195 Ronald Legge, *A Man of Trust, The Life of J.M.S. Coates OBE*, York (1989), p.28.

196 PWA, Halsey, 'Reminiscences', p.5.

197 PWA, 11/5, Catalogue of Two-Day Auction of Office Furniture from Price Waterhouse, 16–17 January 1976.

198 PWA, Southall, 'Staff in Price Waterhouse', p.6.

199 PWA, 58/74, *Notes for Members of the Audit Staff* (1925), p.9.

200 PWA, Southall, 'Staff in Price Waterhouse', p.5.

201 Parker, *Accounting*, pp.42–3.

202 John Orbell, 'The Development of Office Technology' in Alison Turton (ed.), *Managing Business Archives*, Oxford (1991), p.77.

203 PWA, Executive Committee October 1936–March 1945, memorandum for N.E.W. from F.E.W., 4 December 1936.

204 PWA, Executive Committee, note M.C.S. to N.E.W., 7 December 1936.

205 Parker, *Accounting*, p.42.

206 Ibid., p.44.

207 PWA, Box C11, Staff Notebook 1890–1912, pp.170, 174, 44, 72, 195, 51, 61, 103.

208 D.C. Coleman, *Courtaulds, An Economic and Social History Vol. III 1940–1965*, Oxford (1980), pp.30, 31, 327 .

Chapter 7

1 M. Laird Watt, *The First Seventy Five Years, Price Waterhouse Canada*, Montreal (1982), p.22.

2 *Platform*, Summer 1982, 'PMM in the Past', p.20.

3 PMM, 'Volume of Announcements', 1 October 1919, p.11.

4 Ibid., October 1920, p.20.

5 G.B. Pollard, *A History of Price Waterhouse in Europe 1914–1969*, Norwich (1975), p.21; PWA 1/1, Fred Thompson, 'PW & Co. European Firm 1921–1955' (typescript, 4 May 1955), p.1.

6 PWA, Continental Firm, Partners' Meeting, 7 January 1922.

7 PWA, 8/46, Marcel Contil, 'My First Forty Years' (typescript, Paris, 1959), p.2.

8 PWA, Continental Firm, Partners' Meeting, 29–31 October 1935, pp.3–4.

9 PMM, 'Volume of Announcements', March 1921, p.25.

10 Ibid., 1 January 1925, p.32.

11 Alan Hankinson, *The First Tigers, The Early History of Rock Climbing in the Lake District*, Bassenthwaite (1984), pp.71–2.

12 George Seatree, *Lakeland Memories*, R. Scott, Penrith (1923).

13 *The Accountant*, Vol.CXIII, No.3702, 17 November 1945, obituary, p.246.

14 PWA, 34/11, W. Ernest Seatree, *Relation of the Auditor to the Valuation of Inventories (Reprinted from the Journal of Accountancy for September and November 1914)*, Price Waterhouse & Co., New York (1914).

15 Pollard, *Price Waterhouse in Europe*, p.19.

16 Paul Grady (ed.), *Memoirs and Accounting Thought of George O. May*, New York (1962), p.45.

17 Pollard, *PW in Europe*, p.23.

18 PWA, 8/46, Contil, 'Forty Years', p.2.

19 PWA, Senior Partner's Box, letter to N.E. Waterhouse from F.S. Tull, 3 January 1946.

20 Pollard, *PW in Europe*, p.24.

21 PWA, Box C11, Staff Volume, Vol.2, 1890–1924, p.191.

22 Leslie Hannah, 'Visible and Invisible Hands in Great Britain' in Alfred D. Chandler and Herman Daems (eds.), *Managerial Hierarchies: Comparative Perspectives on the Rise of Modern Industrial Enterprise*, Harvard (1980), p.57.

23 Edgar Jones, *Accountancy and the British Economy 1840–1980, The Evolution of Ernst & Whinney*, London (1981), p.175; [Sir Russell Kettle], *Deloitte & Co., 1845–1956*, Oxford (1958), p.115.

24 PWA, 8/36, letter from T.B. Robson to J.B. Inglis, 11 February 1958.

25 Bruce Marshall, *The Bank Audit*, London (1958), p.12.

26 PWA, 1/29, Berlin Office Partnership Matters 1925–29, letter from G.O. May to A.W. Wyon, 12 November 1925.

27 PWA, 6/49, 'Tentative List of British and Continental Clients having Parent or Subsidiary Companies which are Clients of the US Firm' (typescript, n.d.).

28 PWA, Continental Firm, Partners' Meeting, 21 June 1924, p.8.

29 Ibid.

30 Pollard, *PW in Europe*, p. 24.

31 PWA, Continental Firm, Partners' Meeting, 13–14 December 1932, p.6.

32 Ibid., pp.24–25.

33 PWA, 1/29, Berlin Office Partnership Matters 1925–39, Partnership Agreement, 28 November 1931.

34 Pollard, *PW in Europe*, p.25.

35 Paul Theroux, *The Kingdom by the Sea*, London (1983), Harmondsworth (1984), p.335.

36 Pollard, *PW in Europe*, p.25.

37 Ibid., p.26.

38 PWA, Continental Firm, Partners' Meeting, 26–28 October 1936, p.1.

39 Ibid.

40 Eric Bagge, *Off the Record, An Account of Price Waterhouse in Switzerland up to June 21, 1987*, Geneva (1987), p.7.

41 PWA, 1/24, Minutes of Partners' Meeting, 29–31 October 1935.

42 Bagge, *PW in Switzerland*, p.8.

43 PWA, 1/25, Minutes of Partners' Meeting, 26–28 October 1936, pp.1–2.

44 Bagge, *PW in Switzerland*, pp.11–12, 8, 16, 17.

45 PWA, 58/73, Book of Press Cuttings from 1907, 30 June 1930, p.20.

46 Pollard, *PW in Europe*, p.31.

47 PWA, Continental Firm, Partners' Meeting, 8–10 December 1938, p.6.

48 PWA, 6/40, Continental Firm Profit and Loss Account, 9 months to 31 March 1936.

49 PWA, 11/11, 'Continental Partnership Correspondence 1933–1940', letter from W.E. Seatree to A.E. Jones, 3 August 1938.

50 PWA, 11/11, letter from J.W. Webster to N.E. Waterhouse, 6 October 1937, p.1.

51 PWA, 11/11, 'Continental Partnership Correspondence 1933–1940', letter from Fred Thompson to N.E. Waterhouse, 5 October 1937.

52 PWA, 11/11, letter from Charles Evans to G.O. May and N.E. Waterhouse, 2 October 1937.

53 PWA, 11/11, letter from T.L. Ferguson to N.E. Waterhouse, 17 September 1937.

54 K. de Vylder and E. Cooke, *Price Waterhouse Sweden, the first 50 years*, Stockholm (1982), p.14; George R. Thompson, 'Ivar Kreuger – King of Swindlers' in *The Investors Chronicle*, 23 February 1968, p.629.

55 De Vylder and Cooke, *Price Waterhouse Sweden*, pp.16–17.

56 Pollard, *PW in Europe*, p.28.

57 Ibid.

58 Robert Shaplen, *Kreuger, Genius and Swindler*, London (1961), p.142.

59 Pollard, *PW in Europe*, p.29.

60 Grady, *G.O. May*, p.77.

61 PWA, 11/17, Stockholm Office Miscellaneous File 1927–1937, letter, 1 November 1932.

62 PWA, 11/17, *Financial News*, 24 November 1932.

63 PWA, 11/17, letter from Sir Gilbert Garnsey to W.E. Seatree, 27 January 1928.

64 PWA, 11/17, letter from W.E. Seatree to Sir Gilbert Garnsey, 30 January 1928.

65 De Vylder and Cooke, *Price Waterhouse Sweden*, pp.37–8.

66 Edgar Jones, *A History of GKN, Volume 2 1918–1945*, London (1990), pp.195–6.

67 PWA, 13/9, File 'North American Staff Interchange', letter from G.O. May to Sir Albert W. Wyon, 4 January 1929.

68 Ibid.

69 Ibid., 'London Staff to America' (1938).

70 Sir Thomas B. Robson, 'Price Waterhouse and Myself 1923–1966' (typescript, April 1984), p.9.

71 Ibid.

72 W.E. Parker, 'For J.P.P. Some Notes ... and Some Lengthy Reminiscences' (typescript, 1974–7), p.50.

73 D.A. Allen and K. McDermott, *Accounting for Success, A History of Price Waterhouse in America 1890–1990*, Harvard Business School Press, Boston, Massachusetts (1993), p.55.

74 Ibid.

75 Grady, *G.O. May*, p.47.

76 PWA, 'George Oliver May' (typescript, n.d.); *The Accountant*, Vol. CXLIV, No.4511, 3 June 1961, obituary, pp.707–8.

77 A.C. Falkner, 'Price Waterhouse & Co., History of the United Kingdom Firm, The Second Fifty Years 1900–1950', pp.33–4.

78 Sir Harold Howitt, 'PMM & Co.' (typescript, 1966), p.23.

79 PWA, M.C. Spencer, 'A.L.D.' (typewritten note, n.d.).

80 PMM, 'Volume of Announcements', December 1920, p.23.

81 Falkner, 'Second Fifty Years', p.34.

82 PWA, 7/13, 'Memorandum of Mr F.S. Price's Visit to Johannesburg and Pretoria, April and May 1930' (typescript, 17 July 1930), p.7.

83 Ibid., p.8.

84 Ibid., p.15.

85 Denis King and Donald Malpas, *Price Waterhouse in South America, The First Seventy-Five Years 1913–1988*, São Paulo (1989), p.24.

86 Ibid., p.35.

87 Ibid., p.39.

88 Grady, *G.O. May*, p.52.

89 King and Malpas, *PW in South America*, pp.44, 61, 71.

90 PWA, Box 178, 'Report by F.S. Price on his Visit to South America' (typescript, 16 December 1936), p.11.

91 PWA, Box C11, 1920, letter from A.W. Wyon to PW New York, March 1920, p.2.

92 PWA, Minutes of the Partners' Meetings October 1936–September 1948, 7 October 1936, p.9.

93 Ibid.

Chapter 8

1 *Louis MacNeice, Selected Poems*, Faber and Faber, London (1988), p.67.

2 Arthur Marwick, *The Home Front, The British and the Second World War*, London (1976), pp. 20–21.

3 PWA, Partners' Meeting, 22 June 1939.

4 Nicholas A.H. Stacey, *English Accountancy 1800–1954*, London (1954), p.212.

5 PWA, Partners' Meeting, 7 September 1939.

6 Ibid.

7 PWA, 6/27, letter to PW New York from PW London, 4 December 1939.

8 Letter from PW London, 14 September 1939, reproduced from W.E. Parker, 'For J.P.P. Some Notes . . . and Some Lengthy Reminiscences' (typescript, 1974–7), opposite p.42.

9 Parker, 'For J.P.P.'.

10 PWA, 41/15, National Service Christmas Bonuses 1940–42.

11 PWA, Executive Committee, 17 October 1944.

12 PWA, 23/3, File 'Particulars of Service in the Armed Forces, Men Only' (1951).

13 PWA, 58/22, Folder 'War Memorial (1939–45)'.

14 Hilary Sparling, *Paul Scott, A Life*, London (1990), pp.136–7.

15 Sir William Slim, *Defeat into Victory*, London (1956), p.242.

16 S.M. Duncan, 'Personal Recollections' (typescript, n.d.), p.10.

17 *PW Quarterly*, Vol.4, No.2, Autumn 1971, p. 5; ibid., Spring 1981, obituary, p. 2.

18 Parker, 'For J.P.P.', p.58.

19 Ibid., p.64.

20 Ibid., p.65.

21 Ibid., p.66.

22 A.C. Falkner, 'Price Waterhouse & Co., History of the United Kingdom Firm, The Second Fifty Years 1900–1950', p.70.

23 Parker, 'For J.P.P.', p.70.

24 William Ashworth, *History of the Second World War, Contracts and Finance*, London HMSO (1953), p.118.

25 PWA, 6/11, letter from Sir Francis Freemantle to Sir Lawrence Halsey, 19 August 1939.

26 Parker, 'For J.P.P.', p.63.

27 Henry Benson, *Accounting for Life*, London (1989), pp.34, 36.

28 Sir Thomas B. Robson, 'Price Waterhouse and Myself 1923–1966' (typescript, April 1984), p.15.

29 *PWA*, Partners' Meeting, 6 August 1940.

30 Ibid., 29 October 1940.

31 PWA, Executive Committee, 'Memorandum to Staff', 31 October 1940.

32 PWA, Partners' Meeting, 29 October 1940.

33 PWA, Executive Committee, 'Effect of Aerial Attacks on Working Hours', 30 October 1940.

34 Duncan, 'Recollections', p.11.

35 PWA, Partners' Meeting, 7 September 1939.

36 Ibid., 13 December 1939.

37 PWA, Executive Committee, L.W. Shaw, 'Report on the Fire Damage to Premises', 14 May 1941.

38 PWA, 19/10, File 'No. 22 Shepherd's Hill, Highgate', Evacuation Plan by T.H. and F.E.W., 16 June 1941.

39 PWA, Partners' Meeting, 17 June 1941.

40 PWA, 19/10, letter from Price Waterhouse to E.G. Hastings, 6 September 1945.

41 PWA, Partners' Meeting, 22 August 1944.

42 Ibid., 19 September 1944.

43 PWA, 6/41, letter from PW London to PW Peat & Co. Buenos Aires, 13 December 1944.

44 Falkner, 'Second Fifty Years', p.71.

45 PWA, Partners' Meeting, 17 October 1944.

46 Ibid., 6 February 1939.

47 PWA, Executive Committee, 'Memo by M.C.Spencer', 12 June 1941.

48 Ibid.

49 PWA, Partners' Meeting, 17 June 1941.

50 Robson, 'Price Waterhouse and Myself', p.16.

51 PWA, Partners' Meeting, 17 June 1941.

52 PWA, Articles of Partnership, 18 May 1943.

53 PWA, Senior Partner's Box, T.B. Robson and G.E. Richards, 'Memorandum in regard to Certain Partnership Matters', 10 September 1941.

54 Ibid., p.1.

55 Ibid., pp.2–3.

56 Ibid., p.4.

57 Ibid., pp.8, 9.

58 Robson, 'Price Waterhouse and Myself', pp.52–3.

59 PWA, Partners' Meeting, 7 July 1942.

60 PWA, 1/41, Biographical Details L.H. Norman.

61 PWA, Partners' Meeting, 7 July 1942.

62 Ibid.

63 Falkner, 'Second Fifty Years', p.72.

64 Parker, 'For J.P.P.', p.83.

65 Ibid.

66 PWA, Partners' Meeting, 2 April 1940.

67 Ibid., 21 March 1944.

68 Marwick, *The Home Front*, p.133.

69 PWA, 41/41, Folder Girls' Calling-Up, Memo 'Women Staff and National Service' (typescript, 6 December 1943).

70 W.K. Hancock and M.M. Gowing, *British War Economy*, London HMSO (1949), p.163.

71 B.E.V. Sabine, *A Short History of Taxation*, London (1980), p.135.

72 PWA, Partners' Meeting, 6 August 1940.

73 Edgar Jones, *Accountancy and the British Economy 1840–1980, The Evolution of Ernst & Whinney*, London (1981), p.195.

74 PWA, Continental Firm, Partners' Meeting, 6–8 July 1938, p.7.

75 George Pollard, *A History of Price Waterhouse in Europe 1914–1969*, London (1975), p.32.

76 PWA, 21/5, letter from T.W. Webster to J.W.F. Neill, 20 February 1941; letter from W.E. Seatree to N.E. Waterhouse, 2 April 1941.

77 PWA, Continental Firm, Partners' Meeting 5–6 May 1939, p.2.

78 Ibid., p.4.

79 PWA, Continental Firm, Partners' Meeting, 18 August 1939, p.1.

80 Pollard, *PW in Europe*, p.33

81 Ibid., p.35.

82 Ibid., p.36.

83 PWA, 11/11, letter from W.E. Seatree to N.E. Waterhouse, 18 September 1940.

84 PWA, 16/22, letter from T.L. Ferguson to A.E. Jones, 24 October 1940.

85 Pollard, *PW in Europe*, p.34.

86 PWA, 10/14, Van der Burg, 'Memorandum . . . giving a brief summary of the resulting events since May 1940', pp.1–5.

87 Pollard, *PW in Europe*, pp.34, 41, 42.

88 PWA, Partners' Meeting, 6 August 1940.

89 PWA, Executive Committee, 'Memorandum re the Continental Firm', 24 June 1942, p.4.

90 Ibid., p.5.

91 PWA, Partners' Meeting, 7 July 1942.

92 PWA, Executive Committee, 'Memorandum', p.6.

93 Ibid., p.8.

94 PWA, letter from G.O. May, 56 Pine Street, New York, 5 August 1942.

95 Ibid.

96 Ibid.

97 PWA, Partners' Meeting, 30 November 1942.

98 PWA, Executive Committee, letter to Harold Evans from Fred Thompson, Stockholm, 21 September 1942.

99 Ibid., quoting letter from Seatree, 10 August 1942.

100 PWA, Partners' Meeting, 18 May 1943.

101 Ibid.

102 Pollard, *PW in Europe*, p.39.

103 Eric Bagge, *Off the Record, An Account of Price Waterhouse in Switzerland, up to June 21, 1987*, Geneva (1987), p.22.

104 Pollard, *PW in Europe*, p.40.

105 K. de Vylder and E. Cooke, *Price Waterhouse Sweden, the first 50 years*, Stockholm (1982), p.46.

106 PWA, 1/12, letter to T.L. Ferguson from H. Edwards and T.W. Webster, 30 January 1945.

107 PWA, Partners' Meeting, 20 March 1945.

108 PWA, 1/12, memorandum by MCS, 19 February 1945.

109 Ibid.

110 Pollard, *PW in Europe*, p.48.

111 PWA, 1/13, C.H. Evans, 'Re-opening of the French Practice' (typescript, 16 March 1945), p.1.

112 Pollard, *PW in Europe*, p.48.

113 PWA, Evans, 'Re-opening the French Practice', p.2.

114 Pollard, *PW in Europe*, p.43; Parker, 'For J.P.P', p.86.

115 PWA, Partners' Meeting, 17 July 1945.

116 Ibid.

117 Robson, 'Price Waterhouse and Myself', pp.37, 39.

118 Ibid., p.41.

Chapter 9

1 Anthony Sampson, *The Anatomy of Britain*, London (1962), p.466.

2 PWA, 9/8, *Price Waterhouse & Co., 1950 Centenary Dinner*.

3 PWA, 2/8, 'Notes of Speeches at the Centenary Dinner of Price Waterhouse & Co., p.3.

4 PWA, letter from F.S. Tull to N.E. Waterhouse, 3 January 1946.

5 PWA, Articles of Partnership, 18 May 1943; ibid., 23 January 1946.

6 PWA, Partners' Meeting, 18 December 1945.

7 PWA, Partners' Meeting, 15 January 1946.

8 A.C. Falkner, 'Price Waterhouse & Co., History of the United Kingdom Firm, The Second Fifty Years 1900–1950', p.76.

9 PWA, Partners' Meeting, 21 May 1946.

10 PWA, Articles of Partnership, 1949.

11 PWA, Senior Partner's Box, '1946 Arrangements Memorandum by TBR for a Special Committee', 26 December 1945, item 3(a) and (b).

12 Interview E. Jones with A.C. Falkner, 6 November 1989.

13 PWA, Partnership Minutes, '1951 Committee', 25 January 1951.

14 PWA, letter from F.S. Tull to N.E. Waterhouse, 3 January 1946.

15 PWA, letter from Sir Nicholas Waterhouse to 'My Dear Partners', 2 February 1951.

16 Ibid.

17 Ibid.

18 PWA, Partners' Meeting, 8 May 1953.

19 PWA, Partners' Meeting, 'Report of the 1954 Committee', May 1954, p.1.

20 PWA, Senior Partner's Box, 'Report of the 1956 Committee', 1 March 1956.

21 PWA, Senior Partner's Box, letter to A.E. Jones from G.E. Richards, 10 June 1945.

22 PWA, Collection of Partners' Comments, 10 October 1960.

23 PWA, Partners' Meeting, 1 May 1961, p.2.

24 The Accountant, Vol.CLII, No.4798, 2 January 1965, obituary, p.14.

25 PWA, Partnership Minutes, Vol.1, letter from N.E. Waterhouse to the partners, 27 September 1955.

26 Ibid., 'Note to all Partners' from T.B.R., 28 September 1955.

27 Ibid.

28 PWA, Partnership Minutes, Vol.2, 'Report of the 1960 Committee', 6 May 1960.

29 The Accountant, Vol. CLII, No.4798, Sir Thomas Robson, 'Appreciation', p.27.

30 Sir Nicholas E. Waterhouse 'Reminiscences 1877–1960' (typescript, 1961), p.97.

31 PWA, N.E. Waterhouse 'H.J.M.' (typescript biographical note, n.d.).

32 Waterhouse, 'Reminiscences 1877–1961', p.97.

33 Jeffery Meyers, The Enemy – A Biography of Wyndham Lewis, London (1980), p.152.

34 The Times, 30 December 1964, obituary.

35 Waterhouse, 'Reminiscences 1877–1961', pp.81–2, 86.

36 Advertisement: H.R. Harmer Ltd, 41 New Bond Street, sale on 27–30 June 1955.

37 Edgar Jones (ed.), The Memoirs of Edwin Waterhouse, A Founder of Price Waterhouse, London (1988), pp.172–3, pl.44.

38 PWA, Senior Partner's Box, letter from N.E. Waterhouse to Mrs Robson, 30 July 1953.

39 PWA, F.S. Tull to N.E. Waterhouse.

40 Information from J.M. Hamill, librarian, United Grand Lodge of England, 12 May 1992.

41 Interview E. Jones with M.A. Coates, 3 November 1989.

42 Interview E. Jones with M.R. Harris, 17 September 1990.

43 PWA, 23/3, File 'Particulars of Service in the Armed Forces'.

44 PWA, Box C11, Staff Notebook, Vol.3, p.226.

45 Interview E. Jones with W.G.K. Carter, 15 July 1991.

46 Ibid.

47 *PW Quarterly*, Vol.8, No.3, Autumn 1974, 'G.E.Richards', p.2.

48 Interview E. Jones with Mrs J. Pearce, 30 October 1990.

49 Interview E. Jones with M.A. Coates, 3 November 1989.

50 Interview E. Jones with M.R. Harris, 17 September 1990.

51 Interview E. Jones with M.A. Coates, 25 October 1990.

52 Interview E. Jones with Miss A. McDonald, 25 September 1990.

53 Interview E. Jones with W.G.K. Carter, 15 July 1991.

54 PWA, Partners' Meetings 1948–1956, '1949 Committee', 5 May 1949.

55 PWA, Senior Partner's Box, 'Managers' Meeting', 9 February 1951, III.

56 Ibid., III, (2).

57 Falkner,'Second Fifty Years', p.95.

58 Edgar Jones, *Accountancy and the British Economy 1840–1980, The Evolution of Ernst & Whinney*, London (1981), p.268.

59 PWA, 4/5, 'Report on the London Firm for 1953/54'.

60 Ibid., p.2.

61 PWA, Partners' Meeting, 3 December 1962.

62 Ibid., 3 December 1962.

63 Ibid., 25 October 1965.

64 Ibid., 17 September 1946.

65 Ibid.

66 Ibid., 1 December 1947.

67 Ibid., 30 January 1952.

68 *Seventy Five Years of Progress in Accountancy Education, H. Foulks Lynch & Co.*, London (1955).

69 PWA, 8/56, 'Brief for W.E.P.'s Talk to Articled Clerks on 17 January 1958', p.3.

70 PWA, Partners' Meeting, 17 September 1946.

71 PWA, 8/55, 'Recommendations for Articled Clerks' Studies' (typescript, 22 October 1957).

72 PWA, Partners' Meeting, 11 March 1948.

73 PWA, 4/5, 'Report on the London Firm for 1953/1954', p.3.

74 Michael Bishopp, 'Rebuilding of 3 Frederick's Place' in *PW Quarterly*, Vol.8, No.4, p.4.

75 PWA, Partners' Meeting, 'Report of 1961 on Certain Financial Matters', January 1962.

76 PWA, S.M. Duncan, 'Service Company', 1 March 1961.

77 PWA, Partners' Meeting, 'Report of the Ad Hoc Committee on Partnership Administration', 1 January 1964, pp.2–3.

78 PWA, Executive Committee, 18 February 1964, p.2.

79 Ibid., 1 April 1964, p.1.

80 PWA, Partners' Meeting, 1 May 1961, p.1.

81 PWA, Executive Committee, 'Note' by S.M. Duncan, 11 August 1964.

82 PWA, Executive Committee, 'Provision of Technical Information', 24 November 1964.

83 PWA, Senior Partner's Box, 'Staff Pension Scheme', June 1950.

84 PWA, 2/7, *Price Waterhouse & Co., Pension Arrangements*, November 1964, p.3.

85 PWA, Partners' Meeting, 8 July 1947.

86 Sir Thomas B. Robson, 'Price Waterhouse and Myself 1923–1966' (typescript, April 1984), p.22.

87 PWA, Partners' Meeting, 11 March 1948.

88 Interview E. Jones with D. Booth, J.W. Alsop and R. Lovely, 19 August 1991.

89 PWA, 17/10, 'List of Principal Clients arranged by Partner', 6 September 1946.

90 D.C. Coleman, *Courtaulds, An Economic and Social History, Vol. III, 1940–1965*, Oxford (1980), p.218.

91 Ibid., p.224.

92 PWA, 32/18, Analysis of New Work 1957–1963.

93 PWA, Partners' Minutes, Vol.3, 1963–1967, 'Systems Department, Memorandum by Standing Committee', 8 May 1963.

94 PWA, 32/18, Analysis of New Work 1957–1963.

95 PWA, Partners' Newsletter No.6, 10 November 1967, 'Analysis of MCS Assignments for 6 Years to 31 December 1966'.

96 Robson, 'Price Waterhouse and Myself', p.29.

97 J.R. Edwards, *A History of Financial Accounting*, London (1989), p.208.

98 Ibid.

99 Ibid.

100 Robson, 'Price Waterhouse and Myself', p.29.

101 Paragraph 5 of the *Cohen Committee on Company Law Amendment Report*, BPP 1945, IV, 793.

102 Edwards, *Financial Accounting*, p.209.

103 Sir Harold Howitt, 'The Profession of Accounting' in *The Accountant*, Vol.CXXII, No.3934, 13 May 1950, p.537.

104 PWA, Partners' Meeting, 11 March 1948.

105 Sir Thomas Robson, 'Professional Ethics' in *The Accountant*, Vol. CXXXII, No.4184, 26 February 1955, p.237.

106 Ibid.

107 Jones, *Accountancy and the British Economy*, pp.256–60.

108 PMM, 'Firm's offices' (typescript, *c.* 1957).

109 PMM, 'Middlesbrough office' (typescript, 23 April 1959).

110 PWA, Partners' Meeting, 10 September 1962.

111 PWA, Douglas Sandry, 'Notes for KJM' (typescript, 14 April 1975).

112 Interview E. Jones with Douglas Sandry, 15 July 1991.

113 Ibid.

114 PWA, Executive Committee, 7 July 1964.

115 PWA, 2/4, '1867–1967, The First Hundred Years, Howard Smith Thompson & Co.' (typescript, November 1967), pp.1–2.

116 Ibid., p.9.

117 PWA, Partners' Meeting, 28 September 1963, p.3.

118 'Our 125th Anniversary' in *PW Quarterly*, Vol.7, No.1, Spring 1974, p.5.

119 PWA, Executive Committee, 7 July 1964.

120 PWA, 7/23, 'Memorandum by W.B. Morrison on the Development of the Glasgow Office of Price Waterhouse' (typescript, December 1983), p.1.

121 Ibid., p.2.

122 Falkner, 'The Second Fifty Years', p.81.

123 PWA, 'Memorandum by W.B. Morrison', pp.3, 4, 6.

124 Information provided by local history library, Leeds Central Library, 4 January 1993.

125 PWA, 11/8, P.N. Turner, 'Brief Details of Career with Price Waterhouse 1946–1976' (typescript, 1985), pp.1, 3, 4.

126 PWA, 8/25, Douglas Sandry, 'Reminiscences' [n.d.], p.3.

127 Interview E. Jones with D. Booth, R. Lovely and J.W. Alsop, 19 August 1991.

128 PWA, *Articles of Partnership of the Newcastle Partnership, 1939.*

129 Newcastle office, 'Record Book P.W.& Co., Newcastle upon Tyne', 1959, J.M.S. Coates.

130 Information provided by the librarian, United Grand Lodge of England, 12 May 1992.

131 PWA, Partners' Meeting, '1951 Committee', 11 April 1951.

132 PWA, Senior Partner's Box, 'Report of the Committee on Newcastle Partnership Position', 7 September 1960.

133 PWA, Senior Partner's Box, 'Report by the 1960–61 Committee', 17 April 1961.

134 PWA, Senior Partner's Box, 'Newcastle Partnership Arrangements' by T.B.R., 13 May 1958.

135 PWA, Executive Committee, 26 May 1964, 7 July 1964.

136 PWA, Continental Firm, Partners' Meeting, 11–15 September 1945, p.1;

G.B. Pollard, *A History of Price Waterhouse in Europe 1914–1969*, London (1975), p.48.

137 Pollard, *PW in Europe*, p.49.

138 PWA, Continental Firm, Partners' Meeting, 1–6 July 1946, pp.1–2.

139 Ibid., p.50.

140 Ibid.

141 Interview E. Jones with Sir Richard Brooke, 11 December 1990.

142 PWA, European Firm, Partners' Meeting, 11–13 December 1947, p.1.

143 Interview E. Jones with Sir Richard Brooke, 11 December 1990.

144 PWA, European Firm, Partners' Meeting, 11–13 December 1947, p.5.

145 Ibid., 21–25 June 1949, Appendix A, p.1.

146 Ibid., p.2.

147 Eric Bagge, *Off the Record, An Account of Price Waterhouse in Switzerland up to June 21, 1987*, Geneva (1987), p.30.

148 Pollard, *PW in Europe*, p.52.

149 PWA, European Firm, Partners' Meeting, 4–6 July 1951, Appendix H.

150 Pollard, *PW in Europe*, pp.54–5.

151 Ibid., p.57.

152 Ibid., p.58.

153 Ibid., p.62.

154 PWA, European Firm, Partners' Meeting, 15–17 June 1955, Appendix A, p.1.

155 Ibid., Appendix B, p.1.

156 PWA, 27/6, File 'Continental Weekly Staff Summaries 1945–1953'.

157 Pollard, *PW in Europe*, p.62.

158 Ibid., p.72.

159 PWA, European Firm, Partners' Meeting, 1–2 December 1960, p.50.

160 PWA, European Firm, Partners' Meeting, 21–23 June 1961, p.1.

161 Ibid., Appendix A, p.1.

162 Ibid., pp. 72–3.

Chapter 10

1 D.F.Channon, 'Corporate Evolution in the Service Industries' in L.Hannah (ed.), *Management Strategy and Business Development*, London (1976), p.214.

2 Sir Thomas Robson, 'Price Waterhouse and Myself 1923–1966', p.53.

3 PWA, Executive Committee, 6 April 1965: T.B. Robson 'Method of Choosing Future Senior Partner' (4 January 1965).

4 Ibid.

5 PWA, Executive Committee, 6 April 1965: 'Comment by W.E.P. on T.B.R.'s Note', 27 January 1965.

6 *PW Quarterly*, Spring 1981, obituary, p.2.

7 Interview E. Jones with M.A. Coates, 25 October 1990.

8 Interview E. Jones with Lord Benson, 30 March 1992.

9 W.E. Parker, 'Notes for J.P.P. Some Notes ... and Some Lengthy Reminiscences' (typescript, 1974–7), p.108.

10 *Who's Who*, London (1973), p.2476.

11 PWA, 'Staff Notebook', Vol.3, p.65.

12 PWA, Partners' Meeting, 2 June 1966.

13 Ibid., 4–6 June 1970, p.1.

14 *PW Quarterly*, Vol.4, No.2, Autumn 1971, p.3.

15 Interview E. Jones with M.A. Coates, 3 November 1989.

16 *Price Waterhouse Annual Report*, June 1974, p.4.

17 PWA, Partners' Meeting, 6–7 December 1973, p.1.

18 *Who's Who*, London (1989), p.350.

19 PWA, Executive Committee, W.E.P., 'Admissions to the Partnership', 20 April 1966.

20 PWA, Partners' Meeting, 3–4 December 1970, pp.4–5.

21 Ibid., 10 June 1971, p.5.

22 Letter to E. Jones from Sir Jeffery Bowman, 9 August 1993.

23 PWA, Policy Committee, 13–14 May 1975, 57/75.

24 *PW Quarterly*, Winter 1975, 'John Read Departs', p.2.

25 Interview E. Jones with J.L. Read, 11 March 1991.

26 Letter to E. Jones from Sir Jeffery Bowman, 9 August 1993.

27 PWA, Executive Committee, 'Organisation, Report by the Standing Committee to the Executive Committee', 15 March 1965.

28 Ibid.

29 Letter to E. Jones from Michael Coates, 7 March 1994.

30 PWA, 189/2, File 'Organisation': AHC 'Control of Audit Staff in London Office', 6 July 1965, p.3.

31 PWA, 'Talk given by W.E. Parker to members of the London Staff' (typescript 21 December 1966), p.3.

32 PWA, AHC, 'Control of Audit Staff', pp.6, 9.

33 PWA, 'Talk by W.E. Parker', pp.3–4.

34 Interview E. Jones with John Garnett, 21 September 1992.

35 *PW Quarterly*, Vol.5, No.2, Autumn 1972, p.11.

36 PWA, 189/2, 'Organisation', W.E.P., 'Organisation of the London Partnership', 17 January 1966, p.1.

37 PWA, Partners' Meeting, 8 December 1966.

38 Interview E. Jones with W.G.K. Carter, 15 July 1991; *The Reporter*, No.60, October 1988, p.4.

39 Interview E. Jones with A.G. Campbell, 16 April 1991.

40 *PW Quarterly*, Vol.5, No.2, Autumn 1972, 'The National Organisation of the UK Firm', p.11.

41 PWA, Partners' Meeting, 6–9 June 1973, M.A. Coates 'The Firm in the Future', 20 June 1973, p.1.

42 Ibid.

43 Ibid., p.2.

44 Ibid.

45 PWA, Policy Committee, 13–14 November 1973, 109/73, Growth to 1980.

46 PWA, M.A. Coates 'The Firm in the Future' (typescript for the Policy Committee, October 1973), p.2.

47 Ibid., p.4.

48 Ibid., pp.7, 8, 9.

49 PWA, Partners' Newsletter, Vol.4, No.7, 15 November 1968, pp.1, 4.

50 *PW Quarterly*, Vol.8, No.2, Summer 1975, p.27.

51 *Price Waterhouse Annual Review 1983–84*, pp.8, 9, 11, 12.

52 Tony Martin, 'The Top Twenty UK Firms' in *Accountants Weekly*, 20 June 1979, p.25.

53 *Price Waterhouse Annual Review 1987–88*, p.4.

54 PWA, Executive Committee, 'Report of the National Staff Committee', 24 May 1966.

55 Ibid.

56 PWA, 43/2, 'Report by P.L.A. on Staff Planning' (typescript, 14 June 1968), pp.4–5.

57 PWA, 45/12, UK Partners' Meeting, Bournemouth, 4–7 June 1969, 'Managers – Status, Training and Functions' (typescript 9 June 1969),p.1.

58 PWA, Partners' Meeting, 10 June 1971, p.5.

59 Ibid., 2–3 December 1971, p.7.

60 Interview E. Jones with P.L. Ainger, 25 September 1990.

61 Interview E. Jones with M.D. Phillips and B. Mason, 17 January 1991.

62 PWA, 8/63, 'Memorandum for Partners' Meeting on 8 May 1963, Staff Training' by M.R. Harris.

63 PWA, Executive Committee, T.R. Watts, 'Report on Audit Staff Training', 22 July 1966.

64 PWA, 46/14, J.H. Bowman 'Staff Training in the United States Firm'.

65 PWA, Policy Committee, 15–16 May 1973, 67/73.

66 Interview E. Jones with Matthew de Lange, 16 May 1991.

67 PWA, General Committee, 30 January 1967, p.6.

68 Ibid., 29 September 1967, p.5.

69 PWA, 8/72, T.R. Watts, 'London Office Articled Clerks, 1965'.

70 PWA, 8/72, G.C. Francis, 'Oxford University Appointments Committee: Price Waterhouse, 1967'.

71 PWA, Partners' Newsletter, No.14, 18 June 1968, p.1.

72 PWA, Partners' Meeting, 6–8 June 1968, p.8.

73 Interview E. Jones with I.A.C. Macpherson, 7 February 1991.

74 PWA, 12/5, *Facts about your Future with Price Waterhouse & Co.* (*c*.1972).

75 Interview E. Jones with R.A. Shervington, 1 November 1990.

76 Leon Hopkins, *The Hundredth Year*, Plymouth (1980), p.42.

77 *Financial Times Survey*, 13 May 1980, p.iv.

78 PWA, Executive Committee, 1 February 1965, 'Taxation Services', 15 February 1965.

79 H.H. Monroe, *British Tax Review*, No.5 (1979), 'Fiscal Statutes: A Drafting Disaster', p.269.

80 Ibid.

81 PWA, Executive Committee, 6 May 1966, 'Management Consultancy', 4 May 1966.

82 PWA, General Committee, 21 March 1969, p.7, Appendix I.

83 Ibid.

84 PWA, General Committee, 26 March 1971, p.6.

85 Interview E. Jones with E.W. Barnes, 6 July 1992.

86 PWA, General Committee, 17 November 1971, p.7.

87 Ibid., 24 March 1972, p.4.

88 Ibid.

89 PWA, Policy Committee, 18 July 1973, 76/73.

90 *The Accountant*, Vol.CLIX, No.4903, 7 December 1968, obituary, p.771.

91 PWA, 4/8, R.F. Hellis, 'Reminiscences of my Early Years with PW & Co.', (typescript, n.d.), pp.3–4.

92 PWA, Staff Notebook, Vol.3, p.63.

93 PWA, Press Cuttings, Vol.II 1968–1969, *Evening Standard*, 29 November 1968.

94 Ibid., Clive Borrell, 'Hunt for Shot Man's Double' in *The Times*, 30 November 1968.

95 Ibid., *Daily Telegraph*, 17 April 1969, p.25.

96 PWA, General Committee, 17 March 1967, pp.5–6.

97 Ibid., 14 April 1969, p.2.

98 *The Accountant*, Vol.161, No.4945, 27 September 1969, p.407.

99 Interview E. Jones with A.M. Homan, 29 October 1990.

100 PWA, General Committee, 17 March 1967, p.1; 30 January 1967, p.8.

101 PWA, Partners' Meeting, 4–6 June 1970, p.14.

102 PWA, 48/1, 'Development of the Price Waterhouse Style of Notepaper', 4 March 1964.

103 PWA, General Committee, 21 March 1969, p.8.

104 Ibid., 11 November 1969, p.17.

105 Ibid., 26 March 1971, p.10.

106 Ibid., 26 March 1968, p.6.

107 Ibid., 16 May 1969, p.3.

108 Ibid., 15 May 1970, p.6.

109 Ibid.

110 PWA, 12/12, Neville Cheadle, *Southwark Towers, A Case History in Project Management* (reprinted from *Accountancy Ireland*).

111 PWA, General Committee, 17–18 November 1970, p.8.

112 *PW Quarterly*, Vol.3, No.3, Winter 1970, p.5.

113 Ibid., Vol.6, No.3 Autumn 1973, p.2.

114 PWA, 196/4, M.A. Coates' file, 'Southwark Towers Art Objects Working Party' (1974–9).

115 *PW Quarterly*, Vol.6, No.4, Winter 1973, pp.16, 17.

116 *PW Quarterly*, Vol.2, No.1, Summer 1969, p.4.

117 PWA, Partners' Meeting, 6 December 1968, p.8.

118 *PW Quarterly*, Vol.9, No.3, Autumn 1975, pp.16–17.

119 *Price Waterhouse Annual Report June 1975*, p.4.

120 PWA, General Committee, 14 January 1971, p.6.

121 PWA, Partners' Newsletter, Vol.8, No.22, 13 July 1971, p.1.

122 Mark Stevens, *The Big Eight*, New York (1981), p.2.

123 R.J. Briston, 'The UK Accountancy Profession – the Move towards Monopoly Power' in *The Accountant's Magazine*, November 1979, pp.458–9.

124 Ibid.

125 *Accountants Weekly*, 20 June 1979, p.25.

126 Henry Benson, *Accounting for Life*, London (1989), p.143.

127 PWA, 221/8, 'Memorandum for the Partners of Price Waterhouse & Co., Rolls Razor Limited' (typescript, 13 December 1967), p.6.

128 Sir Kenneth Cork, *Cork on Cork*, London (1988), p.61.

129 Ibid., p.63.

130 Ibid., p.69.

131 PWA, 221/15, J.H. Bowman, 'Note to the Policy Committee', 26 February 1976.

132 PWA, 58/12, C.H. Bailey and G.H. Holmes, 'The Companies Act, 1967' (typescript, 2 November 1967), p.2.

133 J.R. Edwards, *A History of Financial Accounting*, London (1989), p.210.

134 Christopher Nobes and R.H. Parker, 'Landmarks in Accounting History' in *Accountancy*, June 1979, p.41.

135 *The Guardian*, 30 July 1968, 'AEI results £14½ million down on forecast'.

136 PWA, Partners' Newsletter, Vol.3, No.20, 6 August 1968.

137 Ibid.

138 Joe Haines, *Maxwell*, London (1988), p.300.

139 Tom Bower, *Maxwell, The Outsider*, London (1988), p.178.

140 PWA, Partners' Newsletter, Vol.5, No.18, 22 September 1969, p.1.

141 Bower, *Maxwell*, p.201.

142 Interview E. Jones with M.R. Harris, 17 September 1990.

143 Bower, *Maxwell*, p.202.

144 Ibid., p.213.

145 Ibid., p.214.

146 Interview E. Jones with M.R. Harris, 17 September 1990.

147 Nobes and Parker, 'Landmarks in Accounting History', p.41.

148 PWA, Policy Committee, 30 July 1975, 109/75.

149 Ibid., 6–7 October 1975, p.8.

150 Ibid., p.9.

151 M. Hallissey, 'Our Worldwide Organisation, A Perspective' (typescript, July 1988), p.32.

152 Ibid., p.33.

153 PWA, European Firm, Partners' Meeting, 19–21 May 1965, p.3.

154 Ibid., 28–30 March 1963, p.4.

155 Ibid., 19–21 June 1963, Appendix B, p.3.

156 Ibid., 5–6 December 1968, p.9.

157 Ibid.

158 Interview E. Jones with Sir Richard Brooke, 11 December 1990.

159 Eric Bagge, *Off the Record, An Account of Price Waterhouse in Switzerland*, Geneva (1987), p.38.

160 Interview E. Jones with P. Granger and A. Peddle, 31 March 1992.

161 D.G. Allen and K. McDermott, *Accounting for Success, A History of Price Waterhouse in America 1890–1990*, Boston (1993), p.199.

Chapter 11

1 PWA, Partners' Meeting, 2–4 November 1976, p.16.

2 *Price Waterhouse Annual Report* (1975), p.5.

3 *PW Quarterly*, Summer 1979, pp.2–3.

4 Interview E. Jones with M.A. Coates, 25 October 1990.

5 Letter to E. Jones from Sir Jeffery Bowman, 9 August 1993.

6 Letter to E. Jones from Ian Mills, 12 August 1993.

7 *PW Quarterly*, Winter 1982–83, p.1.

8 PWA, Partners' Meeting, 5–6 January 1982, p.2.

9 *PW Quarterly*, Winter 1982–3, p.2.

10 M. Hallissey, 'Our Worldwide Organisation, A Perspective' (typescript, July 1988), p.5.

11 Derek F. Channon, *The Strategy and Structure of British Enterprise*, London (1973), p.67.

12 Hallissey, 'Worldwide Organisation', pp.5, 6.

13 Interview E. Jones with I.L.B. Vaile, 14 September 1990.

14 *Price Waterhouse Annual Report* (1979–80), p.7.

15 Interview E. Jones with Andrew Lawton, 23 April 1990.

16 PWA, 212/6, 'Five Year Development Plan: Tax' (typescript, 1975), p.6.

17 PWA, Partners' Meeting, 17 December 1980, p.12.

18 PWA, Partners' Newsletter, Vol.1, No.3, 15 March 1967, p.2.

19 John Orbell, 'The Development of Office Technology' in Alison Turton, *Managing Business Archives*, London (1991), p.8

20 Hallissey, 'Worldwide Organisation', p.6.

21 *Price Waterhouse Annual Report* (1979–80), p.7.

22 Interview E. Jones with E.W. Barnes, 6 July 1992.

23 Ibid.

24 *Price Waterhouse Annual Report* (1979–80), p.7.

25 Interview E. Jones with E.W. Barnes, 6 July 1992.

26 PWA, 212/7, 'MCS Development Plan 1974–1979' (typescript, 15 February 1974), p.7.

27 Interview E. Jones with E.W. Barnes, 6 July 1992.

28 PWA, 212/7. 'MCS Development Plan', p.7.

29 Ibid., p.2.

30 *Price Waterhouse Annual Report* (1979–80), p.7.

31 Interview E. Jones with R.J. Walls, 26 February 1991.

32 Ibid.

33 *Price Waterhouse Annual Report* (1979–80), p.9.

34 Ibid. (1975), p.11.

35 Interview E. Jones with A.M. Homan, 29 October 1990.

36 Interview E. Jones with B.A. Baldwin, 18 April 1991.

37 Interview E. Jones with K. Bell, 4 November 1992.

38 *Price Waterhouse Annual Report* (1978), p.10.

39 PWA, 11/27, *Price Waterhouse Chartered Accountants and Management Consultants* (1985), p.23.

40 Interview E. Jones with M.D. Phillips, 17 January 1991.

41 Interview E. Jones with Matthew de Lange, 16 May 1991.

42 PWA, 230/19, M. Hallissey, 'Price Waterhouse International, Corporate Identity Programme' (typescript, August 1979), p.5.

43 PWA, Partners' Meeting, 17 December 1980, p.5.

44 Ibid., pp.9, 10.

45 Interview E. Jones with R.D. Sandry, 28 February 1991.

46 Interview E. Jones with S.E. Hurley, 25 April 1991.

47 Michael Lafferty, 'The Accountants' Big Bang' in David Rowe (ed.), *The Irish Chartered Accountant, Centenary Essays 1888–1988*, Dublin (1988), p.89.

48 Letter to E. Jones from C.P. Nielsen, 13 July 1990.

49 PWA, Partners' Newsletter, Vol.6, No.19, 28 May 1970, p.2.

50 PWA, Partners' Meeting, 8–9 November 1977.

51 Interview E. Jones with G.H. Stacy, 19 August 1990.

52 *Financial Times*, 13 May 1980.

53 Henry Benson, *Accounting for Life*, London (1989), p.161.

54 Christopher Nobes and R.H. Parker, 'Landmarks in Accounting History' in *Accountancy* (1979), p.42.

55 *Price Waterhouse Annual Report* (1976), p.11.

56 Ibid. (1977), p.6.

57 Ibid. (1975), p.6.

58 Ibid. (1976), p.11; *Price Waterhouse Annual Review* (1982–83), p.23.

59 Interview E. Jones with W.G.K. Carter, 15 July 1991.

60 PWA, Partners' Meeting, 10–11 December 1979.

61 Ibid.

62 Interview E. Jones with Sir Jeffery Bowman, 24 January 1991.

63 PWA, Partners' Meeting, 15 December 1983.

64 Interview E. Jones with P. Granger and A. Peddle, 31 March 1992.

65 D.G. Allen and K. McDermott, *Accounting for Success, A History of Price Waterhouse in America 1890–1990*, Boston (1993), p.239.

66 Interview E. Jones with P.L. Ainger, 25 September 1990.

Epilogue

1 *The Reporter*, Special Edition, December 1988, 'Review of the Year', p.2.

2 *The Reporter*, No.109, November 1992, p.1.

3 PWA, 'Background to the UK Firm's Strategy' (typescript, November 1983), p.4.

4 *Price Waterhouse Annual Review* (1981–82), pp.6–7.

5 Ibid. (1986–7), p.5.

6 *The Reporter*, December 1988, p.2.

7 Ibid., No.109, November 1992, p.2.

8 Interview E. Jones with I.L.B. Vaile, 14 September 1990.

9 Interview E. Jones with E.N. Cheadle, 8 October 1990.

10 Interview E. Jones with P.J. Kiernan, 20 November 1990.

11 Interview E. Jones with R.J. Walls, 26 February 1991.

12 Interview E. Jones with H.J. Hyman, 5 March 1991.

13 *The Reporter*, No.98, December 1991, p.3; Ibid., No.109, November 1992, p.2.

14 PWA, Michael Hallissey, 'Our Worldwide Organisation, A Perspective' (typescript, July 1988), p.6.

15 Ibid., p.7.

16 PWA, 'The UK Firm's Strategy, From the Senior Partner' (typescript, November 1983), p.1.

17 Ibid., p.2.

18 Ibid.

19 Ibid., p.5.

20 Ibid.

21 Ibid., p.7.

22 Ibid., p.8.

23 PWA, 'Background to the UK Firm's Strategy' (typescript, November 1983), p.42.

24 PWA, 'UK Firm's Strategy', p.8.

25 Ibid., p.4.

26 Interview E. Jones with Naomi Stanford, 4 April 1991.

27 Interview E. Jones with M.E. Black, 14 January 1991.

28 PWA, 'UK Firm's Strategy', p.2.

29 Ibid., p.1.

30 PWA, 212/17, J.H. Bowman 'The UK Firm – The Next Stage in Our Development' (typescript, 27 March 1985), p.2.

31 Ibid., p.3.

32 Interview E. Jones with M.A. Coates, 3 November 1989.

33 D.G. Allen and K. McDermott, *Accounting for Success, A History of Price Waterhouse in America 1890–1990*, Boston (1993), p.228.

34 Ibid.

35 PWA, Hallissey 'Our Worldwide Organisation', p.50.

36 Letter to E. Jones from Ian Mills, 12 August 1993.

37 PWA, Hallissey, 'Our Worldwide Organisation', p.51.

38 Allen and McDermott, *Accounting for Success*, p.246.

39 *The Reporter*, No.72, October 1989, p.1.

40 Interview E. Jones with Ian Brindle and John Salmon, 31 January 1991.

41 Interview E. Jones with Graham Stacy, 22 July 1993.

42 *Inquiry into the Supervision of the Bank of Credit and Commerce International*, London HMSO (1992).

43 PWA, 'Background to the UK Firm's Strategy', p.26.

44 Interview E. Jones with Lord Benson, 30 March 1992; and interview E.Jones with Sir Ronald Leach, 5 May 1992.

45 Interview E. Jones with Tony Mallinson, 12 May 1992.

46 Letter to E. Jones from Sir Jeffery Bowman, 9 August 1993.

Sources

MANUSCRIPT SOURCES

The references to the individual chapters should be consulted for a detailed note of the original sources employed. Price Waterhouse have their own archive and this was the principal repository for the study. Those wishing to consult this should apply in writing to the Archivist, Price Waterhouse, Southwark Towers, 32 London Bridge Street, London SE1 9SY. The following record offices, libraries and institutions were also of particular value: Bristol Record Office, Bristol Local History Library, British Library, Business Archives Council, Business History Unit, Guildhall Library, Institute of Chartered Accountants in England and Wales, Manchester Central Library, Public Record Office, Kew, Royal Commission on the Historical Monuments of England, Society of Friends' Library.

JOURNALS

Abacus
Accountancy
The Accountant
The Accountant's Magazine

Accountants Weekly
Accounting and Business Research
Business History
The Economic History Review

PERSONAL RECOLLECTIONS

The following is a list of retired partners and staff of Price Waterhouse who generously agreed to be interviewed:

Peter Ainger
J.W. Alsop
Barry Baldwin
Ernest Barnes
Sir Richard Brooke
Alec Campbell
Michael Carr
Neville Cheadle
Michael Coates

Stanley Duncan
Clifford Falkner
John Fraser
Marmion Garnsey
Patrick Giffin
Eric Gregson
Martin Harris
A.M. Inglis
Ronald Lovely

Ann McDonald

Ian Macpherson

James Mennell

Charles Merriman

Keith Milligan

Dominic Morland

Mrs J. Pearce

David Prosser

John Read

R.H.G. Redshaw

Sir Thomas Robson

Douglas Sandry

George Scheu

J.B. Sewell

Dick Shervington

Eric Walton

Sir Anthony Wilson

Select Bibliography

Allen, David Grayson and McDermott, Kathleen (1993). *Accounting for Success, A History of Price Waterhouse in America 1890–1990*, Harvard Business School Press, Boston, Massachusetts.

Anon. (1955). *Seventy Years of Progress in Accountancy Education, H. Foulks Lynch & Co. Ltd*, London.

Anon. (1965). 'History of the Firm, A.F. Ferguson & Co.' (unpub.).

Anon. (1974). *Harmood Banner & Co., 1805-1974, The Story of a Firm of Chartered Accountants*, London.

Anon. (1974). *The First Sixty Years 1913–1973, Arthur Andersen & Co*, Chicago.

Anon. (1988). *Hill Vellacott, An Historical Account of their Development since 1780*, London.

Arnold, A.J. (1991). 'Secret Reserves or Special Credits? A Reappraisal of the Reserve and Provision Accounting Policies of the Royal Mail Steam Packet Company, 1915–27' in *Accounting and Business Research*, 21.

Ashton, R.K. (1986). 'The Royal Mail Case: A Legal Analysis' in *Abacus*, 22.

Ashworth, William (1953). *History of the Second World War, Contracts and Finance*, HMSO, London.

Bagge, Eric (1987). *Off the Record, An Account of Price Waterhouse in Switzerland up to June 21, 1987*, Price Waterhouse, Geneva.

Baxter, W.T. and Davidson, Sidney (eds.) (1977). *Studies in Accounting*, Sweet & Maxwell, London.

[Benson, Henry] (1954). *A History of Cooper Brothers and Co. 1854–1954*, B.T. Batsford, London.

Benson, [Lord] Henry (1989). *Accounting for Life*, ICAEW, London.

Boys, P.G. (1982). 'The Image of Accountants' in *Accountants Magazine*, 86.

Boys, P.G. (1989). 'Somerset Maugham: Accountant in Bondage' (unpub.).

Boys, Peter (1989). 'What's in a Name' in *Accountancy*, 103.

Brief, Richard P. (1966). 'The Origin and Evolution of Nineteenth Century Asset Accounting' in *Business History Review*, XL.

Briston, R.J. (1979). 'The UK Accountancy Profession – The Move towards Monopoly Power' in *The Accountant's Magazine*, LXXXIII.

Brooks, Collin (ed.) (1933). *The Royal Mail Case*, William Hodge & Co., Edinburgh.

Brown, Richard (1905). *A History of Accounting and Accountants*, Edinburgh.

Bywater, Michael (1985). 'William Quilter (1808–1888)' in *Dictionary of Business Biography*, 4.

Bywater, Michael (1986). 'Josiah Charles Stamp (1880–1941)' in *Dictionary of Business Biography*, 4.

Bywater, Michael and Yamey, B.S. (1982). *Historic Accounting Literature: A Companion Guide*, Scholar Press, London.

Carlisle, Nicholas (1837). *A Memoir of the Life and Works of William Wyon*, London.

Carr-Saunders, A.M. and Wilson, P.A. (1933). *The Professions*, OUP, Oxford.

Chandler, A.D. (1977). *The Visible Hand, The Managerial Revolution in American Business*, Harvard University Press, Cambridge, Massachusetts.

Channon, D.F. (1973). *The Strategy and Structure of British Enterprise*, London.

Channon, D.F. (1978). *The Service Industries, Strategy, Structure and Financial Performance*, London.

Chatfield, Michael (1977). *A History of Accounting Thought*, Robert E. Krieger Publishing, New York.

Chatfield, Michael (1978). *The English View of Accountants' Duties and Responsibilities 1881–1902*, Arno Press, New York.

Cooke, C.A. (1950). *Corporation Trust and Company*, Manchester.

Cooper, Ernest (1921). 'Fifty-seven Years in an Accountant's Office' in *ICAEW Proceedings*, October.

Cork, Sir Kenneth (1988). *Cork on Cork*, Macmillan, London.

Cottrell, P.L. (1979). *Industrial Finance 1830–1914, The Finance and Organization of English Manufacturing Industry*, Methuen, London.

Cutforth, A.E. (1931). *Audits*, 8th edn, Gee & Co., London.

Davenport-Hines, R.P.T. (1985). 'Sir Mark Webster Jenkinson (1880–1935)' in *Dictionary of Business Biography*, 3.

De Mond, C.W. (1951). *Price, Waterhouse & Co. in America, A History of a Public Accounting Firm*, Comet Press, New York.

De Paula, F.R.M. (1934). 'The Form and Presentation of the Accounts of Holding Companies' in *The Accountant*, XCI.

De Paula, F.R.M. (1948). *Developments in Accounting*, London.

De Vylder, K. and Cooke, E. (1982). *Price Waterhouse Sweden, the first 50 years*, Price Waterhouse, Stockholm.

Dennett, Laurie (1989). *Slaughter and May, A Century in the City*, Granta Editions, Cambridge.

Dickens, Charles (1857). *Little Dorrit*, Bradbury & Evans, London.

Dickinson, Arthur Lowes (1908). *Accounting Practice and Procedures*, 3rd edn, New York.

Dicksee, L.R. (1892). *Auditing, a Practical Manual for Auditors*, Gee & Co., London.

Dicksee, L.R. (1897). *The Student's Guide to Accountancy*, London.

Dicksee, L.R. (1915). *Business Methods and the War*, CUP, Cambridge.

Duffy, I.P.H. (1973). 'Bankruptcy and Insolvency in London in the late Eighteenth and early Nineteenth Centuries' (Oxford University D.Phil. thesis, unpub.).

Edey, H.C. and Panitpakdi, Prot (1956). 'British Company Accounting and the Law 1844–1900' in *Studies in the History of Accounting*.

Edwards, J.R. (1981). *Company Legislation and Changing Patterns of Disclosure in British Company Accounts 1900–1940*, ICAEW, London.

Edwards, J.R. (1984). 'Sir Arthur Lowes Dickinson (1859–1935)' in *Dictionary of Business Biography*, 2.

Edwards, J.R. (1984). 'Sir Gilbert Garnsey (1883–1932)' in *Dictionary of Business Biography*, 2.

Edwards, J.R. (ed.) (1984). *Studies of Company Records 1830–1974*, Garland Publishing, New York.

Edwards, J.R. (1985). 'The Origin and Evolution of the Double Account System' in *Abacus*, 21.

Edwards, J.R. (1986). 'Edwin Waterhouse (1841–1917)' in *Dictionary of Business Biography*, 5.

Edwards, J.R. (1989). *A History of Financial Accounting*, Routledge, London.

Edwards, J.R. and Baber, Colin (1978). 'Dowlais Iron Company: Accounting Policies and Procedures for Profit Measurement and Reporting Purposes' in *Accounting and Business Research*, 9.

Emden, Paul H. (1939). *Quakers in Commerce, A Record of Business Achievement*, Sampson, Low, Maston & Co., London.

Falkner, A.C. (1970). 'Price Waterhouse & Co., History of the United Kingdom Firm, The Second Fifty Years 1900–1950' (unpub.).

Farmar, Tony (1988). *A History of Craig, Gardner & Co., The First 100 Years*, Gill and Macmillan, Dublin.

Fielding, Raymond (1992). 'Accounting Practices in the Early American Motion Picture Industry' in *Historical Journal of Film, Radio and Television*, 12.

Fleischman, Richard K. and Tyson, Thomas N. (1993). 'Cost Accounting during the Industrial Revolution: the Present State of Historical Knowledge' in *Economic History Review*, XLVI.

Forrer, Leonard (1917). *The Wyons*, Spink & Son, London.

Fry, Edward (ed.) (1894). *Theodore Waterhouse 1838–1891, Notes of His Life and Extracts from His Letters and Papers*, Chiswick Press, London.

Garcke, Emile and Fells, J.M. (1887). *Factory Accounts, Their Principles and Practice, A Handbook for Accountants and Manufacturers*, London.

Garnsey, Sir Gilbert (1922). *Holding Companies and their Published Accounts*, London.

Garnsey, Sir Gilbert (1926). *Holding Companies and their Published Accounts, Some Further Notes*, London.

Garnsey, Sir Gilbert (1928). *Limitations of a Balance Sheet*, Gee & Co., London.

Garrett, A.A. (1961). *History of the Society of Incorporated Accountants 1885–1957*, OUP, Oxford.

Gower, L.C.B. (1957). *The Principles of Modern Company Law*, 2nd edn, Stevens, London.

Grady, Paul (ed.) (1962). *Memoirs and Accounting Thought of George O. May*, Ronald Press Co., New York.

Graham, John (1977). *The Lowe Bingham Story 1902–1977*, Hong Kong.

Green, Edwin and Moss, Michael (1982). *A Business of National Importance, The Royal Mail Shipping Group 1902–1937*, Methuen, London.

Habgood, Wendy (ed.) (1994). *Chartered Accountants in England and Wales, A Guide to Historical Records*, Manchester University Press, Manchester.

Hancock, W.K. and Gowing, M.M. (1949). *British War Economy*, HMSO, London.

Hannah, Leslie (ed.) (1976). *Management Strategy and Business Development, An Historical and Comparative Study*, London.

Hannah, Leslie (1983). *The Rise of the Corporate Economy*, 2nd edn, Methuen, London.

Hargreaves, E.L. and Gowing, M.M. (1954). *History of the Second World War U.K. Civil Series, Civil Industry and Trade*, HMSO, London.

Hastings, Patrick (1949). *Cases in Court*, London.

Hein, Leonard W. (1978). *The British Companies Acts and the Practice of Accountancy 1844–1962*, Arno Press, New York.

Hopkins, Leon (1980). *The Hundredth Year*, Macdonald and Evans, Plymouth.

[Howitt, Sir Harold] (1966). *The History of the Institute of Chartered Accountants in England and Wales 1880–1965 and of its former Accountancy Bodies 1870–1880*, Heinemann, London.

Howson, Susan and Winch, Donald (1977). *The Economic Advisory Council 1930–1939*, CUP, Cambridge.

Humphries, Robert (1991). *Price Waterhouse Jamaica, Accounting for the First 75 Years*, Price Waterhouse, Kingston.

Jeal, E.F. (1937). 'Some Reflections on the Evolution of a Professional Practice of Accountancy in Great Britain' in *The Accountant*, XCVI.

Jobert, P. and Moss, Michael (eds.) (1990). *The Birth and Death of Companies*, Carnforth.

Jones, Edgar (1981). *Accountancy and the British Economy 1840–1980, The Evolution of Ernst & Whinney*, B.T. Batsford, London.

Jones, Edgar (1984). William Welch Deloitte (1818–1898) in *Dictionary of Business Biography*, 2.

Jones, Edgar (1984). Sir Harold Montague Barton (1882–1962) in *Dictionary of Business Biography*, 1.

Jones, Edgar (1985). Sir Robert Palmer Harding (1821–1893) in *Dictionary of Business Biography*, 3.

Jones, Edgar (1986). Frederick Whinney (1829–1916) in *Dictionary of Business Biography*, 5.

Jones, Edgar (ed.) (1988). *The Memoirs of Edwin Waterhouse, A Founder of Price Waterhouse*, B.T. Batsford, London.

Jones, Haydn (1985). *Accounting, Costing and Cost Estimation, Welsh Industry: 1700–1830*, Cardiff.

Kellett, F.M. (1950). 'Monkhouse, Goddard & Co. 1868–1920, Some Notes on the History of the Newcastle Firm' (unpub.).

[Kettle, Sir Russell] (1958). *Deloitte and Co. 1845–1956*, OUP, Oxford.

King, Denis and Malpas, Donald (1989). *Price Waterhouse in South America, The First Seventy-Five Years 1913–1988*, Price Waterhouse, São Paulo.

Kitchen, J. and Parker, R.H. (1980). *Accounting Thought and Education: Six English Pioneers*, ICAEW, London.

Kohler, Charles (1987). *Five Years Hard! Memoirs of an Articled Clerk*, ICAEW, London.

Lane, Michael R. (1980). *The Story of the Steam Plough Works, Fowlers of Leeds*, Northgate Publishing, London.

Legge, R. (1989). *A Man of Trust, The Life of J.M.S. Coates OBE*, privately printed, York.

Lisle, George (1899). *Accounting in Theory and Practice, A Text-Book for the Use of Accountants*, Edinburgh.

Lisle, George (ed.) (1903). *Encyclopaedia of Accounting*, William Green, Edinburgh.

Littleton, A.C. (1933). *Accounting Evolution to 1900*, American Institute Publishing Co., New York.

Littleton, A.C. and Yamey, B.S. (1956). *Studies in the History of Accounting*, Sweet & Maxwell, London.

Magnus, P. (1958). 'The History of the Institute of Chartered Accountants in England and Wales 1880–1958' (unpub.).

Manley, P.S. (1976). 'Clarence Hatry' in *Abacus*, 12.

Margerison, T. (1980). *The Making of a Profession*, ICAEW, London.

Marriner, S. (1980). 'Company Financial Statements as Source Material for Business Historians' in *Business History*.

Marriner, S. (ed.) (1978). *Business and Businessmen: Studies in Business, Economic and Accountancy History*, Liverpool.

Marshall, Bruce (1958). *The Bank Audit*, London.

Marwick, Arthur (1977). *Women at War 1914–1918*, London.

Maugham, Somerset (1915). *Of Human Bondage*, London.

May, G.O. (1936). *Twenty-Five Years of Accounting Responsibility 1911–1936*, Price Waterhouse, New York.

May, G.O. (1943). *Financial Accounting, A Distillation of Experience*, Macmillan, New York.

Mel, F.H. (1894). *The Accountant*, London.

Millerson, Geoffrey (1964). *The Qualifying Associations*, Routledge & Kegan Paul, London.

Milligan, K.J. (1982). *Centenary 1882–1982, Birmingham and West Midlands Society of Chartered Accountants*, Birmingham.

Moss, Michael and Hulme, John R. (1986). *Shipbuilders to the World, 125 Years of Harland and Wolff, Belfast, 1861–1986*, Blackstaff Press, Belfast.

Murphy, Mary (ed.) (1952). *Selected Readings in Accounting and Auditing, Principles and Problems*, New York.

Nobes, Christopher and Parker, R.H. (1979). 'Landmarks in Accounting History' in *Accountancy*, June.

O'Hagan, H. Osborne (1929). *Leaves from my Life*, John Lane the Bodley Head, London.

Parker, R.H. (1972). *Understanding Company Financial Statements*, Penguin Books, Harmondsworth.

Parker, R.H. (ed.) (1980). *British Accountants, A Biographical Sourcebook*, Arno Press, New York.

Parker, R.H. (1985). 'Sir William Barclay Peat (1852–1936)' in *Dictionary of Business Biography*, 4.

Parker, R.H. (1986). *The Development of the Accountancy Profession in Britain to the Early Twentieth Century*, Academy of Accounting Historians.

Pennington, Robert R. (1959). *The Principles of Company Law*, London.

Pixley, F.W. (1881). *Auditors*, Effingham Wilson, London.

Pixley, Francis W. (1897). *The Profession of a Chartered Accountant*, H. Good, London.

Plender, Lady (ed.) (1951). *Lord Plender, Some Writings and Speeches*, Gee & Co., London.

Pollard, George B. (1975). *A History of Price Waterhouse in Europe 1914–1969*, Price Waterhouse & Co., Norwich.

Pollard, Sidney (1965). *The Genesis of Modern Management, A Study of the Industrial Revolution in Great Britain*, Arnold, London.

Pollins, Harold (1957). 'Railway Auditing – A Report of 1867' in *Accounting Research*, VIII.

Prais, S.J. (1976). *The Evolution of the Giant Firms in Britain*, CUP, Cambridge.

Reader, W.J. (1966). *Professional Men, The Rise of the Professional Classes in Nineteenth Century England*, London.

Reader, W.J. (1975). *Imperial Chemical Industries, A History, Volume Two*, OUP, Oxford.

Reed, M. C. (ed.) (1969). *Railways in the Victorian Economy, Studies in Finance and Economic Growth*, David & Charles, Newton Abbot.

Richards, Archibald R. (1981). *Touche Ross & Co. 1899–1980, The Origins and Growth of the United Kingdom Firm*, London.

Richards, G.E. (1950). 'History of the Firm: The First Fifty Years 1850–1900' [Price Waterhouse] (unpub).

Richmond, Lesley and Stockford, Bridget (eds.) (1986). *Company Archives, The Survey of the Records of the First Registered Companies in England and Wales*, Gower, Aldershot.

Richmond, Lesley and Turton, Alison (eds.) (1992). *Directory of Corporate Archives*, 2nd edn, Business Archives Council, London.

Robinson, H.W. (1983). *A History of Accountants in Ireland*, ICAI, Dublin.

Robson, T.B. (1936). *The Construction of Consolidated Accounts*, London.

Robson, T.B. (1946). *Consolidated Accounts, Principles and Procedure*, Gee & Co., London.

Robson, Sir Thomas B. and Duncan, S.M. (1969). *Consolidated and Other Group Accounts, Principles and Procedure*, 4th edn, Gee & Co., London.

Robson, Sir Thomas B. (1984). 'Price Waterhouse and Myself 1923–1966' (unpub.).

Rowe, David (ed.) (1988). *The Irish Chartered Accountant, Centenary Essays 1888–1988*, Gill and Macmillan, Dublin.

Sabine, B.E.V. (1980). *A Short History of Taxation*, London.

Sampson, Anthony (1962). *The Anatomy of Britain*, London.

Sayers, R.S. (1957). *Lloyds Bank in the History of English Banking*, OUP, Oxford.

Scott, J.D. (1962). *Vickers, A History*, Weidenfeld & Nicolson, London.

Seatree, W. Ernest (1914). *Relation of the Auditor to the Valuation of Inventories*, Price Waterhouse & Co., New York.

Seed, H.E. (1928). *Inspector and Accountant, A Discussion on Mutual Relations*, London.

Sen, R.N. (1981). *In Clive Street*, M.Sen, Calcutta.

Shannon, H.A. (1954). 'The Limited Companies of 1866–1883' in *Essays in Economic History*, 1.

Shaplen, Robert (1961). *Kreuger, Genius and Swindler*, London.

Slinn, Judy (1984). *A History of Freshfields*, privately printed, London.

Squire, Sir John (1937). *The Hall of the Institute of Chartered Accountants in England and Wales*, London.

Stacey, Nicholas A.H. (1954). *English Accountancy, A Study in Social and Economic History 1800–1954*, Gee & Co., London.

Stevens, Mark (1981). *The Big Eight*, Macmillan, New York.

Stevens, Mark (1991). *The Big Six, The Selling Out of America's Top Accounting Firms*, Simon & Schuster, New York.

Supple, Barry (1970). *The Royal Exchange Assurance, A History of British Insurance 1720–1970*, CUP, Cambridge.

Thomson, H. Byerley (1857). *The Choice of a Profession, A Concise Account and Comparative Review of the English Professions*, London.

Turton, Alison (ed.) (1991). *Managing Business Archives*, Butterworth, London.

Walker, R.G. (1977). 'The Hatry Affair' in *Abacus*, 13.

Waterhouse, Edwin (ed.) (1907). *Extracts from the Journals of Mary Waterhouse 1825–1880*, privately printed, London.

Waterhouse, N.E. (1934). *The Liability of Auditors*, Gee & Co., London.

Waterhouse, Sir Nicholas E. (1961). 'Reminiscences 1877–1960' (typescript).

Watt, M. Laird (1982). *The First Seventy Five Years, Price Waterhouse Canada*, Price Waterhouse Canada, Montreal.

Weiss, Barbara. (1986). *The Hell of the English, Bankruptcy and the Victorian Novel*, Lewisburg.

Wilkins, Mira (1989). *The History of Foreign Investment in the United States to 1914*, Harvard University Press, Cambridge, Massachusetts.

Wilson, Charles (1954). *The History of Unilever, A Study in Economic Growth and Social Change*, Cassell & Co., London.

Winsbury, Rex (1977). *Thomson McLintock & Co. – The First Hundred Years*, Seeley, Service & Co., Worcester.

Wise, T.A. (1982). *Peat Marwick Mitchell & Co., 85 Years*, United States.

Witty, Richard A. (1906). *How to Become a Qualified Accountant*, London.

Woolf, Arthur H. (1912). *A Short History of Accountants and Accountancy*, London.

Worthington, Beresford (1895). *Professional Accountants, An Historical Sketch*, Gee & Co., London.

Wyon, Sir Albert (1932). *The Intelligent Auditing of Detail*, Price Waterhouse & Co., London.

Yamey, B.S., Edey, H.C. and Thomson, H.W. (1963). *Accounting in England and Scotland: 1543–1800, Double Entry in Exposition and Practice*, Sweet & Maxwell, London.

Yamey, Basil S. (1989). *Art and Accountancy*, Yale University Press, New Haven.

Appendix: Tables

Summary of Work by Edwin Waterhouse
February–December 1864

Client	Nature of Work	Hours
Queen Insurance Co.	Audit	$82\frac{1}{2}$
Sudlow & Co.	Partnership accounts	85
Terriccio	Accounts and audit	21
Alfred Waterhouse	Accounts and audit	50
British Ice Making Co.	Investigation and audit accounts	48
Carshalton Savings Bank	Accounts	$54\frac{1}{2}$
Hewett Bros.	Accounts	112
Alexander	Accounts	$1\frac{1}{2}$
Drinking Fountain Association	Audit	$15\frac{1}{2}$
F.W. Thompson	Farm accounts	21
John Fowler	Factory accounts	384
Hodson & Son	Investigation and accounts	$11\frac{1}{2}$
Carpenter	Instruction in book-keeping	$2\frac{1}{2}$
Dr R. Gutteridge	Investigation and accounts	10
F.W. Faulkner	Accounts	$31\frac{1}{2}$
Marlborough Club	Accounts	51
J. Horsburgh & Co.	Accounts	21
West Ham Parish	Investigation	$43\frac{1}{2}$
Clergy Club & Hotel Co.	Accounts	$6\frac{1}{2}$

Type of Work	Hours	Percentage
Preparation of accounts (and audit)	839	80
Investigation of accounts (and audit)	113	11
Audit	98	9
Miscellaneous	$2\frac{1}{2}$	–

Source: Edwin Waterhouse, 'Diary, 1864'

TABLE 2
Price Waterhouse Fee Income 1866–1914

	£	Adjusted† £		£	Adjusted† £
1866	9,251	9,070	1891	25,530	35,458
1867	13,931	13,931	1892	28,126	41,362
1868★	19,850	20,051	1893	25,878	38,056
1869	13,108	13,376	1894	27,435	43,548
1870	18,227	18,986	1895	31,712	51,148
1871	14,275	14,275	1896	40,669	66,670
1872	11,954	10,966	1897	47,672	76,890
1873	14,989	13,504	1898	41,640	65,063
1874	15,628	15,322	1899	48,723	71,651
1875	15,535	16,182	1900	43,365	57,820
1876	17,135	18,037	1901	47,821	68,316
1877	18,204	19,366	1902	52,655	76,312
1878	12,946	14,880	1903	57,162	82,844
1879	14,059	16,939	1904	55,839	79,770
1880	14,223	16,163	1905	50,142	69,642
1881	13,658	16,068	1906	53,611	69,625
1882	13,648	16,248	1907	51,390	64,238
1883	12,851	15,672	1908	51,131	70,042
1884	13,682	18,003	1909	52,127	70,442
1885	12,790	17,764	1910	57,687	73,958
1886	15,079	21,854	1911	56,547	70,684
1887	15,201	22,354	1912	62,300	73,294
1888	18,035	25,764	1913	63,091	74,225
1889	21,560	29,944	1914	69,927	82,267
1890	34,542	47,975			

★ Fourteen months
† Adjusted by Sauerbeck-*Statist* index 1867–77 = 100
Fees are defined as billings, plus closing work in progress, less opening work in progress

TABLE 3

Price Waterhouse Profits by Geographical Origin 1866–1914

	United Kingdom £	United States £	Overseas Total %	Total £	Adjusted Total £
1866	7,440	–	–	7,440	7,294
1867	10,837	–	–	10,837	10,837
1868	14,900	–	–	14,900	15,051
1869	8,990	–	–	8,990	9,173
1870	14,677	–	–	14,677	15,289
1871	7,060	–	–	7,060	7,060
1872	7,838	–	–	7,838	7,191
1873	9,192	–	–	9,192	8,281
1874	9,762	–	–	9,762	9,571
1875	9,889	–	–	9,889	9,493
1876	12,230	–	–	12,230	12,874
1877	12,888	–	–	12,888	12,115
1878	8,363	–	–	8,363	9,613
1879	9,573	–	–	9,573	11,534
1880	10,022	–	–	10,022	11,389
1881	9,792	–	–	9,792	11,520
1882	9,934	–	–	9,934	11,826
1883	8,944	–	–	8,944	10,907
1884	9,460	–	–	9,460	12,447
1885	8,773	–	–	8,733	12,185
1886	11,162	–	–	11,162	16,177
1887	10,704	–	–	10,704	15,741
1888	13,123	–	–	13,123	18,747
1889	16,398	–	–	16,398	22,775
1890	26,996	–	–	26,996	37,494
1891	18,399	2,784	13.1	21,183	29,421
1892	20,635	938	4.3	21,573	31,725
1893	16,977	423	2.4	17,400	25,588
1894	18,320	(925)	–	17,395	27,611
1895	22,678	959	4.1	23,637	38,124
1896	30,799	–	–	30,799	50,490
1897	37,383	–	–	37,383	60,295
1898	31,254	2,923	8.6	34,177	53,401
1899	35,986	3,723	9.4	39,709	58,396
1900	30,718	5,670	15.6	36,388	48,517

	United Kingdom £	*United States* £	*Overseas Total* %	*Total* £	*Adjusted Total* £
1901	32,640	3,195	8.9	35,835	51,193
1902	35,727	5,053	12.4	40,780	59,101
1903	39,433	11,244	22.2	50,677	73,445
1904	36,901	5,712	13.4	42,613	60,876
1905	31,941	4,912	13.3	36,853	51,185
1906	34,203	14,151	29.3	48,354	62,797
1907	32,225	6,216	16.2	38,441	48,052
1908	31,578	5,862	15.7	37,440	51,288
1909	32,425	5,530	14.5	37,955	51,291
1910	36,885	6,363	14.7	43,248	55,446
1911	34,751	7,168	17.1	41,919	52,399
1912	39,952	7,004	14.9	46,956	55,242
1913	37,957	7,302	16.1	45,259	53,246
1914	45,433	10,186*	18.3	55,619	65,434

Adjusted by Sauerbeck-*Statist* index 1867–77 = 100

* Including £760 from South Africa and £156 from South America

Note: Profits are stated before taxation, appropriations to/from reserves, partners' salaries and interest on capital accounts

TABLE 4

Fee Income and Profits of the US Firm
of Price Waterhouse 1904–10

	Fee Income $	*Net Profits** $
Year to 30 June 1904	291,890	73,352
1905	280,534	80,840
1906	589,416	102,198
1907	590,025	249,643
1908	627,610	247,442
1909	NA	200,594
1910	NA	294,924

* Before charging depreciation, interest, reserves, etc.

NA: Not available

Source: PWA Box 175, Consolidated Balance Sheets and Profit and Loss Accounts 1904–10

TABLE 5

Price Waterhouse Fee Income 1914–45

	£	Adjusted £
1914	69,927	82,267
1915	64,581	59,797
1916	83,620	61,485
1917	92,624	51,745
1918	102,398	53,332
1919	117,134	56,861
1920	158,445	63,125
1921*	204,412	131,879
1922	207,970	158,756
1923	211,306	163,803
1924	226,407	162,883
1925	232,213	170,745
1926	234,216	185,886
1927	257,724	211,249
1928	278,422	232,018
1929	295,375	256,848
1930	307,257	316,760
1931	319,327	384,731
1932	315,833	394,791
1933	374,076	473,514
1934	354,001	431,709
1935	363,507	432,746
1936	360,128	404,638
1937	379,339	371,901
1938	364,925	401,016
1939	381,334	–
1940	336,859	–
1941	342,677	–
1942	391,043	–
1943	415,764	–
1944	428,891	–
1945	422,994	–

* Including Newcastle profits rather than fees from 1921
Figures adjusted by Sauerbeck-*Statist* index 1867–77 = 100
Index ends at 1938

TABLE 6
Profits of UK Firm by Geographical Origin 1914–45

	United Kingdom £	United States £	Continent £	South America £	South Africa £	Egypt £	India £	Overseas Total %	Total £	Adjusted Total £
1914	45,433	9,270	–	760	–	156	–	18.3	55,619	65,434
1915	37,302	8,033	–	80	–	382	–	18.5	45,797	42,405
1916	45,567	11,200	–	–	–	2,450	–	23.1	59,217	43,542
1917	48,101	13,454	505	–	–	4,300	–	27.5	66,360	37,073
1918	51,149	18,377	1,168	–	–	1,944	–	29.6	72,638	37,832
1919	64,831	24,828	2,020	–	–	1,429	–	30.4	93,108	45,198
1920	76,239	34,482	16,496	–	–	2,051	–	41.0	129,268	62,751
1921	105,524	25,867	4,343	–	–	2,639	–	23.7	138,373	68,080
1922	111,564	20,985	2,000	1,370	–	1,366	766	19.2	138,051	105,382
1923	112,095	22,164	844	1,227	–	1,368	913	19.1	138,611	107,450
1924	114,947	24,281	1,349	2,240	–	1,354	658	20.6	144,829	104,194
1925	116,900	21,743	1,829	2,163	–	1,388	376	19.0	144,399	106,176
1926	120,476	22,029	3,428	2,764	–	1,469	599	20.5	147,975	117,440
1927	131,949	23,259	4,463	170	–	1,468	149	18.2	161,458	132,343
1928	126,779	23,871	3,630	–	–	1,612	1,431	17.4	175,323	146,103
1929	156,500	29,121	4,040	–	–	1,121	–	18.0	190,782	165,897
1930	164,617	30,165	4,040	1,328	–	1,396	–	18.3	201,446	207,676
1931	200,568	27,674	896	6,959	–	893	315	15.5	237,305	298,909
1932	192,701	24,588	1,506	2,580	–	1,456	205	13.6	223,036	278,795
1933	213,564	9,541	4,636	1,344	–	1,747	401	7.6	231,233	292,700
1934	194,623	5,879	4,075	5,990	1,350	1,053	1,231	9.1	214,201	261,220
1935	206,437	12,488	5,403	2,583	–	991	174	9.5	228,076	271,519
1936	196,096	10,788	4,254	2,844	–	978	1,741	9.5	216,701	243,484
1937	208,831	13,598	2,868	3,158	–	–	1,268	10.0	229,723	225,219
1938	191,652	9,842	3,943	3,571	–	686	472	8.8	210,166	230,951
1939	202,330	11,759	3,468	2,940	1,419	1,119	1,187	9.8	224,222	–
1940	164,633	13,469	550	1,168	–	1,509	313	9.3	181,642	–
1941	166,343	9,052	32	2,882	837	2,188	647	8.6	181,981	–
1942	205,274	15,447	–	2,242	282	2,618	1,304	9.6	227,167	–
1943	212,845	9,431	–	4,091	1,058	3,646	2,464	8.9	233,535	–
1944	227,649	24,363	–	3,535	1,134	3,654	3,202	13.6	263,537	–
1945	224,041	20,381	–	3,596	–	4,707	–	11.3	252,725	–

Figures adjusted by Sauerbeck-*Statist* index 1867–77 = 100

Index ends at 1938

TABLE 7

The Continental Firm of Price Waterhouse:
Operating Statistics 1922–34

	Number of Staff	Chargeable Hours	Fee Income (Swiss Fr.)	Profits* (Swiss Fr.)	Number of Offices	Number of Partners
1922	75	100,273	1,477,119	515,359	3	2
1923	85	126,520	1,550,940	685,929	3	2
1924	79	104,775	1,313,236	470,055	4	2
1925	78	101,679	1,377,200	524,428	5	3
1926	149	258,108	2,966,721	1,749,945	5	3
1927	177	262,978	3,267,301	1,230,786	6	4
1928	152	222,076	2,980,820	1,248,504	6	4
1929	157	235,102	3,196,998	1,362,891	6	4
1930	202	293,836	3,758,909	1,631,630	6	4
1931	236	337,792	4,201,750	1,692,908	7	8
1932	229	299,952	3,750,940	1,305,001	7	8
1933	219	308,890	3,845,127	1,499,298	8	7
1934	213	287,129	3,381,029	1,160,079	9	7

* Profits before interest, bonuses and capital losses
Source: PWA, 1/23, Price Waterhouse Continental Firm Statement of Accounts
30 June 1934

TABLE 8

Price Waterhouse Fee Income and Profits 1930–50

	Fees* £	Adjusted £	Profits† £	Adjusted £
1930	307,257	1,365,559	164,617	731,631
1931	319,327	1,520,605	200,568	955,085
1932	315,833	1,540,649	192,701	940,005
1933	374,076	1,879,779	213,564	1,073,186
1934	354,001	1,761,120	194,623	968,274
1935	363,507	1,781,897	206,437	1,011,946
1936	360,128	1,723,100	196,096	938,258
1937	379,339	1,732,141	208,831	953,566
1938	364,925	1,643,806	191,652	863,297
1939	381,334	1,694,818	202,330	899,244
1940	336,859	1,285,721	164,633	628,370
1941	342,677	1,206,609	166,343	585,715
1942	391,043	1,372,081	205,274	720,260
1943	415,764	1,463,958	212,845	749,454
1944	428,891	1,499,619	227,649	795,976
1945	422,994	1,463,647	224,041	775,228
1946	445,466	1,536,089	223,283	769,941
1947	501,094	1,716,075	241,907	828,449
1948	557,258	1,791,826	257,767	828,833
1949	538,002	1,681,256	219,504	685,950
1950	593,496	1,798,472	237,514	719,740

* Includes profits, rather than fees, from Newcastle office, and for the years 1939, 1940 and 1941 includes only profits from both Plymouth and Leeds offices
† Excluding income from overseas partnerships
Figures adjusted by Bank of England's index of consumer prices, January 1974 = 100

TABLE 9

Price Waterhouse Fee Income and Profits 1945–65

	Fee Income		Profits	
	£	£ Adjusted*	£	£ Adjusted*
1945	422,994	1,463,647	224,041	775,228
1946	445,466	1,536,090	223,283	769,941
1947	501,094	1,716,075	241,907	828,449
1948	557,258	1,791,826	257,767	828,833
1949	538,002	1,681,256	219,504	685,950
1950	593,496	1,798,472	237,514	719,740
1951	667,629	1,854,525	298,484	829,122
1952	660,078	1,679,587	262,126	666,987
1953	705,251	1,741,360	298,304	736,553
1954	755,703	1,829,789	311,042	753,128
1955	797,672	1,850,747	330,231	766,197
1956	902,429	1,992,117	346,528	764,962
1957	945,192	2,015,335	327,353	697,981
1958	1,010,264	2,091,644	356,152	737,375
1959	1,095,247	2,253,595	394,398	811,519
1960	1,200,402	2,444,810	443,558	903,377
1961	1,308,864	2,541,483	455,379	884,231
1962	1,456,674	2,748,442	527,527	995,334
1963	†2,343,000	4,338,889	†629,000	1,164,815
1964	2,232,000	4,000,000	636,000	1,139,785
1965	2,820,000	4,828,767	799,000	1,368,151

* Figures adjusted by the Bank of England's index of consumer prices, January 1974 = 100
† 15 months

TABLE 10

Price Waterhouse UK Staffing Levels 1938–51

	Managers	Audit Pool	Tax Dept	Total Staff
pre-1939	24	262	21	457
1944	27	177	24	370
1951	33	266	23	478

Source: Managers Meeting 'Survey of Price Waterhouse', 9 February 1951

TABLE 11
London Office Staff Totals 1939–68

	Partners	Managers	Audit*	Tax	Liquidation	Systems	Other Staff	Total
1939	11	23	253	20	3	–	99	409
1943	10	22	153	20	2	–	99	306
1944	10	22	154	20	2	–	100	308
1945	11	21	140	19	2	–	95	288
1946	12	22	161	20	2	–	92	309
1947	12	20	190	19	2	–	97	340
1948	12	25	177	20	2	–	102	338
1949	13	24	202	22	2	–	108	371
1950	11	24	215	21	2	–	114	387
1951	12	24	216	21	2	–	107	382
1952	12	25	203	21	2	–	107	370
1953	12	27	194	23	2	–	108	366
1954	12	26	198	22	2	–	109	369
1955	13	27	206	22	2	2	105	377
1956	13	28	222	23	2	8	113	409
1957	14	29	222	22	2	9	125	423
1958	14	28	236	23	2	12	132	447
1959	14	28	245	24	2	12	137	462
1960	15	30	280	24	NA	14	131	494
1961	18	31	303	23	NA	19	130	524
1962	18	37	322	25	NA	13	132	547
1963	20	36	351	25	NA	17	138	587
1964	21	45	320	27	NA	26	139	578
1965	22	47	355	32	NA	31	146	633
1966	27	47	347	37	NA	33	161	652
1967	28	46	385	39	NA	34	175	707
1968	32	49	412	40	NA	45	206	784

* Includes Estates, Registration, Transfers and Secretarial, and after 1960 Liquidations
NA: Not available
Source: PWA, 8/54, Summaries of Staff Totals 1939–54, and internal records

TABLE 12
Price Waterhouse UK Staff in 1964

Office	Partners	Managers	Assistant Managers	Professional Staff	Practice Support Staff	Total
London	21	36	19	368	108	552
Birmingham	7	10	4	101	27	149
Bristol	3	3	–	54	13	73
Cardiff	–	1	–	8	1	10
Glasgow	–	1	1	16	2	20
Leeds	1	2	3	22	4	32
Liverpool	–	1	1	14	1	17
Manchester	1	2	2	23	5	33
Newcastle	4	5	3	47	15	74
Plymouth	–	1	–	4	2	7
Total	37	62	33	657	178	967

Source: PWA, 8/62, UK Staff at 30 June 1964

TABLE 13

Financial Record of the Newcastle Partnership 1921–59

	Fee Income £	Profit £	Distributed to London £		Fee Income £	Profit £	Distributed to London £
1921	55,496	23,296	159	1941	44,634	20,803	8,564
1922	52,016	23,782	5,027	1942	46,707	23,245	9,331
1923	55,592	23,809	5,166	1943	48,649	23,768	9,436
1924	55,448	23,606	5,999	1944	51,888	27,230	11,280
1925	50,536	22,476	4,298	1945	52,052	28,362	8,220
1926	47,757	19,481	309	1946	55,311	30,824	8,590
1927	46,785	19,111	1,105	1947	60,080	30,996	7,635
1928	43,372	16,140	4,952	1948	64,558	33,297	11,262
1929	42,477	17,346	3,127	1949	55,248	21,467	7,814
1930	43,728	18,726	2,384	1950	61,055	24,046	9,087
1931	41,566	16,416	4,144	1951	65,723	27,241	10,392
1932	42,196	17,110	954	1952	67,617	26,865	10,710
1933	47,298	22,416	7,412	1953	65,711	25,276	9,552
1934	44,295	19,674	5,766	1954	72,929	29,341	11,546
1935	43,694	19,136	4,086	1955	81,125	36,994	14,125
1936	46,159	21,075	5,845	1956	95,680	45,324	18,341
1937	47,167	21,541	5,551	1957	91,565	39,181	15,494
1938	48,174	22,476	6,993	1958	96,765	37,697	14,117
1939	45,563	19,327	4,789	1959	98,915	38,492	13,587
1940	43,348	19,293	4,767				

Source: 'Record Book P.W. & Co., Newcastle upon Tyne'; PWA, 1/34, Balance Sheets, Newcastle, 1939–48; PWA, 15/3, Balance Sheets, Newcastle, 1932–9

TABLE 14

Price Waterhouse Fee Income and Profits 1965–75

	Fee Income (£000)	Adjusted	Profits (£)	Adjusted
1965–6	2,820	17,301	NA	–
1966–7	3,317	19,862	NA	–
1967–8	3,883	22,189	NA	–
1969	4,671	25,950	919,000	5,106,000
1970	5,700	29,688	1,049,000	5,464,000
1971	6,977	32,603	1,073,000	5,014,000
1972	8,426	36,635	1,657,000	7,142,000
1973	9,921	39,526	2,526,000	9,461,000
1974	11,085	38,093	2,483,000	8,533,000
1975	14,160	39,224	2,275,000	8,707,000

Figures adjusted by the Retail Price Index, 1985 = 100

NA: Not available

TABLE 15
Price Waterhouse UK Staff 1970–94

	Partners	Managers	Students	Other Fee Earning Staff	Practice Support	Total
1970	65	144	333	766	348	1,656
1971	69	139	368	942	399	1,917
1972	71	154	403	795	406	1,829
1973	78	171	441	768	409	1,867
1974	84	251	603	698	431	2,067
1975	87	306	678	567	441	2,079
1976	96	322	689	664	443	2,214
1977	102	351	707	668	457	2,285
1978	113	381	730	682	485	2,391
1979	125	419	784	733	529	2,590
1980	134	471	898	789	615	2,907
1981	155	479	897	789	644	2,964
1982	161	523	898	775	668	3,025
1983	186	515	897	834	678	3,110
1984	208	661	920	1,084	712	3,585
1985	219	692	990	1,019	779	3,699
1986	265	744	1,034	1,186	933	4,162
1987	298	959	1,170	1,173	1,141	4,741
1988	350	1,134	1,224	1,382	1,318	5,408
1989	398	1,260	1,430	1,624	1,868	6,580
1990	463	1,700	1,440	1,308	1,922	6,833
1991	497	1,822	1,483	1,211	2,377	7,390
1992	480	1,507	1,387	1,195	2,096	6,665
1993	471	1,571	1,138	1,151	1,876	6,207
1994	474	1,459	1,171	1,255	1,795	6,154

Figures exclude Middle East and Ireland but include Channel Islands

TABLE 16

Price Waterhouse European Firm Partners and Staff in 1970

	Audit	Tax	MCS	General
Partners	36	3	2	2
Managers	55	13	8	1
Assistant Managers	67	7	7	–
Seniors	239	19	18	–
Assistant Auditors	264	5	2	–
Office Staff	–	–	–	180
Total	661	47	37	183

Source: PWA, European Firm, Partners Meeting, 18–19 June 1970, Appendix I

TABLE 17

The UK Management Consultancy Practice 1976–90

	Fee Income (£000s)	% Contribution to Fee Income	Staff Numbers
1976	581	3.2	NA
1977	698	3.3	79
1978	1,075	4.4	98
1979	1,605	5.8	110
1980	2,072	6.3	152
1981	3,627	8.0	174
1982	4,598	9.0	218
1983	7,250	11.3	254
1984	9,448	14.1	358
1985	13,033	15.9	388
1986	22,500	19.6	500
1987	34,052	23.0	620
1988	47,300	24.0	809
1989	65,460	27.3	1,073
1990	92,300	28.8	1,140

NA: Not available

TABLE 18

Price Waterhouse Fee Income 1975–94

	(£000)		(£000)	Adjusted (£000)	Adjusted (£000)
To Sept 1975	14,160			39,224	
1976	20,276			48,161	
1977	23,771			48,588	
1978	27,972			52,977	
1979	32,598			54,420	
1980	41,682			58,956	
1981	50,503			63,720	
1982	57,528			66,691	
1983	66,685			74,259	
1984	76,615			81,246	
1985	94,292			94,292	
1986	118,823			114,916	
1987	154,662			143,604	
1988	195,115	To June 1988	184,753	172,668	163,498
		1989	238,869		196,116
		1990	320,809		240,667
		1991	387,587		274,690
		1992	395,117		269,889
		1993	383,300		258,300
		1994	384,000		253,100

Figures adjusted by the Retail Price Index, 1985 = 100

Index

(Italicised numbers indicate tables and figures)